Second Language

Published in this series

Second Language Pragmatics

NAOKO TAGUCHI
CARSTEN ROEVER

OXFORD
UNIVERSITY PRESS

OXFORD
UNIVERSITY PRESS

Great Clarendon Street, Oxford, OX2 6DP,
United Kingdom

Oxford University Press is a department of the University of Oxford.
It furthers the University's objective of excellence in research, scholarship,
and education by publishing worldwide. Oxford is a registered trade mark of
Oxford University Press in the UK and in certain other countries

© Oxford University Press 2017

The moral rights of the author have been asserted

First published in 2017

2021 2020 2019 2018 2017

10 9 8 7 6 5 4 3 2 1

ISBN: 978 0 19 420058 5

Printed in China

This book is printed on paper from certified and
well-managed sources

Acknowledgments

Throughout the preparation of this book we received support and encouragement from many colleagues, friends, and students. We appreciate the feedback offered by two anonymous Oxford University Press reviewers on our book proposal. Their critical comments helped shape our vision of this book at an early stage of writing. Thanks also to Gabriele Kasper for reading early versions of several chapters and providing constructive critique and generous support. We are especially indebted to Marta González-Lloret, who served as the external reviewer of the book manuscript and provided many insightful comments. We did our best to incorporate as many suggestions as possible, and we believe that the manuscript improved considerably, thanks to her contribution. We would also like to acknowledge the patience and guidance of Sophie Rogers of Oxford University Press and of our former and current series advisers, Nick Ellis and Diane Larsen-Freeman. Thanks also to Penny Hands for her expert editing work and unfailing attention to detail in combing through our manuscript. Needless to say, we are responsible for any errors that remain. For Naoko, this book project was supported by a sabbatical semester arrangement with the Modern Languages Department at Carnegie Mellon University, and she would like to thank the chair of the department for providing her time to concentrate on this project. Similarly, Carsten would like to acknowledge the sabbatical granted him by the Arts Faculty at the University of Melbourne, which allowed him to complete his portion of the manuscript.

Above all, we wish to acknowledge the fundamental work of Gabriele Kasper and Kenneth Rose, who produced the monograph *Pragmatic development in a second language* (2003). This seminal book served as a source of inspiration for our work over the last decade and for the process of evaluating the current debate in producing our own version of the state-of-the-field. Problems and future directions identified in Kasper and Rose's book offered a starting point for us to assess areas of development in the last decade, and, at the same time, to clarify new research agendas and challenges that can drive the field forward into the next decade.

Contents

I

Second language pragmatics: an introduction

A speaker of English as a second language who has been sick the previous week goes to see his professor to request a copy of the handouts from the past week's lecture, and says: 'I want handouts.' (Roever & Al-Gahtani, 2015, p. 398). Another student in the same situation says: 'Could you give me the handouts for the last time?' (Roever & Al-Gahtani, 2015, p. 399). Both utterances are grammatically well formed and clearly recognizable as requests, but in most English-language university settings they would not be considered equally appropriate. Given the status-unequal relationship between student and professor, the second, more polite utterance would likely be preferred.

In this book we explore how second language learners come to know what to say when and to whom, what factors impact their learning, and how we can research, teach, and assess their ability to use language in social settings. These issues are the domain of second language pragmatics.

What is pragmatics?

In short, pragmatics links linguistic forms and the ways in which they are used in a social context to perform a communicative act. At the same time, it observes how the linguistic act is realized and perceived in that social context.

The field of pragmatics studies aspects of language systems that are dependent on the speaker, the listener, and the context of an utterance. It takes into consideration that the form of language (grammar, lexis, and discourse structure) we use to accomplish a communicative goal is determined by language-internal rules, as well as by social and cultural considerations. Communication missteps occur when we are unaware of sociocultural conventions or norms of language use, which leads to what Thomas (1983) calls 'pragmatic failure' or a failure to convey and comprehend intended meaning. As listeners, we need to interpret both verbal and non-verbal cues in order to understand what is said and what is implied. As speakers, we need to know how to convey our intentions with the level of formality, politeness, and directness required in a situation, or sometimes not to speak at all and communicate intentions only non-verbally. Basic parameters of context, such as speakers' relationships, roles, setting, prior discourse, and assumptions about what other speakers already know or do not know, guide our way of speaking. Our use of language is also bound by consequentiality, because it has a direct impact on the listeners' interpretation of the message, the impression that they form about the speaker, and their subsequent actions.

The origin of the term 'pragmatics' goes back to the 1930s, when Charles Morris (1938, p. 6) first introduced the term to the field of semiotics (the study of signs as elements of communication). He distinguished three areas of inquiry in semiotics: syntax as 'the study of formal relation of signs to one another', semantics as 'the study of the relations of signs to objects to which the signs are applicable', and pragmatics as 'the study of the relation of signs to interpreters'. In short, while syntax and semantics are concerned with what the utterance is and what it means, pragmatics is concerned with what the speaker means by the utterance and how the hearer interprets it.

Morris's definition of pragmatics has since been developed further. A purely linguistic account of pragmatics has shifted toward a more inclusive view of pragmatics that encompasses wider elements of context, agency, and social action. Levinson (1983, p. 9) brings the term 'context' to his definition by referring to pragmatics as 'the study of those relations between language and context that are grammaticalized, or encoded in the structure of language'. Mey (2001), on the other hand, situates pragmatics within a broader frame of society by defining pragmatics as the study of language use and the societal determinants that govern it, namely how speakers use language to achieve personal goals in a society. Thomas (1995, p. 22) views pragmatics as properties emerging in interaction. She contends that meaning-making involves the 'negotiation of meaning between the speaker and hearer, the context of utterance (physical, social, and linguistic), and the meaning potential of an utterance'. Finally, Crystal (1997, p. 301) defines pragmatics as 'the study of language from the point of view of users, especially of the choices they make, the constraints they encounter in using language in social interaction and the effects their use of language has on other participants in the act of communication'. This definition implies Morris's definition of pragmatics that involves the relations between the form and the user of the form. Simultaneously, it introduces the concept of agency by highlighting language users' subjectivity in their choice of the form and the consequence of the choice.

While definitions of pragmatics may vary, several elements stand out as common features: language, meaning, context, and action. Throughout this book we will show how pragmatics involves a complex interplay between linguistic forms, context of use, and social actions.

Cross-cultural pragmatics, intercultural pragmatics, and interlanguage pragmatics

The field of pragmatics has diverged into several sub-fields. This section presents three areas that are particularly relevant to this book: cross-cultural pragmatics, intercultural pragmatics, and interlanguage pragmatics. *Cross-cultural pragmatics* (or transcultural pragmatics) has developed as a field that compares linguistic acts performed by speakers of different languages and cultural backgrounds (Kasper & Blum-Kulka, 1993). This field emphasizes the fact that linguistic and non-linguistic means for realizing a communicative act, as well as the norms and conventions behind the act, are often different across cultures. Research has focused on uncovering these differences to reveal language-specific patterns of pragmatic behavior.

The main premise of cross-cultural pragmatics is that language use reflects the underlying values, beliefs, and assumptions shared by members of the given speech community. Cross-cultural pragmatics is concerned with how, in a given community, certain characteristics of speaking constitute a manifestation of a tacit system of cultural rules that reflect a society's way of speaking.

An excellent study of the influence of cultural norms on ways of speaking is Young's (1994) research on American and Chinese differences in presenting a position in a business negotiation through an extended monologue. Working from an Interactional Sociolinguistics perspective, Young (1994) contrasts the Chinese approach of providing background, reasons, and explanation before making the main point in the American style of leading with the main message and subsequently supporting it. Either way of organizing the message can be confusing to a listener who is expecting a different form of rhetorical organization. Young shows how these different styles are grounded in cultural views of interaction and different worldviews.

Research in cross-cultural pragmatics typically involves contrastive studies of two or more language groups, using comparative data collected independently from different groups. A classic large-scale cross-cultural study was conducted in the 1980s under the title of Cross-Cultural Speech Act Realization Project (Blum-Kulka, House, & Kasper, 1989). In this project, samples of requests and apologies from seven languages were collected using a written questionnaire called the discourse completion test (DCT). By categorizing linguistic expressions of the speech acts across languages using the same coding framework, the researchers were able to reveal culturally specific patterns of the speech act realizations: how many types of expression exist in a particular language, which expressions are considered direct or indirect, and how they vary in different situations. This trend continues today, as seen in various cross-cultural speech act studies. Chen (2010), for example, surveyed compliment and compliment response patterns in 13 languages. In another study, Netz and Lefstein (2016) revealed culture-specific patterns of disagreements in classroom discourse in three countries: the U.K., the U.S., and Israel.

Intercultural pragmatics, on the other hand, studies how speakers who have different first languages and cultures communicate with each other using a common language.[1] This field shares the key idea with cross-cultural pragmatics that culture shapes the way language is used, and that the way language is used shapes culture. However, unlike cross-cultural pragmatics, which compares language use across language groups to study language and culture, intercultural pragmatics examines how people from different cultural backgrounds communicate with each other using a common language, and the effect of different norms and values on communication. For instance, Knapp (2011) shows a cross-cultural miscommunication in an English-language university classroom in Germany, where an Indian student needs to persuade his classmates to let him remain in a project group from which he is about to be excluded for unsatisfactory performance. Instead of talking to his classmates, the student appeals to the lecturer, which Knapp (2011) analyzes as an example of the student following an L1 cultural norm of viewing the lecturer as a holder of absolute power in the classroom in contravention of the local norm. Choosing the lecturer as the recipient of his appeal, rather than his classmates, shows a lack of understanding of the cultural norms and rules of interaction in this situation.

A classic example of intercultural miscommunication is found in *Crosstalk*, a documentary film about interethnic communication. This film was made in the 1970s by the sociolinguist John Gumperz and his colleagues at the University of California, Berkeley. Its aim was to illustrate instances of intercultural miscommunication between South Asians and British people in England. In one example, an Indian applicant failed miserably at a job interview for a position at a British library because he was not aware of interview conventions specific to British culture. Following South Asian conventions of being less direct and less presumptuous in communication, the applicant did not provide straightforward answers to the interviewers' questions and failed to bring up relevant topics. As the film demonstrates, the consequences of these miscommunications can be serious, leading to cultural stereotyping and prejudice.

Studies in the 1980s often emphasized miscommunication and misunderstandings in intercultural communication. However, reflecting globalization and current international communication networks, more recent literature emphasizes mutual intelligibility rather than cultural differences and misunderstandings, with an attempt to examine the process of common-ground-building among intercultural speakers for the purpose of achieving successful communication. Given present-day society, where multilingualism is considered normal and intercultural communication is just one type of communication among others, Kecskes (2014) argues that the current monolingual models of pragmatics need to be revised so they can explain language behavior in multilingual competence. Kecskes observes the following:

> What standard pragmatics assumes about how things work in communication depends on there being commonalities and conventions between speakers and hearers that can hardly be counted on cross-culturally in the same way as in intercultural communication. Commonalities, conventions, common beliefs, shared knowledge, and the like all create a core common ground, a kind of collective salience on which intention and cooperation-based pragmatics is built. (Of course, there are plenty of varieties within these commonalities.) However, when this core common ground appears to be missing or limited, as is the case in intercultural communication, interlocutors

cannot take them for granted. Rather, they need to co-construct them, at least temporarily. So what seems to be happening here is a shift in emphasis from the communal to the individual. It is not that the individual becomes more important than the societal. Rather, since there is limited common ground, it should be created in the interactional context in which the interlocutors function as core common ground creators rather than just common ground seekers and activators, as is mostly the case in intracultural communication. (2014, p. 2)

Kecskes emphasizes the notion of intersubjectivity in intercultural communication. Language that occurs in intercultural communication is something that participants create impromptu during the course of an interaction, going beyond pre-existing linguistic knowledge or cultural frames. Kecskes's observation is reflected in a number of recent studies on lingua franca communication. Those studies reveal that speakers constantly negotiate various norms of interaction, standards of politeness and directness, communication styles, and cultural conventions as interactions unfold (for example, Firth, 2009; House, 2010; Hynninen, 2013; Kecskes, 2012; Verschueren, 2008). Participants either interpret utterances based on their knowledge of their interlocutor's culture, or they create an entirely new standard of communication.

The third sub-field of pragmatics research, *interlanguage pragmatics*, is what this book is about. *Interlanguage*, a classic SLA term first coined by Selinker (1972), refers to a language learner's developing system of a target language which they are learning. Interlanguage pragmatics has evolved as the field that investigates L2 learners' ability to comprehend and perform pragmatic functions in a target language and how that ability develops over time. In the 1990s, Kasper and Dahl (1991, p. 216) defined the term 'interlanguage pragmatics' (ILP) as a branch of SLA that studies 'nonnative speakers' (NNSs') comprehension and production of speech acts, and how their L2-related speech act knowledge is acquired'. This definition has evolved over time to reflect a more expanded concept of pragmatic competence, going beyond just speech acts. Kasper and Schmidt (1996, p. 150) defined the field of ILP as the 'study of the development and use of strategies for linguistic action by non-native speakers'. Later, Kasper and Rose (2002) presented a two-part definition. They claimed that, as the study of L2 use, ILP examines how non-native speakers comprehend and produce actions in a target language; and as the study of L2 learning, ILP investigates how L2 learners develop the ability to understand and perform actions in a target language. More recently, Bardovi-Harlig (2010, p. 1) noted: '[pragmatics] bridges the gap between the system side of language and the use side, and relates both of them at the same time. Interlanguage pragmatics brings the study of acquisition to this mix of structure and use.' Despite these reiterations of the definition of ILP over time, the area of primary research interest remains the same: L2 learners' knowledge and use of language in social interaction.

Interlanguage pragmatics has a close connection with cross-cultural pragmatics and intercultural pragmatics research. Cross-cultural pragmatics takes a view that people in different communities speak in a different way, and that the differences reflect different cultural values and priorities. People speaking according to their own rules or norms of interaction could end up in a 'clash in expectations, and ultimately, misconceptions about the other group' (Boxer, 2005, p. 151). Cross-cultural studies that reveal those differences and similarities can inform interlanguage pragmatics research on the topic of L1 transfer. Because learners' pragmatic behaviors are influenced by their L1 systems, the types of error they make, their causes, and patterns of pragmatic development can be, at least partially, explained by the aspects of L1 pragmatic behaviors and interactional practices that learners transfer to L2. Pragmatic failure (Thomas, 1983) can be explained through cross-cultural findings that have revealed features of L1-derived pragmatic practices. Examples include different views of interpersonal relationships, as with the Indian student in Knapp's (2011) study discussed above, as well as transfer at the level of choices of utterances. For example, Byon (2004) showed that, for requests in Korean as a target language, American learners of Korean used compliments and expressions of gratitude much more frequently than Korean native speakers, and approximately at the same level as an American English-speaking comparison group. This indicates that learners transferred a strategy from their L1, even though it is relatively uncommon in the L2.

Divergences between L1- and L2-based ways of speaking, however, do not always result in communication problems. The view of L1–L2 differences as a source of pragmatic failure has changed drastically due to recent findings in the area of intercultural communication. Intercultural pragmatics, as the study of interactions among people of different language backgrounds, surely informs interlanguage pragmatics because the vast majority of L2 speakers' communication nowadays takes place with other L2 speakers of the target language. In intercultural communication, norms of interaction, conventions, and values cannot be directly transferred from L1 to be put into use. This is because they are often emergent and co-constructed among participants in the process of reaching mutual agreement and creating common ground (Kecskes, 2014). This reality suggests that L2 pragmatic behaviors can be examined only by analyzing what L2 speakers actually do in an interaction; for example, how learners negotiate and interact to achieve mutual understanding with their interlocutors. Methods used to analyze interlanguage pragmatics need to go beyond a traditional framework of pragmatics—that is, what linguistic forms learners use in what context. They need to incorporate different dimensions into the analysis, such as learners' use of communication strategies, learners' mutual orientations to goals of interaction, as well as their context-sensitivity, adaptability, and agency, among other things. The next section presents a more detailed discussion of the agendas and developments in the field of interlanguage pragmatics.

grammatical, discourse & strategic competences
G   D   S

Second language pragmatics

ability to use appropriate form in a specific
(to achieve communicative purposes context.
properly

During the last three decades, second language (L2) pragmatics[2] has established
itself as one of the central areas of investigation in SLA research. Models
of communicative competence (Bachman, 1990; Bachman & Palmer, 1996,
2010; Canale & Swain, 1980) have situated pragmatic competence as an essential component of L2 ability. These models emphasize that communication
missteps can occur from not understanding social conventions or rules of communication, in addition to grammatical, discourse, and strategic competences.
L2 speakers must have pragmalinguistic knowledge (i.e. linguistic tools for
performing communicative acts in the target language). At the same time, they
need sociopragmatic knowledge, i.e. knowledge of cultural rules and norms,
role expectations, and appropriate conduct. These two knowledge types must
be mapped onto each other so learners can choose appropriate linguistic forms
to achieve communicative goals in context.

*model of
communicative
competence*

*praglinguistic
knowledge*

sociopragmatic

*pragmalinguistic
knowledge*

To give an example, the Japanese language has two primary speech
styles—the polite form (the *desu/masu* form) and the plain form (the casual
form)—that occur at utterance-ending position and which index social meanings of formality and distance. Learners need to know specific copulas and
conjugations associated with each form. At the same time, they need to be able
to determine which form or style to use in a particular situation, for example
when speaking to someone for the first time at a party or in a business meeting
(form–function–context mappings).

SLP:
study abt
the choice
of speech
style &
factors
that
influence
that
choice

Recently, however, the relationship between linguistic properties and contextual factors has become complicated by the surge of a discursive approach
to pragmatics (for example, Levinson, 2013). Linguistic behavior appropriate
to context is no longer viewed as a fixed, stable construct. The form–context
relationship is considered to be fundamentally adaptive and contingent. There
is no one-to-one, straightforward correspondence between the form and
context that applies to all situational dynamics. The form–context relationship shifts within the same situation or single interaction corresponding to the
change in interpersonal distance, familiarity, speakers' attitudes and affect,
and the unfolding direction of the talk.

what is
discursive
approach?

form –context
relationship
shifts depend on
interpersonal
distance, familiarity,
speakers' attitude

Using Japanese speech styles as an example, two people meeting for the first
time at a party may start out using the polite form exclusively as an index of
distance, but as the conversation progresses and more common background
and interests are found, the speakers may switch to the plain form as their
primary style, or they may use a mixture of polite and plain forms to express
solidarity and closeness. On parting, however, they may switch back to the
polite form to add formality and ritualistic tone to the closure of conversation. This example shows that situational factors alone do not determine the
choice of speech style. The speakers' style-shifting reflects their adaptability to
the changing direction of talk and their ability to signal transitions between
discourse boundaries.

polite form: index of distance
mixture of polite & plain form: solidarity & closeness
polite form: add formality & ritualistic tone

By the same token, the speakers' choice of speech style could also indicate their adaptability and reciprocity to their interlocutor's linguistic actions. The speakers often design their contributions to discourse in a way that allows them to respond appropriately to co-participants' utterances and actions. Understanding about appropriate ways of speaking—which speech style to use in which situation—is jointly constructed by co-participants. It is a reflection of how participants wish to construct their social relationships with each other in interaction.

In addition to this adaptive, contingent view, subjectivity and agency have recently influenced our understanding of the form–context relationship. Knowing the normative associations between the linguistic form and context is one thing, but actually putting the knowledge into use is another matter because learners' subjectivity is often at work, determining their linguistic choices. Learners draw on their beliefs, values, and personal principles in their linguistic choices and sometimes choose to express their agency by resisting language use that is widely practiced under the community norm. Going back to the example of Japanese speech styles, learners might know which speech style to use in a certain situation, but may not conform to the norms because of their desire to maintain their identity (for example, Siegal, 1996). Some learners may want to project the image of a formal self and choose to use the polite form only, while others prioritize a more casual style and stick to the plain form to express closeness. Here, speech style is not merely a marker of politeness or formality: it is an index of social meaning that one wishes to express in interaction with others.

These descriptions reinforce the idea that pragmatic competence is multi-dimensional and multi-layered. Linguistic knowledge and sociocultural knowledge of social conventions, customs, and norms of interaction form two primary layers of pragmatic knowledge, but the implementation of the knowledge can be a reflection of learners' subjectivity, i.e. how they want to present themselves in social interaction. In addition, understanding and assessment of context, part of sociopragmatic knowledge, is dynamic and changing in nature. Sociopragmatic knowledge is about one's ability to disentangle a complex configuration of context that involves a range of elements (for example, setting, relationship, affect, attitudes, and stance). At the same time, it is about one's ability to detect a subtle change within the elements corresponding to the course of interaction, and to adapt to the change.

Multilingual pragmatic norms

In defining pragmatic competence, we recognize that the monolingual native speaker norm, which echoes SLA research from the early 1970s, needs to be viewed with a great deal of caution. Although native-speaker models have been used to document how L2 learners deviate or diverge from pragmatic norms, poststructuralist discourse has seriously questioned the stability of these norms and the usefulness of the concept of 'native speaker-ness' in increasingly multilingual societies. Researchers need to recognize that people develop diverse perspectives through a variety of intracultural and intercultural experiences stemming from different generational, regional, and social backgrounds and that, as a result, individuals differ in their pragmatic choices regarding ways of projecting politeness, formality, and appropriateness, for example. It is important to consider pragmatic competence in this light; the multi-dimensional, multi-layered concept of pragmatic competence presented in the previous section illustrates how the conceptualization of L2 pragmatics has expanded from its previous focus on monolingual pragmatic behaviors.

Research in L2 pragmatics

Parallel to the evolving definition of pragmatic competence, the field of L2 pragmatics has grown rapidly, as seen in the steep increase in the scope and number of empirical studies produced in the last few decades (see Taguchi, 2017, for a review). In the 1980s and 1990s, cross-linguistic, comparative studies of pragmatics took the lead, as seen in a large body of studies that compared pragmatic behaviors across languages and cultures. Most of these studies were based on the premise that different cultures and languages have different ways of encoding pragmatic notions of politeness or directness into linguistic behaviors, and that these differences often serve as sources of L1 transfer and areas of difficulty in learning.

Having established pragmatics as a discipline, research in the 1990s increasingly focused on instruction and assessment of pragmatic competence. Shifting from the dominant morpho-syntax studies in instructed SLA, researchers started to explore ways to apply formal instruction to the area of sociocultural and sociolinguistic abilities. In the same period, moving away from the mainstream practice of cross-sectional investigation, the field expanded the body of longitudinal studies that directly addressed acquisitional pragmatics. These studies documented evolving patterns of development over a variety of pragmatic targets, ranging from traditional constructs of speech acts and implicature (or comprehension of indirect meaning) to interactional features that facilitate one's participation in speech events (see Taguchi, 2010, for a review). A similar trajectory is apparent for pragmatics assessment which has moved from assessing knowledge of isolated speech acts (request, apology, refusal) to including interpretation of implicature and recognition of routine formulae, and finally participation in extended discourse (see Roever, 2011).

The first decade of this century saw further growth of instructional and acquisitional research, characterized by a more explicit application of mainstream SLA theories to ILP studies, as well as technology applications to teaching and testing. At the same time, the analytical framework of pragmatic competence shifted from 'pragmatics-within-individuals' to 'pragmatics-in-interaction-in-context' by drawing on the concepts of interactional competence (Young, 2002, 2008, 2011) and discursive pragmatics (Kasper,

2006b). With present-day globalization and transnationalism, ILP has further expanded its empirical scope to the areas of intercultural competence (Spencer-Oatey & Franklin, 2009), pragmatics in lingua franca communication (House, 2010), L3 pragmatic acquisition (Alcón Soler, 2013b), and heritage learner pragmatics (Taguchi, Li, & Liu, 2013; Xiao-Desai & Wong, forthcoming). This book brings together these research developments and presents the current landscape of L2 pragmatics.

About this book

The writing of this book was prompted by what we perceived as major changes and advancements in the body of L2 pragmatics literature over the last three decades. The changes and developments which happened within the earlier phase of the field were summarized in Kasper and Rose's (2002) review of L2 pragmatic development. More than a decade after this seminal work, the present book intends to provide a renewed and up-to-date comprehensive overview of the field by summarizing recent research findings, and to problematize the current state in order to take research further.

This book comprehensibly and critically describes the current state of the field, as L2 pragmatics has become increasingly diversified and interdisciplinary since Kasper and Rose's book was published. This is exemplified by the field's growing connections with a broader field of SLA, psycholinguistics, education, and intercultural communication. For example, in the area of instructed pragmatics research, explicit and implicit teaching, guided by Schmidt's (1993, 2001) noticing hypothesis, was the major instructional approach described in Kasper and Rose's book, which included a summary of about ten studies. In recent years, however, empirical investigations have grown rapidly, resulting in a quantitative meta-analysis of 13 studies (Jeon & Kaya, 2006) and synthesis findings of 49 studies on explicit and implicit teaching (Takahashi, 2010). At the same time, new instructional frameworks such as input processing theory, skill acquisition, collaborative dialogue and language-related episodes, and sociocultural theory have entered the field (for a review, see Taguchi, 2015d).

Another area of change is seen in the study of context in pragmatics learning. Study abroad and classroom were the two primary contexts discussed in Kasper and Rose's volume, but the scope of research has expanded to encompass social media and online interaction, immersion, and heritage language learning. More notably, the study of context has gone beyond the analysis of physical environment (for example, study abroad vs. at home). Drawing on the framework of communities of practice (Lave & Wenger, 1991), language socialization (Duff, 2007), and the complex, dynamic systems approach (Larsen-Freeman & Cameron, 2008), recent studies have revealed the intricate interaction between context and individual characteristics in pragmatic development. Finally, Kasper and Rose barely gave a passing mention to the area of pragmatics assessment, which has since grown multifold (Grabowski,

2013; Itomitsu, 2009; Kasper & Ross, 2013; Liu, 2006; Roever, 2005; Roever, Fraser, & Elder, 2014; Walters, 2007; Youn, 2013).

Given these changes and the emergence of new topics over the past decade, we believe that the present book, which brings together recent research and developments in L2 pragmatics research, is a timely addition to the field. We hope that it will serve researchers, teachers, teacher trainers, and students in advanced/postgraduate courses who are looking for an overview of the field, as well as those who wish to build on their current knowledge and further explore options of pragmatics research and teaching.

The structure of this book

This book reviews L2 pragmatics research over eight different topics: (1) disciplinary domain and history, (2) theoretical models for learning pragmatics, (3) research methods in L2 pragmatics, (4) longitudinal studies in pragmatics, (5) individual differences in pragmatics learning and development, (6) contexts for pragmatic development, (7) instruction and assessment of L2 pragmatics, and (8) pragmatics in the era of globalization. We conclude the book with implications of our discussion and directions for future L2 pragmatics research.

Chapter 2 situates L2 pragmatics among academic disciplines, where it occupies a position at the intersection of second language acquisition research and discourse analysis, and overlaps with SLA, second language socialization, speech act research, implicature, interactional sociolinguistics, and Conversation Analysis. We also trace the history of second language pragmatics research from its beginnings in speech-act-based research to the current blossoming of discursive pragmatics.

Chapter 3 surveys applications of major SLA theories to the investigation of pragmatics learning and development. We discuss different theories in five major categories: (1) cognitively oriented theories (the noticing hypothesis and skill acquisition), (2) the output hypothesis and collaborative dialogue, (3) sociocultural theory, (4) language socialization, and (5) Conversation Analysis. Although these theoretical frameworks all focus on revealing the underlying mechanisms that drive learning, they differ in how they view those mechanisms. By featuring key studies in each area, the chapter highlights similarities and differences across theoretical assumptions and their views toward pragmatic development.

In Chapter 4, we critically discuss the major approaches to the collection and analysis of second language pragmatics data. These methods range from receptive judgments of appropriateness, recognition of routine formulae and inferences based on implicatures to productive discourse completion tasks, extended role-plays, elicited conversations, and natural data. We also discuss self-report data, such as verbal protocols. Major data analysis approaches include speech act coding, as well as approaches for the analysis of extended discourse from Conversation Analysis. Our discussion centers around the conclusions that can be validly drawn from data under these approaches.

Chapter 5 focuses on longitudinal studies in L2 pragmatics literature and addresses developmental trajectories of pragmatic competence. L2 pragmatics research has shown some common tendencies of second language learners in terms of the development of their pragmatic competence. We summarize major findings from four key areas: implicature comprehension, including psycholinguistic aspects of development, recognition and production of routine formulae, speech-act-based research on politeness and appropriateness, and research in discursive pragmatics on extended conversation.

Moving away from the topic of commonality in patterns of development discussed in the preceding chapter, Chapter 6 turns our attention to individual variation in pragmatic competence and development. The chapter discusses a range of factors that might explain learners' differential success in acquiring L2 pragmatics, including proficiency, motivation, aptitude, personality, and identity. The chapter also considers the recent complex, dynamic systems approach (Larsen-Freeman & Cameron, 2008) and the reconceptualization of individual difference factors corresponding to this shift (Dörnyei, 2009). It emphasizes that the role of individual characteristics in pragmatic development is best understood in relation to characteristics of the context of learning.

In order to acquire pragmatic competence, learners must have access to the target language and sufficient opportunities for pragmatic practice. Chapter 7 addresses these fundamental conditions for pragmatic development in a broader scope of context of learning. The chapter compares and contrasts characteristics of different learning contexts and how they support pragmatic development similarly or differently. The contexts discussed in this chapter include: study abroad, sojourn, immersion, formal classroom settings, workplaces, and technology-enhanced learning environments (for example, social media, virtual interaction). The chapter summarizes research developments in each context with the purpose of revealing what contextual features contribute to learning pragmatics. The chapter also discusses future opportunities and the challenges involved in researching contexts.

Chapter 8 gives an overview of various approaches to accelerating learners' pragmatic development through instruction, including awareness-raising, deductive and inductive approaches to teaching pragmatics, and explicit and implicit instruction with adapted focus-on-form techniques. It also covers assessment of second language pragmatics, which has developed from a speech act orientation to the representation of a broader construct of pragmatic ability, and the integration of learners' ability to participate in extended discourse. We discuss the problem of ensuring, in pragmatics assessments, sufficient construct coverage and extrapolation in Kane's (2006, 2012) sense while maintaining practicality of measurement.

Chapter 9, the last topic chapter in this book, discusses the present state of L2 pragmatics research in the era of globalization. Today's internationalization and multiculturalism present new research fields in the study of L2 pragmatics. First, this trend reinforces the importance of pragmatic competence in multicultural development. The ability to speak in a culturally appropriate manner is considered critical, as lack of it may lead to cross-cultural miscommunication or cultural stereotyping. Second, due to increasing globalization, pragmatics has identified new issues to consider, such as pragmatic norms in intercultural communication and learning pragmatics in multiple languages. By bringing together a small but emerging body of literature, this chapter discusses these key issues in three broad areas: pragmatics in lingua franca communication, heritage learner pragmatics, and pragmatics in intercultural communicative competence.

Finally, Chapter 10 presents a summary of the topics and research surveyed in the book. We will conclude with a discussion of gaps in, and limitations of, the current literature and propose several thematic areas and directions for future research in L2 pragmatics.

Notes

1. Kecskes (2015) points out differences between intercultural and intracultural communication. Intercultural communication (and intercultural pragmatics) involves an interaction between speakers of different cultural backgrounds using a common language and thus reflects different cultural conventions in the interaction. In contrast, intracultural communication involves an interaction between speakers of a speech community. Such an interaction reflects shared conventions, but individual styles and preferences also exist.
2. In this book, we use the term 'second language' (L2) as a cover term referring to a later-learned language both in a naturalistic environment and instructional settings. We use 'second language pragmatics' interchangeably with 'interlanguage pragmatics'.

2

Disciplinary domain and history

Introduction

By its very name, 'interlanguage pragmatics' (ILP) or 'second language pragmatics' (L2 pragmatics) is an interdisciplinary field, located at the interface of second language acquisition research and pragmatics. In this chapter, we will sketch out some of the major influences on L2 pragmatics that have shaped it into the research area that it is today. Major contributing disciplines have been second language acquisition, general pragmatics and its work on speech acts and implicature, anthropology and its study of politeness, as well as sociology and its sub-field of Conversation Analysis.

Second language acquisition

Second language acquisition (SLA) as a field deals with the learning of a language in addition to one's native language (or native languages, in the case of simultaneous bilinguals), and tries to account for commonalities in learners' developmental trajectories, as well as differences in their rate of learning and ultimate attainment. It tries to elucidate learning processes and understand the individual difference factors (such as age, aptitude, and motivation) that vary between learners and explain differential learning outcomes. (For a detailed overview, see R. Ellis, 2015.)

SLA grew out of work on first language acquisition which showed that people go through predictable stages in acquiring their first language (L1) (R. Brown, 1973); a similar finding was obtained for second language (L2) learners (Dulay & Burt, 1973). Around the same time, Selinker (1972) proposed the concept of interlanguage to explain L2 learners' errors and how learners build up a rule system for a second language. The confluence of work on development and interlanguage can be considered as the birth of SLA.

Since then, SLA has entertained a range of theories to explain second language learning, including the input hypothesis (Krashen, 1985), the interaction hypothesis (Long, 1996), the noticing hypothesis (Schmidt, 1993, 2001), emergentism and complex, dynamic systems theory (de Bot, 2008; N. Ellis & Larsen-Freeman, 2006; Larsen-Freeman & Cameron, 2009), sociocultural theory (Lantolf & Thorne, 2006), and usage-based approaches (Cadierno & Eskildsen, 2015). SLA is thus a field with multiple, co-existing research paradigms. A major paradigmatic shift was initiated through a paper by Firth and Wagner (1997), who critiqued SLA's primarily individualist cognitive orientation and suggested a stronger integration of social context and language use. This opened the door to theoretical approaches that see learning as socially driven, such as sociocultural theory, socialization theory, and Conversation Analysis for SLA (Ortega, 2011).

Pragmatics has been an object of research in SLA since the late 1970s, and its treatment mirrors much of the development of SLA as a larger field. The earliest empirical treatments of pragmatics were studies on L2 learners' production of speech acts and politeness strategies (Kasper, 1979; Scarcella, 1979). The publication of Kasper's (1981) dissertation put interlanguage pragmatics firmly on the map in SLA research. Few studies with a pragmatic focus appeared in the 1980s, but studies through the 1990s and onward were strongly influenced by Schmidt's noticing hypothesis (Schmidt, 1993, 1995, 2001) and to a lesser extent Bialystok's two-dimensional model (Bialystok, 1993, 1994) (see Chapter 3). As the social turn swept through SLA, the range of theoretical frameworks for explaining pragmatic development broadened as well, and studies were done from a sociocultural perspective (Ohta, 2001), a socialization perspective (Cook, 2008; Diao, 2016), and, more recently, a Conversation Analysis perspective (Al-Gahtani & Roever, 2012; Ishida, 2011; Kim, 2012) and an identity perspective (Brown, 2013; Kim, 2014; Siegal, 1996).

Work in L2 pragmatics reflected SLA's interests in describing and explaining developmental trajectories common to learners, as well as the differences in learning processes, rate, and outcomes that differentiate learners. For example, based on longitudinal studies by R. Ellis (1992), Achiba (2002) and Schmidt (1983), Kasper and Rose (2002) describe five stages for the development of requests in English as a target language (see Chapter 5). Another common SLA phenomenon, namely cross-linguistic transfer, has also received attention in L2 pragmatics research. Transfer is the effect of L1 sociopragmatic or pragmalinguistic knowledge on second language pragmatics (but can also proceed from the second to the first language), and can be positive or negative. Transfer has been of interest from the early days of L2 pragmatics research (Olshtain & Cohen, 1983) through to the present (Barron, 2003; Kasper, 1992; Su, 2010), though not a great deal of L2 pragmatics research has focused on it as a phenomenon in its own right.

With regard to individual differences among learners that could explain differential ultimate attainment, a major research area in SLA, namely age of onset (see, Granena & Long, 2013 for a recent overview), has not been much investigated in L2 pragmatics. Similarly, research on motivation has been prominent in SLA (for example, Dörnyei, Henry & MacIntyre, 2014;

individual difference, motivation, not much investigated in L2 pragmatics

≠ SLA & Prag.

Dörnyei, Henry, & Muir, 2015) but much less so in L2 pragmatics. However, both general SLA and L2 pragmatics have paid a great deal of attention to the influence of the linguistic context, usually investigated as learning during study abroad or in technology-mediated contexts. SLA research has focused on gains in accuracy, fluency, and the four skills (listening, speaking, reading, writing) (Freed, 1995; Pérez-Vidal, 2014), while L2 pragmatics research has investigated such areas as pragmatic comprehension (Taguchi, 2007), production of routine formulae (Taguchi, 2013), identity markers (Grieve, 2015), email writing (Alcón Soler, 2015) and discourse participation (Shively, 2011). We discuss research on individual differences in L2 pragmatics in Chapter 6.

where do SLA & prag. connect?

A particular research concern that connects L2 pragmatics and SLA is the role of general language proficiency, especially grammar, in pragmatic performance. Kasper and Rose (2002) follow Bardovi-Harlig (1999) to consider this relationship a central component of the L2 pragmatics research agenda. They show how pragmatic ability can exceed grammatical ability, for example when learners use routine formulae that allow them to produce utterances which they could not generate through their grammatical knowledge alone. By contrast, lack of grammatical knowledge can also serve as a constraint on pragmatic performance, for example when learners' lack of control of conditionals limits their ability to perform polite requests. This research area has broadened from a major focus on grammar to a wider understanding of proficiency, and we explore it in more detail in Chapter 6.

As summarized above, SLA has been the parent discipline of L2 pragmatics and has provided theoretical frameworks and some core research issues. However, the SLA concept of interlanguage only underlies half of the term 'interlanguage pragmatics'. The content of interlanguage pragmatics research comes out of other source disciplines: general pragmatics, including speech act theory, politeness research in anthropology, and research into extended discourse in Conversation Analysis.

General pragmatics

General pragmatics has been a fundamental source discipline for L2 pragmatics; but as a discipline in itself, it is not clearly delineated. Verschueren (2009) shows how pragmatics exists at the intersection of a number of other disciplines, including philosophy, psychology, sociology, anthropology, semiotics, sociolinguistics, psycholinguistics, discourse analysis, and semantics. The original home of thinking about pragmatics was philosophy, where the term 'pragmatic' can be traced back to Immanuel Kant's *Kritik der reinen Vernunft* [Critique of Pure Reason], first published in 1781, in which Kant uses the term *pragmatisch* [pragmatic] to describe a stance that is oriented toward achieving a goal, independent of moral constraints: whatever aids the attainment of that goal is 'good'. Whether an action furthers the attainment of a goal can be learned through empirical experience, not through pure, non-experiential reasoning. This fundamentally empirical and goal-oriented meaning of the term 'pragmatic' then reverberated through the American philosophical tradition of pragmatism, stretching from Charles Peirce through William James to John Dewey and George Herbert Mead. (See Nerlich & Clarke, 1996, for an excellent, detailed treatment of the historical development of pragmatics in philosophy and linguistics.) Pragmatism took up Kant's emphasis on empiricism and impact by emphasizing the utility or usefulness of theoretical concepts for the real world, in Dewey's formulation: 'the inseparable connection between rational cognition and rational purpose' (Dewey, 1970 [1931], p. 24). The wide-ranging, cross-disciplinary impact of pragmatic thought is apparent in the range of different fields in which its fundamental American proponents were located: Peirce in philosophy, James and Mead in cognitive and social psychology, and Dewey in education. Morris, who in his oft-quoted statement from 1937 (published in 1938) coined the distinction between pragmatics, semantics, and semiotics, was a student of Mead's and strongly influenced by Peirce, but he also integrated European thought in his approach.

In Europe, and especially in Britain, thinking about pragmatics can be traced back to the British philosopher Thomas Reid, a contemporary of Kant in Germany. As early as 1785, Reid foreshadowed the concept of speech acts, which, in Austin's later formulation, is still at the heart of pragmatics, by saying: 'The expression of a question, of a command, or of a promise, is as capable of being analysed as a proposition is; but we do not find that this has been attempted; we have not so much as given them a name different from the operations which they express.' (Reid, 1872 [1785], p. 245). These ideas found resonance in the later development of ordinary language philosophy at Oxford, which became the foundation for much work in pragmatics, and especially L2 pragmatics through the concept of speech acts developed by J. L. Austin and the idea of implicature by (Herbert) Paul Grice. At Cambridge, the philosophers Bertrand Russell and Ludwig Wittgenstein took a more formal approach, with Wittgenstein influencing Morris's work in the United States. There was a great deal more work in this area in Europe, especially in the Vienna Circle (Nerlich & Clarke, 1996).

It was the Oxford approach, and especially speech act pragmatics, developed by Austin and later furthered by John Searle, that became fundamental in shaping present-day thinking in pragmatics as an area of language study.

Speech acts and implicature

J. L. Austin was a professor at Oxford when he delivered the William James lectures at Harvard in 1955. Austin had been grappling with a problem in philosophy about the truth value of statements, and showed that many instances of language use cannot easily be evaluated as true or false like logical propositions, but rather as felicitous or infelicitous within their context of occurrence. For example, while it is possible to evaluate the statement 'The moon is made of cheese' as false in its propositional content, this is less possible for 'I'm sorry', 'Have a nice day', 'Can you lend me a few dollars?', or 'I object to this characterization'. Even utterances that look like statements, and could therefore theoretically be judged on their truth value, may carry a force beyond being purely a statement. For example, the utterance 'He is a dangerous man' is, on the surface, a statement that could be judged as true or false (either he is dangerous or he is not), but it can also function as a warning and convey to the listener the message that the person being talked about is a threat that needs to be managed. Rather than a statement, such an utterance is a speech act since it uses language to achieve a real-world effect; or, in Austin's terms, it is an example of 'how to do things with words' (Austin, 1962). What words can actually do and achieve in the real world depends on the context of an utterance; the idea that context impacts meaning and consequent action is at the core of speech act theory.

contexts impact meaning real world effect

Austin demonstrates this for performatives like: 'I now pronounce you husband and wife'. Such statements can succeed or fail as the action of marrying two people depending on context factors, and Austin termed the conditions that an utterance must fulfill to achieve a real-world outcome 'felicity conditions', rather than 'truth conditions'. In the case of a marriage pronouncement, felicity conditions might include, among others, (1) whether the people spoken to wish to be married and are legally eligible to get married to each other, (2) whether the speaker has the authority to perform marriages, and (3) whether the speaker and the hearers are co-present at the moment of speaking. If any of the felicity conditions are not met, the utterance does not have its intended real-world force: if the speaker does not have the legal authority to perform marriages, the couple will not be married, no matter how much they might wish they were, or how convincingly the speaker uttered the marriage pronouncement.

The idea that the context of an utterance determines what that utterance means, what force it has, and how it affects the world is fundamental to speech act theory. However, Austin did not spend much time on defining what makes up context; rather, he described how utterances impact the real world by analyzing speech acts as consisting of three components:

說出的話
- Locution: the actual words uttered and their meaning; for example, 'I' means the person speaking, 'pronounce' means the act of making a legal declaration, 'husband' means a married man, etc.

表達 的意思
- Illocution: the intended real-world force of the utterance; for example, effecting marriage, expressing a wish, making a request, giving a warning, making a suggestion, etc.

正達 到的 real- world effect
- Perlocution: the actual real-world effect of the utterance; for example, two people are now a married couple, a request is granted, someone changes their behavior as result of a warning, etc.

Austin's work was extended by Searle (1969, 1976), who coined the term 'speech act' and classified speech acts into five major categories: representations (for example, complaints, claims, boasts), directives (for example, requests, commands, suggestions, invitations), commissives (for example, promises, pledges), expressives (for example, apology, gratitude, sympathy), and declaratives (for example, declarations, official acts). The speech act is fundamental to research in interlanguage and cross-cultural pragmatics; the ways in which learners perceive and perform requests, apologies, refusals, suggestions, disagreements, offers, invitations, etc. has been the subject of a large number of studies across a range of languages using a variety of research instruments (Kasper, 2008).

However, pragmatics is not just about speech acts. Another significant area of research that has influenced L2 pragmatics is implicature. The concept of implicature sprang from the work of Grice (1975), who noted that meanings are implied in utterances that go beyond the surface meaning of what was said. The part of Grice's work that had the most impact in L2 pragmatics relates to implied meaning created against the backdrop of his four 'conversational maxims'. These maxims account for the fact that interactions tend to rely on both participants making a good faith effort to ensure that the conversation 'works' (Grice's Cooperative Principle). The Maxim of Quantity states that interlocutors will try to make their contribution as informative as required (no more and no less), whereas the Maxim of Quality refers to contributions being truthful to the best of the speaker's knowledge. The Maxim of Relation refers to contributions being relevant and not off-topic, and the Maxim of Manner describes the tendency to be clear, brief, and orderly. Interlocutors can follow the maxims, violate them, opt out (by refusing to engage), or flout them.

It is flouting that gives rise to the type of implicature that has been investigated in L2 pragmatics (Bouton, 1988, 1994, 1999; Taguchi, 2005). When a speaker flouts a maxim, they violate it in such an obvious manner that a competent hearer can clearly see that some additional meaning is intended to be conveyed. For example, flouting the Maxim of Quality by answering the question 'How was the meeting?' with 'I nearly died of boredom.' will lead a competent hearer to conclude that the meeting was extremely tedious rather than that the speaker's heart nearly ceased beating. Similarly, the Maxim of Quantity can be flouted by only giving part of the information requested and letting the hearer infer the rest; for example, 'How do you like my outfit?' – 'I like the hat.' would be understood to mean that the respondent does not like the rest of the outfit. The Maxim of Relation can be flouted by answering the same question ('How do you like my outfit?') with an off-topic response, such as 'What do you think they'll serve for dinner?', which would likely be taken to mean that the respondent does not want to talk about the topic raised by the preceding question. A different way of flouting the Maxim of Relation is by using the 'Pope Q', 'Is the Pope Catholic?' or its variants, which implies that the answer to the original question is affirmative. For example, the response given in the exchange: 'Is this meeting going to be as tedious as the last one?' – 'Is the Pope Catholic?' implies that the meeting is indeed likely to be very tedious. Finally, flouting the Maxim of Manner might involve a question–answer sequence like: 'Do you want to come over for tea?' – 'Well, I'd love to but I've got to pick up Joey from school and then do some shopping and take mother to the doctor, and after that I've got to get dinner ready.' Most competent listeners would draw the conclusion that the speaker will not be able to come for tea even though a clear yes/no answer was never given. Of course, a central assumption in implicature is that the person being addressed is a competent hearer and able to undertake the inferential process required to understand implied meaning. The extent to which this is the case for second language learners and how quickly they can do it has been the central theme of implicature research in L2 pragmatics.

Austin's, Searle's, and Grice's work has been central to L2 pragmatics, and has inspired a large amount of research on the learning of speech acts and some work on the learning of implicature. However, speech act theorists were mostly based in philosophy and did not elaborate on the real-world contextual considerations for performing speech acts: what contextual conditions lead speakers to formulate their speech acts in different ways. This question was addressed from an anthropological perspective through research on politeness.

Anthropology: politeness in context

Two major contributions to L2 pragmatics from anthropology were politeness theory and socialization theory. Politeness theory provided a popular way of thinking about context, and socialization theory provided a way to explain pragmatics learning. We will deal with socialization theory in more detail in Chapter 3, so here we will focus on politeness.

Politeness theory has its roots in sociology and anthropology, notably in Goffman's (1955) sociological work on face, which views face as the image that people project through their talk and behavior in interactions. Penelope Brown and Stephen Levinson, in a fundamental book on linguistic anthropology (Brown & Levinson, 1978, 1987), took the concept of face further by differentiating positive and negative face. Positive face is what interactants want from others: they want to be valued, appreciated, included, and liked by others, and want others to express their appreciation through language and behavior. In Brown and Levinson's (1987, p. 62) words, positive face is 'the want of every member that his wants be desirable to at least some others'. By contrast, negative face is what people do not want others to do: most of all, they do not want to be made to do things that they would not otherwise do. Again, in Brown and Levinson's (1987, p. 62) words, negative face is 'the want of every "competent adult member" that his actions be unimpeded by others'.

In the course of human interaction, the hearer's positive or negative face may be threatened in situations where a speaker expresses disapproval of a hearer or tries to make them do something that they would not otherwise do. For example, a manager telling an employee off for being repeatedly late is threatening the hearer's positive face by criticizing her behavior and thereby not expressing appreciation and inclusiveness. Conversely, an office worker asking a colleague to help with a report is threatening the hearer's negative face by making them do something they would not do out of their own volition. Politeness is used to mitigate these face threats and reduce the likelihood of damage to interpersonal relationships and social disharmony.

Brown and Levinson (1987) investigated how three different communities realized politeness: speakers of Tzeltal, an indigenous language in Mexico, Tamil speakers in Sri Lanka, and speakers of American English. Brown and Levinson identified strategies that speakers use to redress threats to positive and negative face, and found that they were fundamentally the same for all three cultures. For positive politeness, which addresses the hearer's positive face, Brown and Levinson identified 15 different ways ('politeness strategies') in which speakers show that they are on the hearer's side, appreciate the hearer, and share the hearer's wants. In the example of a manager criticizing an employee for being late, an unmitigated criticism ('Don't be late again. Get here on time tomorrow.') can be felt to be offensive and disrupt the interactants' relationship, so the manager could employ positive politeness strategies. For example:

'I know you've been trying to make it on time but please remember
that it's important that we're all at our desks by nine o'clock.'

Positive politeness in this example consists of the manager recognizing the employee's efforts to be on time, using colloquial language to reduce the seriousness of the reproach, depersonalizing the workplace requirement of being at one's desk by nine, and including herself in that requirement. The emphasis on solidarity and being 'in the same boat' appeals to the employee's positive face and mitigates the face threat.

Negative politeness addresses the hearer's negative face, i.e. their desire to be free from interference or imposition. Brown and Levinson distinguish between 'on-record' and 'off-record' strategies. On-record strategies are those used by the speaker to make an audible attempt to address the hearer's negative face. The most important strategy is conventional indirectness, which is commonly expressed with modals. For example:

'Can you help me clean the bathroom?'
'Would you be able to go and get us some watermelon?'
'I was wondering if you would mind giving me a hand with this
report.'

Modals like 'can', 'could', or 'would' and formulae like 'would you mind' or 'I am/was wondering if' are typical realizations of conventional indirectness. Another common strategy, which is frequently combined with conventional indirectness, is hedging. A hedge serves to make a potential face threat seem smaller. For example:

'Would you mind taking a quick look at my report?'
'Could I just borrow a tiny bit of detergent?'

By making the object of the request seem small with the hedge 'a tiny bit of', the burden on the hearer is symbolically reduced as well. Other strategies include:

Be pessimistic: 'I don't suppose you would have any dollar coins,
would you?'
Apologies: 'I'm really sorry to bother you but...'
Acknowledge debt incurred: 'I'd owe you one if you...'

It is, of course, possible and extremely common to combine strategies; for example, conventional indirectness and hedging:

'Can you come over here for a minute?'

In this example, the threat to negative face is verbally mitigated by including a question of ability. The threat is further symbolically reduced by making the amount of time the hearer is likely to spend seem minimal. It is also possible to combine positive and negative politeness strategies; for example, a compliment and a request:

'I've always admired that bracelet. Do you think I could borrow it
sometime?'

One notable feature of on-record strategies for negative politeness is the role of length. In general, the more effort a speaker expends in producing negative politeness, the more polite the utterance appears, though too much politeness can be imply sarcasm. Compare:

'Can you help me with this?'
'I'm terribly sorry to bother you, and I know it's a lot to ask given
how busy you are, but I was wondering if you'd mind giving me a
hand with this for just a second?'

The fact that longer utterances tend to equal more polite utterances has important implications for L2 pragmatics: since longer utterances tend to be more linguistically complex, they are usually outside the reach of lower-proficiency learners, so these learners' utterances may seem unintentionally under-polite. We will have more to say about this issue in Chapter 6, where we discuss proficiency effects on pragmatic performance.

Negative politeness can also be done with off-record strategies, which do not explicitly mention the face-threatening act but violate a Gricean maxim and leave it to the interlocutor to infer what is meant. Off-record strategies can address both positive and negative face. Brown and Levinson show 15 off-record strategies:

- Hinting (violates Maxim of Relation): 'It's cold in here.' (as a request to close the door or turn up the heat)
- Overstatement (violates Maxim of Quantity): 'I texted you a thousand times.' (asking for an explanation of why there was no reply)
- Irony (violates Maxim of Quality): 'Wow, great job.' (when the hearer made a grievous error)

- Vagueness (violates Maxim of Manner): 'Someone didn't pay attention.' (implying that the hearer should have paid attention)

Direct strategies constitute an unmitigated threat to negative or positive face, and are therefore generally avoided, with politeness strategies being used in their place. However, direct strategies are common when the act will benefit the hearer, when the speaker is in a position of unquestionable authority, or in an emergency situation when there is no time to be polite:

'Have another drink.' (host speaking to guest)
'Give me 20 [push-ups].' (drill sergeant speaking to soldier)
'Get out, get out!' (the house is on fire)

In addition to identifying politeness strategies, a fundamental question that Brown and Levinson investigated was how speakers choose the best level of politeness to use. They posited three main factors, which subsequently had a tremendous influence on research in L2 pragmatics: power (P), social distance (D), and ranking of imposition (R). Power (P) describes the degree to which the speaker can make the hearer do what the speaker wants. Fundamentally, this could be due to the speaker having greater physical strength than the hearer, but in most real-world cases, it will be due to the speaker being in a hierarchical relationship with the hearer. For example, in a work situation, a manager normally has higher power (P+) than an employee (P−); on the training ground, a soccer coach (P+) has higher power than a player (P−); in the classroom, a teacher (P+) has higher power than a student (P−). Colleagues at the same level of a corporate hierarchy, classmates in a university course, or fellow players on a team would normally have equal power (P=). Being higher in power means that the speaker has less obligation to redress threats to the hearer's negative face, whereas being lower in power means having to use more politeness. For example, a lecturer asking a student to read a text aloud in class is not required to use much politeness and might only say:

'Tom, you're next.'

In fact, it would invite inferences beyond the simple request if the lecturer said:

'Tom, I was wondering if you would be so kind as to read the next passage.'

This might imply that sarcasm was being used, perhaps because Tom was not paying attention or is known to be recalcitrant. Conversely, if Tom, being in a lower power position, wanted to ask the lecturer to look over his résumé and give him feedback, he would need to use politeness strategies, and might say:

'I wonder if you could take a look at my résumé. I'd appreciate any comments you might have.'

Other factors often play a role in the choice of politeness strategies, for example to what extent an act is a normal and expected part of someone's duties. If the class is about writing résumés and the lecturer has looked at most students' résumés already, the need for negative politeness is reduced since Tom is not making the lecturer do something he would not otherwise do.

There are also cultural constraints that influence the choice of politeness strategies. In some cultures that involve clear hierarchies (for example, Indonesian, Chinese, and Japanese), higher-power speakers are not required to use much (if any) negative politeness with lower-power hearers, so a manager might give direct, bald-on-record commands to a staff member. Conversely, in cultures with a cultural ideology of equality (such as Australian, British, and American), managers would still employ some degree of negative politeness.

Furthermore, it is important to note that power is not inherent in individuals but strongly dependent on contexts and social roles. In a classroom setting, a lecturer is normally more powerful than a student, but that same student might be the lecturer's fitness coach in the university gym and hold more power in that situation.

Social distance (D), another contextual variable in Brown & Levinson, can be glossed as the degree of acquaintanceship: how well the interactants know each other. If they interact frequently, social distance is low (D–). For example, housemates, friends, and close colleagues have low social distance. People who do not know each other have high social distance (D+), for example strangers on the street, a new customer in a shop, or a police officer whom the speaker is asking for directions. Medium social distance exists (D+/–) between people who do not know each other well but have something in common, for example a colleague who works in the same company but in a different department, a classmate to whom one has not spoken before (but who is known by sight), or a professor in the same department, whom one does not know well. As Wolfson (1983) pointed out in her 'bulge theory', based on research on compliments, medium social distance is particularly interesting since it tends to involve more facework than very low or very high social distance.

Social distance is also determined by external context to some extent. For example, two Canadians might not take any notice of each other when passing on the streets of Calgary, but if they are the only Canadians in a tour group consisting of a range of nationalities, they are likely to feel less social distance to each other than to the other members of the group.

The third contextual variable, ranking of imposition (abbreviated by Brown and Levinson as R, but by other authors as I), refers to the 'cost' to the hearer of performing what the speaker requests. This cost can be determined in terms of time, money, effort, or opportunity. It is greatly impacted by how much the hearer has to go out of her way to do what the speaker asks, whether the hearer would have done it anyway or it is part of their professional duties, or whether the hearer receives benefit. High-imposition (R+ or I+) requests cause the hearer a great deal of trouble and require more negative politeness; for example, the hearer is asked to help with a time-consuming task, to lend the speaker a large amount of money, or to give up their plans in order to do what the speaker wants. Asking the hearer to drive to a far-away airport late at night, to lend the speaker $500, or to host the speaker at the hearer's small apartment for two weeks are all high-imposition requests. By contrast, lending the interlocutor a pencil, passing an item at the dinner table, or turning up the air conditioning on a hot day are all low-imposition requests.

As with power and social distance, specific contextual factors play a role in determining the degree of imposition. For a student, asking a professor to write a recommendation letter for a scholarship application is a medium-imposition request, because writing such a letter takes time but is a normal part of a professor's duties. However, asking the professor to provide the letter on the day it is due because the student had only just become aware of the scholarship deadline introduces an element of time pressure that greatly increases the imposition. Similarly, asking to borrow a classmate's pencil is a low-imposition request. However, asking to borrow a classmate's pencil in the last five minutes of an exam when it is the only pencil they have is an extremely high-imposition request.

Brown and Levinson suggest that it is the combination of power, social distance, and imposition that determines how face-threatening a request is, and that this leads to different politeness levels. Where a speaker is lower in power, speaking to someone much higher in power, and the imposition as well as social distance is great, the face-threatening act is very 'weighty', and a large amount of politeness should result. For example, a worker speaking to the president of a large corporation to ask if he could borrow the president's limousine for a day would need to employ so much politeness that making the request would be beyond the reach of any but the boldest interlocutors. Conversely, a company president asking her personal assistant to borrow the assistant's pen to sign a document would not require much politeness at all.

Despite Brown and Levinson's suggestion of a simple summative relationship, there is no principled way of calculating the weight of a face-threatening act and deducing from this how much politeness will be employed. Interlocutors differ in their judgments of the contextual factors of power, social distance, and imposition, and they differ in their choices of politeness strategies. Brown and Levinson's contextual factors are more suitable as rough post hoc explanations of why speakers made certain choices of politeness strategies than as deterministic predictors.

Brown and Levinson's framework has been very influential in L2 pragmatics research, and is widely used to design elicitation instruments and analyze speech act strategies. However, it has been critiqued, most notably from a cross-cultural perspective and a Conversation Analysis perspective.

The cross-cultural critique of Brown and Levinson's framework has focused on its being too ethnocentrically Anglo-American in that it views politeness as a means to an end, i.e. as a way to influence the interlocutor. In contrast to this volition perspective of Western politeness, Ide (1989) claims that politeness in Japanese is fundamentally mandated by cultural norms about how to speak to a specific interlocutor, known as *wakimae* or 'discernment politeness'. Addressing an interlocutor who is higher in Power with honorifics is therefore not so much a strategic attempt at influence but simply a culturally mandated way of speaking. Matsumoto (1988, 1989) also critiques Brown and Levinson's framework as being too individualistic, although Pizziconi (2003) argues for its applicability to Japanese. From a Spanish viewpoint, Bravo (2001, 2012) has criticized the framework for universalizing the need for personal space and freedom of action. Lochner (2013) shows that the concept of politeness and the question of its cross-cultural universality are still very much in flux.

From a Conversation Analysis perspective, Curl and Drew (2008) have shown that different request forms (and different levels of politeness) can occur within the same type of social relationship, and that speakers seem to look to other context factors, such as their degree of entitlement, when selecting certain request forms. They found that speakers tended to use modal verbs (*could, would*) when they were entitled to the object of their request, but used *I wonder if…* prefaces where less entitlement existed. Such a finding is not directly contrary to Brown and Levinson, who do acknowledge that factors other than power, social distance, and imposition can play a role in speakers' assessment of the weight of a face-threatening act. Curl and Drew's findings should be taken as a reminder that a framework like Brown and Levinson's is not deterministic: there is a large degree of speaker agency in linguistic choice.

Brown and Levinson's ideas, in conjunction with speech act theory, were the central research paradigm in L2 pragmatics until the mid-2000s. Since then, a new theoretical paradigm with a well-developed research methodology has entered the scene: Conversation Analysis.

Conversation Analysis

Conversation Analysis (CA) shares some of the theoretical provenance of speech act pragmatics and politeness theory. In a similar way to speech act pragmatics, it echoes the traditions of American pragmatism. And as with politeness theory, it was strongly influenced by the work of Ervin Goffman, with whom the founder of CA, Harvey Sacks, started his Ph.D. (before later changing to Aaron Cicourel). However, CA is fundamentally different in its goals and epistemology from speech act pragmatics and politeness theory.

First and foremost, it is important to realize that CA is a sociological approach that uses language data as a way of understanding how people manage to live together in society. CA aims to uncover the rules that people follow in interacting with each other, which account for conversation not being a chaotic mess but rather displaying 'order at all points' (Sacks, 1984, p. 22). Interactants seem to tacitly share knowledge about the rule system for carrying on a conversation, and this rule system becomes visible and available for inspection by analysts in their interactions (Kasper, 2009). CA therefore subscribes to a radically empirical view reminiscent of the early American pragmatists (for example, William James, 1907), and bases its research on data from naturally occurring conversation, not from data elicited through questionnaires, interviews, or other methods (Hutchby & Wooffitt, 2008). CA does not speculate about what a speaker might have intended to mean, but rather investigates what action an utterance actually accomplishes in the conversation; in other words, how people get the business of daily living done in interaction with each other. Figure 2.1, from a role-play interaction between two Australian-English-speaking men, illustrates some of these points (Al-Gahtani & Roever, 2011; unpublished data). In line 1, A produces an informal greeting and asks B a typical Australian English formulaic question about his well-being. In line 2, B replies to A's question with a formulaic response, and in line 3, A launches into the business of the talk.

This little excerpt demonstrates a great deal of knowledge about interaction on the part of both interactants. For example, B's utterance in line 2 shows that he knows how to deal with a question, namely by responding to it. It also shows that he took the question as a ritual conversation opener that does not require a detailed response. Had he analyzed it as a true topic initiation, intended to elicit a detailed account of his well-being, he would have likely responded with much more detail; however, the form of the question and its sequential positioning at the beginning of a conversation made B's current analysis very likely. A's response in line 3 demonstrates that B's understanding of A's initial question was unproblematic since A does not pursue a more comprehensive answer ('No, I meant, how ARE you, really?'). Instead, he starts the topic of the talk by apologizing, which foreshadows (or 'projects' in CA parlance) an upcoming request. This is a simple and brief interaction, but it demonstrates that both participants share common-sense knowledge about what functions utterances fulfill, given their content and their place in the turn-by-turn unfolding of conversation. The interpretation of others' meanings enabled by shared knowledge is known in CA as 'intersubjectivity', a concept stemming from the work of the phenomenologist Alfred Schutz (Dennis, Philburn, & Smith, 2013).

Just as interactants rely on shared, common-sense knowledge to understand each other's meanings, analysts can also use their common-sense knowledge to make sense of interlocutors' utterances. However, they have an additional tool, known in CA as the next-turn proof procedure (Sacks, Schegloff, &

---

1 **A** hey [name] (.) how are you going:?
2 **B** yeah ↑good
3 **A** sorry to bother you (.) I just [subsequent lines omitted]

Figure 2.1 Everyday interaction (Al-Gahtani & Roever, 2011; unpublished data)

Jefferson, 1974): what understanding of an utterance does the interlocutor display? The interlocutor's response can be taken as evidence for what action an utterance has accomplished in the conversation. In the short example above, B's response in line 2 to A's question in line 1 demonstrates that B took the question as a ritual conversation opener whose social action is to commence the talk, and not a topic initiation that should have prompted him to provide extensive information about his well-being. Did A intend his question that way? This is impossible to say with absolute certainty for the analyst but also for the interlocutor. However, since A does not refute B's interpretation, A's question did indeed function as a conversation opener and B's response as a ritual reply. In its analyses, CA relies exclusively on what is visible in the data in conjunction with the analyst's common-sense understanding. CA avoids using external theoretical frameworks to explain why a speaker phrased their contribution in a certain way, for example to show politeness in the face of low power and high imposition. This is known as CA's 'emic' orientation; it focuses on what utterances mean to the interlocutors and what their actual conversational effect is, rather than adopting an analyst's superimposed 'etic' understanding (ten Have, 2007).

As illustrated in the gloss of the conversation excerpt above, the unit of analysis in CA is the turn rather than the speech act. CA sees turns as accomplishing social actions and interactants building their conversation turn by turn into longer sequences. There are various ways of connecting turns to each other, but a common way is in the form of an adjacency pair, where the first component ('first pair part') makes a particular second component ('second pair part') relevant (Sidnell, 2010). For example, question and answer are a typical adjacency pair, as in lines 1 and 2 of the excerpt. A's question made an answer relevant, and had B not provided an answer in line 2, that answer would have been 'noticeably absent', and very likely A would have pursued it ('Hey, I asked you a question.'). Other adjacency pairs are request and grant/rejection, offer and acceptance/rejection, and greeting and greeting.

CA has investigated several aspects of conversation, guided by its project to demonstrate the orderliness of interaction. In a foundational paper on turn-taking, Sacks, Schegloff, and Jefferson (1974; for an up-to-date overview, see Levinson, 2016) showed that interactants follow rules in taking and giving up the floor, monitor a contribution for transition relevance places (where speakership could change), and leave short gaps between turns. Another central topic in CA is repair, which addresses the question: what conversational practices do interlocutors have at their disposal to deal with 'trouble' in interaction, such as misunderstandings? Schegloff, Jefferson, and Sacks (1977) differentiated types of repair according to who initiates it (speaker or hearer) and who completes it. Further research (see Kitzinger, 2013, for a summary) has investigated repair practices across cultures and in terms of their formulation and sequencing in conversation. CA has also investigated the larger sequential organization of interactions (Schegloff, 2007): its studies on preference organization have been particularly interesting to L2 pragmatics research, since they have shown how social actions like requests are accomplished through extended interactions (Al-Gahtani & Roever, 2012; Drew & Couper-Kuhlen, 2014; Schegloff, 2007).

Preference organization (see Pomerantz & Heritage, 2013, for more detail) describes the phenomenon that not all options for the parts of adjacency pairs are realized in the same way. When a request is made (for example, 'Can you run out to the store and get some milk?'), the interlocutor has two options: to accept the request or reject it. Typically, an acceptance is done through a direct and immediate response (for example, 'Sure, no problem.'), which is known as a preferred second pair part. However, where an interlocutor rejects a request, this is frequently done as a dispreferred second pair part by using delays, hesitations, hedges, explanations, or indirectness, with the rejection implied rather than made outright (for example, 'Well…I'm actually in the middle of this project that I was really hoping to finish, and it's going to take me a little while longer, so…'). The same phenomenon applies to first pair parts, where, for example, offers are generally made as preferred first pair parts (for example, 'Would you like another piece of cake?'), whereas requests are typically made as dispreferred first pair parts, characterized by delaying the request proper through preliminary moves such as giving background, explaining, apologizing, or projecting the upcoming request through a 'pre-pre' (for example, 'Can I ask you a favor?'). It is important to note that 'preference' in CA does not refer to the psychological state of the interactant but is, instead, a technical term describing the structure of first and second pair parts. Generally, first and second pair parts conducive to alignment and social harmony are done as 'preferred', and those that are not conducive as 'dispreferred'.

As should be apparent, a CA perspective on pragmatics is quite different from a speech act or politeness perspective (Heritage, 1990; Schegloff, 1992; Searle, 1992). Whereas speech act and politeness research are interested in what speakers mean and what strategies they use to attain their goals in interaction, CA is interested in how interactants do the work of everyday life through their interactions. CA does not make claims about what speakers might mean but rather what their utterances accomplish. Speech act theory and politeness theory focus on individual utterances and their meaning in isolation, whereas CA looks at utterances in the context of a conversation. Indeed, the notion of 'context' is understood very differently in both traditions (see Kasper, 2006c, for more in-depth discussion). Speech act theory and politeness theory view context as the macro context of the talk in terms of time, location, interlocutors and their power, social distance, and (where relevant) the imposition being put upon the hearer. By contrast, CA has a micro-analytic view of context as being internal to a conversation: A's utterance sets the discourse context for B's subsequent utterance, which sets the context for A's next utterance, so utterances are 'context-shaped' by the preceding utterances and 'context-renewing' for the following utterances (Heritage, 1984, p. 242). CA does not consider external macro context or the relationship between interlocutors in its analyses unless it can be demonstrated that the talk is clearly oriented to these discourse-external aspects.

CA is not an easy fit for L2 pragmatics since its main interest is not related to learning but to the analysis of what language can show about social organization. In addition, CA relies on natural data, which makes it difficult to answer theory-based research questions: a researcher may struggle to find enough exemplars of, say, refusals in a set of natural data to allow solid conclusions. However, the fine-grained microanalytic approach of CA and its attention to the sequential unfolding of interaction are very attractive to second language pragmatics research; and with some work in the area of CA for SLA (Kasper & Wagner, 2014), there is now increasing work on CA for L2 pragmatics, which we will discuss in greater detail in Chapters 3 and 5.

3

Theoretical models of pragmatics learning and development

Introduction

Chapter 2 addressed theoretical frameworks of the *construct* of pragmatic competence by situating the field of L2 pragmatics within overlapping sub-disciplines of pragmatics, communicative competence models, interactional sociolinguistics, and Conversation Analysis. Shifting the focus, this chapter discusses the theories related to the development of pragmatic competence. Developmental research in L2 pragmatics investigates two fundamental issues: changes within the L2 pragmatics systems and influences on these systems (Bardovi-Harlig, 1999, 2013). Hence, developmental studies go beyond a simple description of pragmatic use; they intend to capture changes in pragmatic knowledge and competence from one point in time to another, and to explain these changes by examining possible contextual and individual influences (see also Chapter 5).

This chapter discusses studies relating to pragmatic development and learning, with explicit attention paid to their guiding theoretical foundations. We will address the central question: What mechanisms drive pragmatic development, moving learners from their current stage to a higher stage of pragmatic knowledge? While all theoretical paradigms focus on revealing the underlying mechanisms that drive learning, they differ in how they view those mechanisms. Correspondingly, their views toward pragmatic knowledge and development are different: some view pragmatic knowledge as understanding form–function–context mappings that have to be noticed, attended to, and practiced, in order for the learner to develop, while others view pragmatic knowledge as emerging and evolving in context through an interaction between individual characteristics and pragmatic resources available in context. These different perspectives essentially generate different explanations as to how learners develop their pragmatic competence.

While existing theoretical paradigms are likely to be categorized in a dichotomy between cognitive vs. social or intra-personal vs. inter-personal, our focus in this chapter is not about highlighting these opposing stances or generating debates as to which approach is better than the other. Rather, we take the position that different paradigms and orientations—and essentially different research methods employed under diverse frameworks—collectively strengthen our understanding of the changes within pragmatic systems and influences on these systems.

In this chapter, we will discuss seven different theoretical perspectives of SLA to explain pragmatic development: the two-dimensional model, the noticing hypothesis, skill acquisition theories, collaborative dialogue and language-related episodes, sociocultural theory, language socialization, and Conversation Analysis. By featuring key studies in each area, the chapter highlights similarities and differences across theoretical assumptions and their views toward pragmatic knowledge and development.

The two-dimensional model

The two-dimensional model (Bialystok, 1990, 1993) and the noticing hypothesis (Schmidt, 1993, 1995, 2001) made their first appearances in L2 pragmatics in 1993 in Kasper and Blum-Kulka's edited book *Interlanguage Pragmatics*. In this volume, the editors featured these two cognitive processing theories as influential proposals that could account for L2 pragmatic development. The main difference between these two models is that, while Schmidt's model theorizes the conditions for pragmatic development, Bialystok's model hypothesizes mechanisms behind adults' pragmatic acquisition.

Bialystok distinguishes two aspects of language ability: analysis of knowledge and control of processing. Analysis of knowledge means the ability to structure and organize linguistic knowledge. It refers to the ways in which linguistic knowledge is represented cognitively and how these representations change in the course of linguistic development. Control of processing, on the other hand, refers to one's ability to access this knowledge. It is the ability to focus attention on the relevant part of language information and to select, coordinate, and integrate information in real time in order to arrive at a solution. The model explains that, for children, learning pragmatics involves developing analytic representations of pragmalinguistic and sociopragmatic knowledge, but for adult L2 learners who already possess rich representations of pragmatic knowledge in their L1, this process involves learning a new set of representations while controlling pre-existing pragmatic representations.

Two decades after its appearance, application of this model to L2 pragmatics research has been only marginal. Some early work in L1 transfer made an explicit reference to this model as a post hoc explanation of research findings. For example, Hassall (1997) investigated acquisition of Indonesian request-making by three Australian learners. He showed that positive transfer of L1 pragmatics and use of universal pragmatic knowledge assisted learners' acquisition of request-making forms. However, learners' processing difficulties related to the control of the forms were observed in their slow, choppy production of the forms. These observations lend support to the assumption of the two-dimensional model: adult learners have the representations of pragmatic knowledge, but they struggle with controlling the knowledge in real-time interactions.

More recently, following Kasper's (2001) claim that pragmatic development involves two aspects—acquisition of pragmatic knowledge and gaining automatic control in processing this knowledge in real time—several longitudinal studies traced development at two distinct levels: accurate demonstration of pragmatic knowledge (knowledge of how to perform pragmatic functions) and processing capacity of the knowledge (the speed with which learners access and process pragmatic functions). A series of studies by Taguchi (2007, 2008a, 2008c, 2012) on implicature comprehension in L2 English revealed different pace of development between these two dimensions and the effect of learning context on these differences. Learners in a domestic instructional context showed a greater increase of accuracy scores than that of comprehension speed (measured by response times), but learners in the target language context showed the opposite pattern: greater gains for comprehension speed than for accuracy scores.

Additionally, S. Li (2014) traced development of the speech act of request among learners of Chinese at two proficiency levels in a study abroad setting. Although both groups improved on pragmatic knowledge (as shown in the appropriateness score of request) on a spoken discourse completion task (DCT), only the higher proficiency group improved on fluency (as shown in speech rate when producing request). In other words, the lower proficiency group improved on the ability to produce requests appropriately, but they did not develop their fluency. These studies confirmed that knowledge and processing dimensions do not develop in parallel. Rather, they provide complementary insight into developmental accounts of pragmatic competence, again supporting the two-dimensional model.

The noticing hypothesis

Compared with the two-dimensional model, the noticing hypothesis has received far more attention in L2 pragmatics research as the theoretical grounding that specifies the conditions of pragmatics learning. Application of the noticing hypothesis encompasses both longitudinal and instructional research domains. The impact of this theory is particularly prominent in instructional intervention research, as seen in a large number of studies that used this hypothesis to operationalize their treatment conditions. These studies compared the explicit vs. implicit teaching method, as well as those involving tasks with explicit orientation, such as consciousness raising, input enhancement, and focus-on-form approaches (see Chapter 8).

The noticing hypothesis capitalizes on learners' attention to linguistic forms and their functions as a necessary condition for L2 learning. Schmidt (1993, 1995, 2001) contends that input becomes intake and leads to acquisition if learners notice the input. As such, the primary concern of the noticing hypothesis is the initial phase of input selection and the attentional condition required for its selection. This initial condition is critical for the subsequent phase, i.e. intake and internalization of linguistic forms contained in the input. In essence, attention controls access to consciousness and awareness.

In pragmatics, noticing goes beyond just focus on form(s). Attention to linguistic forms, functional meanings, and relevant contextual features are all necessary conditions for pragmatic input to become intake (Schmidt, 1993). Consciousness and attention refer to a variety of mechanisms, including alertness, orientation, detection within selective attention, facilitation, and inhibition (Schmidt, 2001; Tomlin & Villa, 1994). Critically, attention is not just global alertness to input (Schmidt, 2001). Attention has to be directed to specific learning objects, i.e. form–function–context mapping in the case of pragmatics learning.

According to Schmidt (1995, 2010), attention and awareness are at once complementary and distinct phenomena. Awareness and attention are closely related, because what we are aware of is often what we attend to. In attending to objects, we allow them to enter the level of consciousness. However, awareness of abstract linguistic rules is not a prerequisite to learning. This is evident in the fact that native speakers who have intuitive understanding of the rules in their language often cannot verbalize these rules explicitly. Their implicit knowledge was acquired without conscious effort to learn or awareness of any learning taking place.

Schmidt (1995, 2010) further distinguishes between noticing and understanding. Noticing refers to the conscious registration of specific instances of language that are attended to, whereas understanding refers to a higher level of awareness that involves 'the recognition of some general principle, rule, or pattern' in the event (Schmidt, 1995, p. 29). In pragmatics, noticing involves the detection of pragmalinguistic forms, while understanding refers to relating these forms to their functions, social meanings, and context. Schmidt observes in the following:

> In pragmatics, awareness that on a particular occasion someone says
> to their interlocutor something like, 'I'm terribly sorry to bother you,
> but if you have time could you look at this problem?' is a matter
> of noticing. Relating the various forms used to their strategic
> development in the service of politeness and recognizing their
> co-occurrence with elements of context such as social distance, power,
> level of imposition and so on, are all matters of understanding.
> (1995, p. 30)

The origin of the noticing hypothesis in L2 pragmatics can be traced to the very first longitudinal study on pragmatic development. Schmidt's (1983) three-year case study of the Japanese artist Wes set out to test Schumann's (1978) acculturation model, which posited that learners' social and psychological distance in relation to the target community determines L2 learning.

Low social and psychological distance (for example, L1–L2 cultural congruence, positive mutual attitudes) is considered equivalent to high acculturation, which predicts successful L2 acquisition.

Based on this theoretical assumption, Wes, a 33-year-old Japanese learner of English who had moved to Hawaii, was predicted to be successful in his L2 learning because his social distance in relation to the target community was low, as evidenced by his extensive local network. He maintained a positive attitude and motivation toward integrating into the community. All positive predictors, however, did not lead to linguistic development. Although clear improvement was found in his discourse and strategic competence, almost no progress was found in his grammatical competence. Wes's sociolinguistic competence, on the other hand, revealed his heavy reliance on formulae to convey intentions (for example, using 'please' for requests and 'maybe' for suggestions). He persisted in using non-target-like speech act strategies when speech acts became more complex, indicating that his pragmatic development was only rudimentary.

Schmidt offered a number of explanations for these findings, one of which was Wes's lack of attention to linguistic forms. Wes's cognitive style was judged to be expressive rather than analytic, with consistent focus on message content over form, and a tendency to monitor communication rather than grammar. Learners like Wes need opportunities for processing input in interaction: 'analysing them, formulating hypotheses (which may not be expressible as formal rules but may nevertheless be conscious at some stage of the process, at least through the ability to recognize nativelike linguistic strings), and testing those hypotheses against native speaker speech and native speaker reactions' (Schmidt, 1983, p. 172).

Although Schmidt did not use the term 'noticing' in this 1983 paper, he advocated the critical role of attention and consciousness in the development of formal aspects of language. Attention and consciousness—primary conditions for noticing—serve as mechanisms for pragmatics learning because pragmatics involves formal linguistic aspects that need to be brought into the learner's consciousness. The learner must attend to pragmalinguistic forms and sociopragmatic elements that map onto these forms, and detect the critical form–function connections along with their contextual requirements. Once linguistic, conceptual, and contextual features are processed in short-term memory, they become the candidates for long-term memory, i.e. the stage of internalization. Although noticing alone is not sufficient for input to become intake, without noticing, intake does not occur (Schmidt, 1995).

To our knowledge, no naturalistic longitudinal studies have applied the noticing hypothesis as a priori theory or tested its predictive validity in pragmatics learning. However, this model has offered post hoc explanations for pragmatic development in many studies. The mechanisms for noticing and processing leading to intake have proved expedient to account for how pragmatics learning occurs in a particular moment, for a particular learner.

One general finding, gleaned from longitudinal investigations, is the learners' initial tendency to adhere to simple, one-to-one correspondence between form and function, which is followed with the gradual expansion of the pragmalinguistic repertoire by adopting a new form–function mapping into their system (Taguchi, 2010). Noticing plays a critical role in the entry of a new mapping into the pragmalinguistic repertoire.

Several longitudinal studies have presented evidence supporting this claim. Using the diary study method, Hassall (2006) recorded his own acquisition of leave-taking expressions in Indonesian during a three-month sojourn. At the beginning, the author exclusively used *dulu* in leave-taking, which was too formal for certain occasions. At the mid-point, he began to use another expression, *permisi*, after experiencing misuse and correction. See the following diary excerpt illustrating this learning episode:

> As I was trudging home on the final stretch after a long hot walk, I was called over to chat by two women in the yard of a house nearby. We chatted amiably enough, but I suddenly got the impression that I'd overstayed my welcome – one of them seemed to be casting around rather awkwardly for further questions to ask me. So I rather hastily took my leave, with a *dulu* statement: *Pulang dulu ya* 'I'm going home for now, okay' (literally, 'Go-home for-now, yes'). I said it a bit tensely and unsmilingly and it felt a bit abrupt as I said it. As I then turned to go, one of them said softly, in English, 'Excuse me'. I turned around in puzzlement. She then repeated it in Indonesian: *Permisi*, and laughed. So her 'excuse me' had been a gentle correction: a supplying of what I'd omitted to say. (Diary entry, Padang, Week 2, 9/1/02)
> (Hassall, 2006, p. 39)

Reflecting on this occasion, the author wrote that the native speaker's implicit feedback promoted his noticing of the new pragmalinguistic form (*permisi*). Since the new form occurred in tandem with the familiar form (*dulu*) in the precise context of leave-taking, the author was able to notice the form–function–context association and process it in short-term memory. The new expression eventually entered the author's long-term memory and led to learning. Two weeks later, in a chat with an acquaintance, the author recalled this earlier instance and successfully used *permisi* when he took leave.

Another piece of evidence of noticing as a trigger for pragmatics learning is found in studies in computer-mediated communication (for example, Belz & Kinginger, 2003; González-Lloret, 2008; Kakegawa, 2009). Belz and Kinginger examined the acquisition of German address forms by 11 American college students over a two-month period while engaged in telecommunication with their German peers. The authors documented learners' growing tendency to shift from the formal *V*-form to the informal *T*-form of solidarity. This shift happened only after the learners had received explicit peer feedback on their inappropriate use of the *V*-form (i.e. that it was too polite). See the sample peer feedback:

Now let's correct some mistakes....When speaking to us, don't say "Haben Sie [V] Fragen?" That's much too polite. Say "Habt ihr [T] Fragen?" You would use that polite form with adults you don't know well, for example.

(Belz & Kinginger, 2003, p. 625)

Before receiving peer feedback, most learners did not pick up the *T*-form in their German peers' emails, despite their frequent appearance. This suggests that input exposure alone does not guarantee noticing of the target forms. There has to be some mechanism in place that directs learners' attention to the pragmalinguistic forms and sociopragmatic factors to facilitate their understanding. In this study, explicit peer feedback played that role. It helped learners to notice variants of address forms, their communicative functions, and the social meanings that they encode (formality vs. solidarity). The positive role of noticing is supported further when the results are compared with those from naturalistic learners. Barron (2003) examined acquisition of *T*- and *V*-form among 33 learners of German over a 14-month stay in Germany. DCT data revealed only modest progress: the learners' random switching between these two forms decreased only by 7%.

A general conclusion gleaned from previous studies is that naturalistic development is a slow process, and input exposure alone does not always lead to development. Some external, triggering events, such as feedback and modeling, must occur so that learners can notice and register new form–function–context mappings in their systems. However, previous findings also suggest that there is a limit in the degree of learning that noticing can facilitate. In other words, noticing might be the pre-requisite to learning but does not guarantee acquisition, particularly when the target forms are linguistically complex. Several studies showed that new pragmalinguistic forms increased in frequency, but their appearance remained inaccurate and inconsistent, falling short of complete acquisition (Belz & Kinginger, 2003; González-Lloret, 2008; Kakegawa, 2009).

Belz and Kinginger (2003) revealed cases where inadequate use of the address forms persisted. Although learners were able to disambiguate *T* and *V*, they experienced difficulty in using the forms correctly. This is because German address forms involve number and case categories that need to be accurate when using the forms. They also require the user to make a distinction between singular and plural (for example, there are two second person informal pronouns: *du* for addressing an individual and *ihr* for addressing two or more people), and they affect the conjugation of the verb they control. Hence, the T/V system in German is far more complex than the leave-taking form in Indonesian in Hassall's study, which could be learned as a memorized chunk. Similarly, Kakegawa (2009) reported relatively low accuracy rates of the sentence-final particles in learners' use. Only one particle showed over 80% accuracy rate after the first instruction; the other three remained at a level of 16–57% in accuracy. Hence, the structural and functional property of pragmalinguistic forms can mediate the effect of noticing. Learners might notice and process target pragmatic forms, but whether or not the forms become intake and acquisition depends on the property of the forms and sociopragmatic factors, as well as the learners' readiness.

These widely divergent findings between frequency and accuracy point to the potential need for extending the noticing hypothesis beyond its current focus on the attentional condition and initial stage of input selection. Surely, learning is unlikely to happen without attention, but attention does not invariably lead to learning. Attention to input does not guarantee that the subsequent processing of input occurs. Even if the processing does occur, it may not always lead to long-term memory storage. Indeed, in response to one of the objections to the noticing hypothesis, Schmidt (2010) conceded that the hypothesis needs to be more carefully formulated, acknowledging that some types of learning require more focused attention than others, depending on the difficulty of the target forms and demand on the attentional processes.

Pragmatics learning can be placed on a progression, starting from the initial noticing and conscious registration of pragmalinguistic forms in input, moving toward the level of understanding where learners relate the forms to their functions, social meanings, and contextual elements, and essentially reaching the level of internalization, i.e. accurate, fluent use of the forms in situation. This progression toward mastery may not always be completed. Noticing of target pragmatic features may lead to the subsequent use of the features, but the use may not be immediately characterized as accurate or fluent, depending on the difficulty and complexity of the target features.

Another area of consideration in the noticing hypothesis relates to the factors that facilitate noticing. In the studies discussed above, learner-external factors such as feedback, modeling, and direct instruction were found to assist noticing, but learner-internal factors such as affect, attitudes, and motivation were largely neglected. Yet, individual-level analyses in Belz and Kinginger's study clearly revealed a great individual variation in the production rate of the address forms and sentence-final particles, suggesting that individual learners take advantage of the instances of noticing differently. Belz and Kinginger described one case of non-development—a heritage speaker who was born and grew up in a German-speaking family. Her peers told her to use the *T*-form several times, but she continued to use the *V*-form throughout the semester. The authors attributed the results to her heritage background. Because German was an integral part of her everyday life, peer assistance probably did not serve as a critical moment of noticing and learning for this heritage learner. The findings suggest that feedback can facilitate development, but individual variation also exists in the course of development.

Individual learners' contribution to noticing becomes clearer in Taguchi's (2012) study in an immersion context where students interacted with their English-speaking instructors regularly. Using an oral DCT, the study assessed students' abilities to produce two speech acts: making a request and expressing an opinion. One participant (Shoko, pseudonym) did not produce the target-like bi-clausal request forms (for example, 'I wonder if' + verb) in a formal request situation at the beginning of the study, but the form appeared in her last DCT task at the end of the academic year. In the follow-up interview, Shoko reported that she was conscientious about using the form because of the corrective feedback she received from her teacher. When she sent an email to her instructor to set up an appointment, she wrote, 'I want to talk to you on Tuesday, 25th to talk about my registration. Do you have time?' In response, as shown in Figure 3.1, the instructor told her to use 'I wonder if'.

Shoko,
Well, I do have some time, but you have to learn how to be a bit more polite in your emails. You must use a more polite form with teachers than you do with your friends. For example, with a friend you say 'I want/I need/Let's go' but with a teacher you write:

> I am wondering if I can set up an appointment with you next week sometime to discuss my winter term registration. Are you free at all next week? I look forward to hearing from you.
> Sincerely,
> Shoko

I know it sounds very formal, but you can't email to me the same way you would your friends. The email you sent sounded too demanding. Be careful. I can see you on Tuesday afternoon, okay?
Tom

Figure 3.1 Corrective email feedback from instructor (Taguchi, 2012, p. 160)

Shoko noticed the differences between her request forms and those demonstrated by the instructor. She reacted to this feedback immediately: she revised her email with the bi-clausal request form and sent it back to the instructor. Clearly Shoko took this as an opportunity for pragmalinguistic practice. Because Tom said 'I can see you on Tuesday afternoon, okay?', Shoko's first message had a clear perlocutionary effect. The speech act was complete, and there was no need for the same speech act, other than to practice the pragmalinguistic form. Shoko reported that she knew the form 'I wonder if' as a polite request from her English textbook, but she did not know when to use it, i.e. what level of formality or politeness requires it. The form–function–context mapping clicked when she saw Tom's feedback. Shoko's interest in pragmatics-related language use could be the reason behind this learning. Shoko reported that she paid attention to polite expressions in English in her peers' talk and emails. She also reported changing her way of speaking depending on context: when asking a favor, she said 'could you' instead of 'can you', and used 'I'm afraid' as a politeness marker.

An additional episode here suggests that proficiency also contributed to Shoko's learning. Yosuke, another informant in this study and Shoko's boyfriend, witnessed the whole email exchange between Shoko and Tom. Yosuke also learned that 'I wonder if' is a polite request form and should be used in a situation like this. However, he did not use the form in the DCT because he was not confident with formulating a clause structure after it. Consequently, he avoided it and opted for the simple form, 'please' + verb form. This episode suggests that the emotional reaction and surprise associated with the experience might have facilitated Shoko's learning; Yosuke, however, was still not able to produce the form because of his shaky grammar.

These findings indicate that learners' subjectivity may well interact with noticing. Learners' attitudes and emotion could determine whether they can notice the crucial connections at any moment and take advantage of them to expand their pragmalinguistic repertoire. Shoko's curiosity toward the sociolinguistic aspect of language use and her tendency to observe how people interact with each other may have facilitated her noticing and internalization. Hence, we can conclude that learners with different motivational and attitudinal orientations may exhibit different levels of noticing.

Schmidt (2010) also acknowledges individual variation in noticing. Some learners notice more than others, and individual differences in noticing can affect the pace of learning and ultimate attainment. Motivated learners are more successful than unmotivated learners because they pay more attention to specific aspects of language, not just the content of the message (Tremblay & Gardner, 1995). Motivated learners may also be more persistent in understanding forms in input and achieve higher levels of awareness, leading to more learning. Similarly, recent findings suggest that aptitude, noticing, and learning are related. Mackey, Philp, Egi, Fujii, and Tatsumi (2002) found a relationship between working memory (a component of aptitude) and learners' reported noticing of corrective feedback.

In L2 pragmatics, Takahashi (2005) probably produced the only study on the relationship between noticing and individual characteristics (see Chapter 6). She investigated the effects of motivation in learners' noticing of request-making forms. Japanese EFL students completed a pragmatic task in which they analyzed two transcripts of request-making dialogues. One transcript featured a native-speaker interaction, while the other featured a non-native-speaker conversation. Participants were asked to compare the two versions and spot the differences. They also completed the awareness retrospection questionnaire and indicated their degree of awareness of the target pragmalinguistic forms. Although learners were more likely to attend to non-target pragmatic features such as discourse markers and idiomatic expressions, the learners' awareness of the target request forms correlated with motivation, supporting Tremblay and Gardner's claim that motivated learners tend to notice specific aspects of linguistic information.

In summary, two decades of the noticing hypothesis has seen a continuous growth of the theory in generating empirical studies and implications for pragmatics learning and teaching. In the longitudinal studies reviewed here, the noticing hypothesis has served as a post hoc explanation for how learning of new form–function–context associations occurs. In Chapter 8, we will turn to instructional intervention studies that used the noticing hypothesis as an a priori framework and tested its predictability in generating pragmatics learning.

The idea that pragmatics learning is driven by what learners pay attention to and become aware of in the input seems generally accepted, as seen in the existing longitudinal findings. Pragmalinguistic forms and sociopragmatic factors that are frequent in input are still not acquired until they are consciously noticed in input. Learners must attend to and notice form–function–context mappings of input that they are exposed to if those mappings are to become intake for learning. On the other hand, noticing itself does not guarantee learning, as shown in the variation in the level of achievement between frequency and accuracy of pragmatic features, as well as different degrees of noticing and learning achieved across individual learners.

Future direction with the noticing hypothesis involves continuing specifications of the relationship between noticing, intake, and pragmatics learning. As mentioned in the previous section, the relationship is not straightforward. Learners may notice and process target pragmatic features, but accurate and fluent use of them still requires effort. Specifications of the theory need to go beyond the initial condition of attention, noticing, and processing, and illustrate the precise mechanisms behind the noticing–intake–learning link. In other words, the theory needs to specify how attended pragmatic features become intake and essentially lead to learning. Empirical investigations that set out to investigate the link are necessary.

It is also critical to go beyond the post hoc explanation of noticing and actually collect data of noticing instances from learners' perspectives in a systematic manner. SLA researchers have used a range of methods to examine whether learners actually notice the target linguistic forms in input. Those methods include retrospective interviews, stimulated verbal recall, note-taking, journals and diaries, think-aloud protocols, post-exposure questionnaires and assessments, and eye movement research (for example, Mackey & Gass, 2011). In pragmatics, we have a body of studies that used introspective and retrospective verbal reports in which learners verbalized their thought processes during and immediately after the completion of a pragmatic task (for example, Félix-Brasdefer, 2010). However, these studies have simply gained insights into the reasoning behind learners' performance (for example, perceptions of the situation and influence of the perceptions on their linguistic choice), as well as planning processes of their responses (see Chapter 4). Almost no studies have used interviews to investigate whether learners are able to notice pragmatic forms embedded in input. Future research is required in this direction.

Skill acquisition theories

Application of skill acquisition theories to pragmatics has been scarce. Only three studies exist to date in the domain of instructional research (S. Li, 2012,

2013; Li & Taguchi, 2014). Unlike the noticing hypothesis, whose primary focus is on the initial conditions of input selection, skill acquisition theories inform how learners progress from the initial stage of conscious rule-learning to the end point where learners are able to use rules unconsciously. At the initial stage, performance is slow, cautious, and error-prone, but with practice, performance becomes more rapid and effortless, and eventually becomes automatic and attention-free. This progression is symbolized in a learning curve called the power law of practice in which the logarithm of reaction time or error rate decreases linearly with the logarithm of the amount of practice. A typical learning curve shows the steep decrease in reaction time and error rate at the beginning stages followed by a gradual decrease in response time and errors (DeKeyser, 2007).

Within the skill acquisition theories, Anderson et al.'s (2004) ACT–R (Adaptive Control of Thought–Rational) distinguishes between declarative and procedural knowledge. Declarative knowledge refers to the knowledge of 'what' or facts, which is conscious and can be 'declared' or verbalized explicitly (for example, adding '-ed' to encode the past tense in English). In contrast, procedural knowledge is the knowledge of 'how', which is unconscious, with little access to introspection (for example, using past tense verbs fluently in narrative). The key element in this declarative-to-procedural shift is intensive practice.

Skill acquisition proceeds through three consecutive stages: cognitive, associative, and autonomous (Anderson, 1993). The cognitive stage involves explanations of rules, and, as a result, the rules become chunks of declarative knowledge. This is followed by the associative stage, where the learned rules are practiced. At this stage, a process called proceduralization gradually takes place. Finally, the autonomous stage involves the continuous improvement of a skill to the level that performance becomes fluent and automatic. The automatized behavior resulting from practice is highly domain-specific. A skill acquired in one domain does not directly transfer to another domain (for example, from comprehension to production of sentences).

How is skill acquisition theory relevant to pragmatics learning? Unlike the noticing hypothesis, skill acquisition theories specify how attended form–function mappings (and the knowledge of them) become strengthened and transformed into something more stable and robust (proceduralization). In pragmatics, initial declarative knowledge involves the knowledge of pragmalinguistic forms and their functional meanings, and contextual features associated with the form–function mappings. The mappings become strengthened through their repeated activation via practice. Chunks of declarative knowledge become organized into a condition–action rule: 'if in this situation when performing this function, use this pragmalinguistic form'. Learners begin to rely on this rule instead of the initially learned declarative knowledge. This process results in the qualitative transformation of a declarative knowledge base into procedural knowledge, which requires less attentional resource.

Skill acquisition theories bring several important implications to pragmatic development. First, they describe acquisition as a gradual process, moving from slow and error-prone declarative knowledge to procedural knowledge characterized as fast and error-free. The theories can explain the findings from Belz and Kinginger's and Kakegawa's studies discussed in the previous section. Learners' use of the address forms and sentence-final particles did not reach the stage of fluent, error-free use because they were probably still at the declarative knowledge stage. Practice occurred in their email exchanges with native-speaker peers, but the practice was not extensive enough to bring about a qualitative, transformative change. Multiple forms and functions involved in the practice might have added to the difficulty. Learners were practicing several form–function–context mappings simultaneously (for example, pronouns *du* 'you' and *ihr* 'you all' as a marker of solidarity). As a result, they had limited practice on each mapping.

Skill acquisition theories also highlight the role of practice in L2 pragmatics. Although naturalistic developmental studies make a reference to the opportunity for practice as a mechanism for learning pragmatics, these studies have been interested in capturing a moment of practice, i.e. how it occurred and supported learning. They have not paid much attention to the sustainability of such practice. Instructional intervention studies, on the other hand, have incorporated a variety of tasks as a platform for practice and measured their impact on learning outcomes, but these studies have not incorporated a view of practice as a consistent, repetitive activation of form–function–context mappings. Skill acquisition theories help to conceptualize and implement practice as a vehicle for developing pragmatic competence.

Finally, skill acquisition theories provide ground to conceptualize pragmatic competence as a skill. Traditionally, L2 pragmatics research has emphasized only the declarative knowledge dimension of pragmatic competence. Longitudinal studies have mainly investigated the development of pragmatic knowledge, characterized as learners' accurate and appropriate responses in a pragmatic task. Instructional studies, on the other hand, have targeted the improvement of accuracy and the appropriateness of pragmatic knowledge, and very few studies have provided instruction on fluency or measured this dimension as a learning outcome. Lack of attention to fluency is a curious omission because the declarative–procedural dichotomy is hardly new and goes back more than three decades in Faerch and Kasper's (1984) original model of pragmatic competence, which conceptualized pragmatic knowledge as involving both declarative and procedural components.

Skill acquisition theories offer several implications to the design of instruction. First, in order to promote proceduralization of declarative knowledge, instruction needs to be sequenced (DeKeyser, 2007; Ranta & Lyster, 2007). Instruction should start with developing learners' declarative knowledge by providing explicit information about the target form–function–context mapping. Once the declarative knowledge has established a firmly grounded root in learners' consciousness, systematic practice is needed for proceduralization and automatization. The practice needs to be designed in a way that learners use their declarative knowledge while being engaged in communicative tasks.

A series of studies illustrated how pragmatic development occurred as a function of practice (S. Li, 2012, 2013; Li & Taguchi, 2014). S. Li (2012) investigated the effects of practice in the development of accurate, fluent recognition and production of requests in L2 Chinese. Participants were assigned to three separate groups: an intensive training group, a regular training group, and a control group. The intensive and regular groups first received explicit metapragmatic instruction on request forms to develop their declarative knowledge. After their knowledge base was confirmed, they received systematic practice via receptive-skill activities. The intensive group practiced twice as much as the regular group. The learners' recognition and production of the target forms were assessed by an oral DCT and a listening judgment test (judging whether the form is pragmatically appropriate and grammatically accurate).

Results showed that a larger amount of practice in receptive skills led to more accurate and fluent recognition of the request forms (as measured by response times) but did not extend to fluent production of the forms (as measured by speech rate), although the practice promoted accuracy of production. In other words, declarative knowledge (accuracy) was shared across different skill domains (recognition and production), but procedural knowledge (fluency) was not. Receptive-skill-based practice improved performance accuracy in both comprehension and production tasks, but the effect did not transfer across modalities at the level of fluency.

In a subsequent study, S. Li (2013) focused on the amount of practice needed to promote accurate and fluent use of request-making forms. L2 Chinese learners were divided into different instructional conditions: input-based practice group, output-based practice group, and control group. After receiving metapragmatic instruction on the target request-making forms, the learners practiced the forms over four consecutive days. The input-based group read a dialogue and chose appropriate request-making utterances displayed on a computer screen, while the output-based group produced the requests by typing the forms. Results showed that, regardless of practice modality (input- or output-based), four instances of processing target request-making forms were sufficient for learners to accurately judge and produce target forms, but more than eight instances were needed for them to develop fluency in performance.

Li and Taguchi's (2014) study further adds to the findings on the modality effect of practice. There was an effect of input-based practice on the development of fluency associated with the recognition task (listening judgment) as measured by response time, but no effect was found on fluency associated with the production task (oral DCT) as measured by speech rate and planning speed when producing the request forms. Similarly, there was an effect of output-based practice on the development of fluency associated with the production task, but there was no effect on fluency associated with the recognition task. On the other hand, the input-based and output-based practice both contributed to the development of the accuracy of recognition and production of the request forms. In other words, the effect of practice was skill-specific at the level of procedural knowledge (fluency); but at the level of declarative knowledge (accuracy), the effect transferred across skill domains. The findings suggest that the development of pragmatic processing (fluency) requires skill-specific practice, whereas the development of pragmatic knowledge (accuracy) can benefit from practice in different modalities.

As described above, a small body of existing findings has confirmed several insights from skill acquisition theories. First, pragmatic competence entails knowledge and processing components, which draw on the characteristics of declarative and procedural knowledge respectively. Pragmatic knowledge is represented by the accurate use of the target form–function–context mapping, and pragmatic processing is represented by fluency in accessing the mapping. These dimensions develop separately as a function of practice. There is also a skill-specificity effect: practice in a production task improves fluency in the production of pragmalinguistic forms, but not in the recognition of the forms, and vice versa. Finally, procedural knowledge requires a greater amount of practice to develop than declarative knowledge.

Several issues are left unexplored in pragmatic development as a skill acquisition process. First, because previous studies implemented a short-term intervention spreading over a few practice sessions, they were not able to reveal the gradual, staged improvement of a skill, which starts at the cognitive stage and moves toward the associative and autonomous phase. Future studies could explore a long-term intervention by increasing the amount of practice and by tracking learners over an extended period of time so that they can address the core mechanisms of skill acquisition, i.e. the declarative-to-procedural shift, as applied to pragmatics learning.

Another issue to consider is the generalizability and applicability of the learned pragmatic knowledge to a larger unit of pragmatic performance. Under the skill acquisition paradigm, learning units at the declarative stage are purposely kept as small, discrete units of pragmalinguistic forms (for example, request-making forms) associated with a restricted set of contextual factors (for example, social status of the addressee, degree of imposition) so learners can proceduralize and automatize the component units. A question is whether automatizing the component-level pragmatic knowledge leads to more fluent, smooth, and accurate pragmatic performance at discourse level. For example, does the mastery of a request head act (i.e. a single form that can convey the illocutionary force of a request) promote fluent production of a speech act of request when the speech act involves completing a set of semantic strategies that go beyond the head act itself? Does learning a request form via practice lead to a fluent and accurate production of the form in a role-play task that draws on multiple attentional resources? These questions related to the transfer of lower-order processing to higher-order performance have not been addressed in L2 pragmatics (but see de Jong & Perfetti, 2011, for reading and Fukkink, Hulstijn, & Simis, 2005, for oral fluency), and thus are areas for future research.

Collaborative dialogue and language-related episodes

The three theoretical orientations discussed in the previous sections (i.e. the two-dimensional model, the noticing hypothesis, and skill acquisition theories) are concentrated around the cognitivist-oriented explanations of pragmatic development. In this section, we will turn to a more socially oriented approach that conceptualizes pragmatics learning in interaction as a socially situated activity. We will discuss collaborative dialogue and language-related episodes, which view pragmatic knowledge as jointly constructed among participants in interaction and emerging in goal-oriented, collaborative activities.

(A theoretical perspective to collaborative dialogue originates in the claim that language use is both a form of communication and a social activity (Swain & Lapkin, 1998). Language is considered a psychological tool that enables learners to negotiate and solve cognitively challenging problems. During negotiations and deliberations, learners draw on a pool of linguistic resources to solve a problem, which essentially leads to the learning of the resources.

The concept of language as a psychological tool derives from Vygotsky's (1978, 1987) work, which demonstrated that language is a semiotic tool that mediates cognitive processes. When facing a complex problem, we may talk to another person about the problem or we may talk aloud to ourselves. By using language, we direct our attention to specific features of the task, repeat information, and articulate an action plan to solve a problem, which in turn shapes our thinking. Language 'serves as a tool supporting L2 learning by consciously singling out the L2 as an object to be monitored, reflected upon, and manipulated' (Swain & Lapkin, 1998, p. 329). Swain and Lapkin (1995) present three ways in which language use could mediate L2 learning: (a) generating hypotheses about linguistic rules, (b) assessing the hypotheses, and (c) applying rules or extending the knowledge of rules to new L2 contexts.)

When taking the perspective of language use as a psychological tool, it is necessary to analyze learner interaction for evidence of language used as a tool to support L2 learning. A causality claim between language use and learning can be made when we observe how learners co-construct knowledge of linguistic rules and how this co-construction process leads to linguistic change. Swain and Lapkin (1998) claim that co-construction of knowledge in interaction is language learning in progress: a dialogue that arises during collaborative problem-solving is an enactment of cognitive processes.

Collaborative dialogue serves as a window to examine learning in progress during interaction, and is defined as a dialogue that occurs between speakers as they engage in problem-solving and knowledge-building (Swain, 1998, 2000; Swain & Lapkin, 1998). Previous studies on learner–learner interaction have operationalized the construct of collaborative dialogue through a unit of analysis called language-related episodes (LREs). LREs are defined as: 'any part of a dialogue where the students talk about the language they are producing, question their language use, or correct themselves or others' (Swain & Lapkin, 1998, p. 326). Through collaborative dialogues, learners form and test hypotheses about appropriate and correct use of language, as well as reflecting on their language use. LREs that capture these instances are considered to be useful units for understanding the process and product of L2 learning.

In L2 pragmatics, most of the work that has been done on collaborative dialogue and LREs is seen in the domain of instructional studies, though only sparsely. In fact, a small body of existing studies used collaborative dialogue as an instructional tool, but these studies called it metapragmatic discussion. Metapragmatic discussion occurs when learners engage in a dialogue about pragmalinguistic forms, sociopragmatic factors, and the connection between them, and eventually develop a joint understanding of the principles underlying the connection. Metapragmatic discussion can strengthen pragmatic knowledge because it prompts a deeper level of cognitive processing by requiring learners to think through the rules and explicitly verbalize their thoughts.

A few instructional studies in L2 pragmatics used metapragmatic discussion among students as part of the treatment (for example, Kubota, 1995; Moody, 2014; Nguyen, 2013; Rose & Ng, 2001). However, these studies used metapragmatic discussion in combination with other activities and did not examine the effect of metapragmatic discussion alone in promoting pragmatic development. Takimoto (2012) is one of the few studies that directly investigated whether or not metapragmatic discussion itself can serve as a mechanism for pragmatic development. He compared two conditions for learning request downgraders in English (for example, *Would it be possible to…* or *I'd appreciate it if you…*): consciousness-raising instruction with and without metapragmatic discussion. In a treatment session, both groups compared different request forms and rated their appropriateness. Then they came up with a list of ways in which they could make the request forms more appropriate. One group made a list collaboratively with peers, while the other group worked individually. Development of their knowledge of requests was measured by a written DCT task and an appropriateness judgment task. There was no group difference on the appropriateness judgment test, but the group with metapragmatic discussion outperformed the other on the DCT.

Although Takimoto's study revealed the benefits of metapragmatic discussion in pragmatics learning, he did not examine actual mechanisms of learning during peer-to-peer interaction because there was no analysis on the interaction data. Theoretical interest in collaborative dialogue is about language being used as a cognitive tool that mediates the processes of thinking (Swain, 2006; Swain & Watanabe, 2013). How collaborative dialogue promotes such processes is a key theoretical question that can be addressed only through the analysis of language-related episodes targeting pragmatics.

Taguchi and Kim's (2016) study attempted this. The authors coined the term 'pragmatics-related episodes' or PREs, which involve any part of language production where learners talk about the pragmalinguistic forms they are producing and the sociopragmatic factors they are attending to. The authors analyzed the occurrence of PREs during a collaborative problem-solving task that aimed at developing knowledge of request-making forms in L2 English.

The study was based on three groups of L2 English learners in a junior high school in South Korea. The 'collaborative group' received metapragmatic information on English request forms followed by a dialogue construction task to be done in pairs. Participants received scenarios with pictures of main characters and created a dialogue involving a request based on each scenario. The 'individual group' received the same metapragmatic information and task but completed the task individually by thinking aloud. The control group did not engage in the dialogue construction task. The collaborative group outperformed the individual group on the production of the request head act in the DCT given after the task. However, the advantage of the collaborative condition was short-lived because no group difference was found in a delayed post-test given four weeks later.

Figure 3.2 (adapted from Taguchi & Kim, 2016, p. 430–431) is an illustration of peer-to-peer interaction from the collaborative group (translations in parentheses). In turn 1, Learner 1 shares her understanding of the situation and the type of request form expected in this situation (i.e. polite request). Following the confirmation from her partner, the same learner elaborates on the feature of the request form required in the situation (a 'long' polite request), and in turn 3 she verbalizes 'I was wondering' as a structure to use. This structure is also in Learner 2's cognitive space because she takes over the turn and completes Learner 1's utterance-in-progress by providing a missing clause ('if I could go to'). Here, the target request form, 'I was wondering if I could go to', is jointly constructed.

A similar instance is observed in turns 3–9. In turn 3, Learner 1 starts out with a portion of the target form. Repetition of the verb phrase 'go to' and a missing adverb of place signal a trouble source. Learner 2 acknowledges this problem and completes the turn by providing the location that follows the verb 'go'. Here, Learner 2 co-constructs Learner 1's utterance by providing the other-initiated repair to the trouble source. In turn 9, Learner 1 accepts the repair by repeating Learner 2's word.

In both cases, joint turn construction occurs to solve a language problem. The problem that both parties are attempting to solve is the construction of the target request-making form. The second speaker supplies the crucial piece of a sentence that is necessary to complete the turn-in-progress and establishes a common understanding of the target structure. Note that in both cases, the second speaker completes the turn with a rising intonation (turns 4 and 8). This is a try-marked intonation (rising intonation followed by a pause), which is designed to check the recipient's assessment of the turn

1	**Learner 1**	재명이가, 국어숙제를 집에 놓고 왔대
		(Jaemyong left his Korean homework at home.)
		자율학습시간에 숙제를 가지러 집에 가도 되는지 물어보고 있습니다
		(He is asking if he could go home to get his homework.)
		그러면 먼저, 정중히 부탁해야겠지?
		(Then, he should make a request politely?)
2	**Learner 2**	어
		(Yes.)
(several turns later)		
3	**Learner 1**	그 다음에 공손한 긴 요청문을 사용해야 되지
		(We need to make a long polite request). I was wondering
4	**Learner 2**	if I could go to?
5	**Learner 1**	Go to the home 인가??
		(Is that 'go to the home?')
		Go to home 아니야?
		(Shouldn't it be 'go to home'?)
6	**Learner 2**	I am…
7	**Learner 1**	I was wondering if I could go to…go to
8	**Learner 2**	Go home?
9	**Learner 1**	go home

Figure 3.2 Sample collaborative dialogue (adapted from Taguchi & Kim, 2016, pp. 430–431)

(Sacks & Schegloff, 1979). This upward intonation signals the second speaker's uncertainty about the option and functions as her hypothesis-testing. At the same time, it signals collaborative construction of a form. By offering the first speaker a chance to assess the turn completion unit, the second speaker ensures that they are both on the same ground, contributing to the knowledge-building process. The dialogue provides the learners with opportunities to offer mutual support and to co-construct a complex request form.

This excerpt illustrates the mechanisms of collaborative dialogue promoting the development of pragmatic knowledge. Overlapping talk, other-repetition, and co-construction of sentences were characterized as collaborative orientation in previous literature (for example, Dobao, 2012; Watanabe & Swain, 2008). While interacting around a task, both learners attend to each other's form, negotiate over form, provide feedback and correction, and scaffold each other. They generate hypotheses, assess hypotheses, and apply the resulting knowledge to solve a linguistic problem. During this process, the target pragmalinguistic form becomes salient through recycled use of the form over multiple turns, as well as with prosodic features that accompany the form (for example, rising intonation). Self-monitoring and other-monitoring during this process also promote learning. When learners produce language in a collaborative environment, they do not just produce output; they also have an opportunity to receive feedback from peers while trying to make their language precise (Swain, 2006; Swain & Lapkin, 1998). This collaborative work eventually results in a deeper-level processing of the form, which helps to consolidate learners' pragmatic knowledge and subsequent use of the knowledge.

The concept of collaborative dialogue shares theoretical linkages with the noticing hypothesis in that attention and consciousness are primary requirements for input to become intake and lead to learning. The difference between the two theoretical paradigms is the location of the attention and consciousness. The noticing hypothesis conceptualizes conscious rehearsal of pragmatic features in short-term memory as an individual process occurring within a learner's brain. In contrast, collaborative dialogue views the process as a socially situated activity among participants involved in talk-in-progress. Hence, it is the *collective* attention that helps learners to detect and discover pragmatic features, and to develop understanding of general rules that govern the features. In essence, cognition is on display in public during the process of negotiation and interaction. A close analysis of collaborative dialogue and PREs gives us a clue as to how learners attend to target pragmatic features and how that attention leads to subsequent use and learning, which the noticing hypothesis does not explicate.

Collaborative dialogue also finds a synergy with the skill acquisition perspective in that both paradigms value practice as a mechanism that drives pragmatics learning; the difference lies in their conceptualization of practice. In skill acquisition theories, practice is a solitary activity, implemented as a systematic response to input. In collaborative dialogue, however, practice is conceptualized as a shared social activity in which participants jointly attend to stimulus and solve a linguistic problem. We can also compare these two approaches based on the aspect of practice that they value. In skill acquisition theories, the aspect is quantity. Because reaction time and error rate go down according to how much practice a learner gets, a large amount of systematic and focused practice is considered necessary for proceduralization and automatization. On the other hand, collaborative dialogue emphasizes the quality of practice. Collaborative orientations displayed by participants—cooperative overlaps, repetitions, co-construction of utterances, and turn-taking over a single linguistic item—are all signs of high-quality practice that is likely to lead to quality processing, retention, and learning of the target features. In other words, collaborative dialogue is concerned with the substance of practice, i.e. what participation in a practice means to learners and to their pragmatic development.

Given the paucity of findings on the role of collaborative dialogue in pragmatics, it is pertinent to examine to what extent learners negotiate and co-construct pragmatic knowledge and how these processes result in learning (see Taguchi & Kim, in preparation, for some recent findings). The studies reviewed in this section are all instructional intervention studies that directly tested the efficacy of collaborative dialogue or metapragmatic discussion in producing learning. In future investigation, longitudinal studies in naturalistic settings will add to our understanding of the role of collaborative dialogue in pragmatic development. Those studies will reveal the nature of pragmatics-related episodes or talk around pragmatics occurring in a naturalistic environment. They will show how certain pragmatic features are incidentally picked up for discussion and negotiation, and how those pragmatic features are learned in the microgenesis of interaction. We will review some evidence of this process in our discussion of sociocultural theory and language socialization below.

Sociocultural theory

Following the previous section on the role of interaction in promoting pragmatics learning, in this section we will again direct our attention to interaction, but this time under the neo-Vygotskian paradigm of sociocultural theory. Sociocultural theory also views interaction as fundamentally social and constitutive of the learning process itself. Unlike the cognitivists' approach to SLA, which views interaction as a source of input to be parsed by individual cognitive mechanisms, sociocultural studies conceive of interaction as an impetus for learning. Because language is a means for communication and a tool for thinking, interaction—the place for language use—is learning itself and a competence in its own right.

Sociocultural theory grew out of the work of the Soviet developmental psychologist Lev Vygotsky (1886–1934). Various modifications and extensions made to Vygotsky's original ideas in the contemporary era have given rise to a strand described as 'neo-Vygotskian', which is seen in the work of activity theory (for example, Leontiev, 1981) and cultural-historical activity theory (for example, Cole, 1996). Vygotsky's thinking has also informed SLA and contributed to its theory-building since the 1980s, resulting in over 300 journal articles, book chapters, and dissertations existing to date (Lantolf & Beckett, 2009).

The fundamental tenet of the theory is that individuals' mental functioning is related to cultural and historical context; hence, participation in social interactions and culturally organized activities drives psychological development. According to Vygotsky (1941/1997), 'any function of the child's cultural development appears on the stage twice, or on two planes, first the social, then the psychological, first between people as an intermental category, then within the child as an intramental category' (pp. 105–106). Children or learners acquire new knowledge as they participate in joint social activities.

The central concept of the Vygotskian theme, as identified by Wertsch (1991), is that higher forms of mental activity are mediated by tools and signs. These semiotic means include, for example, language, arithmetic systems, maps, diagrams, and calculators, all of which are useful for solving a problem. From the sociocultural perspective, knowledge is internalized through the use of semiotic tools. Learning is also mediated socially via interaction, as illustrated in the Vygotskian (1978) concept of the zone of proximal development (ZPD). ZPD refers to the domain of knowledge or skill where learners are not yet capable of performing independently, but can perform with assistance from more capable peers. Interactions become successful and lead to cognitive development when they are oriented toward the ZPD.

Language is the central mediating tool for mental development because it regulates cognitive processes and behavior. Children are often observed to engage in private speech to plan or guide their own behavior. As children gain capacity for mental thought, private speech transforms to inner speech, i.e. language used to regulate internal thought without oral verbalization. Self-talk occurs as inner speech, although when an individual is tackling a cognitively demanding task, inner speech re-emerges as a way of regulating thinking.

These key concepts from the sociocultural paradigm generate a number of implications for instruction, assessment, and curriculum. The concept of ZPD suggests the importance of mediation, scaffolding, and guided assistance as ways of promoting learning. In the context of L2 research, a number of studies have analyzed interaction between a teacher/tutor and learner, and illustrated how L2 learning took place as a result of mediation during the novice–expert interaction. A classic study by Aljaafreh and Lantolf (1994) in ESL tutorial settings illustrated a shift from other-regulated to self-regulated performance, as tutors gradually moved from explicit to implicit correction and the learners developed the ability to self-correct. Although traditionally ZPD has been examined in interactions between individuals with disparate knowledge levels, recent studies have expanded ZPD to peer-to-peer interaction, as seen in the surge of studies on collaborative dialogue.

The neo-Vygotskian, sociocultural influence is certainly evident in L2 pragmatics research. The central tenet of the Vygotskian framework—the interdependence of social and individual processes in the co-construction of knowledge—has provided an alternative view of pragmatic knowledge and a renewed explanation as to how this knowledge develops. Sociocultural theory places its emphasis on interaction as learning in its own right. It fundamentally dissociates itself from the noticing hypothesis or skill acquisition theories, which view learning as a solitary activity within individuals' minds. To be sure, sociocultural theory also considers individual cognitive processes, but only on the scale of developmental pathway or as an end point of development. At onset, learning is viewed as a socially situated activity, shared among participants in interaction. Learning is viewed as first social, then individual; first intermental, then intramental; first other-regulated, then self-regulated; first achieved through private speech (external verbalization), then through inner speech. Interaction and mediation within the ZPD are the mechanisms contributing to this shift from assisted to individual, autonomous functioning.

A notable example of sociocultural application to L2 pragmatics is Ohta's (2001) longitudinal study on the acquisition of Japanese among seven learners in formal classroom settings. Ohta collected 34 hours of naturalistic audio/video recordings of classroom interactions over one academic year. The learners wore clip-on microphones attached to individual audio recorders to allow recording of their private speech in class. The data revealed numerous instances of learners' engagement in L2 private speech in three broad categories: vicarious response (covert response during another student's turn), repetition, and manipulation of forms. Private speech occurred as learners tested hypotheses about forms, solved linguistic problems, and analyzed linguistic structures, all of which point to a Vygotskian perspective of language as a psychological tool that mediates cognitive processes.

Ohta examined the learners' development of appropriate listener behaviors, as indicated in their use of acknowledgment and alignment expressions. Acknowledgment is a feedback signal used to show attentiveness in conversation (for example, *so desu ka* meaning 'oh really'), while alignment is an emphatic feedback signal that carries the sentence-final particle *ne* (for example, *ii desu ne*, meaning 'That's great, isn't it?'). Ohta found that students' participation in the interactional routine of the initiation/response/follow-up (IRF) sequence served as a major source of learning this pragmatic behavior. Data revealed the teachers' dominance of the follow-up turn. This had an effect on the students' learning because they were exposed to the teachers' modeling of acknowledgment expressions occurring in the follow-up turn. The students' participation in the IRF routine, supported by the teachers' explicit guidance to use acknowledgment tokens, helped students develop the ability to use assessments and alignments in peer-to-peer interaction.

Kinginger and Belz (2005) also applied a sociocultural perspective to their study; more precisely, they applied methodologies informed by sociocultural theory to carry out a longitudinal, ecologically valid, and detailed observation and documentation of learners' activities. This microgenetic approach allowed the authors to explore in detail how learners' experiences served to shape their use and development of German and French address forms. Grace, the focal participant in the German telecollaboration project, had access to peer assistance from expert speakers of German during her eight-week internet-based correspondence around pedagogical tasks. The authors found that, although Grace gradually learned to adopt the *T*-form of solidarity, which her German peers used exclusively, there were instances in which she did not respond to the peer feedback and continued to use the *V*-form of formality. Follow-up interview data revealed that she had made a conscious decision in opting for the *V*-form because of her limited grammatical knowledge with the category number for the *T*-form. These data demonstrated the learner's agency and identity reflected in her pragmatic choice. Even when learners develop understanding of the social meaning of address forms, they make choices pertaining to their own preferences.

More recently, sociocultural theory has made an impact in the area of instructional research in L2 pragmatics. Van Compernolle (2014) implemented concept-based instruction in teaching sociocultural concepts in L2 French linked to French address forms (*tu/vous*). Concept-based instruction follows Vygotsky's proposal about developing learners' control over theoretical concepts as they are guided through a sequence of activities designed to internalize the concepts. Based on this Vygotskian principle, Gal'perin (1989, 1992) developed the instructional approach that involves providing a complete orientation to the subject matter, materializing the unit of instruction through didactic aids (for example, flow charts and diagrams), and using verbalizations for internalization purposes (for example, self-directed speech reflecting on the concepts). Negueruela's (2008) study was the first to adapt Gal'perin's stepwise procedure to L2 teaching. He introduced grammar-based theoretical concepts in Spanish (for example, aspect and mood) that functioned as tools for thinking and self-regulation. He had students explain to themselves the reasoning behind applying such concepts when constructing meaning. This method essentially helped students to develop conceptual categories with their communicative functionality.

Van Compernolle (2014) demonstrated an application of concept-based instruction to pragmatics teaching. Learners were explicitly introduced to pragmatic concepts of power, social distance, and self-presentation via concept diagrams illustrating two individuals' relationship and stance to each other. These sociopragmatic concepts were linked to the pragmalinguistic forms of *tu* and *vous*, two distinct French address forms that represent the target concepts.

Instruction was conducted via tutorial by having learners verbalize their understanding of the French pronoun distinction. Grounded in the Vygotskian principle of language as a tool for thought, this approach centered on verbalization of metapragmatic awareness. During the tutorial, learners looked at the diagrams and explained the concepts. The tutor assisted the learners' explanations by providing a prompt within their ZPD. Results revealed a marked shift in the learners' thinking process from a conventional understanding of the *tu/vous* distinction to a more nuanced, personal concept-bound understanding of the pronouns. Particularly notable was the learners' increasing reference to the concept of self-presentation guiding their choice, i.e. how they want to present themselves in the situation: close or distant, formal or informal. This means that learners became aware that T/V choices are not merely a response to expected social norms. These findings suggest that, without metapragmatic explanation given top-down, learners can exercise their agency and develop understanding on their own with support provided by the tutor.

In future, we could benefit from additional empirical findings from concept-based instruction focusing on generalizability of learned knowledge. Because this method centers around developing learners' understanding of sociopragmatic concepts, an important question is whether the 'understanding' indeed translates to pragmatic performance, or whether understanding of one pragmatic concept facilitates understanding of other concepts (i.e. transfer of conceptual understanding). Another question is whether the concept-based instruction can assist learners' development of pragmalinguistic knowledge. Available findings are largely limited to the *tu/vous* distinction, but there are other pragmatic concepts that require a number of complex, idiosyncratic pragmalinguistic forms. For example, the concept of face-saving can be expressed through a number of linguistic devices, including lexical and syntactic mitigations, indirect forms, and positive and negative politeness strategies, which often occur in unison in one setting. Whether concept-based instruction can deal with complexity of pragmalinguistic forms (going beyond sociopragmatic knowledge) has not been attested and thus remains a topic for future investigation.

In summary, various ideas and concepts derived from sociocultural theory—mediation, interaction within the ZPD, scaffolding and assistance, private and inner speech, and learning in microgenesis—have been useful in elucidating the mechanisms of pragmatics learning and development. Although the body of findings is small, available studies have illustrated how a Vygotskian perspective can (re)shape our thinking of pragmatics. Critically, these ideas have provided an alternative view to pragmatic development as a process where new, more complex forms of thinking arise and eventually get established. Under the sociocultural perspective, pragmatic development is conceptualized beyond mastery of form–function–context mappings. It involves intellectual transformational processes of understanding what forms mean socially and what role they play in structuring interpersonal relationships and identities. Use of language, implemented through interaction, functions as a semiotic tool facilitating this process.

Most sociocultural research on interaction and its role in pragmatics learning has taken place in classrooms rather than in informal settings. However, interaction between an expert and novice often takes place in a naturalistic environment, such as study abroad, sojourn, or immersion, where learners have daily contact with community members. In those situations, local members may act as expert speakers, working within learners' ZPD and pushing them to a higher level of pragmatic knowledge and awareness. We will review some of these studies in the next section, under the theoretical framework of language socialization.

Language socialization

As Duff and Talmy (2011) summarize, language socialization finds its theoretical roots in a number of research frameworks and disciplines, including: linguistic anthropology (for example, Hymes, 1972; Schieffelin & Ochs, 1986), semiotics (Silverstein, 1976), sociology (for example, Bourdieu, 1977), sociocultural theory (Leontiev, 1981; Vygotsky, 1978), the dialogic approach to language (for example, Bahktin, 1981), cultural psychology (Lave &

Wenger, 1991), and systemic functional linguistics (for example, Halliday & Matthiessen, 2004). Language socialization contends that language knowledge and cultural knowledge are not separate, but acquired together during socialization (Ochs & Schieffelin, 1984). Language socialization is a process in which novices learn to become competent members in a society through interaction with expert members of a society. In this process, language is both the means and the end of the socialization process: novices are socialized *through* the use of language, and they are socialized *to use* language (Ochs, 1988, 1996; Ochs & Schieffelin, 1984; Schieffelin & Ochs, 1986).

The intersection between language and culture, from the language socialization perspective, is symbolized in the concept of *indexical knowledge*. In her discussion of the Indexical Principle, Ochs (1996) contends that socialization is a process of assigning indexical meanings (for example, temporal, special, affective, or epistemic meanings) to particular forms. A linguistic form has the potential to take on a variety of social meanings. For example, epistemic stance (or degree of uncertainty) is indexed through a range of forms, including sentential adverbs (for example, 'maybe' and 'possibly'), modal verbs ('can' and 'could'), hedges, and sentential mood (for example, interrogative structure). These forms constitute other situational dimensions, such as social acts and social identities. For example, the adverb 'maybe' can index the epistemic stance of certainty (or lack thereof) but also the act of giving advice or making a suggestion, as in 'Maybe you should get some rest'. In the indexical view, language is a tool for creating, maintaining, and negotiating social acts, activities, and identities (Ochs, 1996).

Language socialization involves acquiring this indexical knowledge. It is a process through which novices develop their 'understanding of linguistic forms [and] their indexical potential (i.e. the situational constellations of by whom, for what, when, where and to what ends forms are conventionally employed) in co-ordination with co-occurring linguistic forms and other symbolic dimensions of the situation at hand' (Ochs, 1996, p. 414). Language socialization emphasizes the agency of a language user, who chooses particular linguistic forms to construct social situations. Language socialization research examines how novices are guided by expert members to learn the semiotic processes of indexes through their participation in interactional routines.

In the context of L2 learning, Duff and Talmy (2011) present several characteristics of L2 socialization research. First, unlike studies under the cognitivist SLA, the object of investigation under the language socialization approach goes beyond aspects of a linguistic code (for example, grammar and lexis) and extends to the knowledge of culture, social knowledge, ideologies, and identities, among others. Duff and Talmy observe:

> In contrast to a restricted and decontextualized view of language as a neutral transmitter of information made up of morphemes, syntactic structures, lexis, and pragmatic norms, language socialization conceives of language as one of a multitude of in-flux, contested, and

ever-changing social practices that in part constitute particular dynamic communities of practice. Language socialization also differs from the cognitivist SLA in its focus on the local, social, political, and cultural contexts in which language is learned and used, on historical aspects of language and culture learning, on contestation and change across timescales, and on the cultural content of linguistic structures and practices.

(2011, p. 96)

As the excerpt illustrates, cognitive theories such as the noticing hypothesis and skill acquisition theories view pragmatic knowledge as discrete pragmalinguistic forms linked to their functions and contextual parameters. These theories conceptualize pragmatic development as a predictable, linear process that occurs within individuals as a function of noticing and amount of practice. In contrast, language socialization observes L2 learning in the macro and micro contexts in which language is actually learned and used. This approach emphasizes the concept of language *praxis* (Bourdieu, 1977). Learners develop an understanding of the indexical relationship between language and social meanings through recurrent observation and participation in everyday practices with community members. To this end, access and participation in social activities, as well as affordances of learning contexts, are the key components of L2 socialization. When learners do not have access to opportunities for practice, L2 development and ultimate attainment are inevitably restricted (Duff, 2012).

Contingency is another characteristic of language socialization, because outcomes of the socializing process are fluid and unpredictable (Duff & Talmy, 2011; Zuengler & Cole, 2005). Socialization can lead to the development of linguistic competence and internalization of cultural values and communicative practices, but it can also result in, intentionally or unintentionally, unsuccessful or unanticipated outcomes such as the incomplete understanding of L2 or peripheral position in the L2 community (Duff & Talmy, 2011). Although the unpredictability of learning outcomes is also assumed in other theories, the difference is that the qualitative, ethnographic methods taken by L2 socialization studies can explain why development did or did not happen.

Learners might unintentionally fail to conform to the norms that local members try to induct them into because, unlike L1 learners, L2 learners often lack sufficient access to competent speakers and legitimacy in full social participation due to their L2 learner identities or other identities imposed by the local community (Duff, 2003; Isabelli-Garcia, 2006; Morita, 2004, 2009; Norton, 2000). On the other hand, learners may intentionally not conform to L2 norms and linguistic practices in order to exercise their agency and adopt differing L2 options as a way to signal their identity (see Chapter 6). Unlike L1 learners, L2 learners already have a repertoire of linguistic and cultural practices in their native language. Learners might find that what local members consider appropriate language practices actually conflict with their own cultural and personal values. As a result, they might resist conforming to the community norms and even go so far as to attempt to socialize the locals into their own cultural practices. This phenomenon is observed precisely because of the object of examination in the L2 socialization research, i.e. acquisition of indexical knowledge or the meaning potential of linguistic forms. Language is not just a system of code. It is a 'system of symbolic resources designed for production and interpretation of social and intellectual activities' (Ochs, 1996, p. 407). Because linguistic forms encode cultural values and norms, enactment of the values through language can sometimes be difficult for learners if these values are in conflict with their own.

The L2 socialization process is also multidirectional (Duff & Talmy, 2011). Participation in social routines with more proficient community members facilitates learners' development, but proficient members are also socialized into their expert roles by learners. The experts learn from L2 learners about their distinct communicative needs, the cultural values that they bring into the practice, and their history and prior experiences that shape their stance toward L2 learning. Hence, as Duff and Talmy claim, L2 socialization is a bi- or multidirectional process that affects both novices and experts, and is accomplished collaboratively by both parties.

These various dimensions involved in L2 socialization—acquisition of indexical knowledge, contingency and unpredictability of learning, and multidirectionality of socialization outcomes—are particularly relevant to pragmatics learning. The interdependence of linguistic and sociocultural knowledge is the core of pragmatic knowledge, because pragmatics involves knowledge of linguistic forms and their social functions in context. The language socialization approach ensures that researchers direct their attention to this indexical aspect of language use when examining pragmatics learning. In addition, because pragmatics-specific concepts such as politeness, formality, and face-saving become meaningful only in real-life social interactions, analysis of authentic communicative practices, which is mandated in L2 socialization research, is useful for L2 pragmatic analysis. Perlocutionary effects carried by pragmatic behaviors also certify that pragmatic development is potentially contingent and multidirectional: successful pragmatic performance, or the outcome of pragmatics learning, depends on how learners' pragmatic behaviors are perceived and accepted by community members.

One of the criticisms of L2 socialization research has been its tendency to emphasize the macro or social aspects of L2 learning over micro, linguistic-level analyses of language development. Although a macro standpoint allows an analysis of communicative events and their linguistic affordances, as well as ecologies of the L2 learning process, it does not replace a fine-grained, micro-level analysis of learners' linguistic forms and how they change over time during socialization. Thus, critics say that a narrower, more linguistic-focused analysis will make language socialization theory more relevant to the field of SLA (R. Ellis, 2009).

This criticism, however, does not apply to L2 pragmatics because there is a wealth of pragmatic socialization studies that focused on specific pragmalinguistic features and tracked their change in the everyday activities of language users. A variety of pragmatic features, social events, social identities of the learners and their expert interlocutors, and occasions of explicit and implicit socialization have been examined in these studies. An example is Hassall's (2006) study on his own learning of L2 Indonesian (cited previously). When the author took leave with the expression *Pulang dulu, ya?* ('I'm going home, OK?'), a native speaker corrected him by modeling the appropriate leave-taking form in the situation (*permisi*). Similarly, in Belz and Kinginger's (2003) study, peer feedback in a CMC setting played a facilitative role in socializing L2 German learners into the use of *T*-form as an index of solidarity. Taguchi (2012) also revealed that teacher feedback worked to socialize an ESL learner into using appropriate request-making forms. Ohta (2001) showed how L2 Japanese learners in the classroom were socialized into the role of an empathetic listener by learning expressions of acknowledgment and alignment. Other notable examples include Kanagy's (1999) study on the L2 Japanese socialization of classroom routines in a kindergarten; D. Li's (2000) study on the acquisition of requests among immigrants at work; Ishida's (2009, 2011) study on the development of Japanese listener responses in a homestay setting; and Shively's (2013) study on peer socialization in L2 Spanish humor.

As a set, studies of this sort have illustrated a dual process that learners undergo in their socialization process: socialization *to use* language and socialization *through* the use of language (Schieffelin & Ochs, 1986). Through guided assistance provided by community members, learners are socialized into the use of particular pragmalinguistic forms and their sociopragmatic meanings. Learning to use these forms and their meaning potential socializes learners to become competent members of a given community. Daily routines—a casual chat with neighbors, routine interactions in a classroom and workplace, and synchronous online communication—all serve as a platform where socialization and learning occur. These studies have also confirmed that, by examining daily interactional routines, L2 socialization research addresses and goes beyond the analysis of words, phrases, and sentences to deal with the indexical or pragmatic meaning of these forms within a larger interpersonal discourse context.

Below we will review three L2 pragmatics studies that have explicitly adapted the socialization approach to reveal the dual process of L2 socialization and acquisition of indexical meaning (Cook, 2008; Diao, 2016; DuFon, 2010). These studies revealed instances of both explicit and implicit socialization. Explicit socialization involves overt teaching of local norms and values, modeling of desired linguistic demeanors, and direct feedback and correction given to learners' inappropriate linguistic behaviors. Although explicit socialization might be more salient and effective, implicit socialization is probably more ubiquitous. Local members may implicitly signal linguistic and sociocultural information by using particular pragmalinguistic forms in front of the learners or providing repairs to learners' pragmatic language use. A variety of data used in these implicit and explicit socialization studies—diaries, field observations, conversation data, and interviews—also help us to understand what it takes to uncover a moment of explicit and implicit socialization in a naturalistic setting.

DuFon (2010) examined how L2 Indonesian learners were socialized into the practice of leave-taking and simultaneously into cultural values and beliefs associated with leave-taking routines. In Indonesian culture, the words *permisi* and *pamit,* which convey the sense of asking permission to leave, are directed to someone in authority. Using these words at leave-taking (i.e. *permit*-ing) is more than just saying goodbye. Because *permit*-ing essentially asks permission, it encodes cultural values of showing humility and respect for those of higher status. Hence, *permisi* and *pamit* are indexical forms that constitute a social structure: they define the social identities of the participants and the social act that they intend to accomplish. Gaining understanding of the social and indexical scope of these forms is a process of socialization.

DuFon found that novices (in this case, the learners) often struggled to adapt to the practice of *permit*-ing as a way of redefining their relationship with their local interlocutors, simply because this cultural practice was foreign to them. In those cases, both experts (native speakers) and novices (the learners) negotiated and collaboratively constructed the definition of leave-taking. Explicit socialization into these forms and cultural values occurred through native speakers' direct corrections. For example, when the learner (the author of the study) visited a school administrator's office to receive a report card and started leaving the office, she was told to be polite and *permit* the administrator. The author recalled this instance as a 'powerful lesson', teaching her the norm of showing respect to a higher-status person by asking his permission to leave. Implicit socialization, on the other hand, occurred through learners' observations of the contexts in which *permit*-ing is not necessary. One such context was saying goodbye to someone who is of an equal or lower status. The author learned this when her host brother said *saya berangkat* ('I'm leaving') to her at leave-taking. This phrase simply announced his departure, without asking permission.

While DuFon illustrated instances of socialization through field notes and self-report data, Cook (2008) presented micro-level analyses of dinnertime conversation in a homestay context to illustrate explicit and implicit socialization in microgenesis. The focal pragmatic feature analyzed in the study was Japanese speech style: the polite and plain forms that appear at the utterance-ending position. Although the polite form is typically associated with formal speech and the plain form with informal speech, speakers often shift between these two forms in a single conversation in order to negotiate interpersonal distance and to index different voices and social identities.

Cook's data showed how expert members of the society (i.e. host family members) socialized American learners of Japanese into this indexical knowledge of speech style during dinnertime talk. Cook observed that family members predominantly used the plain form among themselves and with the learners, which in turn socialized learners to use the plain form in daily interactions at home. By using the plain form, learners and host family members co-constructed the *uchi* (in-group) context and created social meanings of solidarity, familiarity, and informality.

However, the participants at times shifted to the polite form in a marked manner in order to create a *soto* (out-group) identity. These shifts to the polite form indirectly indexed various social identities related to responsibilities in the family or voices of people outside the family in their roles. For instance, the participants shifted to the polite form when they were in charge of activities at hand. A host mother shifted to the polite form when she was talking about the food that she had just prepared, signalling her identity and authority as the provider of food in the household. On another occasion, a host mother shifted to the polite form when she was explaining to a learner about Japanese language and social customs, which indexed the self-presentational stance and highlighted her identity as a knowledgeable person. Another instance of style-shifting was found when host family members directly took on the voices of others, for example mimicking the voice of a mailman or a customer. Using the polite form on these occasions was a way to index the voices of people outside the family (*soto* or out-group), socializing the learners to use appropriate voices in different contexts and social roles.

See Figure 3.3, a dialogue between Greg (G) and his host mother (HM), for illustration (Cook, 2008). In line 3, the host mother talks about the food she has just prepared using the plain form. Then, in line 5, she switches to the polite form (*tsukurimashita* 'made') when she paraphrases what she said

1	**HM**	*doozo* =			
		please			
		'please'			
2	**G**	*hai (2.0)*	*nn <u>soba</u>?*		
		yes	um soba noodles		
		'yes, uh soba noodles?'			
3	**HM**	*kyoo*	*wa*	*ne*	*<u>yakisoba</u>* =
		today	Top	FP	fried noodles
		'It's fried noodles today.'			
4	**G**	= *un*			
		yeah			
		'yeah'			
5	**HM**	*hisashiburi ni*	*yakisobba*	*o*	***tsukurimashita.***
		after a long time	fried noodles	O	made
		'I cooked fried noodles for the first time in a long time.'			

Figure 3.3 Conversation between Greg and his host mother (Cook, 2008, p. 78)

in line 3. By using the polite form, she presents herself as someone who is in charge of cooking for the household, signalling her identity as a caretaker.

Notably, the learners also style-shifted to the polite form for the exact interactional functions, i.e. foregrounding particular aspects of their social identity and quoting others in different contexts, although the frequency was much smaller than that of host family members. For example, one learner switched to the polite form when he responded to his host mother's question about an English word as a way of signaling his authority and expertise in the English language. These findings indicate that implicit socialization into Japanese speech style was constant in dinnertime routines. The learners gradually developed their indexical knowledge of the polite form through their recurrent observation and participation in this social activity. While implicit socialization was pervasive, explicit socialization was also found in the data. Host family members sometimes modeled appropriate voices in certain social situations and provided metalinguistic explanations about polite language and gendered speech.

Diao's (2016) study also illustrates explicit and implicit socialization in dual process (socialization to use language and socialization through language), but unlike the other two studies, she revealed the bi-directionality of socialization outcomes, i.e. socialization affecting both novices and experts. She analyzed conversations among three American learners of L2 Chinese and their Chinese roommates in a college dorm in Shanghai and described instances of peer socialization of gendered Mandarin practices. Her analysis focused on the participants' use of affective sentence-final particles and their discussion about the social meanings they projected.

Affective sentence-final particles (ASPs), such as *a/ya, la, me, o, eh/ye*, are common in Chinese conversations and index multiple social meanings including affect and politeness. They are also increasingly becoming indexes of gender, as women frequently use them as a linguistic resource in order to enact an infantilized, powerless, female persona. Through the analysis of the use of ASPs, participants' gendered linguistic practices became apparent.

One female learner, Ellen, used ASPs during a conversation with her Chinese roommate, Helen. This happened right after Helen had commented that Ellen's way of speaking sounded like a man. Following this comment, she immediately changed her way of speech in a playful manner, by adding the particle *a* to her utterance with a girl-like high pitch. These instances indicate that Ellen was aware of the indexical meaning of the ASP and used it as a strategy to project a cute female persona. During interaction, Helen constantly provided backchannel cues ('right, right, right') to Ellen, which functioned to support Ellen's understanding of the ASP. Here, the learner and her peer collaboratively achieved socialization into the gendered speech.

Diao also presented a case where ASPs became a way of policing sexual orientation between a male learner (Tuzi) and his roommate (Li). Li noticed Tuzi's frequent use of ASPs and told him not to use them because he sounds 'like a gay or a woman'. In fact, Tuzi's habit of using ASPs came from his previous experience when he spent six months in southern China where ASPs are routinely used among locals of both genders. Li helped Tuzi understand additional social meanings of ASPs, for example, that in Shanghai they are indexical of sexual orientation. Socialization here took place bi-directionally. Tuzi was socialized into varied meanings of ASPs by Li. At the same time, Li was socialized into his expert role in instructing the learner about norms of ASPs in the local community. These findings add to Schieffelin and Ochs's (1986, p. 165) claim that, in social interactions, participants are not only learning ways of interacting, but also 'socializing each other into their particular world views as they negotiate situated meaning'.

Ellen and Tuzi's linguistic practices evolved around the dimension of gender, but a difference between these two cases was the outcome of socialization. Ellen's use of ASPs was accepted as a way of displaying a female persona, whereas Tuzi was sanctioned against using ASPs because they were incongruent with his heterosexuality. Results showed divergent patterns in the production of ASPs: while Ellen's ASP frequency increased by 8% from the first conversation to the last conversation at the end of the semester, Tuzi's frequency dropped by 9%.

In summary, these studies illustrate how language socialization acts as a mechanism for pragmatics learning. Pragmatics learning is embedded in cultural practices in situ in a community of users of the language. Learners develop an understanding of pragmalinguistic forms and their indexical meanings (for example, *permit*-ing as a signal of respect; the plain and polite forms as resources for projecting various social identities; sentence-final particles as an index of sexuality) through routine interactions with expert members of the community. Socialization into pragmatic language use happens explicitly through the experts' modeling, correction, and provision of metapragmatic information, as well as implicitly through observation of the experts' pragmatic performance. The result of this process is socialization into the local community through language use. The language socialization framework expands the scope of the analysis from pragmalinguistic and sociopragmatic knowledge alone to other knowledge bases, including knowledge of culture, norms, and social practice, and generates a broad description of the cultures and communities, of which pragmatics learning is a part.

Future research should continue cultivating ways to apply the socialization approach to pragmatic analysis, perhaps with more in-depth examination of pragmatic abilities and how they evolve over the course of study. Although existing studies are largely longitudinal, involving regular observations of learners' social participation over an extended period, these studies do not always have a parallel form of systematic, cyclical documentation of learners' pragmatic abilities. As a result, we do not know how pragmatic abilities changed as a function of socialization or whether the change is stable or ephemeral. According to Ortega and Iberri-Shea (2005), longitudinal research, by design, involves the conceptual focus of capturing change, with an emphasis on establishing antecedent–consequent relationships by tracking L2 learning in its context. Future pragmatic socialization studies should commit to these definitions of longitudinal research by incorporating systematic data collection on pragmatic abilities through a cyclical use of comparative tasks and analytical tools. In turn, learners' changing pragmatic abilities can be linked to a critical moment of explicit and implicit socialization to reveal the influence of context, culture, and community shaping learners' pragmatic development.

Conversation Analysis

While CA is being increasingly used as an approach to the analysis of L2 pragmatics data (for example, Al-Gahtani & Roever, 2012, 2014 a, b, 2015b; Lee & Hellermann, 2014; Pekarek Doehler & Pochon-Berger, 2011, 2015), it cannot easily be applied to <u>explaining learning</u>, which has traditionally been the <u>fundamental goal of L2 pragmatics research</u>. CA is not designed as a theory of learning, but rather as an analytical approach for describing social conduct whose main objective is to explain how people manage their social relations moment by moment through talk. In fact, studies comparing groups of participants or the same participants at several points in time are uncommon in CA, and until Zimmerman (1999) argued for the value of horizontal (cross-sectional) or vertical (longitudinal) comparisons, there was little rationale in CA to compare at all. In addition, CA has a strongly anti-mentalist stance (Kasper, 2009; Markee & Seo, 2009), emphasizing observable data and behaviors and declining to speculate about possible motivations, intentions, or cognitive processes since these are not available to interactants. By contrast, most <u>theories of L2 pragmatics discuss cognitive processes of learning</u> and <u>mental representation</u>.

At the same time, CA's microanalytic approach, its extreme attention to minute details of unfolding talk, and its rigorously emic perspective requiring that any analytic conclusion be substantiated with data make CA an attractive tool in SLA research. In addition, its provenance as a sociological theory concerned with social conduct makes it particularly interesting for L2 pragmatics. But how can the large disparity between CA's lack of interest in learning and downright hostility to cognitive processes be reconciled with L2 pragmatics' traditional cognitive and acquisitional agenda?

There are three broad ways of dealing with this issue, which we explain in more detail below:

- make L2 pragmatics primary and use CA as an analytic tool without subscribing to its epistemology (Al-Gahtani & Roever, 2014 a, b; Taguchi, 2014a)
- combine CA with an exogenous theory that accommodates learning (for example, Cekaite, 2007; Hellermann & Cole, 2009)
- practice 'pure CA' (Jenks, 2010) and take a descriptive, shared cognition view of learning (for example, Kasper, 2009; Markee & Kunitz, 2013).

Making L2 pragmatics primary

These studies use CA as an analytical tool within an L2 pragmatics study while relaxing some of CA's fundamental assumptions, including reliance on natural data, entirely bottom-up data analysis without pre-existing target features or categories, and no speculation about mental processes. These types of studies might use role-play data rather than natural data (Al-Gahtani & Roever, 2012), investigate pre-existing research questions (Al-Gahtani & Roever, 2014 a, b; Huth, 2010), and not just contrast practices to demonstrate that learning must have occurred but actually use 'mentalist' constructs like proficiency, noticing, and knowledge to explain and model learning (Al-Gahtani & Roever, 2012, 2013, 2014b; Taguchi, 2014a).

For example, in their study of insert and post-expansions in L2 Arabic requests, Al-Gahtani and Roever (2014b) designed a language use situation that would elicit requests from learners at four different proficiency levels in an institutional interaction with an administrator. Al-Gahtani and Roever (2014b) then identified and categorized these sequences and compared them between learner groups. In the final analytic step, they explained differences between groups by means of noticing, cognitive processing, and knowledge representation.

In a similar vein, Taguchi (2014a) investigated the use of incomplete sentences by learners of Japanese as a second language before and after a 12-week study abroad period in Japan. While she recorded and analyzed learner interactions that were not specifically designed to elicit incomplete sentences, she explicitly built on previous research in the area. Undertaking vertical comparison in Zimmerman's (1999) terms, Taguchi found a much greater use of incomplete sentences for the purpose of joint turn construction and efficient communication post-sojourn. She views this change as an expansion of learners' functional abilities and improvement in their interactional competence to co-construct conversations. To explain how learning occurred, she takes a broad noticing perspective, interpreting her findings on this feature of Japanese as evidence 'that learners picked it up naturally as they were exposed to naturalistic conversation and observed how and when incomplete sentences occur and what functions they play' (p. 530).

These studies, and others done in the same tradition (Al-Gahtani & Roever, 2012; Youn, 2013, 2015; Zhang, 2016), make the L2 pragmatics research program primary and use CA in a limited way as a research tool that is helpful in analyzing interaction and in its micro-features.

Combining CA with exogenous theory

Studies combining CA with exogenous theory tend to try to strike a balance between CA and the exogenous theory by emphasizing the social aspect of interaction and minimizing any 'mentalist' approach to analysis. Theoretical stances that have been taken include sociocultural theory (van Compernolle,

2011b; Ishida, 2011), language socialization (Cekaite, 2007), and community of practice (Hellermann & Cole, 2009).

An application of sociocultural theory is exemplified in van Compernolle's
(2011b) study of Oral Proficiency Interviews (OPIs) and the role of repair.
He analyzed appropriate and inappropriate learner responses to questions in
OPIs using CA, and noted that little repair work is initiated by learners, even
though such work could open up learning opportunities. Van Compernolle
(2011) then used his data to support a proposal for a pedagogical intervention to improve learners' use of repair through concept appropriation based
on Vygotsky's (1997) model of concept-based instruction. Van Compernolle's
connection between the CA-based data analysis and his pedagogical proposal
is relatively loose: he demonstrates a particular learner practice and then suggests a pedagogical approach for improving that practice, which follows
sociocultural theory. From a CA perspective, the analysis could have stood
on its own and, in turn, the pedagogical suggestion could have been informed
by an analysis other than CA. Whether the use of a pedagogical intervention
based on concept appropriation actually would lead to learning and change
learners' practices was not investigated by van Compernolle. Ishida (2011)
also interpreted her L2 Japanese learner's changes in listenership as a recipient of storytelling from a sociocultural perspective. As was the case for van
Compernolle (2011b), Ishida's (2011) use of sociocultural theory was quite
separate from her CA-based analysis, only occurring in the latter half of her
discussion of her findings.

Cekaite (2007) analyzed a second language learner's changes in classroom
participation from a language socialization perspective. Following an L1
Kurdish immigrant child during her first year in a Swedish immersion classroom for refugees and immigrants, she documented the learner's development
from quiet non-participation to very active but at times inappropriate participation, for which she received negative feedback from teachers and other
students. Finally, the learner displayed appropriate and expected classroom
participation patterns. Cekaite (2007) analyzes the learner's development as
a process of learning how to design interactional contributions that were
acceptable within the frames of various classroom activities. Cekaite ties
her interpretations of her data more closely to the theoretical framework of
socialization than van Compernolle (2011b) does in that she demonstrates
changes in the learner's interactional competence and explains these changes
by means of socialization theory. This way she exploits the microanalytic
strengths of CA for supporting her theory-based conclusions.

A popular theoretical framework combined with CA is community of
practice (Lave, 1988; Lave & Wenger, 1991), which describes a community
characterized by the members' mutual engagement, a shared goal, and a
common repertoire of practices. New members are initially at the periphery of the community and over time can move toward full participation.
Hellermann and Cole (2009) showed how an adult learner of English in an
ESL classroom moved from the use of minimal contributions and interactional

routines to more elaborate language use and engagement in a variety of practices related to disengaging from tasks. Hellermann and Cole (2009) interpret their findings as indicative of development from peripheral participation to full participation in task disengagement within individual sessions and, more dramatically, over a 16-month period. Similar to Cekaite (2007), Hellermann and Cole (2009) use their CA analyses to support their interpretations of the learner's change in level of participation.

Hauser (2011) provides a response to Hellermann and Cole's (2009) study, demonstrating that the use of an exogenous theory can be problematic. Hauser is critical of Hellermann and Cole's (2009) equating of increasing participation with increasing linguistic sophistication and questions the overall usefulness of the community of practice framework for CA-based analyses of learning. He argues that Lave and Wenger (1991) saw participation not primarily as participation in interaction but as participation in setting-relevant activities, which may or may not be interactionally constituted. Hauser (2011) expresses concern that the use of exogenous theory in CA-based studies can be a poor fit for the data and lead to a theory being imposed on the data that accounts for it inadequately.

Practicing 'pure CA'

Hauser's (2011) position is similar to the one proposed by Kasper (2009) and Wootton (1997), who consider CA sufficient for developmental studies without adducing an exogenous theory. Kasper (2009) and Kasper and Wagner (2011) argue against the need for an exogenous theory and emphasize that the results of whatever intra-psychological processes might occur in participants are available to interlocutors and analysts through the interaction. Researchers can identify differences in interactional practices over time or between groups, and document development by describing qualitatively different practices without employing exogenous theory or speculations about invisible mental states.

Pekarek Doehler and Pochon-Berger (2011) report a study that considered development rather than learning, emphasizing the 'products of learning' (p. 238) rather than the processes. They compared disagreements from classroom data between learners of French at two different proficiency levels and identified differences in sequential organization and turn design of the disagreement turn. Higher-proficiency learners implemented typical sequential organization of disagreements as dispreferred actions by using sequential delay, token agreement, and mitigation. By contrast, lower-proficiency learners showed much less design of disagreements as dispreferred actions. Pekarek Doehler and Pochon-Berger (2011) do not use exogenous theoretical concepts to account for learning and go further in that they only consider observable changes. They therefore describe differences between groups, which are evidence of the development of interactional competence, but they do not theorize about the cognitive reality of these changes within learners. Similarly, in a longitudinal case study of a learner of L2 Spanish, González-Lloret (2011) shows development in the learner's responses to troubles talk (mentions of unpleasant, undesirable or difficult events) in online chats with her L1 Spanish interlocutor. Whereas in earlier interactions the learner largely takes the telling of troubles as information, in later interactions she responds with elaboration, sympathy and her own experience, thereby displaying affiliation with the troubles-telling. González-Lloret (2011) does not engage in deliberations on how the learner may have noticed, processed, or acquired trouble talk responses either; instead, she focuses on the observable learning outcomes.

Summary: CA as/within L2 pragmatics

Whether a researcher considers CA to be sufficient for investigating L2 pragmatics or sees a need for more or less cognitivist theoretical accounts of learning primarily depends on the researcher's own epistemological stance. Researchers approaching L2 pragmatics from a CA perspective focus on interactional patterns, practices, and features, and 'learning' from this perspective is constituted by changes in these patterns, practices, and features. It is not of great interest to these researchers what caused these changes in terms of learners' knowledge about L2 sociopragmatics and pragmalinguistics. Also, their view of interactional competence as being co-constructed (Kasper & Wagner, 2011; Mehan, 1979) makes it pointless to focus on individual learners. Rather, they show evidence of the outcomes of learning without explaining how and why learning occurred, and what learners' visible performance means for their invisible competence. This 'pure' approach has been taken by the majority of CA-based studies in L2 pragmatics but can be critically viewed as a 'black box' approach to learning: the 'pure' approach does not deny that cognitive processes occur, but it is not interested in exploring them. This would make it very difficult to design instructional interventions, which rely on understanding why and how learners learn.

By contrast, researchers interested in L2 pragmatics learning from a cognitive perspective (or a socio-cognitive perspective) tend to use CA as an analytic tool whose findings are then interpreted through the lens of a theory that accounts for learning and models how learners' cognition changes in the process of learning. Such a 'CA-informed' approach can still follow CA principles closely in data analysis by employing detailed transcription, the next-turn proof procedure (Sacks, Schegloff, & Jefferson, 1974) for justifying the labelling of social actions, and CA analytic categories, such as adjacency pair and pre-expansion, post-expansion, and insert expansion (see Chapter 4 for more detail on CA categories). However, subsequent to analysis, researchers explain the differences and similarities found with the help of one of the theories outlined in this chapter. Some of the questions that might be asked are: What do the results show about learners' pragmalinguistic and sociopragmatic knowledge? Have they been socialized into particular practices? Has learned, declarative knowledge been automatized? Does their increased proficiency allow them to produce request forms that were previously outside their reach? Answering questions like these would be considered undue speculation by 'pure' CA research, but for researchers following cognitive paradigms, they are essential for understanding L2 pragmatics learning.

Overall, we believe that CA can make a significant contribution to L2 pragmatics research, but some degree of epistemological compromise will be involved. For studies aiming to explore L2 pragmatics learning, CA is probably more useful as an analytic toolkit than as a research paradigm.

Chapter summary and directions for future research

This chapter has discussed seven distinct SLA theories as applied to L2 pragmatics research. Our discussion has evolved around the central question: What mechanisms drive pragmatic development and move learners from their current stage to a higher stage of pragmatic competence? We have observed that different theoretical paradigms conceptualize pragmatic knowledge differently and offer different explanations as to how pragmatic competence develops.

The two-dimensional model (Bialystok, 1993) views pragmatic competence as entailing two aspects: analysis of knowledge and control of processing. This conceptualization is also found in Faerch and Kasper's (1984) model that theorizes pragmatic competence as involving declarative and procedural knowledge. The end goal of pragmatic development, based on these models, is to acquire pragmatic knowledge and gain automatic control in using the knowledge in real time. These models explain the nature of pragmatic competence by expanding the scope of the analysis from knowledge to processing. Existing findings do indeed provide evidence that these two dimensions do not develop in parallel (for example, S. Li, 2014; Taguchi, 2012). However, these models do not explicate how the two dimensions develop. In other words, underlying mechanisms that trigger and impel development are missing from the models.

Those mechanisms are explained by the noticing hypothesis and skill acquisition theories. The noticing hypothesis (Schmidt, 1993, 2001) emphasizes the role of awareness and consciousness in promoting the entry of declarative knowledge into learners' systems. Hence, the initial phase of input selection and attentional condition is the primary concern of the noticing hypothesis. The idea that input becomes intake and leads to acquisition only if learners notice the input has been widely accepted in general SLA research. Specifically, the contribution of the theory to pragmatics is seen in the theory's specification of the object of noticing. In pragmatics, noticing goes beyond just focus on form(s). Attention to linguistic forms, functional meanings, and relevant contextual features (i.e. form–function–context mappings) is necessary for pragmatic input to become intake (Schmidt, 1993).

But the critical question is how the transition from noticing to intake and learning happens. Previous studies illustrated the instances in which learners noticed the form–function–context mappings, but learners showed incomplete use of the attended mappings at a later period (Belz & Kinginger, 2003; Kakegawa, 2009). Surely attention and consciousness are primary conditions, but they are not the only conditions needed for learning to take place. A good illustration of this is Taguchi's (2012) study, which revealed contrasting outcomes of noticing between two focal participants, Shoko and Yosuke. Shoko learned the request form through feedback and modeling in her instructor's email, but Yosuke did not learn, or at least failed to demonstrate his learning, despite the fact that he saw the same email and noticed the target form. These findings indicate that there have to be additional mechanisms in place, beyond noticing, that promote learning. More explicit attention to the noticing–intake–learning link is necessary to fully account for the mechanisms of pragmatic development.

Skill acquisition theories represented in the ACT–R model (Anderson et al., 2004) attempt this. Like the two-dimensional model, the ACT–R conceptualizes knowledge as involving declarative and procedural knowledge. Similar to the noticing hypothesis, the ACT–R model places emphasis on the role of attention and consciousness because these are the primary characteristics of the declarative knowledge base. But unlike the other two models, skill acquisition theories specify the process underlying the shift from the declarative to procedural knowledge. Through repeated activation (or practice) of declarative knowledge, chunks of declarative knowledge become organized into a condition–action rule, i.e. 'if in this situation when performing this function, use this pragmalinguistic form'. As a result, declarative knowledge transforms into procedural knowledge, which requires less attentional resource. The end point of acquisition is the stage of automatization where performance becomes rapid and error-free.

Existing findings have revealed the development of accurate, fluent execution of form–function–context mappings as a function of practice (S. Li, 2012, 2013; Li & Taguchi, 2014), but these studies largely focused on the proceduralization of knowledge and did not attend to the process involved in the formation of declarative knowledge. Learners received explicit information about pragmatic rules in one setting, and their mastery of knowledge was confirmed. Only after this was confirmed did learners move on to the practice stage. Hence, these studies gave primary explanatory power to practice as a mechanism that strengthens knowledge. Consolidation of pragmatic knowledge was expected to occur at the practice stage through repeated application of knowledge in pragmatic tasks.

Socially oriented theoretical paradigms (collaborative dialogue and languaging (Swain, 2006; Swain & Watanabe, 2013) and sociocultural theory (Vygotsky, 1978)) offer an alternative explanation to the consolidation of pragmatic knowledge. These two theories contend that pragmatic knowledge is co-constructed among participants in interaction and emerges from talk around problem-solving. This process helps consolidate pragmatic knowledge because it prompts a deeper level of cognitive processing by having learners negotiate their understanding of pragmatics. This process is in line with sociocultural theory, which claims that verbalization mediates cognition and leads to a deeper understanding of a concept. Concept-based instruction can prompt learners to verbalize their reflections of sociological concepts, which in turn consolidates understanding of concepts and linguistic forms that index the concepts. With respect to the mechanisms of pragmatic development, sociocultural theory gives central explanatory power to verbalization through mediation: evidence of learning is gleaned from the quality of learners' verbal protocols (evidence of thinking through concepts).

Language socialization theory adds a new perspective to pragmatic development. Because of the theory's attention to language and culture, L2 socialization research is committed to examining naturalistic interaction in a sociocultural context. In a similar way to the paradigms of collaborative dialogue and sociocultural theory, language socialization values interaction in a socially organized activity, but the locus of interaction is much broader: community, culture, and society. As a result, conceptualization of pragmatic competence is broader, including indexical knowledge, cultural values, norms, ideologies, and identities. Pragmatic development is not limited to the acquisition of pragmalinguistic and sociopragmatic knowledge, but extends to the understanding of how these knowledge bases work in a community, which essentially leads to the establishment of membership in that community. Hence, pragmatic development is viewed as a dual process of socialization. A learner is socialized to use language through participation in daily routines, which leads to their acquisition of pragmalinguistics and sociopragmatics. At the same time, through pragmatic language use, a learner is socialized to become a competent member in the community. Pragmalinguistics and sociopragmatics are resources that learners draw on during this socialization process.

As with collaborative dialogue and sociocultural theory, the language socialization theory contends that consolidation of pragmatic knowledge happens through assisted interaction in social activities. However, unlike other paradigms, this theory draws on learners' real-life experiences in authentic situations. Noticing and intake occur in learners' own individual contexts with people they interact with regularly. The immediacy and relevance associated with interaction and participation essentially strengthen learners' pragmatic knowledge. Interaction is highly contextualized, embedded in their everyday discourse. As a result, attended pragmalinguistic and sociopragmatic knowledge becomes salient and memorable.

Conversation Analysis might be the 'odd one out' among the theories discussed in this chapter since it does not have much interest in learning, at least where learning is understood as a change in knowledge representations. Being rigorously, even rigidly, bottom-up and data driven, pure CA research contents itself with describing outcomes of learning which can be identified in changing interactional practices, rather than 'speculating' about mental processes. While this stance is probably too constraining for most L2 pragmatics researchers interested in acquisition, a less orthodox version of CA can be beneficial to pragmatics research. CA has amassed a huge amount of research on interaction and created a solid yet flexible set of analytic tools, which is highly suitable for investigating learners' development in their ability to participate in extended interactions. CA is highly suited to analyzing sequential organization of talk and identifying subtle as well as more dramatic changes. Using CA as a methodology in L2 pragmatics research or combining it with a theory like socialization theory or sociocultural theory is a fruitful way of exploiting the methodological power of CA without fully subscribing to its epistemology.

We have outlined mechanisms of pragmatic development under seven distinct theoretical paradigms. From the accumulated body of research, we can certainly observe a growing variety in the theoretical epistemology underpinning pragmatic development. Although these theoretical frameworks differ in how they view pragmatic knowledge and underlying mechanisms for pragmatics learning, they all consider the consolidation of pragmatic knowledge to be crucial in development. The noticing hypothesis emphasizes attention and awareness as primary conditions for the consolidation to take place. Under skill acquisition theories, consolidation of pragmatic rules occurs through repeated, conscious application of the rules. Sociocultural theory and collaborative dialogue view verbalization as a means for externalizing understanding of pragmatic concepts, which in turn facilitates internalization of the concepts. In language socialization, the driving force for the consolidation of pragmatic knowledge is recurrent participation in social activities with more proficient members.

We hope that this theoretical diversity in the current field will continue with more empirical data coming from the recent frameworks discussed here, and with the addition of new theories drawn from broader disciplines of SLA, psychology, and education. One framework that has not been fully incorporated into L2 pragmatics is the Cognition Hypothesis (Robinson 2011). The hypothesis claims that more complex tasks promote more interaction, leading to language development. Robinson proposes two dimensions of task complexity: resource-dispersing and resource-directing. The former involves task features that impact learners' attention and processing capacities (for example, availability of planning time), while the latter refers to the features that pose cognitive demands in such a way that they direct learners' attention to specific aspects of language. This principle can be applied to L2 pragmatics such that task complexity promotes consolidation of pragmatic knowledge. The Cognition Hypothesis could serve as an alternative theoretical framework that enriches our understanding of mechanisms behind pragmatic development. Kim and Taguchi's (2015, 2016) studies are samples in this direction. These studies adopted the Cognition Hypothesis to develop instructional tasks for teaching requests in L2 English. Results showed that cognitive complexity (rather than pragmatic complexity) generated a greater amount of interaction (Kim & Taguchi, 2016). There was a positive effect of task complexity in the retention of learning (Kim & Taguchi, 2015).

Dynamic Complexity theory Another recent theory that deserves more attention in L2 pragmatics is dynamic complexity theory. Corresponding to the recent paradigm shift and social turn in SLA, there has been increasing attention given to dynamicity and complexity of L2 acquisition in a social context. Dynamic Systems Theory (DST) (de Bot, 2008; Verspoor, de Bot, & Lowie, 2011), complexity theory (Larsen-Freeman & Cameron, 2008; Larsen-Freeman, 2012), and emergentism (N. Ellis & Larsen-Freeman, 2006; MacWhinney, 2006) are major forerunners in this trend. These approaches view L2 development as a dynamic, non-linear process, emerging from socially co-regulated interactions between multiple influences in context. Learning is characterized as non-linear, irregular, and unevenly paced, involving a great degree of inter- and intra-variation. Recently, DST-specific terminologies and methods have emerged in the field to illustrate variability and non-linearity in L2 development (for example, Lowie & Verspoor, 2015; Verspoor, de Bot, & Lowie, 2011). These new ideas have potential to lead to innovation in the theory-building of L2 pragmatics. We will provide more detailed accounts of DST in Chapter 6, where the topic of individual differences in pragmatics development will be discussed.

4

Research methods in L2 pragmatics

Introduction

The question of research methodology in L2 pragmatics is a long-standing concern, and justifiably so: how data is collected and analyzed is crucial for determining what conclusions can be drawn. Methods can be categorized according to how data is collected, for example via elicitation, observation or experiment (Golato & Golato, 2013), or according to the kind of data that results from a study. Taking the latter perspective, resulting data can be classified along reception/production lines as receptive judgment data, non-interactive production data, and interactive production data. Receptive judgment data results from metapragmatic judgment instruments, whereas non-interactive production data results from production questionnaires like discourse completion tasks (DCTs). Interactive production data results from role-plays, elicited conversations, and natural interactions. Supplementary data about language users' cognitive processes is rendered by verbal reports. We will discuss each type of data and look at some typical research instruments. Finally, we will outline data analysis procedures.

Receptive data

Metapragmatic judgments

Metapragmatic judgment items (also known as 'acceptability judgments' or sometimes 'appropriateness judgments') elicit respondents' perceptions about a pragmatic feature, most commonly their impression of the appropriateness of a stimulus utterance, but also their perception of power, social distance, or imposition, or their comprehension of implied meaning. Metapragmatic judgment tasks allow researchers to draw conclusions about participants' awareness of target language pragmatic norms, their perception of pragmatic meanings, and their pragmatic intuitions. Since these tasks do not elicit productive abilities, they do not support conclusions about learners' deployment of pragmatic knowledge; but at the same time, they can access pragmatic knowledge more directly than they could in tasks where responses are mediated (and possibly contaminated) by learners' speaking and writing ability. Metapragmatic judgment tasks only require comprehension, which tends to put less pressure on learners' developing L2 system than production.

The stimulus materials in metapragmatic judgment tasks are most commonly items composed of written scenarios with target utterances for learners to judge on a Likert scale, as shown in Figure 4.1. The descriptions of the scenarios commonly vary the social relationships between the imaginary interlocutors along the lines of power, social distance, and imposition. Roever, Fraser, and Elder (2014) used this type of item as one component of a test battery to assess learners' knowledge of English sociopragmatics. They asked test takers to rate target utterances on a five-point Likert scale ranging from 'very impolite' via 'entirely appropriate' to 'far too polite'. A variation on this approach is to provide the task input via audio (Taguchi, 2011a; Li & Taguchi, 2014; Takimoto, 2009), or to alter the judgment task, as Takimoto (2009, 2012) did. He adapted a magnitude estimation method for metapragmatic judgments by providing several request utterances as responses for a scenario, and having learners rate them on an 11-point Likert scale with the first request serving as the anchor and the others to be rated proportionately to the first.

Susan is leaving work and realizes that she just missed the train home. The next train is in an hour. She asks her colleague, Patrick, who lives near her, for a ride:

Susan   'Patrick, I just missed my train. Can I catch a ride with you?'
Patrick   'No, you can't.'

How appropriate is Patrick's response?

Entirely inappropriate	Mostly inappropriate	Somewhat inappropriate	Somewhat appropriate	Mostly appropriate	Entirely appropriate

---

Figure 4.1 Metapragmatic judgment item

Employing a slightly different approach, Bardovi-Harlig and Dörnyei (1998) conducted a much-replicated study (Niezgoda & Roever, 2001; Schauer, 2006) on learners' perception of the severity of pragmatic versus grammatical errors. They presented their scenarios as brief video clips and then asked learners whether the final utterance was in some way faulty (a binary yes/no judgment), and, if so, how serious the problem was on a six-point Likert scale ranging from 'not bad at all' to 'very bad'. Similarly, Li and Taguchi (2014) gave learners scenarios for requests in Mandarin as a foreign language as aural and reading input, and then played a request utterance, asking learners to judge whether it was pragmatically appropriate and grammatically accurate, pragmatically inappropriate and grammatically accurate, or pragmatically appropriate and grammatically inaccurate.

Instead of providing a rating scale, some studies have used a multiple-choice approach, asking learners to choose from different response options. Matsumura (2001, 2003) created scenarios that required giving advice to the imaginary interlocutor and asked ESL learners to choose from three options for an advice utterance with a fourth option of not giving advice.

Metapragmatic judgment items can also be used to investigate whether different groups of participants have similar perceptions of the context variables of power, social distance, and imposition (Blum-Kulka & House, 1989). For example, Economidou-Kogetsidis (2010) employed three-step Likert scales to elicit her participants' perceptions of these social variables in her DCT scenarios given to native speakers of British English and L1 Greek-speaking learners of English (see Chang, 2011, for a similar approach). Such an approach can be valuable in generating explanations for differences in groups' responses on a productive instrument since different perceptions of social variables are likely to lead to different politeness choices in utterances.

Metapragmatic judgments have also been used for other target constructs, including knowledge and perception of swear words in English as L1 and L2 (Dewaele, 2016), knowledge of routine formulae (Bardovi-Harlig, 2009), and perception of how social relationships affect the use of address pronouns in L2 Spanish (Villarreal, 2014).

Comprehension

Another type of receptive task is the pragmatic comprehension task. Taguchi (2005, 2011b) used comprehension tasks to assess L2 English learners' comprehension of conversational implicature. The difference between metapragmatic judgment and implicature comprehension is the construct under study. The former deals with learners' perception of a pragmatic feature (for example, understanding of the context in which a pragmatic feature occurs; assessment of appropriateness of a particular pragmatic feature in a given situation), whereas the latter relates to learners' inferential ability. In order to comprehend implicature, learners need to understand the Gricean maxims of relevance and arrive at the most plausible interpretation of indirect meaning based on contextual information. To assess this ability, Taguchi used a computer-delivered multiple-choice listening test. She played audio-recorded conversations including implicature to ESL learners and asked them to choose the correct interpretation of the target indirect utterance out of four possible interpretations, as in the sample item in Figure 4.2.

Taguchi's task adapted the psycholinguistic approach by using a measure of comprehension response times along with accuracy scores. Response times have been used widely in psycholinguistics research. Response time data is considered an indirect reflection of the ease or difficulty involved in processing information, as well as the relative amount of linguistic, cognitive, and affective resource required for this processing. Taguchi's study measured the amount of time (in milliseconds) taken to comprehend implicature correctly.

Mike	Why are you working so hard, Nancy?
Nancy	Hey Mike. My medical exam is coming up next week. You know I took it before, but I have to get a better score to get into a medical school.
Mike	What was your score before?
Nancy	Ten fifty.
Mike	I'd be happy with seven hundred. (target implicature utterance)

1. *Mike thinks Nancy's exam score is good. (correct interpretation)*
2. *Mike thinks Nancy's score is poor.*
3. *Nancy is a medical school student.*
4. *Nancy's medical school exam is next month.*

Figure 4.2 Implicature comprehension item (Taguchi, 2011b, p. 919)

The results shed light on the relationship between the degree of indirectness reflected in implicature and the amount of effort required for comprehension.

Response time data did indeed reveal that the type of implicature affects the degree of processing effort. When the proposition was immediately accessible, L2 English learners' comprehension was better and utterances took a shorter time to comprehend. This was the case for conventional implicature, in which indirect meaning was encoded through conventional linguistic and discourse strategies. Because conventions trigger routinized associations in long-term memory, conventional utterances, even in indirect form, do not require extensive processing and are thus comprehended quickly. In contrast, when the proposition is not salient, learners took a longer time to comprehend implicature. This was the case for non-conventional implicature, which requires more extensive processing of linguistic and contextual cues to arrive at meaning. With the absence of conventional features that link form with meaning, non-conventional implicature requires both bottom-up processing of linguistic information and top-down processing of contextual cues, leading to longer response times, as revealed in Taguchi's results.

However, more recently, Taguchi, Gomez-Laich, and Arrufat-Marqués (in press) found that visual cues, rather than conventionality, could facilitate comprehension. Using a video-based multimodal instrument, the authors examined L2 Spanish learners' comprehension of implicatures and irony. Contrary to their expectations, non-conventional implicatures (indirect opinions) had faster comprehension speed than conventional implicatures (indirect refusals). This was likely the result of visual cues that accompanied the indirect opinion utterances. When people express dislike, their emotions usually appear in facial expressions and gestures. These non-verbal cues probably sped up the comprehension of negative indirect opinions. In other words, visual cues reduced the cognitive load, leading to shorter response times.

In another study, Holtgraves (2007) collected response time data to assess online comprehension of speech act utterances. Native and non-native English speakers read 24 speech act utterances displayed on a computer screen. In the experimental items, the target utterance was followed by the speech act verb naming the utterance (for example, the speech act verb 'offer' following the utterance 'If you need some help just give me a call.'). In the control items, the target utterance did not perform the speech act. Participants were asked to determine whether the letter string that appeared after the target utterance was a real word or a non-word. (Non-words, such as 'adivse' and 'rejcet' were provided so that participants did not always expect the target letter string to be a word.) Native speakers' response times were faster in speech act utterances than in control utterances. However, non-native speakers' response times were not significantly different between these two utterance types.

As shown above, several studies have taken advantage of recent technology to adapt the psycholinguistic framework, measuring response times as an additional dimension of implicature comprehension beyond accuracy. L2 learners' speedy selection of the correct implied meaning has served as an alternative indication of their ability to detect the speaker's intention encoded in implicature.

Analyzing metapragmatic judgment data

The analysis of metapragmatic judgment data in L2 pragmatics research depends on whether learner data is considered a sample of perceptions, or whether it is evaluated for its similarity to a target language norm. In other words, are researchers just interested in learners' pragmatic intuitions, or do they want to measure the extent to which learners' perceptions agree with native speakers' perceptions?

If the research goal is simply to collect learners' perceptions, Likert-scale responses are commonly scored by assigning every step on the scale a numerical value. For example, a five-step Likert scale ranging from 'entirely inappropriate' to 'entirely appropriate' might have a value of 1 for 'entirely inappropriate' increasing to 5 for 'entirely appropriate'. Averages per scenario (or per group of scenarios based on common settings of power, social distance, and imposition) can then be computed and compared between groups, as was done, for example, by Chang (2011). Chang collected appropriateness judgments of refusals in English from L1 Mandarin-speaking learners and native American English speakers. She then computed mean appropriateness ratings for each refusal and compared the groups statistically with a t-test, thereby uncovering areas where learners and native speakers had different perceptions of appropriateness. Similarly, Bardovi-Harlig and Dörnyei (1998), in their classic study, computed average ratings for error severity from their EFL sample in Hungary and their ESL sample in the United States and compared the ratings with a t-test between samples. They also compared ratings for grammatical and pragmatic error severity within samples. This allowed them to find out whether EFL and ESL learners differed in their view of the severity of pragmatic and grammatical errors, and which error type each group considered more severe.

Analyses progress differently if judgments are evaluated for their agreement with a target language norm. The first issue concerns the assignment of point values to different levels on the rating scale based on native-speaker judgments. Matsumura (2001) handled this by giving his instrument to a native-speaker comparison group and then assigning scores to the learners' responses based on the rank order of native-speaker preferences. If a learner chose a response that the majority of native speakers had chosen, the learner's response received four points. If the learner's response choice corresponded to the one chosen by the second largest native-speaker group, the learner's choice received three points, and so on. Matsumura then computed scores for his learners, and compared scores collected at various times during their study abroad in Canada to trace longitudinal development.

Roever, Fraser, and Elder (2014) chose a somewhat different approach. Where a learner judged the appropriateness of a target utterance in line with the majority of the native-speaker comparison sample, the learner's judgment received two points. If they judged it in line with the next two largest native-speaker groups, they received a score of one point, provided each native-speaker group encompassed more than 10% of the native-speaker sample. In all other cases, the learner's response received a score of zero. Roever, Fraser, and Elder implemented a 10% hurdle to ensure that learners would get points only for judgments endorsed by larger numbers of native speakers, since these native-speaker samples are more representative of the overall population. Roever, Fraser, and Elder used the scores from their metapragmatic judgment tasks as part of an overall score on their sociopragmatics test.

Assigning scores based on native-speaker judgments is complex for several reasons. Most importantly, it assumes a native-speaker standard in pragmatics, when in fact a learner standard might be more appropriate: learners are not always expected to behave like native speakers, and tend to be given more leeway should their language use be outside accepted norms (House, 2009, 2013; Kasper, 1995). In addition, a native-speaker standard does not apply to lingua franca communication, where a language is used as a medium of interaction between people with L1s that are both different from each other and different from the lingua franca. (For more about this, see Chapter 9.) Even where a native-speaker standard applies, native speakers do not necessarily agree overwhelmingly on an appropriate response or acceptable appropriateness level. Giving scores based on proportions of native speakers that chose a particular rating implies that the majority's view is more appropriate or correct than the minority's, but that may not be the case. In a case like Matsumura's, native speakers might find several options possible and inoffensive, and simply choose the one that they feel fits best. In other words, just because a smaller number of native speakers find a response 'entirely appropriate' does not mean that the majority find it 'entirely inappropriate' or would be offended by a learner saying it. Also, the comparison sample of native speakers is likely to be a convenience sample, which is not representative of the whole population or relevant to the target domains in which the learner operates.

Furthermore, there is an issue with converting interval-level frequencies of choosing a particular option to ordinal-level ranks expressed as Likert-scale values: assigning point values with equal intervals (5, 4, 3, 2, 1) to response options implies that the difference in acceptability between an option worth five points and an option worth four points is the same as between an option worth two points and an option worth one point. That may not be true, however: the four-point option may just be slightly less suitable than the five-point option, whereas the one-point option may be entirely inappropriate and cause grave offence, while the two-point option might be clumsy but inoffensive.

The issue of equal distances between the levels of a Likert scale also applies to cases where researchers just collect learner perceptions and do not score them against a native-speaker norm. Take the example item above: just because one learner judges the utterance to be 'mostly inappropriate', which could be converted to a score level of two, and another learner judges it to be 'mostly appropriate', which would give a score level of four, does not mean that the second learner considers the utterance exactly twice as appropriate as the first. In fact, with ordinal data generated using Likert scales, the notion of 'twice as much' does not make sense; and, technically, Likert-scale data cannot be used to compute means or standard deviations, or to run statistical procedures like t-tests. However, it is often used in that way in reality, and there is discussion in the statistical literature about the legitimacy of treating Likert-scale data like interval data (Jamieson, 2004; Carifio & Perla, 2007). J. D. Brown (2011) suggests that it is legitimate to analyze Likert-scale data by means of statistical procedures provided the data is not at the item level but consists of sums of items. This means that researchers could add up ratings from several items grouped by context variable (power, social distance, imposition), or just for the entire instrument, and then apply statistical procedures to the resulting totals. This is how Bardovi-Harlig and Dörnyei (1998) as well as Takimoto (2009) proceeded: they used totals for the entire metapragmatic judgment questionnaire in their inter-group and intra-group comparisons, which is defensible, whereas the t-test analyses in Chang's (2011) and Economidou-Kogetsidis's (2010) studies are conducted at the item level, which is not advisable.

Overall, metapragmatic judgment tasks offer insight into respondents' pragmatic perceptions, especially their sociopragmatic knowledge, and have the additional advantage that they do so while being less affected by proficiency than productive tasks. However, they do not allow conclusions as to learners' pragmatic performance, and usually put less emphasis on pragmalinguistics.

Non-interactive production data

Discourse completion tasks

Discourse completion tasks (DCTs) are a type of production questionnaire (Kasper, 2008); they are the most classic and widely used pragmatic production task (for example, Bella, 2012; Li & Taguchi, 2014; Nguyen, 2013; Taguchi & Kim, 2014). In their basic format, they are written tasks in which research participants write down what they would say in a situation which is laid out in the DCT prompt. Figure 4.3 shows an example of a DCT item aiming to elicit a request. The participant might provide a response like in Figure 4.4.

You are at work, and writing a report that is due by the end of the day. You don't know how to create a graph for the report from a spreadsheet but your colleague Jane in the next cubicle is very good with spreadsheets. You get along well with Jane and often help each other. You decide to ask Jane to show you how to create the graph. She is at her desk reading a document. You walk up to her and say: _____

Figure 4.3 DCT item

'Hey Jane, I've got a favor to ask. Can you help me make a graph for my report? I'm a bit stuck.'

Figure 4.4 Possible participant response for DCT item

DCTs are very much in the tradition of speech act research and politeness research, as described in Chapter 2. They elicit individual speech acts and the dependent variable is usually the politeness level of the participant's response, instantiated through choices of pragmalinguistic expressions and strategies. Prompts need to clarify the relationship between the imaginary interlocutor and the respondent in terms of power, social distance, and imposition, just as they do for metapragmatic judgments. Prompts also need to contain sufficient information for participants to construct a response; it has been shown that more information in the prompt leads to more external modification in responses (Billmyer & Varghese, 2000). It is also important in the item design phase to ensure the plausibility of the scenarios for the respondents through member checking (Tran, 2013), where members of the target population are asked how likely or common the situation described in the prompt is. This ensures that respondents can imagine themselves in the situation given in the prompt and respond realistically. (For more discussion of DCT design, see Roever, 2015; Sweeney & Hua, 2016.)

While the basic DCT item shown above is the most common type, DCTs have numerous variations. For example, the situation can be turned into a dialogue, with the imaginary interlocutor (Jane, in the above example) providing an opening utterance (Bardovi-Harlig & Hartford, 1993b), or an utterance following the gap. The latter is known as a 'rejoinder', and studies have shown that positive or negative rejoinder affects respondents' speech act production (Johnston, Kasper, & Ross, 1998; Rose, 1992). For assessment

[margin notes:] measure politeness level through choices of pragmalinguistic expressions & strategies

dialogue DCT

purposes, rejoinders can be used to constrain the range of possible responses in assessment instruments (Roever, 2005). Another variation on DCTs is the multi-turn DCT, where respondents are asked to fill in the gaps in a conversation (Cohen & Shively, 2002; Roever, Fraser, & Elder, 2014). This type of DCT has not been widely used and its similarity to natural conversation, or lack thereof, is still awaiting investigation. A more extreme variant, the Interactive DCT (Martínez-Flor, 2013), requires participants to write out a dialogue in response to a prompt. DCTs can also be oral (ODCT), asking participants to respond to prompts in the spoken modality (Li & Taguchi, 2014). Finally, the DCT prompts themselves can be enhanced with cartoons (Flores Salgado, 2011; Rose, 2000) or video (Schauer, 2004; Tada, 2005).

A receptive type of DCT is the multiple-choice DCT (MCDCT), where participants choose the most situationally appropriate response from a number of response options (Hudson, Detmer, & Brown, 1995; Liu, 2006; Tada, 2005). This is essentially the same as a metapragmatic judgment task, but MCDCTs are usually designed to have one correct response, with the other options being clearly unacceptable distractors. It is worth noting that MCDCTs tend to be difficult to construct in terms of developing attractive but clearly inappropriate distractors (Brown, 2001; Yamashita, 1996).

DCTs have been widely used in interlanguage and cross-cultural pragmatics research. The largest study in these areas ever completed, Blum-Kulka, House, and Kasper's (1989) Cross-Cultural Speech Act Realization Project (CCSARP), used DCTs to collect speech act data from 1,946 participants from seven native language backgrounds, illustrating the great practicality of DCTs: they can elicit a large amount of data under controlled conditions from a large number of respondents in a short period of time.

However, DCTs have serious limitations in terms of the conclusions that they allow and the range of research questions that they can help to answer. DCTs elicit offline knowledge (Félix-Brasdefer, 2010). In other words, they show participants' knowledge of the strategies available to produce a speech act, but they do not show what participants would actually say in real-world interaction. This is likely due to a combination of factors, including the under-specification of context in the prompt, the lack of any real-world consequences of the response, and two major differences between DCTs and actual interactions: the lack of time pressure for formulating a response and the DCT's non-interactiveness, i.e. the absence of a discourse context of previous utterances. This final point is quite crucial: since DCTs only contain one gap, they do not allow the sequential unfolding of interaction and do not enable conclusions about respondents' ability to engage in extended interaction. Take the example response to the DCT item in Figure 4.3: in a real-world setting it would actually be very strange for the speaker ('You') to walk up to Jane and deliver the request as a one-shot monologue. It is much more likely that it would unfold as a conversation, such as the imaginary interaction in Figure 4.5.

While the dialogue in Figure 4.5 is imaginary, it illustrates that interactions need not contain an on-record request (for example, 'Could you help me put in

1	**You**	Hey Jane.
2	**Jane**	Hey, what's up?
3	**You**	I've got a favor to ask.
4	**Jane**	Sure, what is it?
5	**You**	I'm working on this report [Jane nods] and I need to put in a graph based on
6		my spreadsheet.
7	**Jane**	Ok.
8	**You**	Yeah, and I'm not sure how to do that.
9	**Jane**	Oh, shouldn't be hard, let me take a look.

Figure 4.5 Conversation with Jane

a graph?') since the situational context and discourse context make the requester's intention fairly clear, and interlocutors such as Jane are likely to preempt the request with an offer. (Schegloff, 2007, gives several examples from natural data.) DCTs would not be able to capture this feature of requesting, and they force participants to make on-record requests, which they might not make in a similar real-world situation. Furthermore, in a DCT, the imaginary interlocutor is no more than a prop, whereas in reality, interactions are co-constructed between two speakers, and one speaker's discursive choices impact what kind of pragmatic-discursive abilities the other speaker must deploy. For example, if Jane had said in line 4, 'I'm kind of busy now', line 5 and subsequent turns would have looked radically different.

The difference between DCT data and natural data was empirically demonstrated in a widely cited study by Golato (2003), who first collected naturally occurring compliment responses and then created a DCT based on the situations in which the naturally occurring compliment responses were embedded. She used the compliments themselves as opening utterances before the gap, and gave her DCT to a sample comparable to the one that had provided the natural data, with some respondents being members of both samples. She found that the DCT elicited responses which did not occur in the natural data and that the relative frequency of preferred responses also differed between the instruments. In a later study, Economidou-Kogetsidis (2013) used requests from service encounters to demonstrate greater overlap between DCT and natural data in terms of strategies used, though the frequency distributions were noticeably different between DCT and natural data in her results as well. Studies like Golato's made it clear that DCTs do not provide information about actual language use but rather about pragmatic intuitions (Kasper, 2008) and the repertoire of speech act strategies that language users have at their disposal. Where findings regarding repertoire of pragmatic strategies or offline knowledge are the target of a study, DCTs are useful instruments, but they do not support conclusions about people's actual, real-world language use.

Analyzing non-interactive production data

DCT data is commonly analyzed by coding DCT responses as strategies (aka semantic formulae) and then counting the frequency of occurrence of each coding category. Frequency counts can be compared between different combinations of context variables (power, social distance, imposition) within the same group of participants, or between different groups of participants. Since different speech acts are constructed from different sets of semantic formulae, several coding schemes exist. For the much-researched speech acts of request and apology, the fundamental coding scheme was developed by Blum-Kulka, House, and Kasper (1989) in the Cross-Cultural Speech Act Realization Project, and has been adapted by later studies (Al-Gahtani & Roever, 2015a; Economidou-Kogetsidis, 2013; Hồ, 2013). For requests, the coding scheme distinguishes between the 'head act', which is the request proper, and 'supportive moves', which serve to make acceptance more likely. 'Alerters', which get the imaginary interlocutor's attention, are also coded. For example, take the sample response to the DCT item in Figure 4.3:

'Hey Jane, I've got a favor to ask. Can you help me make a graph for my report? I'm a bit stuck.'

CCSARP would classify the Alerter as an Attention Getter ('hey') and a first name ('Jane'). The following part ('I've got a favor to ask') is a supportive move preceding the head act, and it would be coded as 'Getting a precommitment', since it gauges whether the hearer is even willing to entertain the upcoming request. The head act itself ('Can you help me make a graph for my report') would be coded as 'Preparatory' (sometimes also 'Query Preparatory') since it asks for ability or willingness. CCSARP also contains categories for the perspective taken in the request (in this case, 'Hearer dominance'), and syntactic modification of the request itself (in this case, 'Interrogative'). The last part of the response ('I'm a bit stuck'), is another supportive move and would be coded as a 'Grounder'.

Not all categories need to be coded in every study, and researchers can modify existing schemes. For example, in her comparative study of natural and DCT data, Economidou-Kogetsidis (2013) focused only on coding head acts, and used more detailed coding categories, for example sub-dividing the category of 'Query Preparatory' into 'Query Preparatory Ability' and 'Query Preparatory Willingness'. Coding categories exist for several speech acts in addition to requests, including apologies (Cohen & Olshtain, 1981; Kondo, 2010; Liu & Ren, 2016), complaints (Boxer, 2010; Do, 2013; Olshtain & Weinbach, 1987), refusals (Beebe & Cummings, 1996; Eslami, 2010; Shishavan & Sharifian, 2016), compliment responses (Ishihara, 2010; Lin, Woodfield, & Ren, 2012; Manes, 1983), with less work on expressions of gratitude (Eisenstein & Bodman, 1993; Intachakra, 2004), disagreements (Malamed, 2010; Rees-Miller, 2000), and advice/suggestions (Decapua & Dunham, 2007; Li, 2010; Martínez-Flor, 2010).

[margin note: none of the coding approach is unproblematic]

Although well developed and widely used, the coding approach to speech act analysis is far from unproblematic. In a strident critique, Kasper (2006c) criticized the researcher-led, etic orientation of speech act coding and argued for a discursive perspective informed by Conversation Analysis. On the one hand, she highlighted technical problems with coding schemes, such as the placement of contradictory sub-categories under the same overarching category. For example, in the CCSARP apology coding manual, the categories 'Explicit self-blame' and 'Refusal to acknowledge guilt' were both sub-categories of the super-category 'Taking on responsibility' (Blum-Kulka, House, & Kasper, 1989, pp. 292–293), even though a refusal to acknowledge guilt is actually a rejection of responsibility. On the other hand, Kasper raised the more fundamental concern that coding schemes lead researchers to interpret respondents' meanings without a procedure for validating these interpretations. This results in several viable interpretations of the same speech act, since an utterance like 'I wouldn't mind another glass of wine' could function as a statement of fact, a request for a refill, a reproach to a non-attentive host, a conciliatory gesture after the speaker had threatened to leave earlier, or an acknowledgment that the wine is better than the speaker had previously claimed. Which of these interpretations is taken to be the intended meaning depends essentially on the researcher's intuition, but it is of course more obvious in DCTs, where carefully crafted prompts are specifically designed to elicit certain illocutions. However, an analytic approach to pragmatic meaning should also be able to account for natural data, which coding schemes like CCSARP struggle to do.

[margin note: CCSARP: coding approach]

Another approach to analyzing DCT data is to have raters score responses in terms of target features (see Hudson, Detmer, & Brown, 1995, for details on developing scales), most prominently appropriateness (Takimoto, 2009), but also other features, such as use of downgraders and overall correctness (Li & Taguchi, 2014). This is mostly done in assessment and effect-of-instruction studies, which we will discuss in Chapter 8.

The coding approach to analyzing DCT data is well established and allows comparability between studies. However, it suffers from inherent shortcomings, and the resulting analyses are subject to the overall critique that has been applied to the use of instruments such as DCTs for collecting pragmatics data.

Interactive production data

In this section we will describe three types of interactive production data: role-plays, elicited conversation, and natural interaction. We will also discuss the analysis of interactive production data.

Role-play

Role-plays are often seen as a good compromise between a structured, standardized data collection procedure and natural data. Role-plays can be 'closed' or 'open'. Closed role-plays are the same as oral DCTs (Félix-Brasdefer, 2010), and only allow a single oral response to a prompt (Li & Taguchi, 2014). Open role-plays, on the other hand, elicit an interaction between the participant and a trained interlocutor, or between two participants. Role-plays are usually based on role-play cards explaining the situation and the relationship between interlocutors. Similar to a DCT prompt, the card may specify who speaks first. Usually, the two role-play interlocutors cannot see each other's role-play card, and the role-play can be set up so that the interlocutors' goals are in direct conflict (as was the case with the request–refusal role-play in Gass & Houck, 1999), or so that complications must be resolved (Al-Gahtani & Roever, 2012). The prompt can also specify whether a resolution must *be reached* be reached, though that is generally left to the participants. When a trained interlocutor conducts the role-play with a participant, the interlocutor can implement pre-planned resistance to extend the role-play by introducing complications (Al-Gahtani & Roever, 2012; Ross & O'Connell, 2013).

Since open role-plays do not usually follow a detailed script, leaving conversations to be co-constructed by interlocutors, no two role-play interactions, even if based on the same prompts, are likely to be identical. This raises the thorny issue of standardization vs. authenticity. The more instructions are provided to a trained interlocutor of how to conduct the interaction, the more comparable role-plays with different participants are likely to be. Youn (2013, 2015) increased standardization by giving both learners and trained interlocutors detailed role-play instructions that specified what speech act to produce at the beginning, middle, and end of the conversation, without providing the actual wording. Given that Youn's study was an assessment study, such an emphasis on standardization may be justified, but it detracts from the moment-by-moment co-construction of an interaction, as would occur in a natural setting. By contrast, Grabowski (2009, 2013) also used open role-plays in an assessment study, but only provided situational background information, without guidance on the conversational structure. She did, however, specify the speaker's emotional state; for example, 'make sure your partner knows that you are upset' (Grabowski, 2013, p. 153). This lesser degree of standardization made the conversations elicited by Grabowski more co-constructed 'on the fly' like real-world interactions, but it also made them less directly comparable. In non-assessment-focused L2 pragmatics research, role-play interactions tend to privilege openness over standardization and generally provide a few prompts with some notes for the interlocutor stating how compliant they should be (Al-Gahtani & Roever, 2012; Bella, 2014).

As with other research instruments, the fundamental questions relating to role-plays concern validity. What kind of conclusions do they allow? What do they tell researchers about participants' pragmatic ability? While open role-plays are interactions similar to natural talk, in that they elicit moment-by-moment, co-constructed interactions, they are not exactly the same as natural interactions. At the simplest level, people play roles in role-plays, rather than themselves, so they necessarily imagine how someone in the given

validity, issue with role-play interaction

Strengths : similar to natural talk , co-constructed interactions role would be likely to act or speak. The impact of this can be minimized by asking them to play roles that they have experience with, for example having participants who are students play the role of students (as in Youn's 2015 study). It is not advisable to ask participants to play roles they have never had in real life (for example, 'You're a customs officer…') because they lack the members' knowledge required to act out these roles realistically. Also, similar to DCT prompts, the scenario in a role-play is never sufficiently specified since instructions are kept short and interactants do not share a common history in their roles.

Even if participants play roles that are familiar to them, role-plays have no stakes, unlike in the real world, where actual concerns are addressed. As Ewald (2012) showed in a comparison between real-world direction giving and direction giving in role-plays, real-world participants gave much more detailed directions and constantly monitored and repaired their production, whereas role-play participants' directions were shorter and less helpful. Ewald sees the real-world stake of a driver potentially getting lost as strongly impacting the linguistic production in the natural data. Finding a destination in the role-play, on the other hand, was not actually at stake, and participants therefore paid less attention to being precise. Besides a lesser focus on real-world outcomes, face (in the Brown & Levinson, 1987 sense) is less at stake in role-plays since participants can shield their actual face with the simulated face of the role.

Furthermore, a role-play is inalterably different from a real-world interaction in that participants orient to two social situations: the situation simulated in the role-play, and the role-play as a social situation in itself. Participants are aware that they are in a role-play and that their performance will be in some way viewed, analyzed, or evaluated by a third party other than themselves and the interlocutor. This became obvious in Ewald's (2012) role-plays, where some participants asked the role-play interlocutor for an evaluation of their performance at the end of the task.

Being aware of being viewed, analyzed, or assessed leads role-play participants to recipient-design their behavior to the extraneous third party as well as the interlocutor, and to choose a particular type of self-display. This was impressively shown in a study by Stokoe (2013), who compared recordings of police interviews between police officers and actual suspects with recordings of simulated interviews between police officers and suspects played by actors, done as part of ongoing professional development for police officers. She stresses that police participants in both settings ranged from less experienced to highly experienced officers. Stokoe focused on the opening portion of the interviews and found that actual and simulated interviews were similar overall, but that simulated interviews showed a great degree of elaboration and explicit performance of social actions, which made some phases of the simulated interviews noticeably longer than in the real interviews. Stokoe interpreted these findings as participants orienting to the assessed nature of the simulated interviews and displaying their interviewing abilities more overtly for the benefit of the assessor. By contrast, in the real interviews, participants were focused on accomplishing a task and did not spend time making their interviewing skills 'interactionally visible and "assessable"' (Stokoe, 2013, p. 165). This focus on making one's pragmatic abilities visible to the researcher was also found in a study comparing role-play and natural data by Bataller (2013). She collected native speaker data from service encounters in a cafeteria in Spain and role-plays of such service encounters. She found that role-plays were nearly twice as likely as natural data to have opening and closing phases, requests in role-plays were more elaborate while natural requests tended to be brief and elliptical (echoing an earlier finding for L1 Spanish requests by Félix-Brasdefer, 2007), and nearly one third of role-play interactions used address terms indicating social distance (*usted*), which did not occur in natural data.

However, just because role-plays do not generate data that is identical to natural interactions does not mean they are hopelessly tainted. Several studies have found that role-play participants demonstrate interactional abilities that they also need in real-world interactions. For example, Okada (2010) used role-plays from Oral Proficiency Interviews (OPIs) to show that ESL learners interacting with a trained native-speaker interlocutor were able to display their ability to recognize the function of an interlocutor utterance as opening a service encounter; they were also able to understand interlocutor silence as repair initiation, and implement politeness levels appropriate to the simulated situation. Similarly, Huth (2010) had L2 learners of German role-play phone conversations with each other and found that the sequential organization of openings was similar to natural conversations: learners oriented to different possible second pair parts as being differentially preferred (in a CA sense of preference), and they responded to a compliment in a similar way as has been attested to in natural data (including strong L1 English transfer). Al-Gahtani and Roever (2012) also showed that L2 learners of English in role-plays with a trained interlocutor oriented to the preference organization of requests. However, this was primarily the case for learners at lower-intermediate level and above, suggesting an interplay between proficiency and the deployment of interactional abilities. Finally, Al-Gahtani and Roever (2015b) compared the occurrence of multiple requests in interactions with second language learners of Arabic in both natural and role-play settings, and found no difference in the occurrence of multiple requests between the two settings.

Elicited conversation

Elicited conversation is a rarely used method in L2 pragmatics research, though it holds promise. To obtain elicited conversation data, a researcher puts dyads or groups of participants together and gives them general instructions on what to do, for example to discuss a topic such as 'the role of English in the world' (Baumgarten & House, 2010), to get to know each other (Svennevig, 2000; Taguchi, 2015c), or to solve a task together (Hanafi, 2015;

Zhang, 2016). Even though the conversation is arranged (the interactants are brought together by the researcher, and they may be given a topic or task to discuss), elicited conversations differ from role-plays in that participants do not have to imagine themselves in a fictitious situation acting out a role that is additional to their social role of being role-play participants. In elicited conversations, interactants are entirely themselves. It should be noted, though, that their awareness of being recorded, and knowledge of the fact that the recordings will later be viewed by a third party, may impact what they say and how they say it.

observer's paradox

While no direct comparisons between data from elicited conversations and natural interactions exist, it is likely that elicited conversations produce data fairly typical of natural conversational practices. For example, in Svennevig's (2000) study of first encounters between unacquainted dyads, he found elements of topic organization also reported in the CA literature based on natural data.

elicited conversation = natural conversational practices

Elicited conversation is a promising approach for L2 pragmatics research, as it allows researchers to design tasks which increase the likelihood of particular target features occurring. For example, Zhang (2016) investigated agreements and disagreements in intermediate and advanced learners of Mandarin as a second language. He paired each learner with a Mandarin native speaker (and included a native comparison group), and asked them to solve a decision-making task, for example ranking several candidates according to their suitability for a scholarship, given the candidates' background and eligibility. While the tasks were fictional, participants were asked to come to an agreement, which led to lengthy negotiations. Zhang identified differences and similarities between the groups, for example similar preference organization for disagreement, which also mirrored findings based on natural data (Kotthoff, 1993; Pomerantz, 1984) and classroom data (Pekarek Doehler & Pochon-Berger, 2011).

what's some preference organization for disagreement

Elicited conversation deserves more attention in L2 pragmatics research since it avoids the suspension of disbelief that role-plays require, and it can be designed to elicit a range of conversational practices and target speech acts.

selling point of elicited conversation

Natural interaction

Natural data is often held up as the 'gold standard' of L2 pragmatics data because it shows how language users talk in the real world and therefore most directly enables conclusions to be drawn about pragmatic abilities. Natural data is non-elicited data, over which the researcher has no influence. In order to establish whether data is natural, the researcher might ask: 'If I were not involved, would the data look the same?' If the answer is 'yes', we are dealing with truly natural data; however, this is not as straightforward as it might seem. For example, is data still natural when participants have unguided, unelicited interactions, but they know that they are being recorded, as is the case in nearly all studies using natural data in L2 pragmatics? In such cases,

to determine if data is natural

the same issue applies as for role-plays, where participants might be influenced by their awareness of an unseen 'second audience', so even apparently natural data may not be exactly identical to the way participants would act outside the research situation.

In addition, Bardovi-Harlig (2013) highlights the problem that natural data does not allow much researcher control, and it may therefore be more difficult to answer a pre-existing research question. Also, different exemplars of data are not necessarily comparable. Both of these consequences are problematic for L2 pragmatics research.

[handwritten margin note: problem with natural data. · not much control]

In L2 pragmatics research, studies are usually undertaken to answer a research question, which in turn is based on an existing theory. While L2 pragmatics research generally does not follow a strong Popperian hypothesis-testing approach (Long, 2007) but rather a weaker exploratory approach, it normally aims to answer a pre-determined question. In other words, the data is just a tool used to arrive at findings that are generalizable beyond the specific data set and provide information about a general phenomenon, for example how L2 learners at different proficiency levels produce requests (Al-Gahtani & Roever, 2012). This more researcher-driven, top-down perspective contrasts with traditional CA research, which takes a bottom-up perspective and advocates 'unmotivated looking' (Psathas, 1995) to discover interesting phenomena in the data. This means that any natural data is useful to CA research, but for L2 pragmatics research, only data that helps to answer a specific research question is useful; and a random set of natural data, being uncontrolled by the researcher, may simply not be helpful for finding answers to a research question. For example, if a study intends to investigate requests made by learners at different proficiency levels, a useful data set would need to contain a reasonable number of instances of requests made by learners at each proficiency level. That is not difficult to control in role-plays, but it is very difficult to bring about as natural data. How do we ensure that we get enough instances of requests? How do we ensure that several proficiency levels are represented? How do we even ascertain speakers' proficiency levels if the data is collected in a natural environment where researchers cannot test the speakers?

The second concern with natural data is comparability, which can also be viewed as standardization. With role-plays, the role-play prompt can have a built-in complication (Al-Gahtani & Roever, 2012) or a trained interlocutor can introduce complications or show a degree of resistance (Ross & O'Connell, 2013; Youn, 2013). This ensures that role-plays produced by different participants with different interlocutors are comparable to each other to some degree, although interlocutor variability (Brown, 2003) and the unscripted nature of co-constructed talk always limit comparability. With natural data, however, there is no guarantee of comparability whatsoever: the illocutionary force of requests might vary, different interlocutors might put up vastly different degrees of resistance to a request, and different contexts of language use might impact talk differentially, such as requests on a phone hotline (Curl & Drew, 2008), or between acquaintances (examples in Schegloff, 2007). Standardization can be improved by keeping the language use situation constant, for example by focusing on service encounters (Shively, 2011) or interactions with an administrator (Al-Gahtani & Roever, 2014 a, b), but interactions can still progress quite differently.

In addition to issues of usefulness of data and standardization, there is a problem with research ethics in the case of natural data. If interactants' data is recorded and analyzed for a research study, they should normally be asked to give informed consent. Asking interactants to give consent to their data being used for research purposes prior to data collection is likely to lead to similar observer effects as we outlined for role-plays, so how 'natural' would natural data be under those circumstances? However, an exception may apply where interactions are in plain public view. Shively's (2011) collection of interactions with service providers in shops did not require consent of the service providers since all interactions occurred in public and the identity of the service providers was anonymous.

While there are limitations and challenges in obtaining natural data for L2 pragmatics studies, several studies have been done that involved natural data and resolved these problems in different ways.

One set of studies involves longitudinal case studies of a learner, or small numbers of learners, interacting in casual settings with an interlocutor. For example, Ishida (2009) and Kim (2009) asked study abroad learners to record their natural interactions with friends or host families, and used the resulting data to investigate the changes in a single learner's use of a sentence final particle in Japanese and a discourse marker in Korean respectively. Similarly, Ishida (2011) showed how an L2 Japanese learner developed her ability to be an active recipient in interactions with a native speaker over the course of a year's study abroad, and Kim (2012) followed two ESL learners over nine months in their interactions with a native speaker and highlighted opportunities for language learning which arose from the negotiation of recognitional reference (i.e. terms that make it clear who or what is being referred to). The single-learner studies such as Ishida's (2009, 2011) and Kim's (2009, 2012) sidestepped issues of sufficient data, standardization, and ethics by focusing on target phenomena that are pervasive in conversational data, such as recipientship, and following the same learners and interlocutors throughout the study. While the linguistic environments in which the target phenomena occurred were not standardized (which might weaken conclusions as to development), the benefit of naturally occurring data can be argued to outweigh this drawback. In addition, a case study has limited value in terms of generating generalizable conclusions, so the weaker degree of standardization involved is less problematic. Ethical considerations are also not particularly complex in these studies since the only requirement for researchers would be to obtain permission from participants to have their data recorded.

Another type of study collects data in language classrooms; this has the advantage that learners' proficiency levels are known and the controlled environment of the school facilitates recording. Classroom-based studies have covered a variety of areas such as turn-taking (Cekaite, 2007), engagement with tasks (Hellermann, 2007, 2008; Hellermann & Cole, 2009), storytelling (Hellermann, 2008), topic management (Lee & Hellermann, 2014), and repair (Hellermann, 2009). For example, Lee and Hellermann (2014) demonstrate how storytelling practices change longitudinally by analyzing the case of one learner, and how they differ cross-sectionally by comparing data from learners at different proficiency levels. For their longitudinal data, they relied on recordings of a conversation circle of English teachers in South Korea, who met weekly for conversation practice over a ten-month period. Lee and Hellermann contrast one participant's early and late topic shifts, and show how the participant accomplished smoother shifts by making use of marking devices in the later session. For their cross-sectional analysis, they compare story openings by lower- and higher-level learners in ESL classrooms, and find that lower-level learners lack prefatory moves before opening the story, and therefore rely on sequential placement of their contribution, context-setting, and the acting out of story content.

Data from instructional settings is necessarily limited in the activity types it can contain. While learners can be recorded working on tasks, telling stories, and interacting with the teacher, researchers might be less likely to find compliment responses, apologies, or interaction in activity contexts like service encounters.

A third type of study collects data in a particular type of real-world setting, and thereby tries to maintain a degree of standardization. For example, Shively (2011) had seven second language learners of Spanish doing study abroad in Spain record service encounters in which they made requests at three time points over a ten-week period. She demonstrated that for some (though not all) learners, request realizations moved from a more indirect American English norm to a more direct Spanish norm. Al-Gahtani and Roever (2014 a, b) also collected service encounter data with students of Arabic as a second language at four proficiency levels. The learners engaged in two service encounters with an administrator in a university setting at the beginning and end of a five-month period to ask for a class or an exam to be rescheduled. The encounters were unobtrusively recorded, with the learners being unaware of the recording and the administrator having been told that the recording was being carried out to evaluate the learners' progress. Consent was obtained retroactively. Al-Gahtani and Roever (2014 a, b) analyzed their data for insert expansions and post-expansions as well as the occurrence of multiple requests, and found clear differences between lower and higher proficiency groups.

Both Shively (2011) and Al-Gahtani and Roever's (2014 a, b) studies used service encounters, which provides some standardization since goals and physical settings are similar across request exemplars. Using service encounters also ensured that requests would occur frequently since requesting service is at the heart of a service encounter. In Shively's (2011) study, learners knew that they were recording their encounters, but service providers were unaware that they were being recorded, which raises issues of consent. Shively argues that consent is unnecessary for recording talk during a service encounter in a public place since such talk is likely to be overheard by several third parties, and speakers would not say anything that they would not want others to hear. In Al-Gahtani and Roever's (2014 a, b) studies, learners did not know they were being recorded, but due to the institutional setting of the study, it was unproblematic to obtain consent after the data collection. However, in both cases at least one party to the interaction knew they were being recorded, and this may have affected the interaction.

In both studies the setting was quite specific, which raises an empirical question as to the extent to which the ability to make requests in service encounters generalizes to requests in other interactions. This issue actually goes to the heart of what it means to be a competent interactant: interactional practices vary between settings and situations, and while general interactional abilities are probably useful across contexts, norms of communication do differ. More research on this issue is needed to determine the exact generalizability of findings from natural data collected in specific settings.

Analyzing interactive data

Interactive data can be analyzed within theoretical frameworks that take sequential interaction into account, such as Conversation Analysis. However, it is also possible to analyze such data from a speech act perspective and to use coding of interaction similar to DCTs (Bataller, 2013; Economidou-Kogetsidis, 2013). While the choice of analytic approach depends on the research question, we generally recommend that a data analysis approach take as many features of the data into account as possible. Using a speech act coding approach for interactive data does not make optimal use of the richness of this type of data since it cannot capture the sequential unfolding of interaction. We will focus on a Conversation Analysis approach for analyzing interactive data given that CA has built up a large corpus of studies and provides a clearly defined and well-established analytical toolset. It is, of course, also possible to use other analytic approaches, such as interactional sociolinguistics (see Gumperz & Cook-Gumperz, 2012, for an overview) or critical discourse analysis (Fairclough, 2013), depending on the study's research focus and the analyst's theoretical orientation.

Transcription

The first step in analyzing interactive data is transcription; this is quite a crucial step since analysts will be working with transcripts, not the actual, spoken, recorded data. This makes careful and detailed transcription essential. Transcribing is not simply a matter of putting spoken words on paper; in fact, as Ochs (1979) argued in a famous paper, transcription is theory.

(For another classic work on transcription, see Edwards & Lambert, 1993; for a more recent discussion, see Jenks, 2011.)

How a transcript is done in terms of detail depends on the analyst's interests. Take a simple verbal utterance like 'How are you?' said in a casual setting to a friend who the speaker is happy to see. Most likely, in reality, a speaker would not pronounce every single word slowly and carefully 'how (pause) are (pause) you' but rather produce something like 'howahya'. So should it be transcribed orthographically as 'how are you', or closer to the actual pronunciation as 'howahya', or even phonetically as /haʊ ɑːʳ jə/? The orthographic option, 'how are you', is less accurate but easier to read in a transcript, while 'howahya' is closer to reality but harder to parse for readers, and the phonetic transcription requires specialist training to produce and read with ease. And what if there is emphasis on 'are'? This might be rendered as 'howAHya'. But the more non-orthographic a transcript becomes, the more reader-unfriendly it becomes. The hard truth is that there is no perfect and 100% accurate transcription of spoken language. The analyst always makes a decision about the type of transcript to be produced, and that decision influences what becomes available for analysis and later to readers. Transcription decisions need to be guided by the analytic focus of the study, i.e. the target feature to be focused on needs to be represented with a high degree of accuracy.

While decisions about transcription are the analyst's responsibility, there are common practices for transcription depending on the analyst's theoretical orientation. One of the most commonly used transcription systems in L2 pragmatics research is the one developed for CA by Gail Jefferson. (See Hepburn & Bolden, 2013, for an overview, and Jefferson, 2004, for explanation of symbols.) This system tries to strike a balance between precise rendering of what was said and reader-friendly representation by showing talk as it sounds without resorting to phonetic symbols. It also displays pauses, overlaps, and latches (i.e. instances of a next turn immediately following the previous turn with no pause). As an example, take the modified excerpt in Figure 4.6 from a role-play conversation between Ahmed and Bob about borrowing a laptop late at night (modified from Al-Gahtani & Roever, 2011).

1	**A**	Um: (0.5) Bob
2	**B**	[Yeah]
3	**A**	[I'm] freakin out
4	**B**	Whuz happen [ing?]
5	**A**	[My] computer died I've got my la- my con-

Figure 4.6 Sample CA transcription (modified from Al-Gahtani & Roever, 2011)

In line 1, Ahmed produces a hesitation marker (um), which is lengthened (:), followed by a 0.5 second pause and then Bob's name. In line 2, Bob acknowledges Ahmed's utterance as a prelude to another action with a go-ahead signal (yeah), which overlaps with the beginning of Ahmed's next utterance in line 3, which is indicated by the square brackets around the overlapping portions in both utterances. Note also that Ahmed's 'freaking out' in line 3 was heard by the transcriber as 'freakin out' and was thus transcribed. Similarly, in line 4, Bob is inviting Ahmed to tell his story by saying 'What's happening?', which is shown as 'whuz happening', with the question mark at the end indicating a rising tone. Again, there is an overlap with the first part of Ahmed's description of the problem in line 5, which gets off to a rough start with two cutoffs (incomplete words): 'la-' and 'con-', the cut-offs indicated by a hyphen.

We hasten to add that this transcript is actually a *very* rough representation of what Ahmed and Bob actually sound like in terms of voice range, volume, and accent, but it gives a basic impression of how their interaction went. The CA approach to transcription can be modified to focus on a specific feature, for example Jefferson's famous paper on laughter (Jefferson, 1984b).

Transcription is a time-consuming and painstaking task, and requires transcribers to listen to the data repeatedly. It is even more challenging as multimodal transcription where eye gaze, body torque, and gesture are part of the analysis (Heath & Luff, 2013). Traditionally, transcription is seen as an essential component of the data analysis process in CA since the analyst becomes familiar with the data while transcribing, and develops hypotheses about possible target phenomena to investigate further. (For a more detailed description of the CA research process, see ten Have, 2007.) However, in a 2015 debate on the potential benefits of using automated transcription engines for CA, Moore (2015) argued that automated transcription offers the benefit of being able to work with larger data sets and provides a rough 'first pass' transcription for the analyst to refine, while reducing overall workload. Bolden (2015) argues against this approach and emphasizes the importance of close familiarity with the data. A similar question arises with regard to the outsourcing of transcriptions to paid transcribers, which has the advantage of reducing the analyst's workload but also limits the researcher's opportunity to become familiar with the data.

We take a nuanced but practical position on this issue, and on transcription as a whole. Deep familiarity with one's data set is essential for 'classic' CA research, which starts with unmotivated looking; i.e. the analyst becomes acquainted with the data and in the process stumbles upon features worthy of analysis. Such an approach requires the analyst to know their data set extremely well in order to determine if a target phenomenon is interesting and pervasive enough to warrant investigation. However, in L2 pragmatics research, the data collection procedure is often designed to elicit a specific target phenomenon, such as request (Al-Gahtani & Roever, 2012, 2014 a, b) or agreement/disagreement (Zhang, 2016). In that case the analyst does not need to *discover* the research target so much as *identify* it in the data, which has its own challenges, as we will outline below. In this case, outsourcing or automatization of transcription is less problematic, assuming, of course, that the researcher checks the draft transcript against the data.

In the absence of paid transcribers or automatic transcription engines, a researcher investigating a pre-existing research question may also decide to initially produce an orthographic first pass transcription of all the data, then identify occurrences of the target phenomenon, and only create detailed, CA-level transcripts for those sections of the transcript where the target phenomenon occurs. This would still enable the researcher to build a collection of detailed transcripts of occurrences of the target feature without spending large amounts of time and effort on those parts of the data that do not aid in answering the research question. Note that this approach would be very problematic from a classic CA perspective, since by <u>focusing on a pre-determined target phenomenon, researchers lose the emic perspective of primarily making sense of interactants' meanings and might miss other phenomena in the data;</u> but this is a compromise that is unavoidable in studies guided by research questions.

A final issue with transcription that comes up with second language work concerns levels of transcription. Where data is in the language in which researchers are writing their paper, display of excerpts is unproblematic. However, if the data is in another language, researchers need to add translations, and matters get even more complex if the language does not have an alphabetic, left-to-right script. Consider Figure 4.7, a data excerpt from Al-Gahtani and Roever (2015b). The original data was in Modern Standard Arabic, whose script is non-alphabetic, right-to-left. As this excerpt demonstrates, Al-Gahtani and Roever (2015b) showed three levels of transcription, including the Arabic Romanization, a direct word-for-word translation and an idiomatic translation. They omitted the transcription in Arabic script, which sidesteps the issue of right-to-left writing direction. However, a possible way to include the target language script, which makes reading easier for readers who are familiar with the target language, is to show the excerpt entirely in the target language script first, followed by the three-level transcript shown in Figure 4.7.

[handwritten margin note: data of different lang]

```
1  I   ánt   fii   áy      mustawaa?
       you   in    which   level
       Which level are you in?
2  P   al-mustawaa    ar-raab'
       level          four
       Level four
```

Figure 4.7 Conversation data in Modern Standard Arabic (Al-Gahtani and Roever, 2015b, p. 419)

Identifying the target

In a study conducted to investigate a particular social action (in CA terms) or speech act, the <u>target action must be identified in the data</u>. Take the dialogue in Figure 4.8 from Al-Gahtani and Roever (2011, unpublished data). To identify the request in this excerpt, a researcher uses their own common-sense knowledge of what a request looks like, coupled with the CA technique of the next-turn proof procedure: whatever the interlocutor orients to as a request is likely to be the request. In general, an interlocutor shows that they interpreted an utterance as a request by granting or rejecting it. Common-sense member's knowledge suggests that the request is in line 10 ('can I use your computer') because this conventionally indirect formulation is typical of requests. Indeed, Bob orients to Ahmed's turn from lines 8–11 as containing a request, since Bob starts a refusal in line 12, and then elaborates on it in lines 14–17. This sequence of the social actions of request–refusal is the 'core adjacency pair' (Schegloff, 2007). Had Bob not responded to Ahmed's request, Ahmed would have likely pursued a response. It is important to note, however, that sometimes <u>second pair parts in adjacency pairs do not follow the first pair part immediately but the parts can be separated by an insert expansion</u> (see Schegloff, 2007, for more on this).

insert expansion in adjacency pairs

1		((knocking))
2	**B**	Yes?
3		(1.5)
4	**A**	Um: (0.5) Bob,
5	**B**	[Yeah]
6	**A**	[I'm] freakin out
7	**B**	Whuz happen [ing?]
8	**A**	[My] computer died, I've got my la- my
9		con- assignments due tomorrow I only need a couple of
10		hours to do it can I use your computer I: (0.7) (.) I'll
11		pay you I'll buy you a carton of beer whatever you want.
12	**B**	You came at the absolute wrong time
13	**A**	I'm <u>so</u> [sorry]
14	**B**	[I have an-] I'm <u>so</u> sorry I <u>really</u> would love
15		to help you out (1.0) but I've got an assignment due
16		tomorrow at eight o'clock and it's eleven now so I need
17		(.) a <u>mini</u>mum [lines omitted]

Figure 4.8 Conversation leading to a request (Al-Gahtani and Roever, 2011, unpublished data)

Utterances preceding the core-adjacency pair, to the extent that they lead toward it, are known as pre-expansions, for example 'I'm freakin out' in line 8. However, talk that is not directly related to the upcoming request would not be considered a pre-expansion. There is relatively little pre-expansion work in the excerpt above, but in other cases we find a great deal more pre-expansion to give the interlocutor sufficient background and project the upcoming request (see, for example, Al-Gahtani & Roever, 2012).

A response to a request can be followed by more talk, known as post-expansion (Schegloff, 2007), though the extent of the post-expansion tends to depend strongly on whether the request was granted or refused. Request acceptances usually have minimal post-expansions—often just an expression of gratitude—since there is no reason for much negotiation once a request has been accepted. However, rejected requests can be followed by lengthy post-expansions, with the requester trying to change the interlocutor's mind. As a case in point, the present interaction continued for another 36 lines before concluding (not shown here for reasons of space). Al-Gahtani and Roever (2014b) investigated insert expansions and post-expansions of requests in Arabic as a second language, and compared how these practices differed as a function of learners' proficiency level.

Once exemplars of the target social action (for example, request) have been identified in the data, researchers can use them to build a collection and identify patterns, regularities, and differences. Where the research interest is about comparing how a social action is carried out between groups (cross-sectionally), or between different points in time (longitudinally), researchers can compare how certain specific features of the target social action are realized at different levels of a target background variable, most commonly proficiency (for comparison in CA, see Zimmerman, 1999). For example, Pekarek-Doehler and Pochon-Berger (2011) compared disagreements by L2 learners of French at lower and higher proficiency levels based on features such as the sequential positioning of a disagreement in relation to a turn that included an opinion (immediately adjacent or delayed), placement of the disagreement component as turn-initial or later in the disagreement turn, occurrence of explanations or accounts in addition to the disagreement, and the linguistic format of the disagreement. While CA would advocate a data-driven approach to the identification of features to be compared, it is preferred for L2 pragmatics research that findings from previous studies also be taken into account. It should be noted that this approach of identifying the target features of the study is essentially a coding approach: the data is abstracted to more general categories (turn design, sequential placement of disagreement turn) and different exemplars are compared using these categories. The difference between CA and a coding approach like CCSARP is that CA develops the categories from the data at hand, whereas CCSARP applies a pre-existing coding scheme.

When researchers compare groups or performances at points in time, the use of quantification in CA is generally limited (see Schegloff, 1993, for a skeptical discussion of quantification and Stivers, 2015, for a more liberal perspective). While in the past broader quantitative categories were employed (for example, 'in most cases', and 'exceedingly rare') without giving precise counts, the use of frequency counts is now more common in CA work on first language (for example, Clayman & Heritage, 2002; Heritage et al., 2007) and second language data (Pekarek Doehler & Pochon-Berger, 2011). Nevertheless, the focus in CA work is on the careful explication of interactional practices and their functions, with coding and counting a secondary concern that is undertaken with some apprehension (see Stivers, 2015, for caveats).

The CA approach to interactional data is a powerful tool for careful and detailed analysis, while still allowing abstractions of patterns that can be compared between groups of interest. The large research database amassed by CA since the 1960s supports research well, although much less work exists on interactional practices in languages other than English. CA data analysis is also ideally done in data sessions involving a group of researchers, at least in the initial stages. Seeing patterns in interactional data takes a great deal of practice and is aided when several analysts work on the data together.

Verbal protocols

Verbal protocols, also known as verbal reports or 'think-aloud' protocols, are introspective self-report procedures which provide a different kind of data than the instruments we have discussed so far. Verbal protocols generate data *about tackling* tasks, not data *resulting from* tasks. There are two types of verbal protocol: concurrent and retrospective. In concurrent verbal protocols, learners are asked to say what they are thinking while they are working on tasks, whereas in retrospective verbal protocols, they complete the task first and then report what they were thinking.

The idea behind verbal protocols is that they offer direct access to the cognitive problem-solving steps a learner performs in working memory when dealing with the task (Ericsson & Simon, 1993). Learners are able to report on the outcomes of cognitive operations, for example word retrieval, while the operation itself is normally automatic, below the level of consciousness and therefore not reportable. Analyzing learners' reported series of cognitive states allows researchers to infer what abilities are mobilized while the learner is working on the task, what strategies learners are using, and what problems they encounter in the process of performing a task.

In order for concurrent verbal protocols to be elicited, participants work on a task in an individual session with the researcher (Ericsson & Simon, 1993). While a few studies in L2 pragmatics have had pairs of learners provide commentary on their task processes (Chen, 2015; Woodfield, 2008, 2010), this is not standard methodology for concurrent verbal reports. Concurrent verbal reports usually begin with explicit instructions to participants to say whatever they are thinking while solving the task, not to direct their comments at the researcher, and to keep talking continually. Participants are then given some practice tasks similar to the actual tasks to make them comfortable with the slightly strange situation of 'talking to themselves' with a researcher and a recording device in the room. While they undertake the target tasks, the researcher's only role is to remind them to keep talking whenever they fall silent. (From a practical perspective, it is worth noting that not all participants are equally good at providing verbal protocols, as some people seem to find it extremely difficult to verbalize their thought content while others are able to do so without any problems. In studies using verbal protocols, researchers need to build in a 'buffer' when deciding on participant numbers to ensure that enough data is obtained. In our experience, about one in five people will not provide adequate verbal protocol data.)

In order for retrospective verbal protocols to be elicited, learners are asked to reconstruct what they were thinking, usually focusing on specific aspects of their experience and supported by a replay of their responses (stimulated recall, see Gass & Mackey, 2000, for more detail). Due to the rapid decay of information in working memory, retrospective verbal protocols should ideally be done immediately after task completion. They may access memories of particularly salient aspects of the experience of solving the task, but they will primarily rely on reconstructions of experiences, unlike concurrent verbal protocols, which access outcomes of cognitive operations in situ. Retrospective protocols commonly include reflection and explanation, and they are usually elicited through interview questions from the researcher (see Robinson, 1992, and Woodfield, 2010, for comparative studies).

There has been a great deal of controversy in SLA research about the use of verbal protocols (summarized in Bowles, 2010), questioning whether the data generated truly represents thought content (veridicality), whether verbalizing affects task solution processes (reactivity), and whether participants are actually able to follow the instruction given in concurrent protocols to verbalize without regard to a listener (recipient design). While it is likely that participants' utterances are somewhat recipient-designed (Sasaki, 2008), and findings on veridicality and reactivity differ (Bowles, 2010), Cohen (2013) expresses optimism about the usefulness of verbal protocols as research instruments, and we cautiously share his optimism: verbal protocols can provide interesting insights into participants' thinking but are subject to so many limitations that they should primarily serve as supplemental information to enhance the analysis of primary data.

Verbal protocols have been used in L2 pragmatics research to investigate instrument effects (Woodfield, 2008), to gain insight into learners' cognitive processes (Chen, 2015; Félix-Brasdefer, 2008a; Nguyen, 2014) and their pragmatic development (Ren, 2014), and to validate assessment tools (Roever, 2005). In a study investigating DCTs, Woodfield (2008) had six native English speakers provide verbal reports in pairs while completing a DCT eliciting requests, and found that the reports offered insight into participants' handling of the research instrument, including their resistance to one-shot responses and uncertainty about under-specified situation prompts. Félix-Brasdefer (2008a) used retrospective verbal protocols to probe the cognitive processes of learners of Spanish as a second language. He had the learners complete two role-plays with refusals to invitations, and then asked them what they were

attending to while formulating their refusals, what language they were thinking in, and how they felt about the role-play interlocutor's insistence after the
learner had declined the invitation. These directive questions are typical of
retrospective verbal reports. Félix-Brasdefer also employed stimulated recall
by replaying the recording of the interaction when participants answered his
questions.

A different use of retrospective verbal protocols was shown in Ren (2014).
He collected retrospective protocols from 20 ESL learners at three points
over 10 months during the learners' study abroad sojourn in the U.K. The
learners performed refusals using a DCT with a picture illustrating the situation. After completing the DCT, Ren asked the learners what they had
attended to in formulating their answers and why they thought they had
responded in that particular way, supported by stimulated recall. He found
that learners attended more to sociopragmatic cues from the first to the
second data collection session, and there was evidence that their pragmatic
knowledge changed over time and became more target-like.

Finally, verbal reports have also been used in general language testing
research (for example, Barkaoui, 2011; Plakans & Gebril, 2012). In assessment of L2 pragmatics, Roever (2005) employed concurrent verbal protocols
in the piloting and validation of a test of ESL pragmalinguistics. In the validation phase he had six English native speakers and six non-native speakers
provide concurrent protocols as they were answering the test items. He identified task solution processes specific to the content tested (for example,
reasoning for implicature, prediction of correct response option for routines)
and found differences between the native and non-native speaker groups,
with non-native speakers engaging much more frequently in overt response
planning for speech act items. Roever interpreted this outcome as supporting
a test construct of three separate but related types of pragmatic knowledge.
It also supported the test's ability to distinguish between highly proficient and
less proficient test takers.

Verbal protocols have a place in L2 pragmatics research, but, like all research
instruments, their usefulness is limited to particular purposes. Concurrent
verbal protocols can provide an insight into the steps that learners follow in
tackling a task and what they attend to at each step. This is useful information
for instrument design and test validation; but, of course, interactive tasks are
precluded from concurrent verbal protocols since learners cannot simultaneously engage in a conversation and verbalize their thought content. Only
retrospective protocols are an option for such situations; the information
they provide is quite different, though no less interesting. While participants
in concurrent protocols should not explain their thinking, because doing so
may alter thought content (Ericsson & Simon, 1993), such reflection is often
encouraged in retrospective protocols and appears to provide researchers
with information about why learners responded to a task in a certain way. We
caution that it in fact provides information about why learners *think* they
responded to a task in a certain way. Researchers need to be very clear that

retrospective protocols are reflections on actions—at best reconstructions of what learners might have been thinking—and can only render candidate explanations for actions. The actual cognitive steps of solving the task are irretrievably lost. Retrospective protocols can serve as debriefings that collect learners' emic views of why they said and did what they said and did, but these are ex post facto views and interpretations, not reflections of sequences of momentary cognitive states.

Analysis of verbal protocol data

The analysis of verbal report data relies primarily on content coding (see Schreier, 2014, for an overview). After transcribing the spoken data, researchers need to segment the data and assign codes to classify the segments into categories. While there is a great deal of variation in coding approaches (see Flick, 2014; Miles, Huberman, & Saldana, 2014), the process of developing codes can primarily be based on the data, or based on the research goal of the study. In the bottom-up (also known as inductive or data-driven) approach, the researcher identifies patterns in the data and groups segments that follow these patterns into categories, which are then labeled and their characteristics outlined. In discourse analysis, CA is an example of an analytic tradition that uses this type of approach to identify discursive practices in the data. In the top-down (also known as deductive or theory-driven) approach, the researcher uses an existing coding scheme and applies it to the data, collecting exemplars that correspond to the existing coding categories. This is similar to the CCSARP approach in speech act coding.

Both approaches have advantages and drawbacks: bottom-up, data-driven generation of coding categories tends to account well for the data and represent it closely. However, different studies can arrive at very different coding schemes, making comparison and accumulation of knowledge about a phenomenon difficult. This approach also does not fit well with a research design where data is elicited specifically to answer a research question. On the other hand, top-down, theory-driven generation of coding categories tends to be more practical where a specific, pre-determined feature is of interest and where comparability with other studies is important. However, top-down coding can struggle to fit data into pre-defined coding categories, and the analyst may be forced to discard a large amount of data in order to focus narrowly on a pre-defined question.

Which approach is used depends on whether researchers are trying to identify phenomena in the data without preconceived notions about likely findings, or whether they are investigating a specific question, which is usually the case in L2 pragmatics research. For example, in Ren's (2014) study, the questions posed in the retrospective interview provided the foundation of a coding scheme. Since Ren was interested in learners' attention to socio-pragmatic, contextual features and other factors impacting their response, he established two major coding themes: situation features and learner factors.

He subdivided the 'learner factors' category further into two sub-categories: pragmatic difficulty and sources of knowledge. While Ren's overall category system was based on his research interest in investigating to what extent and why learners' sociopragmatic awareness develops during study abroad, specific sub-categories are often developed inductively out of the data. This mutual shaping of a coding scheme between theory and data is typical, and represents a position between bottom-up and top-down approaches, aiming to optimally exploit the data from the perspective of a particular research question.

Chapter summary and directions for future research

In this chapter we have reviewed widely used research instruments in L2 pragmatics, grouped along the lines of interactiveness and productive vs. receptive mode. The key concern with the use of any research instrument is what information it can provide and what kinds of research questions it can answer. Non-interactive receptive instruments, such as metapragmatic judgments, allow researchers to draw conclusions about learners' pragmatic perceptions, most commonly their intuitions about sociopragmatic appropriateness. This is useful information since sociopragmatic knowledge guides and constrains pragmalinguistic choices. However, receptive instruments do not support conclusions about learners' likely real-world pragmatic performance.

Non-interactive productive instruments, like DCTs, support conclusions about the repertoire of pragmalinguistic strategies which learners have at their disposal, and about how these pragmalinguistic tools relate to their sociopragmatic perception of the context variables encoded in the scenario. However, due to the offline nature of cognitive processes involved in answering DCT items and the non-interactiveness of DCTs, no conclusions can be drawn about what learners would actually be able to do in real-world interactions. While DCTs are practical, their usefulness for answering research questions is limited: learners' pragmatic intuitions are better elicited with metapragmatic judgment tasks, and their pragmatic performance is better elicited with interactive productive tasks, which does not leave much room for the use of DCTs. We only see a useful application of DCTs in cases where the research purpose is to explore the repertoire of strategies for implementing a specific speech act that learners have at their disposal. No conclusions can be drawn as to whether they can and will use these strategies in real-world interactions. We also see a role for DCTs in cases where responses are very brief, one-turn utterances in real-world interaction, such as expressions of gratitude or routines, or where the response is lengthy, and in written form, such as an email. Indeed, email communication is becoming a more heavily researched area (Alcón Soler, 2013a; Félix-Brasdefer, 2012; Zhu, 2012), and DCT-type items are legitimate in eliciting learner emails. There is also possible usefulness in multi-turn DCTs, where learners reconstruct a conversation; however, this type of instrument still needs more research to ascertain what conclusions can be drawn from it. Overall, we are very skeptical about the usefulness of the 'classic' one-shot DCT. Given the serious criticism that has been leveled against it, any use of a DCT should be thoroughly justified.

Interactive productive methods are better approximations of actual pragmatic performance in that they require coherent talk and moment-by-moment co-construction of conversation with an interlocutor. They therefore elicit online performance and provide data on learners' ability to interact in the target language, but they are logistically less advantageous than non-interactive methods since the talk generated must be painstakingly transcribed and analyzed. Researchers also need to be aware of participants' orienting to the social situation of being a research participant, which affects their performance, except in rare cases of completely natural data. While natural data often serves as a yardstick of data quality, it is difficult to obtain in a way that makes it useful for answering specific research questions. We recommend that researchers privilege interactive production data, simply because it is richer and more authentic than non-interactive data, thereby bolstering the strength of conclusions to be drawn from the study.

Finally, we see value in verbal report data, but mostly as supplemental information to collect emic explanations of participants' pragmatic choices and performances. In the case of interactive data collection, verbal report data can only be retroactive, and thus reflects the participants' hypotheses about their performance more than cognitive processes actually underlying this performance.

Methods for data analysis depend greatly on the type of data and researchers' epistemological orientation. We recommend using methods that capture as much of the information in the data as possible. For interactive data, it is difficult to look past the Conversation Analysis approach, with its detailed probing of spoken interaction and massive research base. For non-interactive production data and verbal report data, coding schemes need to be used, but they should not be imported wholesale without reflection; rather, they must be well anchored in the data, incorporating bottom-up and top-down aspects in their design. Metapragmatic data can be easy to analyze in the case of perceptions or dichotomously scored (correct/incorrect) items, but becomes much more difficult to handle when scores are benchmarked against a native-speaker norm. We prefer to use metapragmatic data primarily as perception data in its own right (without native-speaker benchmark) or scored dichotomously (correct/incorrect) rather than trying to measure it against native-speaker preference distribution.

In conclusion, the choice of data collection method and approach to analysis depends crucially on the goal of the study and, in turn, it crucially determines what contribution the study can make. We urge researchers to be thoroughly aware of the conclusions that different methods can defensibly support, and to design studies accordingly.

5

What learners have in common: pragmatic development

Introduction

In this chapter we will discuss findings on developmental trajectories in the learning of L2 pragmatics. Our focus will be on the stages that learners typically traverse rather than on explanations for their differential rate of learning and their differential ultimate attainment. We will discuss research on how individual differences may impact learning in Chapter 6, and the impact of the learning context in Chapter 7.

Similar to other areas of L2 pragmatics research, the vast majority of work in the area of development has been done on speech acts, with recent research also describing development of interactional abilities. Significantly less research exists on the learning of routine formulae and implicature. Wherever possible in this chapter, we will rely on findings from longitudinal studies (for a review, see Taguchi, 2010), which have the advantage of following the same learners over an extended time period, enabling researchers to detect changes in knowledge and performance. The drawback of longitudinal studies is the risk of subject mortality, particularly over long time periods, as well as the large and unwieldy amount of data that is generated by repeated measurement. Because of this, longitudinal studies tend to involve few participants; in the twelve production studies included in Taguchi's (2010) review, participant numbers range from 2 to 35.

In some cases, where no longitudinal studies are available to illustrate pragmatic development, we will use findings from cross-sectional studies which group learners according to a background variable (usually proficiency), and then compare the groups. The disadvantage of this approach is that it involves a leap of faith in assuming continuity in development between groups. For example, it assumes that current lower-intermediate learners will become like current upper-intermediate learners in the future. This is not guaranteed, however, since learning conditions might change. Still, cross-sectional studies are able to suggest developmental pathways. A small number of studies combine both approaches (for example, Al-Gahtani & Roever, 2014 a, b,

2015 a, b; S. Li, 2014), comparing groups of learners and also following the groups over a time period and collecting longitudinal data.

Speech acts

Development of requesting has been the most thoroughly investigated area of development research in L2 pragmatics. In early longitudinal studies, Ellis (1992) and Achiba (2002) investigated the request development of ESL learners, though sample sizes were very small. Ellis's study followed two young ESL learners in a British classroom setting for a year in one case and one-and-a-half years in the other, whereas Achiba investigated the request development of her seven-year-old daughter during a 17-month stay in Australia. Based on these studies, Kasper and Rose (2002) proposed five stages of request development:

- Pre-basic stage: This stage is essentially non-pragmatic in that learners' language resources are so limited that they use whatever they have to get their message across. Very short utterances dominate, and there is no apparent politeness or orientation to social relationships.
- Formulaic stage: Learners use chunks, routine formulae, and imperatives to make requests. There is little evidence of deployment of sociopragmatic knowledge, but high-frequency constructions and formulae do occur.
- Unpacking stage: Learners start using conventional indirectness ('Can you...') and increasingly analyze formulae. They start to make pragmalinguistic choices based on social context variables (for example, power, social distance, and degree of imposition).
- Pragmatic expansion: Learners' repertoire of pragmalinguistic tools increases, with utterances becoming more syntactically complex and including more mitigation.
- Fine tuning: Learners' mapping of pragmalinguistic tools and sociopragmatic rules becomes increasingly target-like, and utterances are recipient-designed for particular interlocutors and situations.

Later longitudinal research on English as a target language has supported Kasper and Rose's (2002) stage sequences for requests (for example, Barron, 2003; Schauer, 2009; Woodfield, 2012), as has cross-sectional research (for example, Göy, Zeyrek, & Otcu, 2012; Savić, 2015; Trosborg, 1995), and research for some other target languages, including Greek (Bella, 2012), Spanish (Félix-Brasdefer, 2007), and Mandarin Chinese (S. Li, 2014).

However, studies by Shively (2011) and Bataller (2010) for L2 Spanish, as well as by Al-Gahtani and Roever (2015a) for L2 Arabic, highlight the interplay of pragmatic development and target community pragmatic norms. In Shively's (2011) study, L1 American English-speaking learners of Spanish in a study abroad context recorded their service encounters over a one-semester period. The author found a move from an American English politeness norm of using conventional indirectness ('*puedo comprar ciento gramos de jamon especial de la casa?*' 'Can I buy a hundred grams of the special house ham?')

to a more direct Spanish politeness norm ('*cien gramos de este salchichon*' 'A hundred grams of this salami.'). Shively (2011) ascribes her learners' use of less complex requests to socialization into the Spanish norms of making requests in service encounters by observing other customers and receiving negative feedback (lack of service) when transferring their L1 American English politeness norm. Similarly, Al-Gahtani and Roever (2015a) conducted a combined cross-sectional and longitudinal study of the development of L2 Arabic requests with learners from a variety of L1 backgrounds at four levels of a Modern Standard Arabic intensive program in Saudi Arabia. Collecting data longitudinally (at the beginning and end of the teaching semester) and cross-sectionally (across the four program levels), Al-Gahtani and Roever (2015a) found that learners at the lower levels shifted exclusively from making direct to indirect requests between the beginning and end of the teaching semester. However, at the second highest (upper-intermediate) level, the shift reversed: while the majority of learners had been making indirect requests at the beginning of the semester, they were making direct requests at the end, and this tendency was also found at the highest (advanced) level. In fact, lower-level learners only moved from making direct to indirect requests, whereas higher-level learners only moved in the opposite direction. Directness in requests, though usually modified by religious formulae, is the Saudi norm, so learners at the upper-intermediate and advanced levels must have realized that their indirect request production (enabled by their improving Arabic proficiency) was not target-like and thus started using direct request-making forms. Due to the fact that learners with a variety of L1s were involved in Al-Gahtani and Roever's (2015a) sample, it is impossible to know if learners were transferring their L1-based request behaviors at the lower levels or if a more general developmental phenomenon was at work, where learners might follow a strategy of erring on the side of being more polite once their pragmalinguistic ability allows them to do so. This is not an unreasonable strategy since being too polite is less likely to cause interpersonal conflict than not being polite enough. However, when it leads to non-target-like production, the majority of learners seem to notice the gap between their own theories of L2 politeness and the target-like norms, and adjust their utterances accordingly. It should be noted that not all learners moved to making more direct requests in Al-Gahtani and Roever's (2015a) or Shively's (2011) studies, with some learners in Shively's study citing personal choice as their reason for not following L2 norms.

Some research also exists on other speech acts besides requests. Development in apologizing has been researched fairly widely (Chang, 2010; Edmondson & House, 1991; Rose, 2000; Trosborg, 1995; Warga & Schölmberger, 2007), though few studies have been longitudinal. Overall, studies on apology revealed similar tendencies found in studies on request, with learners expanding their pragmalinguistic repertoire of apology strategies, and moving from formulaic to more complex apologies (Chang, 2010; Rose, 2000). In an oft-cited cross-sectional study, Rose (2000) compared second, fourth, and sixth graders in Hong Kong in their EFL apologies. He found that second graders were able to use apology IFIDs (illocutionary force indicating devices, for example, 'I'm sorry.') at the same level as fourth and sixth graders, but there were clear differences in their use of supportive moves. For example, offers of repair ('I'll get you a new one.') were not used by second graders, rarely used by fourth graders, and heavily used by sixth graders. Promise of forbearance ('It won't happen again.') only started to emerge among sixth graders, who used apology intensifiers and acknowledgments of responsibility much more frequently than the other groups. Rose (2000) also collected L1 data, which showed very little effect of year level, indicating that the use of supportive moves is dependent on increased L2 competence and that certain L2-specific pragmatic moves are less accessible to learners at a lower-proficiency level.

A finding specific to apologies is the 'waffle phenomenon' (Edmondson & House, 1991) among intermediate-level learners, who have been found to show excessive politeness in their apologies, probably due to non-target-like sociopragmatic knowledge. This phenomenon is similar to the initial tendency toward non-target-like indirectness which Al-Gahtani and Roever (2015a) found for requests, and indicates that mapping of sociopragmatic and pragmalinguistic knowledge continues up to high levels of development.

Other speech acts have been given less attention in developmental studies. Matsumura (2001, 2003) conducted a longitudinal study on learners' perceptions of ESL advice-giving expressions with Japanese study abroad learners in Canada, and found that most development occurred in the first month after arrival, with little improvement three months later. Barron (2007) and Ren (2012) investigated refusals by study abroad learners, and Bella (2014) did a cross-sectional study of refusals with learners of Greek as a second language. Barron (2007) found that her Irish English-speaking learners of L2 German spending a year studying abroad in Germany moved toward the target language norms in terms of upgrading refusals of offers; for example, '*Mir geht es wirklich gut.*' ('I really am fine.') when refusing an offer of help after a minor accident. Ren (2012), on the other hand, found in his refusal study that ESL learners' repertoire of refusal strategies increased during their nine-month stay in the U.K. Similarly, learners in Bella's (2014) study increasingly replaced direct refusals with indirect ones as they increased in proficiency level.

In a classic study on suggestions and responding to advice, Bardovi-Harlig and Hartford (1993a) found that ESL learners in status-unequal encounters with advisers in a U.S. university context learned role-based expectations, which helped them to avoid refusing the adviser's suggestions by putting suggestions forward themselves. They also learned to use acceptable reasons when refusing advisers' suggestions; for example, a clash with another course rather than a desire to sleep in.

Overall, developmental studies in the speech act tradition have shown that learners tend to shift from using brief, formulaic utterances to longer and more complex utterances, use more modifications in and around the head act, and develop toward the target language norm in terms of directness and indirectness. This developmental trajectory can be accounted for pragmalinguistically in terms of learners' greater automatization of their linguistic knowledge, which allows them to produce more complex speech act formulations and add supportive moves without great effort. This enables them to make their production more polite and less direct since polite and indirect utterances tend to be longer and more complex. Sociopragmatically, learners develop toward more fine-tuned understandings of social relationships, and the cultural norms that impact interactions. Mapping pragmalinguistic knowledge and sociopragmatic knowledge is an ongoing process but one that can start in earnest only when learners have a sufficient pragmalinguistic repertoire that gives them options, and allows them to assign certain pragmalinguistic choices to certain constellations of sociopragmatic contextual factors.

Extended discourse: markers of interactional competence

Recently, there has been increasing research on the development of learners' ability to participate in extended discourse. Some of these studies have also looked at speech acts; for example, requests (Al-Gahtani & Roever, 2012, 2014 a, b), disagreements (Pekarek Doehler & Pochon-Berger, 2011; Zhang, 2016), and suggestions (Tran, 2013b). These studies have been cross-sectional, whereas a number of longitudinal case studies have taken an interactional perspective and investigated issues such as turn-taking (Cekaite, 2007), repair (Hellermann, 2011), listenership (Ishida, 2011), or topic shifts (Lee & Hellermann, 2014). Another set of cross-sectional studies has investigated the differences in interactional competence between learners at different levels of L2 proficiency (Galaczi, 2014; Ikeda, 2016) in order to identify what aspects of interaction can be isolated to distinguish differences between learners with lower or higher interactional competence. We will take a similar perspective here, and discuss some markers of interactional competence that have emerged from previous research. We will start with the most well-attested markers—preference organization and topic management—which have each been investigated in several studies. Other possible markers, including reliance on the interlocutor, non-minimal post-expansions, and orientation to the interlocutor's social status will also be briefly discussed.

Preference organization

In Conversation Analysis (CA), preference organization describes a type of sequential organization that applies to certain second pair parts such as disagreements and refusals, which occur as responses to social actions like giving an opinion or making a request (see Pomerantz & Heritage, 2013, for details on preference organization). Preference organization also applies to certain first pair parts such as requests and complaints, which are intended to elicit a response from an interlocutor. While preference does not refer to an interactant's desire to be told certain things and not others (for example, to have a request accepted rather than refused), it is the case that preferred social actions promote social harmony and affiliation between interlocutors, whereas dispreferred social actions show that interlocutors are disaffiliated and such actions may therefore threaten social harmony (Heritage, 1984). Preferred actions are done without delay, preliminary moves, hesitation, or mitigation, whereas dispreferred actions are usually done late in a sequence, are hedged and mitigated, and are preceded by hesitations and preliminary moves such as explanations, accounts, and pre-commitment checks. When applied to the request sequence, this sequential placement allows the person receiving the request to signal an upcoming rejection early on without actually having to perform it on the record, or to pre-empt the request with an offer.

In studies with ESL learners and second language learners of Modern Standard Arabic (MSA), Al-Gahtani and Roever (2012, 2013, 2014 a, b) showed that learners became increasingly likely to use conventional preference structure by deploying preliminary moves with increasing proficiency. In their cross-sectional study of MSA learners undertaking an intensive program in Saudi Arabia (Al-Gahtani & Roever, 2014b), the authors collected near-natural service encounter data, and found that the majority of learners in the lowest proficiency group did not produce any preliminary moves before the request (for example, explanations or accounts), and made their request right after the opening sequence of the interaction. At the next level, the number of learners using preliminary moves doubled over a five-month period, but many used only minimal preliminary moves, as demonstrated in Figure 5.1, from a conversation between a learner (L) and a university administrator (A). Preceding the excerpt, a greeting sequence had occurred.

1	L	*al-jadwul*	*tağiir-a*	*mina aš-šabaah*	*élaa*	*al-masaa*
		the timetable	changed	from the morning	to	the evening
		The timetable has been changed from morning to evening.				
2	A	*na'am.*	*šahiih*			
		Yes	true			
		Yes, true				
3	L	*ánaa*	*ábğaa*	*šabaa:ħ (0.2)*	↑*faqt.*	
		I	want	morning (0.2)	only	
		I want morning only.				

Figure 5.1 Conversation opening with minimal pre-expansion (Al-Gahtani & Roever 2014b, p. 630)

In line 1, the learner produces a preliminary move in the form of a statement that contextualizes and projects the upcoming request. The administrator confirms the veracity of the statement in line 2, followed by the request in line 3. This is a case of a minimal use of preliminary moves; multiple preliminary moves became more common as levels increased. At the upper-intermediate level, three-quarters of learners used preliminary moves, and at the advanced level, the number approached 100%.

This pattern mirrored the situation of Al-Gahtani and Roever's (2013) ESL learners, where preliminary moves occurred in fewer than half of the role-plays at the lowest of three levels, and conversations like that in Figure 5.2 were common in a role-play between the researcher acting out the role of professor and the learner acting out the role of student. After the greeting sequence in lines 1 and 2, the learner immediately produces a request without any preliminary moves. However, an orientation to the dispreferred nature of the requesting in this case is apparent in the indirect formatting of the request itself.

1	L	Hi doctor.
2	R	Hello.
3	L	Can I have handouts for last week?

Figure 5.2 Conversation opening without preliminary moves

However, learners at the next two higher levels invariably used preliminary moves, for example in Figure 5.3 after a greeting sequence. In this excerpt, the learner starts off with an availability check and a general pre-pre (Schegloff, 1980), which lays the groundwork for subsequent preliminary moves, in line 1. After the researcher, playing the role of professor, has confirmed availability and offered the learner a seat, the learner produces an explanation for the upcoming request in line 3, which, after a go-ahead from the interlocutor, continues in line 5, followed by the request itself. Other interactions included even more explanations and accounts before the request was made.

1	L	do you have some time…I want to tell you something?
2	R	yeah, for sure have a seat.
3	L	thank you. last week I was absent [
4	R	[yeah
5	L	I don't have…handouts…so can you please give it to me?

Figure 5.3 Conversation opening with preliminary moves

In her assessment studies of learners at three proficiency levels producing ESL requests, Youn (2013, 2015) reports similar findings, with lower-proficiency learners not following a sequence organization that marks their requests as dispreferred actions.

While requests are first pair parts, developmental patterns have also been found with second pair parts. Pekarek Doehler and Pochon-Berger (2011) compared disagreement sequences in pair discussions in L2 French. Their participants involved lower-level learners in their fourth year of high school French in Switzerland and higher-level learners in their eighth year of high school French. They found that lower-level learners' disagreements were organized like preferred actions: they occurred exclusively in the turn that immediately followed the statement to which the disagreement related, and in 98% of cases, the disagreement turn started with an overt, explicit disagreement marker, such as *non* (no) or *mais* (but). While the upper-level learners also overwhelmingly used immediate disagreements, delayed disagreements also started to emerge, indicating that learners were starting to use sequence as an interactional resource to minimize overt disaffiliation. In the immediate agreement turns, upper-level learners used fewer polarity markers ('non') and in some cases made their disagreement non-turn-initial by means of token agreement ('yes, but'), which lower-level learners did not do.

Investigating agreements and disagreements in elicited conversation in L2 Mandarin, Zhang (2016) paired intermediate-level learners and advanced learners with native speakers, and had them negotiate solutions to complex scenarios. While both learner groups structured their disagreements as dispreferred actions with clarification questions, explanations, and accounts preceding an outright disagreement, Zhang found differences in the formatting of disagreements between the groups. For example, Mandarin native speakers and advanced learners formatted some counter-arguments as questions, which intermediate-level learners did not do. Also, intermediate-level learners did not use expressions that stressed common ground before presenting counter-arguments, and they did not use the inclusive discourse marker 吧 (ba). When emphasizing their disagreement, neither the intermediate nor the advanced learner group upgraded disagreements by using exacerbating discourse markers such as 唉 (ai) or 呀 (ya), which the native-speaker group used. For agreements, Zhang found two sequential types: agreement immediately following the interlocutor's opinion, and delayed agreement. The idea of delaying agreement seems to run contrary to typical preference organization, where actions indicative of affiliation and conducive to social harmony are done without delay. However, since Zhang's data involved extended negotiation and compromising to arrive at a mutually satisfactory solution, it is perhaps not surprising that agreement was often only given reluctantly and followed lengthy persuasion sequences. When delayed agreement occurred, native speakers and advanced learners signaled their reluctance by including disagreement components in the final agreement term, and by using modal particles and formulaic expressions. None of these devices were used by intermediate learners, who also generally signaled their agreement more explicitly than advanced learners and native speakers. Due to the need for extended negotiations, Zhang's study only included learners with a fairly high degree of proficiency and fluency in L2 Mandarin, which may explain why all his learners were able to exploit sequential organization for carrying out dispreferred social actions such as disagreement and reluctant agreement.

These studies suggest a developmental pattern for learners' production of preferred and dispreferred actions. At the initial stage, learners focus on getting their message across efficiently without preliminary moves or delaying a dispreferred action sequentially, and without much mitigation work in the turn in which the action occurs. This is presumably because introducing explanations and accounts or complex semantic formulae would unduly stress learners' linguistic processing capability.

As learners' automatization of access to linguistic knowledge and their fluency increase, they start to exploit sequentiality as a means of marking an action as dispreferred. They begin to use preliminary moves, although they may initially use a small number of moves, mostly for the purpose of orienting the interlocutor to the topic of the upcoming talk. Greater facility with the target language allows learners to produce more sophisticated pre-sequences, which project the target social action (Pekarek Doehler & Pochon-Berger, 2015), for example by getting pre-commitments from the interlocutor, and making a detailed argument for supporting their upcoming request or disagreement. More interactionally competent learners also make greater use of turn-constructional features such as solidarity markers (stressing commonality, expressing concern for the interlocutor) and semantic formulae that reduce the disaffiliating force of the request or disagreement.

There is much less research on preferred actions such as agreements and offers. These actions should require fewer linguistic and interactional abilities than dispreferred actions since they can often be done bald-on-record without much linguistic adornment or sequential delay. However, as Zhang's (2016) work demonstrates, preferred actions can be sequentially carried out as dispreferred actions, for example, to indicate reluctance in the case of agreements. It is unclear to what extent lower-ability learners would be able to use sequential resources for that purpose. Also, the formatting of the action itself with a disagreement component indicating resistance before agreement appears to be available only to high-ability learners.

Topic management and collaboration

Assessment studies (Galaczi, 2008, 2014; Gan, 2010; Youn, 2013) and longitudinal case studies (Ishida, 2011; Lee & Hellermann, 2014) have investigated how managing topics in conversations relates to levels of interactional competence. Galaczi (2014) compared learner dyads at proficiency levels B1, B2, C1, and C2 in the Common European Framework of Reference (CEFR) undertaking a speaking test. She found that interactions between learners at B1 level (threshold/intermediate) were characterized by non-elaborated topics, lack of connection with the interlocutor's previous utterance, and disjunctive topic shifts, where a new topic is introduced abruptly without transitioning from the previous topic. B1 learners tended to focus on their own topics and did little work on elaborating topics introduced by the interlocutor. They also left noticeably longer gaps and pauses between turns than is common in native conversations, and they displayed few listener responses such as backchannels, assessments, or other overt expressions of interest, engagement, and affiliation. Overall, their conversations appeared like sequences of barely connected monologues, showing little collaboration in discourse.

Learners at B2 level (vantage/upper intermediate) showed more collaborative construction of the conversation, elaborating their own and the interlocutor's topics, at times co-producing complex clauses, and generally leaving shorter gaps between turns. Topics were developed over several turns by both interlocutors, and the interlocutors deployed questions to invite co-participant contributions. Topic shifts were also more closely tied to the topic under discussion, for example, transitioning by focusing on one aspect of the topic. However, there were still notable gaps between some turns, and disjunctive topic shifts still occurred.

Learners at C1 and C2 level (advanced/effective operational proficiency and mastery) displayed the highest degree of collaboration and topic development. They reacted quickly to each other's turns, not usually leaving large gaps, and showing overlap and latching. Learners extended and developed their own and the interlocutor's topics, and their topic transitions appeared smoother and followed a stepwise pattern (Jefferson, 1984a; Sacks, 1992) rather than being abrupt and involving disjunctive topic change.

Ishida's (2011) case study of an L2 learner of Japanese as a listener to her Japanese host mother's tellings shows a similar trajectory in terms of moving from being a mere recipient to being a collaborator in the telling. The learner initially produced few assessments but over time became more actively involved in the telling by providing commentary, second stories (related tellings of her own experiences), and eventually using a second story telling to add to the host mother's topic.

Galaczi's (2014) and Ishida's (2011) findings show that learners' ability to collaboratively construct topics evolves as their interactional competence increases. Higher-ability learners design their contributions to relate more obviously to the interlocutor's preceding contribution, extending topics the interlocutor has initiated, and transitioning to other topics by linking to them through common aspects. They also show more listenership and respond with minimal gaps, thereby creating a sense of conversational flow and collaboration. Lower-ability learners may struggle more with joint topic development since their linguistic competence may not be entirely at the same level as their interlocutor's competence. As a result, the topic initiated by the interlocutor may push them outside their comfort zone, which they try to regain by initiating a topic of their own. This effect may be particularly pronounced in a testing setting like Galaczi's study, where learners may feel they need to display their linguistic abilities to an examiner rather than create shared understanding with another interlocutor. The prevalence of disjunctive topic transitions observed in low-ability learners can also be explained by a combination of linguistic ability and communicative setting: finding links between topics that can be used for stepwise transition is cognitively demanding and requires activation of relevant vocabulary, which may be beyond the learners' processing ability when they are simultaneously having to deal with comprehension of input and formulation of their next contribution. In addition, if learners prioritize displaying their linguistic ability over conversing, smooth topic transition is not a necessity. Supporting this, topic management was found to be a discriminating characteristic of learners' ability levels in Youn's (2013) assessment study as well. Youn distinguishes between high-level performance with smooth topic transitions and the use of transitional markers, and intermediate-level performance with abrupt topic shifts involving the deployment of unrelated content.

Similarly, in a longitudinal case-study of an L1 Korean speaker of English, Lee and Hellerman (2014) showed that, after a ten-month period, the learner was able to mark topic transitions when engaged in storytelling through the use of transitional markers ('but', 'as we know') and content organization; for example, including the year an event happened in an extended telling about the history of space exploration. By contrast, in an earlier story telling, the learner did not use markers of topic change: she launched into a new topic but then repaired this abrupt change by explicitly announcing the new topic ('I want to tell about the spi- spiritual lectures', Lee & Hellermann, 2014, p. 777).

In summary, development of the ability to manage topics seems to progress across a fairly broad developmental spectrum, from low-ability learners not marking topics explicitly, to more able learners using transitional markers but at the same time still shifting topics abruptly, and high-ability learners shifting topics by linking the previous topic with the next. Joint management of topics also seems to develop, from little engagement with the interlocutor's contributions and a focus on elaborating on one's own topics, to collaboratively working through topics by taking up and extending each other's contributions.

Signaling a need for support

Al-Gahtani and Roever (2012) examined how low-proficiency ESL learners, who were probably roughly at A2 level (elementary) of the CEFR, managed to successfully complete request role-plays. They found that learners frequently produced the request early in the interaction without preliminary moves, in a similar way to Figure 5.2. However, this did not lead to an automatic failing of the request. Instead, in two-thirds of the interactions with low-proficiency learners, the interlocutor elicited the background for the request after it had been made, as in Figure 5.4, where the learner (P) (playing the role of a busy student) is asking the researcher (I) (playing the role of his housemate) to go get some bread for him.

The learner begins by putting his request on the record in line 3. This is followed by a repair from the researcher in line 6, and a confirmation by the learner in line 7. At this point, the learner-driven request sequence has come to a close, but rather than accepting or rejecting the request, the researcher asks questions providing a candidate account for the learner's request in line 8, and phrasing the request with more detail in line 10. It appears that the learner's early requesting and brief (non-elaborating) response in line 5 prompted the researcher to take on most of the interactional work and elicit the information that the learner could have provided before the request. However, this

1	P	↑Excuse me::
2	I	yes
3	P	I (.) want bread
4	I	Ok
5	P	Yea::h
6	I	So:: you want bread?
7	P	Yes:: (.) it is <u>e</u>nough in the ( )
8	I	.hhh (.) >you mean< there is <u>n</u>othing: in the fridge?
9	P	Yes
10	I	So:: (.) you <u>wa</u>::nt me to <u>g</u>o:: to the superma::rket and <u>g</u>et some bread for <u>y</u>ou.
11	P	<u>Y</u>es
12	I	Ok (.) I'll go ↑now and <u>g</u>et it for <u>y</u>ou

Figure 5.4 Interlocutor takes control of conversation (Al-Gahtani &
Roever, 2012, p. 50)

interactional pattern did not occur in any of the higher-level groups, indicating that <u>low-ability learners can use the interlocutor as a resource</u> to <u>accomplish social actions by proxy</u>. Low-ability learners seem to rely on their interlocutors' cooperation, and 'borrow' interlocutors' linguistic ability to accomplish actions by putting the request on the record and then working out the details. This pattern does not show much orientation to affiliation and social harmony; it is similar to learners at the first two stages of Kasper and Rose's (2002) five stages of request development (pre-basic and formulaic).

There is another facet to this phenomenon of an interlocutor-led conversation: the learner's less-than-perfect opening seems to signal to the interlocutor that they need to make the learners' task as easy as possible. Al-Gahtani and Roever (2012) note that with low-ability learners, the role-play conductor in their ESL interactions avoided complicating questions, which had been built into the role-plays to make the learners' task more challenging. In fact, the interlocutor would often grant the learners' request with no further enquiry or some yes/no questions as shown above. Similarly, in Al-Gahtani and Roever's L2 Arabic studies (2014a, b) of MSA data, the interlocutor (who was a university administrator without interlocutor training) did not ask low-ability learners for reasons for their request but simply confirmed receipt, as in Figure 5.5.

After a greeting sequence (not shown), the learner immediately makes his request in line 1 that classes be taught in the morning. The administrator provides linguistic repair in line 2, and the learner confirms the interlocutor's understanding, upon which the administrator provisionally grants the request. By contrast, in some dialogues with high-level learners the administrator quizzed the learner about his reasons for wanting to change the class time.

1	**LOW**	*ánaa*	<u>*áb*</u>*ǧaa*	*šabaa:ħ (0.2)*	↑*faqat.*
		I	want	morning (0.2)	only
			I want morning (0.2) only.		
2	**ADM**	*turiid*	*aš-šabaaħ?*		
		You	want the morning		
			Do you want the morning?		
3	**LOW**	*na'am*			
		yes			
			Yes		
4	**ADM**	*sawfa*	<u>*nuħaa::wil*</u> *taǧiir,*	*al-muhaaḍaraah (.)*	
		Will	we try	change the lecture (.)	
			We will try to change the lecture (.)		

Figure 5.5 Interlocutor does not elicit reasons (Al-Gahtani & Roever, 2014a, p. 200)

The interlocutor's brevity with low-proficiency learners in both studies may be due to the likely effort required to have an extended conversation with a low-proficiency conversationalist. It appears that the learner's sequentially signaled lack of interactional competence impacts what the interlocutor does (elicit explanations) and does not do (engage in extended talk). From a developmental perspective, low-ability learners appeal to the interlocutor's ability to simplify and facilitate the interaction, whereas higher-ability learners exert a greater degree of control over the course of the conversation.

Other interactional features

Other features, which seem to change with learners' developing interactional competence but have been investigated less often, include post-expansions (Al-Gahtani & Roever, 2014), turn completion (Youn, 2013), and formality (Al-Gahtani & Roever, 2012; Ikeda, 2016).

Post-expansions are sequences that follow the core adjacency pair (request–acceptance/refusal, opinion–agreement/disagreement). They are frequently minimal (acknowledgment, thanks) and come after preferred second pair parts, but they can be non-minimal (i.e. extended) where the second pair part was dispreferred, for example where a request was refused. After receiving a refusal, the unsuccessful requester may follow up with a non-minimal post-expansion, for example by trying to negotiate further. Al-Gahtani and Roever (2014a) found that non-minimal post-expansions in the MSA data occurred only with learners at the highest proficiency level.

Youn (2013) found unconventional turn construction by lower-ability learners, with turn-internal pauses and disfluencies that made it difficult at times for the interlocutor to determine if a turn had ended. This is exemplified in Figure 5.6, which was preceded by native-speaker interlocutor J suggesting

1	P	hm:: (1.0) how about the:
2	(1.0)	
3	J	does- it does work for you? right?= ((laugh))
4	P	=yeah I think it's [xx
5	J	[oh why not?
6	P	I think how about the (1.0) uh: Saturday because it's weekend

Figure 5.6 Unclear turn structure due to pausing (Youn, 2013, p. 75)

Tuesday for a meeting to discuss a class project with ESL learner classmate P (Youn, 2013).

In line 1, P starts a counter suggestion but does not complete the sentence, instead leaving a one-second pause. J takes the long pause as a completion point, and produces the next turn in line 3, checking acceptance of her earlier suggestion of a Tuesday meeting. In line 4, P apparently indicates the unsuitability of Tuesday as a meeting day since J in line 5 asks for a reason why her suggestion is not taken up. In line 6, P utters his suggestion in a similar format as line 1 with an equally long pause before proposing Saturday and giving a reason. This 'choppy' delivery was common among low-ability learners, leading to repair initiations on the part of the interlocutor.

With regard to orientation to interlocutor social status, Al-Gahtani and Roever (2012) report that only high-ability learners showed differences in sequence design between lower-status and same- or higher-status interlocutors. With lower-status interlocutors, some of Al-Gahtani and Roever's advanced ESL learners integrated accounts in the request turn, as in Figure 5.7 (unpublished data from Al-Gahtani & Roever, 2009), where the learner (A) plays a professor asking a student (I, the role-play conductor) to let his classmates know that class is canceled. Figure 5.7 starts right after a greeting sequence. A makes the request in line 1 without any pre-expansion and follows up with a reason in line 4. Al-Gahtani and Roever (2012) ascribe this organization to the learner displaying a sense of entitlement attached to a

1	A	uhm I would like you know to…I would appreciate if you could tell your classmates
		that we have no class today [
2	I	[.hh
3	A	uhm because…I have an appointment with the head of the department [
4	I	[I see
5	A	so we could not…we will not make you know class today

Figure 5.7 Orientation to social status (unpublished data from Al-Gahtani & Roever, 2009)

more powerful social role, which obviates the need for checking interlocutor availability or willingness.

By contrast, in an interaction where the same learner (A) played a student and the interlocutor (I) played a professor, the learner used preliminary moves before the request. Figure 5.8 (Al-Gahtani & Roever, 2009) is preceded by a greeting sequence. The learner (A) shows classic dispreferred sequential organization for his request, beginning with the dispreference marker 'well' in line 2, followed by an account, and an explanation in line 4, before making the request proper in line 6. This high-ability learner appears to be able to make fine differentiation in interactional organization, whereas lower-ability learners tend not to adapt their sequential structure to the interlocutor. Ikeda (2016) shows a similar finding with higher-level learners displaying interactional orientation to interlocutor status more strongly than lower-level learners.

```
1   I   good. thank you. how can I help you ?
2   A   well, actually I missed you know the class…last Monday [
3   I                                                          [.hh
4   A   and I couldn't you know able to…get the notes for that class [
5   I                                                                [yeah
6   A   could you please you know…give me these notes ?
```

Figure 5.8 Sequential organization as a dispreferred action (Al-Gahtani & Roever, 2009)

Overall, interactional abilities seem to develop over a series of broad stages:

- Egocentric: Learners have little ability to treat conversation as a social activity that requires shared understanding. They focus on getting their message across, regardless of threats to social harmony, and they show little collaboration on developing topics. They rely strongly on the interlocutor for successfully completing the interaction, assisting in creating shared understandings, and making allowances for their lack of attention to social harmony.
- Basic mutuality: Learners begin to create shared understandings with the interlocutor by implementing some elements of preference organization and showing some engagement with interlocutors' topics. However, efficient communication is still important so they sacrifice expression of some of their own stances (for example, signaling reluctance or contesting an undesirable request outcome) in order to complete the interaction quickly.
- Shared understandings: Learners recipient-design their contributions to take into account the interlocutor's understanding and their social relationship. They can organize their talk recognizably, and show uptake of

interlocutor utterances by displaying evidence of listenership and elaborating on topics. Efficiency of communication is less important and learners privilege the maintenance of social harmony while conveying their position.

Implicatures, routines, and other pragmatic targets

Learners' development in a range of areas other than speech acts and interaction has also been investigated. In this section, we will focus on implicatures and routine formulae, and briefly summarize other research.

Implicature

Developmental research in implicature has shown that different types of implicature develop differentially. In a series of studies with ESL students in a U.S. university, Bouton (1988, 1994, 1999) found that implicature which was accessible from its context and the utterance's semantic meaning ('idiosyncratic implicature') was easier to decode for learners and was learned to a higher level than implicature which relies on the hearer's knowledge of its structure ('formulaic implicature'). An example of idiosyncratic implicature is simple conversational implicature, which draws on flouting the maxim of relevance; for example, A: 'Where is the mixer?' – B: 'Check the cabinet.' Without saying explicitly that Speaker B knows or believes the mixer to be in the cabinet, Speaker B's utterance implies such knowledge or belief (in addition to an understanding that A is actively looking for the mixer rather than enquiring after its location out of general curiosity).

In contrast, formulaic implicature includes such types as indirect criticism, where an irrelevant part is disingenuously praised to imply dislike of the whole ('How did you like their new house?' – 'Nice driveway.') and the infamous Pope Q, in which a question is responded to with a question that has the same answer ('Are we going to get in trouble?' – 'Is the pope Catholic?'). Bouton found that learners' comprehension of idiosyncratic implicature was high (close to 90%), even when first arriving in the U.S., and then increased quickly toward native-speaker levels. However, their comprehension of formulaic implicature was much weaker on arrival and took longer to approach native-speaker levels, in some cases over four years. Learners' comprehension of formulaic implicature stayed clearly below that of native speakers.

Roever (2013) had a similar finding with formulaic and idiosyncratic implicature in a test for high-proficiency ESL learners and native English speakers. Learners' scores on formulaic items were lower than on idiosyncratic items; and only on formulaic indirect criticism items did learners with more than one year's residence perform better than learners with less than one year's residence. It can be concluded that this type of implicature was learned over time (contrary to Bouton's 1994 findings).

exposure
& proficiency

In fact, it is less exposure and more proficiency that matters for the development of implicature comprehension, as studies by Taguchi (2011b) and Wang, Brophy, and Roever (2014) showed (see also Chapter 6 on proficiency as an individual difference factor). Taguchi compared three groups of EFL learners: high-proficiency learners with one-year study abroad, high-proficiency learners without study abroad, and low-proficiency learners without study abroad. She found that both high-proficiency groups outperformed the low-proficiency groups on all comprehension accuracy and response-time measures, but these two groups did not significantly differ from each other, with one exception: high-proficiency learners with study abroad performed better than those without study abroad on the comprehension of non-conventional implicatures, which were designed to be more opaque and require stronger listener inferencing.

A similar finding of the close connection between implicature comprehension and proficiency was obtained by Wang, Brophy, and Roever (2014), who showed that length of residence had only a negligible effect on learners' scores on a test of idiosyncratic and formulaic implicature, but that proficiency had a strong effect, with learners in their fourth year of high school EFL scoring twice as high as third-year learners, and learners in their sixth year scoring over four times as high as third-year learners.

These findings show that implicature develops hand in hand with learners' proficiency, and that learners comprehend more transparent types of implicature earlier than implicature that requires culture-specific background knowledge (like the Pope Q), follows a particular discourse pattern (like indirect criticism), or has opaque meaning (like non-conventional implicature). Wang, Brophy, and Roever (2014) attribute the proficiency-dependence of implicature comprehension to learners' need to first fully comprehend the surface meaning of an utterance. Once their proficiency is at a level where they have no comprehension problems, they are in a position to realize that the apparent mismatch between the utterance containing the implicature and the one preceding it is not due to a lack of listening ability on the part of the learner but is in fact intentional and requires listener-inferencing to resolve. In the case of non-conventional implicatures, Taguchi (2011b) suggests that their higher frequency in the target language setting (as opposed to the classroom setting) may account for a residence effect, and the same is likely true for the formulaic implicatures examined by Roever (2013). No study has investigated learners' ability to produce implicatures.

Routines

For routine formulae, the picture is somewhat more complex since recognition and production of situationally appropriate formulae require different skills. Recognition is less dependent on proficiency and more on repeated experience with a formula, whereas productive ability is additionally affected by proficiency. For recognition of routine formulae, length of residence has been shown to be strongly influential. Roever (2012) found that two months' residence in an English-speaking country led to an increase from 48% to 68% on a test of comprehension of formulae in L2 English. By the end of 12 months' residence, learners scored 78%, and learners with 24 months' residence or more scored 88%. However, not all formulae were equally learnable: while 'Hello' for answering the phone and 'Nice to meet you' for first encounters was known by the vast majority of learners without residence, 'Do you have the time?' took about a year to learn, and the restaurant routine 'Can I get you anything else?' was only firmly established after two years.

In a series of studies, Bardovi-Harlig (2009, 2010, 2014) explored the relationship between recognition and production of routine formulae (which she calls 'conventional expressions') with ESL learners at four levels of a pre-university intensive English program in the U.S. She found that, overall, learners' recognition of formulae was similar to their production ability, and both increased noticeably from the lowest (low-intermediate) to the second lowest (intermediate) level. Recognition then flattened out, whereas production continued to increase, albeit slowly. Interestingly, even at the highest level, learners were able to recognize and produce two-thirds of the routines tested, which indicates that some routines are not learned quickly, as Roever (2012) also found. Routines like 'Thanks for having me' and 'Excuse the mess' were least known to learners. Bardovi-Harlig (2014) showed that mapping pragmalinguistic forms of routines to sociopragmatic usage conditions is not always straightforward, because up to a third of learners were not able to make a distinction between 'Nice to meet you' as a routine for first meetings and 'Nice to see you' as a routine for subsequent meetings. Similarly, Bardovi-Harlig (2009) found that some expressions are highly recognizable to learners but not produced much; for example, 'I'm looking for…' and 'I'm just looking' in service encounter situations.

Studies on routine formulae indicate that development in learners' recognition and production ability for routines is non-linear and related to both exposure and proficiency. With even short residence, learners' recognition of some common formulae increases quickly, but their repertoire then grows more slowly over time. Production seems to be restricted to a limited range of expressions, and the exact usage conditions for some formulae are established over time, especially when similar formulae exist.

Other targets

There has been some more diffuse work on other aspects of pragmatic development. Shively (2013) reports a case study of how an American English-speaking study abroad learner in Spain developed humor, moving from transferring humorous L1 expressions and 'deadpan' humor to explicitly marking humor, relying on shared background knowledge, and adopting expressions and ways of speaking from his interlocutors and the larger community. Shively's study takes a socialization perspective and highlights the interplay of subjective choice and input, as well as feedback from interlocutors for a learner who values humorous interaction and seeks out ways of being humorous in the L2.

Waring (2013) shows how adult ESL classroom learners in the U.S. changed their responses to routine enquiries like 'How was your weekend?', adapting to teacher expectations of providing accounts of leisure-time activities rather than accounts of work-related activities or routinized responses. Teacher feedback conveyed to learners the sociopragmatic rules of this classroom practice, and continual use improved their pragmalinguistic ability to respond without delay or need for additional prompting. Waring's study also emphasizes that interactional practices are learned locally: it is entirely appropriate in everyday conversation to respond to an enquiry about one's weekend with a formulaic response or by recounting work-related activities. However, in the particular setting and with the particular interlocutor in Waring's study, a specific practice is expected and learned by learners.

Hassall (2013) and Barron (2006) report studies on study abroad learners' development of the use of address terms in Indonesian and German, respectively. Hassall's (2013) study demonstrates strong development in high-frequency address terms in vocative slots but less movement toward the Indonesian norm with address terms in the pronoun slot. He ascribes this difference to the novelty of vocative address term use for his participants, and the competition with the widely taught address term *anda* for the pronoun slot. Barron (2006) shows modest development in the address pronoun use of her Irish English-speaking study abroad learners in Germany. While learners moved toward the L1 norm in informal, less complex situations, they still showed a high degree of inappropriate switching between address terms to the same interlocutor and non-reciprocal address term use (for example, responding with an informal address term after being addressed with a formal term). Barron's and Hassall's studies illustrate the complexity of address term learning in the face of little feedback from interlocutors on inappropriate address term use, little opportunity to encounter and practice a wide variety of address terms in the language classroom, and learners' possible perception of being positioned outside the target language community and therefore not needing to control the subtleties of the L2 address system.

Chapter summary and directions for future research

The overall developmental trajectory for pragmatic abilities progresses along a continuum with two poles. At the low-ability end, learners lack in sociopragmatic knowledge (which can be understood as social intuition) and pragmalinguistic repertoire. Their processing ability is constrained by little automatization of vocabulary retrieval, utterance building, and parsing. Low-ability learners' L2 pragmatic performance is therefore characterized by simplification, with their production focusing on achieving task targets but taking little account of social relationships and the interlocutor's wants

and needs, or connecting to the interlocutor through achieving mutual understanding. While learners understand and can use some high-frequency routine
formulae, non-literal and implied language use is difficult for them where it
involves more than simple inferencing.

As overall L2 competence develops and learners' sociopragmatic and pragmalinguistic knowledge and ability for use increase through socialization,
practice, and experience in target language use situations, learners' pragmalinguistic repertoire broadens, offering them choices of how to express
a proposition, as well as allowing them to develop and test interlanguage
hypotheses of how these pragmalinguistic choices match their sociopragmatic
knowledge. As learners become more able to incorporate social 'niceties' in
their production, they can recipient-design their utterances more specifically
to the interlocutor and situation, and collaborate with the interlocutor in
building a conversation rather than relying on the interlocutor to carry the
conversation. Learners know different routine formulae that can be used in
the same situation, employ colloquial language, and understand more opaque
and formulaic implicature. However, learners may at times overgeneralize the
use of pragmalinguistic tools or map them inaccurately to sociopragmatic
rules; they may not comprehend sarcasm or indirect criticism; and they may
make small errors in their use of routine formulae, or confuse similar formulae
with different sociopragmatic constraints.

At an advanced stage of pragmatic ability, learners' general L2 proficiency
is so high that they have little to worry about in terms of automatization for
production and comprehension in the target language. They can deploy a
wide range of linguistic tools for pragmalinguistic purposes and have broad
experience in a range of social situations. Their sociopragmatic knowledge
and understanding of social relationships and cultural rules and norms is
also fine-tuned and intuitive. This is not to say that learners even at advanced
levels of pragmatic ability are native-like: they may not have sociopragmatic
knowledge of subtle role expectations (for example, in the boss–employee
relationship), and they may choose to assert their identity by deploying pragmalinguistic tools that are non-normative. Also, they are likely to struggle in
formal situations which require complex vocabulary and careful pragmatic
choices, or language use contexts that they are not used to. However, these
learners are fully capable of engaging in extended interactions, expressing
speech intentions and propositions conventionally (and, if they desire, strategically), differentiating style levels of colloquial and more formal language
use, comprehending less transparent types of implicature, and using a wide
range of routine formulae.

Research on pragmatic development has made significant progress, but
there is still a great deal of work to do. Future work on speech acts should be
embedded in extended interactions and could involve such (less-researched)
speech acts as advice or complaint, or preferred social actions such as agreement. It is important to consider the language use situation for these speech
acts, whose sequential organization and linguistic formatting depends greatly

on the activity type in which they are embedded, for example disagreements in friendly conversations and disputes (Kotthoff, 1993). This leads to a deeper question of the transferability of pragmatic knowledge between contexts, as well as language users' understandings of the differences between activity types and external contexts.

While we have outlined some broad developmental trajectories, work needs to continue on identifying distinguishing markers of different levels of interactional competence. Describing how higher- and lower-ability learners accomplish the same task and in what aspects they differ in their interactional performance is important for the design of diagnostic tests and pedagogical interventions. We should also hear the learners' voices more in this regard, and find out what aspects of interaction learners subjectively found challenging, where they thought they performed well, and what they are uncertain about.

In the case of implicatures and routine formulae, it is time to leave the laboratory; we know nothing about learners' own use of implicature. While such data will be difficult to come by, it is not impossible to gather. It would require recordings of learners' interactions with others, preferably longitudinally. Such data would serve as an extremely rich resource for many research questions. Similarly, for routine formulae, it would be very interesting to collect recorded data from learners' interactions, even if that is limited to service encounters. We suspect that learners use a far smaller range of routine formulae than they can recognize or generate examples for, but of course, so may native speakers.

We recognize that a learner's development is closely tied to their input and interaction opportunities, to the rate at which their proficiency increases, and to learner characteristics such as motivation, aptitude, and identity. We will explore the relationship between learning and these learner-internal and learner-external factors in the next two chapters.

6

What differentiates learners: individual characteristics

Introduction

Shifting from Chapter 5's focus on commonality in patterns of pragmatic development, this chapter turns our attention to individual variation in pragmatic competence and development. Individual differences (ID) are defined as 'dimensions of enduring personal characteristics that are assumed to apply to everybody and on which people differ by degree' (Dörnyei, 2005, p. 4). Because large variations are often found among learners in their pace of learning and ultimate success in mastering an L2, studies of individual characteristics have been striving to identify ID factors that explain the variations and predict success in L2 learning (for a review, see Dörnyei, 2005, 2009; Dörnyei & Skehan, 2003; R. Ellis, 2005).

Two decades ago, Kasper and Schmidt (1996) drew attention to the dearth of research in pragmatic development and stressed the need to profile L2 pragmatics as an area of inquiry in SLA research. They proposed 14 basic questions about SLA that are applicable to L2 pragmatics research, three of which were directed toward the role of individual characteristics (motivation, personality, and age) in pragmatics learning. Because the study of individual differences has been a featured research area in SLA, 'making the area one of the most thoroughly studied psychological aspects of SLA' (Dörnyei, 2005, p. 6), individual differences is an essential topic of study in pragmatics that helps to align L2 pragmatics with mainstream SLA research.

Although the study of individual differences helps strengthen the pragmatics–SLA connection, it also highlights the uniqueness of pragmatics as a site of analysis, which, in turn, motivates us to explore learner characteristics that are specific to pragmatics learning. Pragmatic competence is unique in that many aspects of this competence are inseparable not only from cognitive considerations but also from sociocultural practices and individuals' orientations toward these practices. To become able to communicate intentions appropriately, learners need refined knowledge of linguistic systems and the skills to implement the knowledge in real-time interaction. To this end, pragmatic abilities draw on threshold-level proficiency and cognitive capacities. Yet, because of the sociocultural nature of pragmatic competence, input and opportunities to engage in social interaction are vital for pragmatic growth. Pragmatics is also inseparable from personal considerations. The politeness and formality of learners' performance reflect not only their linguistic abilities but also their personalities and styles, for example preferences and beliefs about how formal or polite they want to sound in a given situation. In short, pragmatic competence entails linguistic and cognitive components, but it is also fundamentally social and personal. Because of these unique features inherent to pragmatics, there might be a specific set of individual characteristics that uniquely affect pragmatics learning.

Two decades after Kasper and Schmidt's (1996) seminal paper, the body of ID studies in L2 pragmatics has grown rapidly to address a taxonomy of individual characteristics. We can categorize the current literature into two major lines of study. One line of literature is found in a group of quantitative studies that followed a traditional approach, grounded in the field of psychology, by treating individual characteristics as fixed, discrete variables. Those studies, through experimental tasks, have measured ID factors in a group of learners and have examined both the descriptive and predictive relationships with learners' pragmatic competence. A variety of ID variables have been examined according to this paradigm, including age, gender, motivation, cognitive variables, personality, and proficiency.

Another line of research is found in qualitative approaches that focus on the *learner* rather than on learner characteristics. In this approach, individual characteristics such as personality, motivation, and attitudes are no longer viewed as fixed, discrete variables isolated from other individual characteristics or contexts of learning. Rather, they are examined in connection with other traits that dynamically change and cumulatively arise within a learner as he/she interacts with a context. Dörnyei argues the following:

> Scholars have come to reject the notion that the various traits are
> context-independent and absolute, and are now increasingly
> proposing new dynamic conceptualizations in which ID factors enter
> into some interaction with the situational parameters rather than
> cutting across tasks and environments.
> (2005, p. 218)

The context-dependent, situated approach to individual characteristics is also found in L2 pragmatics research. Under the umbrella of identity and subjectivity, some studies show that learners' pragmatic choice is often a reflection of their desired identity—how they want to be perceived in a situation—and does not always coincide with their knowledge of normative pragmatic behaviors in a local community. Other studies pursue an explicit application of the complex, dynamic systems approach to language learning (N. Ellis & Larsen-Freeman, 2006; Larsen-Freeman, 2012; Larsen-Freeman &

Cameron, 2008; Verspoor, de Bot, & Lowie, 2011) and reveal how individual characteristics and context of learning interact with each other and jointly shape the course of pragmatic development.

This chapter reviews current literature in these two lines of study. The two approaches, i.e. the quantitative and qualitative approaches, present fundamentally different ways of conceptualizing individual characteristics in pragmatic development. Taking the cognitive-componential approach, the quantitative approach treats learner characteristics as categorical, static traits that are measurable as a general tendency, while the qualitative approach treats individual characteristics as evolving in flux in interactions between learner and context. Although these differences are fundamental, we consider these two bodies of study to be complementary rather than competing, and maintain that they mutually strengthen the connections between pragmatics and SLA research. In the first part of this chapter, we will review quantitative studies under the cognitive-componential approach in four main areas of ID factors: proficiency, cognitive variables (aptitude, working memory, and lexical access skill), motivation, and personality. We have selected these four individual characteristics simply because of the availability of studies in these areas. In the second half of the chapter, we will review qualitative studies under the dynamic, interactive approach to individual characteristics. We will review studies within the framework of identity and subjectivity, as well as within a dynamic systems perspective that investigates individual characteristics as situated and evolving in the context of learning.

The cognitive-componential approach to individual characteristics

Proficiency

In mainstream SLA research, proficiency has usually been placed outside of the common list of ID factors (for example, Dörnyei, 2005; R. Ellis, 2005). However, Dörnyei (2009) made the point that language proficiency should be treated as an ID factor, emphasizing that proficiency is the equivalent of general intelligence; it refers to the amount of a learner's domain-specific knowledge, or more specifically, linguistic knowledge of the target language (for example, knowledge of grammar, vocabulary, and discourse).

When accounting for differential pragmatic performance by learners, proficiency is by far the most widely researched individual difference factor. As we illustrate below, the effect of proficiency has been investigated for speech acts, implicature, routine formulae, extended discourse, and a small range of other pragmatic features. We will begin with a discussion of how proficiency has been conceptualized in second language acquisition and language testing research before discussing L2 pragmatics studies that use proficiency as an explanatory or grouping variable.

The proficiency construct

Any investigation into the effect of second language proficiency on pragmatics will benefit from reflection on the concept of 'proficiency' as a construct; most authors who employ 'proficiency' as an individual difference variable do not explicitly define what they mean by the term. As Gass and Selinker (2008) point out, the most common ways of classifying learners by proficiency in SLA research are institutional level (based on an institutional placement test or simply year level in a program), standardized test (for example, TOEFL, TOEIC, IELTS, PTE, etc.), and researcher-designed tests (for example, C-tests) or impressionistic judgment.[1] The same approaches are common in interlanguage pragmatics research, as will become apparent in our discussion below, but they carry the same problems as they do in SLA research, most importantly that the absence of a common proficiency benchmark across studies makes comparability difficult. However, at the core of the issue lies the question of what proficiency is. This question has been tackled in two ways: through models and scales of second language competence, mostly coming out of language testing, and through psycholinguistic research into second language processes, mostly coming out of SLA.

Models of second language competence include the well-known models of communicative competence by Canale and Swain (1980), Canale (1983), Bachman and Palmer (1996, 2010), and, to a lesser extent, Purpura (2004) and Celce-Murcia, Dörnyei, and Thurrell (1995). The most recent model by Bachman and Palmer (2010) distinguishes between language knowledge and strategic competence. The latter includes planning and decision-making processes while the former is subdivided into organizational and pragmatic knowledge, with organizational knowledge incorporating vocabulary, syntax, phonology, cohesion, and rhetorical organization. Pragmatic knowledge includes knowledge of language functions, essentially illocutionary knowledge, and knowledge of sociolinguistic features like genre, dialect, register, idiomaticity, etc. While pragmatics plays a strong role in Bachman and Palmer's conceptualization, this part of their model has barely been implemented in language scales and tests, which are primarily organized along the lines of skills (listening/speaking/reading/writing), for example TOEFL, IELTS, and PTE. For example, the speaking scoring guide for TOEFL does not explicitly mention pragmatic aspects of language but measures delivery, language use, and topic development (Educational Testing Service, 2014). Similarly, the IELTS speaking band descriptors score fluency and coherence, lexical resource, grammatical range and accuracy and pronunciation (IELTS, n.d.). PTE scores content, oral fluency, and pronunciation (Pearson, 2014b).

Even scale descriptors for the various speaking subscales of the very extensive and highly influential Common European Framework of Reference for Languages (CEFR, Council of Europe, 2001) do not make explicit mention of pragmatics, and are primarily functionally oriented. The CEFR contains dedicated subscales for sociolinguistic and pragmatic competences, but as these are not part of the scales for skills, it is questionable how much CEFR users would integrate them in skills-based assessments. The upshot is that conceptualizations of proficiency include pragmatics, but actual measurement of proficiency is more reflective of the degree to which learners control grammar, vocabulary, phonology, and text organization features.

The other approach to proficiency is more process-oriented and focuses not only on what learners know but also on how they use their linguistic knowledge in processing language input and output. Hulstijn defines 'language proficiency' as:

> …the extent to which an individual possesses the linguistic cognition necessary to function in a given communicative situation, in a given modality (listening, speaking, reading, or writing). Linguistic cognition is the combination of the representation of linguistic information (knowledge of form-meaning mappings) and the ease with which linguistic information can be processed (skill).
>
> (2011, p. 242)

Hulstijn, Schoonen, de Jong, Steinel, and Florijn's (2012) study compared learners at two adjacent levels of the CEFR (B1 and B2) and found that higher-level learners performed better on all grammatical subtests and had greater vocabulary knowledge than lower-level learners. More target-like pronunciation was also associated with higher proficiency, and (less strongly) faster lexical retrieval and faster sentence building. In a related study, de Jong, Steinel, Florijn, Schoonen, and Hulstijn (2012) found that speaking proficiency was largely explained by knowledge of vocabulary and grammar, speed of lexical retrieval and sentence building, and pronunciation ability. Similarly, in a study investigating specific features of L2 Russian grammar, lexis, morphology, phonology, and collocations that could serve to explain ratings on the ILR scale (Interagency Language Roundtable, n.d.), Long, Gor, and Jackson (2012) found that specific micro-features could be identified that distinguish larger ILR levels (2 vs. 3) as well as immediately adjacent ones (2 vs. 2+, 2+ vs. 3).

In summary, while models of second language proficiency include pragmatics, assessment measures usually do not include it to any great extent. Where learners are grouped by proficiency according to test scores on standardized tests, 'proficiency' is likely to mean knowledge of grammar and vocabulary; and if speaking test scores are used, pronunciation may also have an influence, as might processing speed. Where learners are categorized according to years of instruction rather than by formal measures, similar factors are likely to differentiate them, since classroom learning tends to privilege grammar and vocabulary.

While this reality of how proficiency is conceptualized is problematic from a construct perspective, it is actually rather helpful for researchers. By effectively employing 'pragmatics-free' proficiency estimates, researchers can determine the relative impact of organizational competence (in Bachman and

Palmer's terms) on pragmatics without the circularity that would arise by relating pragmatics to a proficiency measure that includes it. Given the strong impact of vocabulary and grammatical knowledge on proficiency, it will mostly be these two aspects of learners' linguistic competence whose effect on pragmatics we are probing; indeed, the connection between grammar and pragmatics has long been an area of interest in second language pragmatics research (Bardovi-Harlig, 2013; Kasper & Rose, 2002).

Proficiency and speech acts

Overall, it has been found that proficiency conveys advantages for speech act comprehension and production, although most research has focused on production. In general, higher-proficiency learners tend to be less direct, more appropriate, have a wider repertoire of semantic formulae, use more modification and provide more explanations, reasons, and accounts. This has been found for a variety of speech acts, with most research on requests (Bella, 2012; Félix-Brasdefer, 2007; Hill, 1997; Roever, 2005; Rose, 2009; Tada, 2005; Taguchi, 2006, 2007; Pinto, 2005; Trosborg, 1995), apologies (Maeshiba et al., 1996; Rose, 2000; Sabaté i Dalmau & Curell i Gotor, 2007; Shardakova, 2005; Roever, 2005; Tada, 2005; Trosborg, 1987), and refusals (Allami & Naeimi, 2011; Bella, 2014; Chang, 2009; Félix-Brasdefer, 2004; Sasaki, 1998; Taguchi, 2007; Vilar-Beltran & Melchor-Couto, 2013). Little to no research investigating the impact of proficiency has been done on other speech acts, although some exists for disagreement (Dippold, 2011; Geyer, 2007; Kreutel, 2007).

For example, Bella (2014) investigated refusals by learners of L2 Greek at three proficiency levels as assigned by an institutional placement test oriented toward the CEFR (Council of Europe, 2001): lower intermediate (around B1), intermediate (around B2), and advanced (around C1). Bella also included a native-speaker comparison group, and employed three open role-plays, varying power and social distance, and analyzing the data in a speech act framework. Invariably, the use of semantic formulae associated with directness decreased with increasing proficiency level, though the drop was more pronounced between lower-intermediate and intermediate learners than between intermediate and high-intermediate learners. The number of indirect strategies used showed the opposite tendency and increased with proficiency level, as did learners' use of adjuncts. Interestingly, even the advanced learners were never equivalent to the native-speaker comparison group, using between 50% and 100% more direct formulae than native speakers. Learners also used more lexical and phrasal downgraders with increasing proficiency; but again, native speakers used more than twice the number of downgraders as even the advanced group.

While Bella (2012, 2014) analyzed her participants' production of requests and refusals qualitatively, Lee (2013) assigned appropriateness scores to his learners' refusals. His participants were two groups of Korean EFL learners, divided into a lower- and a higher-proficiency group by their scores on a standardized English test, the TOEIC. Lower-proficiency learners had TOEIC scores between 500 and 690, whereas higher-proficiency learners had TOEIC scores between 700 and 945. The study also included a native-speaker comparison group. Lee collected closed role-play data varying power and social distance, which he operationalized as familiarity with the interlocutor. Learners' production was scored on a scale of 0 to 5 by three native-speaker raters, and, following Taguchi (2011a), Lee also measured learners' task-planning time, speech rate (number of words per minute), and length of pauses. Lee found that the lower-proficiency group scored on average a third of a score level below the higher-proficiency group, but differences were minute for situations where the interlocutor had higher or equal power. Lower-proficiency learners also used a smaller number of semantic formulae than high-proficiency learners, though the distribution of semantic formulae was roughly similar, with the only striking difference being greater use of apology/regret by both Korean groups compared to the English native-speaker group, and less use of dissuasion.

Roever, Wang, and Brophy (2014) investigated the effect of proficiency, length of residence and gender on a sample of 229 EFL and ESL learners. Their participants consisted of high school students in Germany in their third to ninth year of EFL, university students in Germany majoring in English, university students in the lower and upper levels of an ESL program at a U.S. university, and ESL graduate students majoring in second language studies at a U.S. university. Learners completed Roever's web-based test of ESL pragmalinguistics (Roever, 2005, 2006), whose speech act section contains DCT items with rejoinders testing requests, apologies, and refusals. Results revealed a strong effect for proficiency on speech act performance on a DCT with rejoinders. Compared to a baseline of third-year EFL learners (seventh graders), fifth-year learners had 50% higher scores; and the highest-scoring group (ESL graduate students) had nearly four times the score of the lowest-scoring group. Interestingly, gender was also a significant predictor for speech act scores, with female test takers performing 25.4% better than male test takers.

In contrast to speech act production, little research has focused on the effect of proficiency on learners' pragmatic perception of speech act appropriateness, and the existing findings are largely mixed. In a classic study of pragmatic and grammatical awareness, Bardovi-Harlig and Dörnyei (1998) compared low- and high-proficiency learners' judgments (based on self-assessments) of the severity of pragmatic errors, and found that the high-proficiency learners rated pragmatic errors as significantly more severe than did low-proficiency learners in both the ESL and EFL groups, though with a small effect size. Niezgoda and Roever's (2001) replication with a high-aptitude Czech EFL group and an ESL group did not find significant proficiency effects on rating of pragmatic severity. In a recent study, Roever, Fraser, and Elder (2014) assessed learners' English proficiency by means of a C-test and administered a pragmatic appropriateness questionnaire as part of a larger test battery. The latter encompassed judgment of appropriate discourse and appropriate conventional expressions, as well as multi-turn DCTs and production of conventional expressions. In a regression analysis for their main ESL sample, they found that the speech act appropriateness judgment section was the least affected by proficiency, while the multi-turn DCT section was affected six times more.

The strong effect of proficiency on speech act production is likely due to an interaction between task type, modality, and learner factors. Most speech act tasks are productive measures and require writing or speaking of the target speech act. Higher-proficiency learners probably find these easier due to their larger vocabulary, greater availability of exemplars of language use, and greater automatization of access to their language knowledge. Automatization in particular is helpful as it leaves more processing space for fine-tuning utterances and producing adjuncts and supportive moves, which lower-proficiency learners find especially difficult (for example, Bella, 2012, 2014; Rose, 2000). By contrast, proficiency effects on speech act perception (appropriateness judgments) seem to be rather weak, as shown in Niezgoda and Roever (2001) and Roever et al.'s (2014) findings. Complete linguistic processing may not be necessary in pragmatic perception because the learner's job is to read a pragmalinguistic form appearing in the scenario and evaluate its appropriateness on a multiple-choice test. In contrast, when producing pragmalinguistic forms, learners' morphosyntax must be accurate so the illocution encoded in the forms is understood correctly. Because of the greater linguistic processing involved in production, proficiency effects might appear more strongly in production than in perception.

Even though proficiency itself does not necessarily convey advantages in terms of sociopragmatic knowledge, it is helpful in producing utterances that require greater politeness, which generally gets rewarded in rated instruments. Politeness across languages requires longer utterances (Brown & Levinson, 1987), and in English it requires the use of modals and interrogative sentence structures, which are complex and not easily available to lower-proficiency learners (Salsbury & Bardovi-Harlig, 2000). The proficiency effect wanes in receptive tasks, where learners' judgments of target language appropriateness are more strongly based on their sociopragmatic knowledge.

Proficiency and implicature

Proficiency has a strong effect on comprehension of implicature in terms of learners' accuracy of comprehension and their processing speed. This effect has been variously demonstrated in a series of studies by Taguchi (2005, 2007, 2008b, 2009, 2011b), Roever (2005, 2006, 2013), and others (Cook & Liddicoat, 2002; Garcia, 2004; Roever, Wang, & Brophy, 2014; Yamanaka, 2003). Taguchi (2011b) compared three groups of EFL learners in Japan: a lower-proficiency group and two higher-proficiency groups, of which one had study abroad experience and the other did not. She administered a computer-based test of implicature comprehension, comparing conventional implicatures (routine formulae and indirect refusals) and non-conventional implicatures. Conventional implicatures convey meanings through fixed linguistic forms or through the conventions of language use specific to the situation (for example, giving an excuse when refusing someone's invitation). Non-conventional implicatures, on the other hand, are more dependent on the specific discourse context (for example, indicating a negative opinion of a movie by saying 'I was glad when it was over').

Taguchi found significantly higher scores for the two higher-proficiency groups over the lower-proficiency group, and this difference was very pronounced for conventional implicatures, with the average of the higher-proficiency groups exceeding the lower-proficiency group by 77%. The difference was smaller for non-conventional implicature, with 34% higher scores for the high-proficiency groups. In both cases, the native-speaker comparison group scored higher than any of the learner groups. Taguchi also measured response times, and found that the two higher-proficiency groups responded significantly faster than the lower-proficiency group, which was 30–36% slower in its responses. The native-speaker group was far faster than any of the learner groups.

Roever, Wang, and Brophy (2014) also found that proficiency had a strong effect on implicature comprehension of EFL learners. One additional year of instruction above the third-year baseline doubled implicature scores, and the highest-scoring group had scores over five times higher than the third-year baseline group. Of the three predictors (gender, exposure, proficiency) in this study, proficiency was the only significant predictor for implicature comprehension.

The strong effect of proficiency on implicature (an effect that is even stronger than that on speech acts) can be explained by the nature of implicatures and their processing. Implicatures do not have a great deal of sociopragmatic functionality, i.e. the relationship between the interlocutors in terms of power or social distance is not particularly important for implicature comprehension, and politeness does not figure greatly in implicatures, at least in the way they have been researched. Rather, implicatures are textbook cases of pragmalinguistic items, and pragmalinguistics is the language-facing part of pragmatics (Leech, 1983). In addition, processing implicature requires advanced proficiency for the learner to realize that a non-literal meaning is implied through a flouting of a Gricean maxim (Grice, 1975). Learners at lower proficiency levels may not understand the literal meaning of the utterance and as a result would not be able to detect a flouting of a maxim, which arises out of a mismatch between the question by the interlocutor and the literal, apparently unrelated meaning of the response.

Strong proficiency effect on implicature can also be interpreted from the perspective of the L1–L2 interface. Comprehension of implicature might be more strongly influenced by learners' L1-based inferential skills than L2-specific pragmatic knowledge. Whether in L1 or L2, the ability to seek the relevance of a message is part of innate human cognition. Through socialization, we develop the ability to detect a mismatch between literal meaning and implied

[margin note: explanation for the effect of prof on implicature]

meaning, and to make inference of the implied meaning by using contextual cues. Hence, unless it is culture-specific implicature such as irony, relevance processing in L1 can be directly transferable to L2. High-proficiency learners are more advantaged than their low-proficiency counterparts in applying these L1-based inferential practices to L2, simply because they have basic abilities and skills (grammar, vocabulary, and listening) that they use in this process.

Proficiency and routine formulae

While not absent, the impact of proficiency is less pronounced for routine formulae (see Chapter 5 for the discussion of formulae). Roever (2012) investigated the recognition of routines by five groups of EFL learners from third to eighth year of secondary EFL. Among learners without residence in the target language community, recognition scores increased from an average score of 36% to an average score of 50% over five years of instruction. This is an appreciable increase, but it is noteworthy that for learners with just two years' residence in the target language community, the average score was 88%, which indicates that the effect of residence abroad greatly outweighs the effect of proficiency.

Bardovi-Harlig and Bastos (2011), on the other hand, compared production and recognition of routines among four groups of ESL learner levels from low intermediate to low advanced, based on placement in an intensive English program. There was no significant effect of proficiency on the recognition of routine formulae (conventional expressions), which was measured with a self-report task in which learners indicated how often they had heard the target conventional expressions. However, for the production of conventional expressions measured with a spoken DCT, proficiency was a significant predictor.

In a production study with three groups of Japanese learners of English, Taguchi (2013) found that the higher-proficiency group with study abroad experience consistently outperformed the lower-proficiency group without study abroad experience on appropriateness, speech rate, and planning time when producing routines on a DCT task. However, the higher-proficiency group without study abroad experience did not outperform the lower-proficiency group on appropriateness and planning time; they only outperformed the lower-proficiency group on speech rate, emphasizing again that proficiency is less important with routine formulae than exposure.

Finally, in Roever, Wang, and Brophy's (2014) regression study, proficiency was a significant predictor for recognition of routine formulae, but not as strong as for implicature and speech acts. The highest-scoring group scored 3.5 times above the lowest-scoring group for routines, compared to nearly 4 times above for speech acts and over 5 times above for implicature. Exposure was another significant predictor for recognition of routine formulae.

Taken together, these studies point to a weaker role of proficiency in recognition of routine formulae but a certain impact on their production. This is

probably due to routine formulae being short, with little linguistic complexity. This facilitates their comprehension and production and puts them in
reach even of low-proficiency learners, since they only need to recognize and
reproduce a chunk without necessarily having to parse it semantically and
grammatically. This is not to say that routine formulae do not benefit at all
from proficiency, especially in their production: routines are not entirely and
exclusively formulaic but frequently contain 'slots' whose completion benefits from proficiency, or the formula itself may have a certain level of flexibility.
While 'Have a nice day' can be learned, recognized, and reproduced as a
chunk with minimal analysis, asking for the time can be accomplished formu-
laically in a variety of ways (Taguchi, 2013): 'Do you have the time?', 'Do you
know the time?', 'Can you tell me what the time is?', etc. There is room for
inappropriateness, error, and misunderstandings here, and greater proficiency can help to reduce the likelihood of incorrectness. This would be even
more pronounced with formulae that have a 'slot-and-frame pattern' like
'Would you mind ... ?'. In themselves, these formulae are not difficult; however,
their completion into a sentence requires a fairly high degree of proficiency.
Overall, routine formulae are less susceptible to proficiency effects due to
the lesser degree of creative construction required in their processing, understanding, and production.

Proficiency and extended discourse

Recent research has increasingly compared learners at different proficiency
levels with regard to their ability to produce social actions in extended discourse, and has found some effect of proficiency in this area as well (for
example, Dippold, 2011; Pakarek Doehler & Pochon-Berger, 2011; Zhang,
2016; see Chapter 5). For example, Dippold (2011) found a similar proficiency effect with the organization of agreement and disagreement by three
groups of native-English-speaking second language learners of German in
their first, second, and final year of university study in the U.K. More advanced ✳
learners also delayed their disagreement, and produced more extensive
post-expansions.

Al-Gahtani and Roever (2014b) report a parallel finding with the preference
organization of requests by second language learners of Saudi Arabic at four
proficiency levels, determined by their placement in the Arabic as a second
language intensive program. Learners were interacting with a native speaker
of Saudi Arabic in an institutional setting. As their proficiency level increased,
learners were more likely to organize their requests as dispreferred social
actions by prefacing the request with explanations and accounts. Lower-level
learners by contrast were more likely to make their requests without prefacing, often leading to interlocutor-initiated repair.

In Figure 6.1 (Al-Gahtani & Roever, 2014b), a beginning-level learner is
requesting that a lecture time be moved to the morning at the beginning of the
teaching semester. After greeting the interlocutor (a university administrator)
in line 1 and receiving a return greeting from his interlocutor in line 2, the

learner immediately launches into the core business of the talk by putting his request on the record in line 3 without any preliminary moves. The interlocutor responds with a repair initiation in line 4, and the learner repeats part of his original utterance in line 5. The interlocutor then rephrases the learner's request as a yes/no question in line 6, and the learner confirms it in line 7. By contrast, consider the same learner's request performance toward the end of the five-month intensive teaching semester in Figure 6.2, where the learner's proficiency had significantly increased.

In Figure 6.2 (Al-Gahtani & Roever, 2014b), the learner is requesting that an exam be rescheduled so that it is not on the same day as another exam. After an exchange of greetings in lines 1 and 2, the learner does not launch straight into the request but rather provides background information to the interlocutor first, stating his level in line 3 and the reason for his visit in lines 6 and 7. After a go-ahead signal from the interlocutor in line 8, the learner states his request in line 9, and the interlocutor seems to comprehend it without any trouble. This trouble-free interaction is in stark contrast to that in Figure 6.1, where the interlocutor initiated repair twice to clarify the request. The dialogue in Figure 6.2 flows much more smoothly since the learner followed the typical preference structure of a request through the inclusion of preliminary moves and delay of the core request move. Presumably it was the learner's

---

1 **BEG** *as-salaam-u   'alaykum*
         peace   upon you
         Peace be upon you (hello)
2 **ADM** *'alaykum-u   as-salaam*   (.)   *tafaḍal*
         upon you   peace.   (.)   come in
         Peace be upon you (hello)   (.)   Come in
3 **BEG** *óriid-u   al-muḥaaḍarah   (o.2)   šabaa:ḥa-n*
         I want   the lecture   (o.2)   morning
         I want the lecture (o.2) in the morning
4 **ADM** *turiid-u   maaźaa?*
         Want   what
         What do you want?
5 **BEG** *al-muḥaa::ḍarah   (o.1)   šabaaḥa-n*
         the lecture   (o.1)   morning
         The lecture (o.1) in the morning
6 **ADM** *turiid-u   waqt   al-muḥaaḍarah   án takuun-a   fii   ↑aš-šabaaḥ?*
         you want   time   the lecture   to be   in   the morning
         You want the lecture time to be in the morning?
7 **BEG** *na'am*
         yes
         Yes

Figure 6.1 Request without preliminary moves (Al-Gahtani & Roever, 2014b, pp. 633–634)

1	**BEG**	*as-salaam-u 'alaykum.*
		peace upon you
		Peace be upon you (hello)
2	**ADM**	*wa: 'alaykum-u as-salaam*
		and upon you peace
		Peace be upon you, too (hello)
3	**BEG**	*ána (0.3) ↑ta:lib fii al-mustawa (.) al-áw-wal*
		I (0.3) student in the level (.) one
		I'm (0.3) a student in level (.) one
4	**ADM**	*áhlan*
		welcome
		Welcome
5		(0.4)
6	**BEG**	*ána::(.) ána jét-u élayk-a (0.2) bi-xušuuš,*
		I (.) I came to you (0.2) regarding
		I (.) came to you (0.2) regarding
7		*émtihaa:n (0.2) al-qawaa'id. wa al-qiraaáh=*
		exam (0.2) Grammar and Reading
		the Grammar and Reading (0.2) exams
8	**ADM**	*=na'am*
		yes
		Yes
9	**BEG**	*nuriid-u fii kul-i yawm (.) maadah ↑waahidah*
		We want in each day (.) subject one
		We want one subject in each day
10	**ADM**	*tayyb (.) ma: ésmuk?*
		Okay (.) what your name
		Okay (.) what's your name?

Figure 6.2 Request with preliminary moves (Al-Gahtani & Roever, 2014b, p. 634–635)

higher proficiency that made it easier for him to produce these additional moves.

Related analyses based on the same data corpus showed that higher-proficiency learners were also more likely to produce post-expansions, with longer, non-minimal post-expansions limited to the most advanced group (Al-Gahtani & Roever, 2014b). Higher-proficiency learners were also more likely to employ multiple requests in the same turn (Al-Gahtani & Roever, 2015a), which is a practice that is recipient-designed to increase likelihood of acceptance.

Also working in a Conversation Analysis tradition, Al-Gahtani and Roever (2012, 2013) found notably different overall discourse organization in role-played request interactions with four levels of Saudi ESL learners, as determined by program level and a C-test. With increasing proficiency, learners used more preliminary moves and sequentially delayed the request. With learners at the lowest level, the interlocutor took the initiative in the interaction, producing more first pair parts and eliciting accounts and explanations. In addition, only advanced learners showed evidence of attention to power difference.

In another study, Youn (2013) used role-plays with learners at three proficiency levels (advanced, intermediate, low-intermediate) based on TOEFL and IELTS scores to identify interactional features that are correlates of proficiency levels. She found that learners were more able, with increasing proficiency, to complete adjacency pairs, interpret meaningful pauses, and steer the conversation with less assistance from the interlocutor, which mirrors Al-Gahtani and Roever's (2012, 2013) findings. Advanced learners also showed greater sensitivity to the context by providing accounts and displaying institutional knowledge.

Working within Purpura's (2004) framework, Grabowski (2013) compared three groups of learners at the intermediate and advanced levels of a community ESL program and post-university admission (expert) ESL speakers. Based on ratings from expert raters, she found that learners' ability to show psychological appropriateness (i.e. display affective stance) and sociocultural appropriateness (i.e. metaphor, idiomatic language, production of speech acts where required) improved in line with their proficiency, but their sociolinguistic appropriateness (use of identity markers, relationship indexicals for power and social distance, adherence to social norms) was not much affected by their proficiency.

Overall, greater proficiency helps learners to produce extended discourse, in particular with regard to features beyond the core 'business' of the talk, i.e. moves beyond just a pure request or disagreement. Such pre- and post-sequences require extra effort, and low-proficiency learners' lesser degree of automatized access to their linguistic knowledge under the pressures of real-time interaction leads them to concentrate on getting their central message across and relying on the interlocutor to elicit further moves, such as accounts or explanations. Higher-proficiency learners, on the other hand, are able to participate more fully in the discourse and take control of it when required by implementing preference structure and thereby foreshadowing the type of core utterance that will follow.

Proficiency and other aspects of L2 pragmatics

Besides the 'mainstays' of interlanguage pragmatics research, a small number of other pragmatic features have also been investigated with regard to proficiency effects. Tran (2013a) compared two groups of learners of L2 Vietnamese on their performance of address forms in Vietnamese. Learner level was assigned by a university placement test, but the higher-proficiency group also generally had longer residence in Vietnam. Advanced learners' choices of address terms were generally more similar to native speakers' than pre-intermediate learners', but both groups deviated notably from the native-speaker baseline in some scenarios. Another study on address forms was conducted by Takenoya (2003). She compared three proficiency groups of L2 Japanese learners in a U.S. university (proficiency determined by a placement test) on their production of Japanese address forms. Similar to Tran's findings, no significant group difference was found in the production of address forms, indicating that address forms are relatively easy to learn, even for lower-proficiency learners.

Focusing on the noticing of address terms by learners of Russian as a foreign language, DeWaard (2012) showed Russian film clips to four levels of foreign language learners of Russian from two different U.S. institutions, whose proficiency level had been determined by their level in a tertiary Russian program. She found no significant proficiency effect, though group sizes were very small and in one institution the effect size of the difference between the lowest- and highest-level groups was large (d = .95). The absence of significance despite a large effect size may indicate that a proficiency effect was present, but due to the small group sizes the statistical analysis did not have enough power to detect it.

In a study on discourse markers, Wei (2011) compared intermediate and advanced Chinese EFL learners' use of pragmatic markers, which establish discourse coherence (for example, 'actually', 'you know', 'anyway', etc.). She used data from Oral Proficiency Interviews (OPIs), with learner level determined by OPI scores. She found that advanced learners used 32% more pragmatic markers as the ratio of pragmatic markers to total words. In another study using OPI, Geyer (2007) also found the proficiency effect in L2 Japanese learners' use of self-qualification expressions, i.e. pragmatic markers used to mitigate disagreement, involving three connectives: *demo*, *kedo*, and *ga* (all of which carry contrastive meaning of 'but' or 'although'). Novice learners largely relied on the connective *demo*, but advanced learners frequently used the connective *kedo*, which requires the most complex grammatical structure, suggesting that higher-proficiency learners have a greater repertoire of pragmatic markers.

Proficiency and L2 pragmatics revisited

It is readily apparent that proficiency (in its abbreviated meaning of grammar and vocabulary knowledge) is an important factor in pragmatic competence and performance. This is not surprising since higher-proficiency learners have more vocabulary and a wider range of grammatical structures. This helps them understand implicature, produce speech acts at different levels of politeness, and participate in extended discourse. Their greater automatization in accessing their linguistic knowledge makes language production less effortful and frees up processing space for fine-tuning their production to the interlocutor, the situation, and their interactional goals.

However, grammar and vocabulary are not everything. Learners' sociopragmatic knowledge of target community norms, their judgment of pragmatic appropriateness, and their knowledge of highly frequent situation-bound routine formulae is less related to their proficiency and shows strong influences of socialization through extended exposure and interaction within the target language setting. For example, in DuFon's (2010) study, learners of Indonesian were socialized into the practice of asking for permission at leave-taking through their participation of routine activities, and this socialization process occurred regardless of their proficiency level. Knowledge of what to do when and to whom, as Fraser, Rintell, and Walters (1981) put it, is learned through observation of models, feedback from others on behavior, and repeated experience of a wide variety of social situations. Proficiency helps in this regard since it opens up language as another input channel, but it is just one of several channels and is nearly irrelevant to learning proxemics and other types of non-verbal behavior. Very little research exists on these extra-linguistic aspects of second language pragmatic competence.

future research direction

Research into the effect of proficiency could use a longitudinal design by following learners as their proficiency increases and tracking their pragmatic development simultaneously. Bardovi-Harlig and Salsbury's (2004) work is a good model because it clearly shows that the patterns of pragmatic development are, in part, constrained by learners' grammar. The study traced the development of the speech act of disagreement by ESL learners over a year. They found that a learner with a high type/token ratio of modals (i.e. a high number of different modals appearing in speech) developed the ability to use a variety of modal forms to qualify disagreements in conversations. In contrast, a learner with a low type/token ratio repeatedly recycled the same modal expressions, suggesting that grammatically weak learners are constrained by their small range of modal expressions.

Future research is needed in this area to examine pragmatic development with an in-depth analysis of specific, related grammatical sub-systems. Independent analyses of learners' knowledge of grammatical forms and their occurrence in specific sociocultural functions could reveal how the knowledge of the forms mediates the pace and pattern of development in the pragmatic functions that necessitate the forms. Since very few longitudinal studies have actually examined the presence or absence of the target pragmalinguistic knowledge, separate analyses of grammar and pragmatics will help to illuminate the effect of proficiency on pragmatic development.

Cognitive variables *(aptitude × WM)*

In contrast to proficiency, cognitive characteristics have been examined only sparsely in L2 pragmatics research. We have only one study on language aptitude and another on working memory; this contrasts starkly with the general trend in SLA, where aptitude is one of the 'big two' individual difference variables next to motivation (R. Ellis, 2005, p. 531), and working memory has recently become the most prominent topic in language aptitude studies (DeKeyser & Koeth, 2011; Dörnyei, 2005). If cognition governs the mechanisms behind how we learn, remember, problem-solve, and pay attention, learning pragmatics—which also draws on abilities and processes of understanding and acting—is likely to be affected by one's cognitive capacities. For this reason, the effect of cognitive abilities on pragmatics learning is worth investigating. As with proficiency, this effect can tell us the extent to which general capacities of understanding and acquiring new knowledge underlie one's ability to perform well on socioculturally oriented language tasks.

Foreign language learning aptitude, the most studied cognitive variable in SLA, is defined as 'some characteristic of an individual which controls, at a given point of time, the rate of progress that he will make subsequently in learning a foreign language' (Carroll, 1974, p. 320). Language aptitude is claimed to predict how well and quickly an individual can, relative to other individuals, learn a language at a given time and under certain conditions. The most famous test of language aptitude, the Modern Language Aptitude Test (MLAT), was created by Carroll and Sapon (1959), who envisioned aptitude as consisting of four dimensions: (1) phonemic coding ability, (2) grammatical sensitivity, (3) inductive learning ability, and (4) associative memory. Another famous instrument, the Pimsleur Language Aptitude Battery (PLAB) (Pimsleur, 1966), shares a similar taxonomy with MLAT (measuring verbal intelligence and auditory ability), but it addresses a broader construct by including motivation as one of the components.

In L2 pragmatics, no studies have examined the relationship between language aptitude and pragmatic competence, so correlation coefficients between these variables are not available. However, Li's (in press) study explored the effect of aptitude on pragmatics learning under different instructional conditions. In this study, one L2 Chinese group received input-based training on the speech act of request, in which they assessed the grammaticality and appropriateness of the request expressions. The other group practiced the same materials using the output-based program: after reading a dialogue and assessing the degree of imposition, they typed the request expression on the computer screen. Instructional effects were measured by a listening judgment test (LJT) and an oral discourse completion test (ODCT).

Both treatment conditions were considered to demand the aptitude for explicit rule learning (Robinson, 2007, 2012). Because one of the underlying constituents for this aptitude complex is 'metalinguistic rule rehearsal' (MRR), Li used Carroll's MLAT to measure grammatical sensitivity, rote memory, and working memory, which underlie the MRR factor. In the input-based condition, learners with a larger working memory capacity became faster at responding to the listening test items after the training. For the output-based group, a significant correlation was found between rote memory and planning speed on ODCT, and between grammatical sensitivity and speech rates on ODCT. Hence, gains in different aspects of pragmatic performance were related to different dimensions of language aptitude, and the patterns of the relationship were different between the input-based and output-based groups.

Li's study adds to the current research program in aptitude–treatment interaction, which claims that aptitude and the type of instruction interact with each other to influence learning (Robinson, 2007, 2012). Certain instructional methods might be effective for some learners but not for others depending on their specific abilities. Because optimal learning is considered to occur when the instruction aligns with learners' cognitive resources, this research program aims to identify optimal combinations of aptitude variables that influence learning under certain instructional conditions. Although existing instructional studies in pragmatics have revealed a relative advantage of explicit over implicit teaching, Li's results imply that this generalization may not be so straightforward when aptitude comes into the picture. Implicit teaching could work better for learners with specific aptitude complexities.

Traditionally, language aptitude has been treated as a monolithic construct that affects learning as a whole. A more recent approach to aptitude is actually moving in the opposite direction: decomposing the aptitude construct into its constituents and assessing their independent impact on L2 learning. Notably, Dörnyei (2005, p. 34) explicitly states that there is no such thing as language aptitude: 'foreign language aptitude is not a unitary factor but rather a complex of basic abilities that are essential to facilitate foreign language learning'. This trend is seen most clearly in the intensive research in working memory that the field has accumulated in recent years. Following Miyake and Freedman's (1998, p. 339) claim that 'working memory for language may be one (if not the) central component of this language aptitude', research on working memory alone has gathered steam. This trend is seen in a number of studies that demonstrated positive relationships between working memory and L2 proficiency, as well as the effect of working memory on instructed L2 learning (for a review, see DeKeyser & Koeth, 2011; Juffs, 2014; Juffs & Harrington, 2011). The trend is also seen in new models of language aptitude tests, for example the High-Level Language Aptitude Battery (Hi-LAB) (Doughty et al., 2010), which is designed to predict language learning advantages at ultimate L2 achievement. A recent study showed that one of the working memory constructs—phonological short-term memory—along with associative memory and implicit learning skill, successfully identified participants with high L2 achievement (Linck et al., 2013).

In L2 pragmatics, there are only a few studies that align with the component-based analysis of language aptitude. For instance, Taguchi (2008b) examined whether accurate and speedy comprehension of implicature is related to listening proficiency and two cognitive variables: working memory and lexical access skill.

Working memory is considered a component of listening because processing acoustic stimuli is subject to memory constraints. Lexical access skill (the ability to retrieve word meaning quickly) also supports comprehension because comprehension involves the lower-level processing of attending to and assigning meaning to linguistic stimuli. Working memory and lexical access can jointly contribute to comprehension. Speedy processing of lexis can free up learners' memory space. As a result, more working memory becomes available for higher-order processing such as implicature comprehension.

Contrary to this expectation, only one variable—lexical access skill—significantly correlated with speedy processing of implicature (measured by response times), explaining 25% of the variance. Working memory bore no relationship to comprehension speed or accuracy. Similar findings were obtained in a longitudinal study. Taguchi (2008a) found that development in implicature comprehension over a four-month study abroad period significantly correlated with the initial-level lexical access skill, but correlation was found only with gains in comprehension speed, not with accuracy scores. The correlation coefficient was much smaller than that of the single-moment study, explaining 11% of the variance.

This section has reviewed research on the role of cognitive variables in pragmatics learning. Available findings suggest that cognitive factors, especially aptitude and lexical access skill, may strongly support pragmatic competence and development. These conclusions reinforce the notion that, like grammar and lexis, learning pragmatics draws on the general cognitive mechanisms of memory, attention, and processing that apply to any type of learning.

It was more than a decade ago that Robinson (2005, p. 50) asked the important question: What are the aptitude components that predict acquisition of pragmatic abilities? In his model of 'aptitude complexes', Robinson situates pragmatic ability as a higher-level competence, which is supported by lower-level aptitude components, such as self-presentation and impression management (Goffman, 1967), mind-reading (Baron-Cohen, 1995), non-verbal sensitivity (Archer, 1983), self-efficacy (Bandura, 1986), and openness to experience (Costa & MacRae, 1985). To date, no research has seriously tested this framework to find out if there is such a thing as 'pragmatics aptitude'. To answer this question, it is necessary to present a clear framework of pragmatic competence to explicate what abilities make someone pragmatically competent, and to then link those abilities to cognitive and personal traits that may support those abilities.

Similarly, new frameworks of aptitude testing could inform pragmatics learning. Grigorenko, Sternberg, and Ehrman (2000) recently developed an aptitude test called CANAL-FT (the Cognitive Ability for Novelty in Acquisition of Language as Applied to Foreign Language Test). This test is based on Sternberg's (2002) triarchic theory of human intelligence that conceptualizes intelligence as consisting of three components: analytical, creative, and practical. Analytical intelligence encompasses the ability to analyze, compare, and evaluate. Creative intelligence is called on when one has to cope with novel situations and problems using past experiences and current skills. Practical intelligence involves the ability to adapt to a changing environment and find a fit between oneself and the demands of the environment.

The CANAL-FT and Sternberg's theory of human intelligence present a radically different view of language aptitude. Shifting from Carroll's (1974) paradigm—where aptitude was viewed as a stable, fixed construct immune to influences from the environment—Sternberg situates language aptitude as a dynamic system that fluctuates depending on experiences. Sternberg conceptualizes language aptitude as the ability to cope with novelty and adapt to a changing context. Because much of language learning is about dealing with novel information and the challenges that an environment offers, L2 success hinges on the ability to implement new knowledge when solving novel problems. Although no studies have applied the human intelligence theory to pragmatics, future research in this direction is promising. Because form–function–context associations in pragmatics are not stable across situations, learners must learn how to adapt their resources in response to situational dynamics. Learners who have a high level of creative and practical intelligence might excel in pragmatics learning because of the shared attribute of adaptability.

Motivation

Motivation is one of the 'big two' ID factors in SLA research, attracting considerable interest from both researchers and teachers alike over the last three decades. The popularity of motivation research originated over three decades ago in Gardner's (1985) socio-psychological model of motivation that situated integrative motivation as the central construct. This socially oriented conceptualization of motivation, i.e. motivation arising as one's desire to learn a language for successful interethnic communication and cultural affiliation, has shifted over time toward more situation-specific accounts of motivational phenomena (for example, Crookes & Schmidt, 1991; Dörnyei, 2000, 2001, 2005). These shifts and changes have further intensified researchers' and teachers' interest in understanding motivational processes as well as their mechanisms in driving successful L2 learning.

This intense interest in motivation in SLA research, however, has not penetrated the field of L2 pragmatics. In the existing literature, motivation is often used as a post hoc interpretation of empirical findings, explaining why one group excelled over the other on pragmatic tasks or why some students made faster progress in developing pragmatic abilities than others. In Niezgoda and Roever's (2001) study, EFL learners in the Czech Republic detected a higher number of pragmatic and grammatical errors in speech acts and judged both error types as more serious than ESL learners did. The researchers attributed EFL learners' superior pragmatic awareness to their high level of motivation; they were enrolled in a highly selective teacher education program with a strong commitment to becoming English teachers. Cook (2001), on the other hand, found that only a minority of learners of Japanese as a foreign language were able to recognize appropriate speech styles. Successful learners tended to have specific goals of working or studying in Japan, or communicating with Japanese people, indicating their higher-level motivation.

Kasper and Rose's (2002) seminal volume reviewed only one study (Takahashi, 2005, which was an unpublished manuscript at the time) that assessed motivation as an independent variable and examined its effect on pragmatics learning. Remarkably, this situation stays almost unchanged over a decade later. To our knowledge, only a few new studies have been published in this area, including Takahashi's (2005) original study, which appeared as a journal article (Takahashi, 2005). This situation could be a reflection of the fact that in recent studies, motivation has been analyzed qualitatively in context. We will discuss those qualitative studies later, in the section on the dynamic, interactive approach to individual characteristics, but here we will first summarize Takahashi's (2005) study, which examined how motivation and proficiency affect EFL learners' awareness and noticing of pragmalinguistic forms embedded in written dialogues. The target forms included: bi-clausal request-making forms in English (for example, 'I was wondering if you could' + verb phrase), idiomatic expressions, and discourse markers. EFL students in a Japanese university received implicit instruction in which they analyzed dialogues for the target pragmalinguistic features. After the instruction, they indicated their degree of awareness of the target forms on a seven-point Likert scale. Participants who were intrinsically motivated to learn English were more likely to notice target request forms and idiomatic expressions. These findings suggest that intrinsic motivation may help to direct learners' attention to pragmalinguistic forms that are perceived to be important for communication. Together with Li's study on the aptitude–treatment interaction, Takahashi's findings contribute to our understanding of the interaction of ID factors and pragmatics learning.

The claim regarding the connection between motivation and attention has been confirmed more recently in Takahashi's (2015) study. She found that, in situations where the learners were not explicitly shown or taught the request forms, learners with stronger communication-oriented motivation and a higher listening proficiency were more likely to notice the target bi-clausal request forms in input than those with lower-level proficiency and motivation. In contrast, these variables did not play a significant role in learning requests as measured by oral DCT tasks. In other words, more proficient and motivated learners reported noticing the target forms more frequently, but their noticing did not lead to the accurate production of the forms. These findings indicate that pragmatic awareness and performance are in separate domains and are affected differently by motivation. Awareness without sufficient form–function analysis of the target pragmatic features in input is likely to lead to inadequate learning outcomes, despite high-level motivation and proficiency.

Although Takahashi's study did not reveal the motivation–performance link, Tajeddin and Moghadam's (2012) study found such a link when different types of motivation were assessed. They developed surveys measuring two types of motivation: general pragmatic motivation and speech-act-specific motivation. The former addressed cultural familiarity, appropriacy, and communication needs, measured by 42 Likert-scale items ranging from 'strongly agree' to 'strongly disagree'. Figure 6.3 shows some sample items.

The speech-act-specific motivation focused on the motivation to make speech acts of request, refusal, and apology (for example, 'I like to learn how

Cultural familiarity
'I need to learn cultural norms when I learn English.'
Appropriacy
'When I am learning English, I pay attention to the situations in which conversations happen.'

*Figure 6.3 Likert-scale items measuring motivation (Tajeddin &
Moghadam, 2012, p. 359)*

to be polite when I request.'), as measured by 12 Likert-scale items. Regression analysis revealed that speech-act-specific motivation had a significant impact on the participants' speech act production (assessed by DCT), although the variance explained by that motivation was very small (r-square=.08). General pragmatic motivation, however, had no impact. The findings indicate that motivation specific to certain areas of pragmatic performance may better account for learners' pragmatic performance.

Ushioda (2016) recently advocated the need for future research that examines motivation 'through a small lens' to reveal how motivation connects with specific psycholinguistic processes of SLA or development of specific linguistic features. Such a study could essentially generate a situated, evidence-based analysis of how classroom instructors can help enhance students' motivation to maximize learning. Along this line, further replication of Takahashi's study would be useful to examine the relationship between types of motivation and pragmatic awareness among different treatment conditions, L1/L2 groups, and proficiency levels.

Another direction of future motivation research in pragmatics is to closely align with the current trend of motivation research that conceptualizes motivation as a process-oriented, situated construct, rather than a static, robust attribute that determines learning behavior. As Dörnyei (2009, p. 188) says, 'the timeless and context-free stability of IDs is an illusion'; motivation, attitudes, and affect change from time to time, from situation to situation. Under this recent epistemology, the psychometric tradition of measuring motivation and categorizing people according to motivation type—integrative vs. instrumental motivation (Gardner, 1985) or extrinsic vs. intrinsic motivation (Deci & Ryan, 1985)—is no longer current.

We can observe recent developments of motivation research in several areas. One is the process-oriented conceptualization of motivation that explicitly acknowledges the dynamic, changing nature of motivation with time (Dörnyei, 2001, 2005; Ushioda, 2009). Dörnyei and Otto (1998) (also Dörnyei, 2001) proposed a model that distinguishes three phases of motivational process: (1) preactional stage or the motivation generation stage that involves selection of specific goals; (2) actional stage concerning how generated motivation is maintained in the process of achieving the goal; and

(3) postactional stage involving the learners' retrospective evaluation of how things went. This model can account for the temporal variation and progression of motivation, i.e. how motivation changes over time during L2 learning.

Another recent approach to L2 motivation research is the L2 Motivational Self System (Dörnyei, 2005; Dörnyei & Chan, 2013), which also illustrates the interaction between individual characteristics and context. This model specifies that motivated learning is organized according to three components: ideal L2 self, ought-to L2 self, and L2 learning experience. The ideal L2 self refers to what one wishes to become as an L2 speaker, while the ought-to L2 self describes the attributes that one believes one ought to have to meet expectations. The third dimension, L2 learning experience, situates motivation within the immediate learning context and experience (for example, influence from the teacher and peers, experience of success).

These process-oriented, context-dependent approaches could be applied to the study of motivation in learning pragmatics. The three stages of motivation (preactional, actional, and postactional) can serve as a useful framework, particularly in a study abroad context, to illustrate how motivation toward learning sociocultural norms of interaction changes over time, corresponding to learners' experiences. Similarly, the ideal image of an L2 speaker and the ought-to L2 self can be examined through a pragmatics lens to reveal attributes and qualities that learners perceive to be important in order to function appropriately in a social context. These attributes and qualities can be cross-examined with learners' experiences to see what kinds of opportunities for pragmatics-related interaction are available in a context that might support those qualities.

Most recently, this process-oriented, context-dependent approach to motivation has shifted to incorporate a dynamic systems perspective in its research program (de Bot, 2008; Dörnyei, 2009; N. Ellis & Larsen-Freeman, 2006; Larsen-Freeman & Cameron, 2008). These two approaches share an underlying view of motivation as an organic process that emerges through complex interrelations among elements in context. In L2 pragmatics, several qualitative studies have presented rich descriptions of pragmatic development in context, and in most cases, motivation has emerged as one of the core individual characteristics that underlie and guide the process of pragmatics learning. We will discuss those studies in the last section of this chapter.

Personality

Personality is a relevant ID factor in pragmatics because personality is a dynamic set of characteristics that uniquely influences people's actions in a range of social situations. How people react in a certain situation—how they perceive things, people, and events in a situation, and how they form a judgment about them—is the domain of personality. People perform a pragmatic act in certain ways based on their perceptions of situational dynamics and their judgment about expected behaviors in, and outcomes of, a situation.

Although people's learned knowledge (both linguistic and sociocultural knowledge) and their previous experiences determine their choice of pragmatic act, people's traits are also a determinant because they are directly responsible for how these people think and conduct themselves in a general sense.

There are several personality models and theories in the field, and each one offers a different perspective on the constructs of personality. Eysenck and Eysenck's three-factor model (Eysenck & Eysenck, 1985) presents three components—extraversion, neuroticism, and psychoticism—as basic, biologically based categories of temperament. The 'Big Five' model (Goldberg, 1992; McCrae & Costa, 2003), the most widely used taxonomy in the field, is an extension of Eysenck and Eysenck's model. It presents five dimensions that are considered fundamental to our social and interpersonal relations with others (see John, Naumann, & Soto, 2008, for a review). The five dimensions and their related characteristics are:

- extraversion (sociable, talkative, assertive, emotionally expressive)
- agreeableness (sympathetic, kind, affectionate, cooperative)
- consciousness (organized, goal-directed, self-disciplined)
- neuroticism (emotionally unstable, anxious, moody, tense)
- openness (curious, creative, adventurous).

Costa and McCrae (1985) developed a 240-item survey called NEO-PI (NEO Personality Inventory) that measures the Big Five dimensions.

While the NEO-PI measures personality traits that come in different degrees, the Myers-Briggs Type Indicator (MBTI) (Myers & Briggs, 1976), another major instrument, classifies people according to type. The MBTI is based on Carl Jung's theory that proposed three binary personality types as fundamental to human personality: extroversion–introversion, sensing–intuition, and thinking–feeling. Myers and Briggs added a fourth dichotomy, judgment–perception. Extroverted types prefer to focus their attention on the outer world, while introverted types focus on the inner world. Intuitive types prefer abstraction and imagination, while sensing types are empirically inclined and prefer details. Thinking types follow rational principles and objective criteria in making decisions, while feeling types follow subjective criteria and value empathy and harmony. Judging types favor a planned, orderly way of doing things and prefer closure, while perception types prefer spontaneity and like to keep things open-ended. The MBTI is designed to measure these personality types. It includes 93 questions, which help to categorize people into a combination of types.

These models of personality and measurements have been applied to L2 pragmatics studies, although the body of literature on these applications is still very small. The central question pursued by these studies is whether learners' personalities make a difference in their ability to comprehend or perform pragmatic functions, and, if so, which dimension(s) have the most direct impact. Existing studies have uniformly found a statistically significant relationship between personality and pragmatic abilities, providing evidence that personality factors underlie how learners perform pragmatic tasks. However, when separate traits are analyzed, existing findings are far less conclusive, indicating that not all traits have an equal effect. Different traits show different patterns of relationships depending on the constructs and measures of pragmatic competence, as well as other learner- and context-level factors that mediate the relationship.

Verhoeven and Vermeer (2002) examined the relationship between communicative competence (organizational, strategic, and pragmatic competence) and personality determined by the 'Big Five' model. Participants were L1 Dutch children and L2 Dutch-speaking children in elementary schools in the Netherlands. Pragmatic competence was measured by a role-play task in which the children acted out a variety of speech acts (for example, greeting and thanking). Findings revealed a moderate correlation between pragmatic competence and one personality dimension: openness to experience. The fact that this dimension also correlated with organizational and strategic competences indicates that learning in general, at this age, seems to depend primarily on this trait. What is interesting is that pragmatic competence did not correlate with any other traits, in contrast to organizational and strategic competences, which correlated with extraversion. These findings point to the unique characteristics of pragmatic competence, suggesting that other factors may contribute to individuals' ability to produce speech acts.

When we turn to adult L2 learners, however, we find different results between the 'Big Five' model and pragmatic competence. Kuriscak (2006) conducted a large-scale study that examined the impact of a number of characteristics on Spanish learners' requests and complaints (measured by DCT), as well as on their perceived difficulty in producing the speech acts (rated on a seven-point scale). Participants were 292 college students enrolled in advanced-level Spanish courses in the U.S. Personality was assessed on three traits: extraversion, neuroticism, and social desirability (perceived importance of projecting a desirable social image).

Regression analyses revealed that learners who were more proficient and scored higher on extraversion produced more mitigations and upgraders in the speech acts. In addition, learners who scored higher on the neuroticism scale and lower on social desirability perceived the DCT scenarios to be more imposing and difficult to respond to. These findings are sensible considering the nature of the personality traits. Extroverts, being more outgoing, expressive, and talkative, probably produced more language, and their production featured a greater amount of mitigations and upgraders. Similarly, more proficient learners were more skilled at producing increasingly elaborate speech acts featuring modifications. Neuroticism and social desirability, on the other hand, affected perception, but not production. Learners who were anxious, tense, and self-conscious probably felt a greater degree of psychological pressure in performing face-threatening speech acts than those who were less neurotic. Lower scores on the social desirability scale indicate a greater desire to maintain positive face. Because of their stronger orientation to positive face, learners who were concerned about social image might have felt uneasy with the scenarios that involved a potential face-threat to the addressee.

Looking into the same 'Big Five' traits and speech acts, Verhoeven and Vermeer (2002) and Kuriscak's (2006) studies produced remarkably different findings. Extraversion and neuroticism, two personality traits that affected production of modifications or perceived difficulty in Kuriscak's study had no effect on the ability to role-play speech acts in Verhoeven and Vermeer's study. One explanation is the age of the participants and the context of learning. Sociability and emotional stability may not be the factors that affect children's pragmatic performance when they are in the target community, because in their everyday interaction with same-age peers, they are immersed in those speech acts. This situation is different for college students in a domestic, formal, institutional context, where they have to actively seek opportunities for practice. Emotional stability and an outgoing personality could make a difference in this opportunity-seeking process: adults who are more active and less reserved might be able to find more opportunities for practice and become familiar with elaborate speech act expressions.

Another explanation is the potential interaction between personality traits and aspects of speech acts analyzed. When speech acts are analyzed for fluency or amount of language produced in the time limit, extraversion might be an advantage, as shown in Kuriscak's study, where extroverts produced more external modifications (mitigations and upgraders) than introverts did. Verhoeven and Vermeer, on the other hand, did not find the extraversion effect, potentially because they did not analyze the length of speech. When the focus was placed on overall illocutionary force, the extraversion–introversion dichotomy did not make a difference: whether active or passive, the participants were similar in their ability to convey intention.

Neuroticism, on the other hand, was the significant predictor for *perception* of the DCT situations in Kuriscak's study. This trait did not play a role in Verhoeven and Vermeer's study, but again, they did not measure children's perceived difficulty in responding to the role-play situations (although they measured speech act productions in role-play). In a sense, the findings of these two studies are complementary because neuroticism had no effect on the actual production of speech acts in Kuriscak's study, and affected perceptions of speech acts only. Because neurotic people tend to consider themselves to be less capable of solving a problem, this trait may affect learners' perceived confidence in coping with a language task. As shown in Kuriscak's study, learners who were high in neuroticism were less self-assured about the DCT task and perceived the speech acts in the DCT task to be difficult to produce, and they attributed their difficulty to their lack of vocabulary and personal reasons (for example, shyness, confrontation).

Confidence in performing a pragmatic task, then, seems to be grounded at both the linguistic and social levels. Learners must have confidence (and thus feel easy) in handling linguistic demands. At the same time, they have to be comfortable with navigating imagined social situations in the task.

Confrontation and imposition implied in the scenarios present a challenge because of perceived negative consequences in social relations. Learners who have a neurotic tendency seem to identify this challenge to be more serious than do their less neurotic counterparts. This challenge, however, remained at the level of perception and did not affect the actual performance. These findings indicate that the personality effect is not uniform and fluctuates depending on the constructs and measures. We can also conclude that a more specific operationalization of pragmatic competence (for example, perception of scenarios, use of semantic strategies), rather than a global pragmatics construct (for example, success in communicating illocutionary force), might reveal more meaningful relationships with personality traits.

The last study we will summarize here also contributes to our understanding of the role of mediating variables on the relationship between personality and L2 pragmatics: in this case, 'time'. Previous L2 pragmatics studies on personality (or ID factors in general) were almost exclusively confined to a single-moment design by examining the relationship between personality and pragmatic competence at a single point in time, and very few studies have addressed the role of personality from a developmental perspective. However, if we consider that individual characteristics are not fixed but change with time, personality effect could also change in response to changing pragmatic abilities. To understand the role of personality in pragmatic *development*, rather than performance at a given point of time, a longitudinal study with repeated measures design is necessary.

Taguchi (2014c) investigated the impact of personality traits on the development of L2 English learners' production of speech acts (requests and opinions). Speech acts were measured by a spoken DCT given three times over a two-semester period. Learners' personality was measured using Keirsey's (1998) temperament sorter that draws on the Myers-Briggs Type Indicator. The hierarchical linear model was used to assess the main effect of time on changes in speech acts (appropriateness and fluency), and the interaction effect of time and personality (entered as covariate) on the changes.

The feeling–thinking dimension showed a significant interaction effect with time on the appropriateness of speech acts. It was the 'thinking' types who increased the score in the first (but not the second) semester. However, the 'feeling' types had started out with a significantly higher appropriateness score than the 'thinking' types, and used more indirect expressions in their requests. The same personality dimension also revealed a significant interaction effect with time on fluency. The 'feeling' types became faster at planning for their production, although the effect was limited to the first semester.

The complex interaction between personality traits, outcome measures, and time found in this study once again confirms that personality effect is not constant across different traits, aspects of pragmatic competence examined, or timescales. The indirectness of the 'feeling' types could be a reflection of their tendency to value empathy and personal relations. These characteristics that initially differentiated their speech act performance from their 'thinking' counterparts were no longer factors after a semester, once the 'thinking' types (presumably) gained more linguistic experiences and resources to refine their speech acts. The 'feeling' types also improved in planning speed, possibly reflecting their tendency to make a decision more promptly based on emotion than their 'thinking' counterparts, who are more analytically oriented and careful in proceeding with a task. Interestingly, this 'feeling' effect disappeared again in the second semester, which indicates that learners' gained experience and proficiency might outweigh their initial pragmatic variation coming from personality.

This section has reviewed L2 pragmatics studies that treated personality as a distinct, independent variable by measuring the construct using a psychometric questionnaire, and examined the relationship between personality and pragmatic development. Although the body of literature is small, existing findings suggest that, when viewed as a categorical variable, personality has an impact on learners' speech acts. Open-mindedness was found to be related to children's ability to convey communicative intentions in speech acts (Verhoeven & Vermeer, 2002). Among adult learners in a foreign language context, extraversion had an effect on the degree of elaboration added to speech acts through mitigations and upgraders (Kuriscak, 2006). In the same context, neuroticism had an effect on learners' perception, characterized as the degree of imposition and psychological difficulty that they experienced in responding to the situations. In a longitudinal study, learners' preferred way of decision-making—using logic and moral values—had an effect on their gains in speech acts (Taguchi, 2014c). The personality–pragmatics contingencies indicate that how learners think, feel, and behave in general underlies their approach to, and performance in, pragmatics-oriented tasks.

Another notable tendency that emerged from the existing findings is a complex interplay between personality and pragmatic constructs. There is no one personality trait or dimension that explained learners' variation in pragmatic behavior consistently over different outcome measures or different timescales. This tendency is also seen in a larger area of SLA. Dörnyei (2005) claims that there is an interaction between personality factors and context-specific variables. Certain types of learning situations or the nature of tasks that learners engage in could favor one personality type over the other. This means that the personality–learning relation is, to a great extent, a function of contextual features.

Similarly, personality can be just one of many variables that affect the way learners respond to their learning environment and tasks. Dörnyei observes:

Personality traits can in many ways be compared to the ingredients of a cooking recipe and it is known fact that a good cook can usually prepare a delicious meal of almost any ingredients by knowing how to combine them. In a similar vein, one can argue that we should not expect many strong linear relationships (expressed, for example, by correlations) between individual personality traits and achievement, because successful learners can combine their personality features to best effect by utilizing their specific strengths and compensating for their possible weaknesses (Brown, 2000).

(2005, p. 24)

The field of pragmatics could certainly take up this cooking metaphor and examine the combined effect of, or interrelationship between, personality traits and other individual characteristics on pragmatic competence and development. Rather than isolating personality from other learner-level factors, personality can be conceptualized as one of several variables that constitute even more complex composite constructs. Future research calls for a study that is explicitly designed to investigate this interaction among individual and contextual-level variables.

The dynamic, interactive approach to individual characteristics

Identity, subjectivity, and agency

Previous sections reviewed L2 pragmatics studies on a range of learner-level factors, including proficiency, cognitive abilities, motivation, and personality. These quantitative studies treated individual characteristics as fixed, categorical traits. They measured the effect of these characteristics within a group of learners and assessed the characteristics' relationships to pragmatic competence and development. In the remaining part of the chapter, we will turn to qualitative studies that have taken the dynamic, interactive approach to the study of individual characteristics. Studies in this category have focused on individuals rather than groups, and have provided a situated analysis of the influence that learner characteristics have on pragmatics learning. First, we will focus on identity as an individual characteristic.

A growing body of SLA studies has explored the relationship between identity and L2 learning, elevating identity to a central concern in the second language acquisition process (Block, 2007; Norton & MacKinney, 2011; Pavlenko & Blackledge, 2003). This rise in identity research originated in the recent 'social turn' (Block, 2003), characterized as a shift from a cognitive, psycholinguistic approach to SLA to an approach that emphasizes social dimensions of L2 learning. While the majority of the SLA research in the 1970s and 1980s investigated learner characteristics as isolated factors that affect learning, current identity theorists are concerned with the diverse social and historical contexts in which learners are situated, and how learners accommodate, resist, or negotiate the diverse positions that those contexts offer them. Norton observes the interaction between language, identity, and context in the following:

I foreground the role of language as constitutive of and constituted by a language learner's social identity…It is through language that a person negotiates a sense of self within and across different sites at different points in time, and it is through language that a person gains access to or is denied access to powerful social networks that give learners the opportunity to speak.

(2013, p. 45)

Social identity was originally defined as 'part of individuals' self-concept which derives from his knowledge of his membership of a social group (or groups) together with the emotional significance attached to that membership' (Tajfel, 1974, p. 69). This static, individualistic view of identity, however, does not fit well in the current poststructuralist era. Poststructuralists reject the idea that individuals have pre-determined identities or that identities are fixed. Instead, they conceptualize learner identity as multifaceted, fluid, a site of negotiation, and subject to change (Block, 2007; Norton, 1997, 2013; Norton Peirce, 1995; Norton & McKinney, 2011). They consider identity to be dynamic and alterable, and able to be constructed and reconstructed in the course of L2 development, depending on learners' relationships with others and how they wish to position themselves in the L2 world. Multiple identities might conflict with each other at times, causing learners to struggle with selecting a particular identity to assert in a given situation. To understand the role of identity in L2 learning, it is crucial to consider the *agency* of individual learners in selecting, enacting, and negotiating their identity.

According to LoCastro (2003), agency, or individuals' capacity to act and make their own choices, refers to a self-reliant capacity that works with volition and power to bring about an effect on, or change in, one's behavior. Agency is closely connected to subjectivity: learners are considered active agents who create new social positions for themselves. In learning pragmatics, for instance, learners do not always passively observe target pragmatic norms by using honorifics or formal terms to address someone older and superior. When the norms contradict their desired social identity, learners might contest those norms. In this section, we will review L2 pragmatics studies that document this phenomenon of identity as a site of struggle (Norton, 2013).

A classic study by Siegal (1994, 1996) describes how four European women in Japan negotiated conflicts between the L2 community norms and their desired identities as scholars and professionals. One participant, Arina, expressed strong distaste for Japanese women's way of speaking because it sounded too feminine and humble, and conflicted with her desired identity: an independent Western woman. She rejected using honorifics even when she was making a speech in public. She opted for the polite form (the *desu/masu* form), which she viewed as a neutral form. Another participant, Lisa, overused the plain form even when speaking to someone older and superior, when, in fact, the polite form was clearly the norm. Finally, Mary, a visiting scholar at a Japanese university, frequently used the polite modal verb *deshoo* instead of using honorifics. *Deshoo* is an epistemic marker indicating that the presented information is known to the addressee. However, it sounds condescending when interlocutors are not in a close relationship because—depending on intonation—it sounds as if the speaker is challenging the addressee's knowledge. Mary used *deshoo* purposefully to express a polite stance, but her strategy failed in the eyes of native Japanese speakers.

Clearly, these participants evaluated gendered linguistic practices and the social meanings of these practices through their own lens. When their evaluations clashed with their own identity and how they wished to present themselves in Japanese society, they 'created their own language system based on their perceptions of Japanese women's language and demeanor and their awareness of their position in Japanese society' (Siegal, 1994, p. 344). Lacking in these women was the *emic* view of those linguistic practices and the social meaning of the practices. The women in Siegal's study probably over-interpreted the social meaning of honorifics, designating it as a speech for women with less power and lower social status. In the absence of an *emic* understanding of the honorifics, they were probably not aware of the social consequences of their pragmatic choices: how their chosen styles were perceived and received in the local community. Even if they were aware, local members might not have reacted negatively to their pragmatic demeanor because of their status as 'foreigner'. For instance, Mary's inappropriate speech was not viewed as a pragmatic failure by the male professor because she was categorized as a *gaijin* (foreigner) who had no obligation to conform to the norm, which was not her chosen identity but one assigned by the members of the local community.[2]

Around two decades after Siegal's study, we have a handful of L2 pragmatics studies that situate identity as the central topic. A trend seen in the more recent studies is the use of multiple data sources in their investigation. These studies used a DCT, a role-play task, or a conversation task to elicit learners' pragmatic knowledge, and then conducted a follow-up interview to gain insights into learners' responses. The purpose of the interview was to explore learners' insider perspectives to determine why they responded the way they did. By cross-examining learners' pragmatic performance and their perception data, researchers can explore whether the knowledge that learners demonstrate in tasks accommodates or diverges from the target language norms. In the case of diversion, researchers can examine if it is due to learners' lack of knowledge of L2 norms or due to their subjective resistance to these norms. In the case of accommodation, researchers can explore what caused learners to intentionally accommodate the target norms.

Using a DCT and role-play task, Ishihara and Tarone (2009) investigated pragmatic choices in speech acts among seven L2 learners of Japanese in a U.S. university. Retrospective interviews revealed instances in which several learners resisted using high-level honorifics and gendered language use because of their L1-derived beliefs in egalitarian social relationships. Masuda (2011) examined the development of six Japanese learners' use of the sentence-final particle *ne*, a linguistic marker for agreement, assessment, and alignment expressions. One participant intentionally avoided using *ne* because he perceived it to be a marker of female speech, an impression that he gained from Japanese pop media. Here, we observe how the learner's lack of an *emic* view of the particle usage combined with his masculine subject position. Absence of this particle in his conversation with his peer and instructor was not a result of his lack of pragmalinguistic knowledge. Rather, it was caused by his limited sociopragmatic knowledge of *ne* combined with his wish to explicitly implement his masculine identity.

Brown (2013) adds another dimension to the study of identity and L2 pragmatics by revealing how multicultural identity can affect pragmatic choice. He analyzed DCT data and recordings of naturalistic conversations and interviews to chart acquisition of Korean honorifics (*contaymal*) by four learners of Korean during a year-long stay in South Korea. He found that the learners were not utilizing their near-perfect knowledge of honorifics demonstrated in DCT for a range of reasons. In the case of one heritage learner, Daniel, this was because of his conflicting multiple identities: first as a speaker of German, having grown up in Germany; second as a heritage Korean speaker; and third as a learner of Korean who was trying to master his ancestral language. Daniel was caught between his desire to establish himself as a 'real Korean', by using locally normative honorifics fluently, and his desire to honor his Western background, which favors egalitarianism in language use. He felt difficulty in 'adapting to a social structure in which there was no equal basis' (Brown, 2013, p. 294) and asked his younger subordinates to downgrade to casual speech when speaking to him. But these occasional deviations from the target norm cast Daniel in the role of a foreigner who falls short of Korean norms, despite his inherited Korean identity, competence in Korean, and his strong desire to integrate into the Korean community.

While these studies on L2 pragmatics reveal why learners in the West often experience resistance to pragmatic norms practiced in some Asian cultures, another recent study reveals the identity conflict in the opposite L1–L2 dynamics: Asian learners studying English in the United States. In Kim's (2014) study, Korean students in a U.S. university completed a DCT and role-play task in English. Follow-up interviews found instances of learners' intended accommodation and divergence from target pragmatic norms. Compliment response was one such area. Although the learners did not reject compliments in order to signal modesty—which is a value commonly attributed to Asian culture (Saito & Beecken, 1997)—they felt uncomfortable with emulating the typical American response that involves just saying 'Thank you', and added unique semantic moves (for example, humble expressions) to their responses as a way of negotiating conflicting social identities. Similarly, in performing the speech act of request, some learners resisted target norms when speaking to someone younger. They used direct forms in requests (imperative requests) to intentionally position themselves as an older interlocutor, a choice that was motivated by their L1-based norms. This is the case of negative L1 transfer, as the following interview excerpt reveals:

At the shopping mall, I saw the [American mothers] saying, 'Would you like to have cereal, honey?' to their children…We [Korean mothers] don't use such polite forms with children in Korea. I would lose dignity as a mother [if I used polite forms with children].
(Kim, 2014, p. 97)

These findings clearly point to the importance of considering learners' subjectivity and agency when analyzing speech act data. Typical methods of L2 data analysis have involved categorizing semantic strategies in a speech act, and comparing the patterns with baseline data collected from native speakers or advanced speakers of the target language. A conclusion about learners' competence is based on how their patterns approximate or deviate from the baseline. However, if learners' subjectivity and values co-regulate their pragmatic choice, their deviation from baseline practices does not necessarily mean that they lack knowledge of the target norms. Rather, their deviation is an indication of their cultural identity. Kim's participants used extra semantic strategies in compliment responses, not because they did not know that those strategies were redundant but because they used them as a solution for their conflicting identities. L2 learners do not always follow target norms blindly; they sometimes exercise their agency and adopt differing L2 pragmatic options as a way to signal their identity.

Kim's data shows language use as a site for struggle (Norton, 2013). Learners felt pressure to comply with the target pragmatic norms, but at the same time they were uncomfortable with adopting the L2 norms due to their desire to express their subject positions. The findings are particularly revealing because the participants in Kim's study were all highly motivated and willing to use the target pragmatic options as long as they knew them. Despite being motivated, they still resisted the target norms, or at least experienced inner struggles between conflicting pragmatic norms. Kim interpreted this from the point of view of learner investment:

Participants selected pragmatic norms in a way that positioned them in social relationships and ultimately enabled them to invest in their social identities. This finding corresponds with the theoretical notion of investment delineated by Norton (1997; 1995)…they [learners] chose the pragmatic norms in the hopes of good returns, such as recognition of talent by their professor or respect from their children.
(2014, p. 98)

In the studies featured above, learners rejected pragmatic norms that they perceived to be incongruent with their L1 cultural values. Another line of literature documented inconsistency in the sense of self or self-identity as a cause of learners' resistance. Liao (2009) analyzed the use of English discourse markers (for example, 'you know', 'like', and 'well') by L1 Chinese graduate teaching assistants (TAs) in a U.S. university. She found that one female participant used discourse markers far less frequently than others. This was because the informal and colloquial image associated with discourse markers was incompatible with the professional teacher persona that she wanted to project. Fernandez's (2013) study also revealed learners' resistance to 'young-speak', stemming from their desired identity. She found that one L2 Spanish participant in a study abroad program in Argentina did not increase her use of informal Spanish, despite exposure to informal language use. She maintained that certain lexical items were 'bad' words, and she avoided them even though there were no real offensive connotations. Her stance, in part, came from her desire to present herself as a serious, conservative student.

This section has reviewed recent studies on identity as a learner characteristic in pragmatics learning. When we discuss individual characteristics, we typically expect that certain characteristics have a positive influence on pragmatics learning; for instance, intrinsic motivation facilitates recognition of pragmalinguistic forms, or high-level language aptitude accelerates the learning of pragmatic features in an instructed setting. Lack of such a positive relationship is determined simply as 'no effect'. However, as shown above, the majority of the studies on identity reviewed here revealed its influence in the opposite direction: Learners' identity and agency worked against adopting normative pragmatic behaviors, or put them in a conflict where they had to negotiate between different identities in their pragmatic choice. Some learners resisted what they perceived to be native speakers' pragmatic norms, while others chose to meet these expectations despite their discomfort with them. In either case, research has shown that how learners construct themselves as L2 speakers, and what identities they wish to project, could impede their implementation of pragmatic knowledge. Learners rely on their beliefs, values, and personal principles in their linguistic choices and sometimes choose to express their agency by not accommodating those norms.

Existing findings clearly demonstrate the determining role of learner agency and subjectivity in pragmatic choices, whether that is driven by L1-derived identity or self-identity. They also point to the complexity of the means by which learners negotiated identities and invested in the use of the L2 pragmatic norms. Bardovi-Harlig (2001) presented a list of the factors that are considered to affect pragmatic development, a list which includes input, instruction, proficiency, length of stay in the target language community, and L1 language and culture. Current findings suggest that learner identity can be added to this list. L2 learners do not passively 'pick up' and internalize L2 pragmatic norms through exposure. The learners' position in the L2 society, consciousness about their goals of L2 learning and use, and consciousness of the self (LoCastro, 2003, p. 297) equally influence their pragmatic performance and development. As Norton and McKinney (2011, p. 86) state, 'failing to consider the centrality of learners' identities will produce an inadequate understanding of SLA'. This point certainly applies to current L2 pragmatics research.

Agency and subjectivity affecting L2 performance reinforce the uniqueness of pragmatics. Learning pragmatics involves learning linguistic behaviors that are reflective of the values and norms in a given culture. When learners' L1 and L2 cultures do not share the same values and norms, or when learners feel resistance to L2 norms, linguistic forms that encode target norms are not practiced. In the areas of grammar and lexis, those cases are treated as instances of negative transfer or L1 interference that are largely unconscious, but in pragmatics learners make conscious decisions about whether to accept or resist target pragmatic norms (Taguchi, 2011c). Learners' decisions are guided by the identity that they desire to project in relation to others, which is based largely on their personal or L1-derived values and experiences.

Existing findings also send a message that we need to interpret pragmatic change with caution. Most longitudinal studies expect upward change in the data as a positive effect of time in pragmatic development. However, several studies (Fernandez, 2013; Masuda, 2011) found that upward change did not occur in some learners. If identity and agency are an extension of learners' pragmatic performance, we need to reconceptualize what counts as development. Development is not always signaled by an increase in numerical data, or approximation toward the native-speaker norm. Learners' decisions *not* to conform to normative practices could be viewed as a change and development, because it strongly indicates their understanding of local practices, and their self-expression reflects where they situate themselves in these practices.

Future challenges in the study of identity and pragmatics lie in the implications of these findings. We have observed that learner identity, subjectivity, and agency form a complementary explanation for why learners, intentionally or subconsciously, exhibit non-target-like pragmatic performance. But where do we go from here? Future research should move beyond mere description of this resistance phenomenon and extend to applications of the findings. One such area is instruction. Although pragmatics should always be taught by taking learners' subjectivity into consideration, the question is what form of instruction is possible if learner identity becomes part of teaching. Some researchers argue that possible consequences of selecting certain pragmatic behavior should be made clear to learners, although choosing how to behave should be left to them according to their own learning goals (Judd, 1999). Others think that we need to assess who the students are and what needs they have for their language study, and to select the pragmatic norms to teach depending on their needs (Ishihara & Tarone, 2009). Still others take the variationalist approach to pragmatics teaching, emphasizing the importance of exposing students to multiple differing norms of behavior within a community or across cultures, and encouraging learners to consider different intentions and motivations associated with pragmatic variation (Brock & Nagasaka, 2005; Ishihara & Cohen, 2010). There is yet another approach that teaches 'self-presentation', along with power and social distance, as a concept to consider when making pragmatic choices (van Compernolle, 2014). Future research lies in a more systematic application of these learner-centered, agency-based approaches to pragmatics teaching.

Another challenge for the future involves re-conceptualizing pragmatic norms. Target norms have been assumed in the previous studies in order to reveal how learners 'deviate from', 'resist', or 'diverge from' the assumed norms. However, the concept of native-speaker norms has been challenged in the current poststructuralist discourse and in multilingualism, where a uniform standard for pragmatic behaviors is seriously questioned (see Chapter 9). People exhibit immense variation in their ways of projecting politeness or formality because of their diverse experiences and perspectives. If there is no single norm operating in the local community, the initial step for a study on identity should be to determine what learners perceive to be local norms and where their perceptions come from. The focus should be placed on discovering 'salient norms' instead of 'target norms', and on investigating learners' orientation to—and understanding of—local pragmatics practices.

Individual differences in the complex, dynamic systems approach

As mentioned in the previous section, the field of SLA has recently undergone a paradigm shift, characterized as a move from positivist, cognitively oriented, and quantitative research to the poststructuralist, socially oriented, and qualitative paradigm (Block, 2003; Firth & Wagner, 1997; Lafford, 2007; Zuengler & Miller, 2006). The study of individual characteristics has also found itself in the midst of this paradigm reform. The most notable trend in this reform is the view of individual characteristics as dynamically changing and evolving characteristics contingent upon context. This trend is emphasized by Dörnyei (2009), who situates the complex, dynamic systems approach as a way to study individual variation and learner characteristics.

Dynamic Systems Theory (DST) (de Bot, 2008; Verspoor, de Bot, & Lowie, 2011), chaos/complexity theory (Larsen-Freeman & Cameron, 2008; Larsen-Freeman, 2012), and emergentism (N. Ellis & Larsen-Freeman, 2006; MacWhinney, 2006) are all related strands under the recent SLA epistemology that situates language development as a dynamic, non-linear process, emerging from socially co-regulated interactions between multiple influences in context. Below is a summary of the central terminologies of this theoretical paradigm.

- *Dynamicity and non-linearity*
  Language development is a non-linear process in which cognitive, social, and contextual factors continuously interact and co-regulate the course of L2 development over time. Different aspects of language abilities demonstrate different paces and rates of change, and a change in one aspect does not directly cause a change in other aspects. The developmental curve

is non-linear, involving backslidings, jumps, and stagnations (Larsen-Freeman & Cameron, 2008).

- *Variability*
  Unlike traditional quantitative studies that consider variability as 'noise', which should be controlled or regulated in statistical analyses, the dynamic systems approach considers variability as an invaluable source of information: variability data provide details of individual learners' developmental trajectories that are otherwise masked in the analysis of group means (N. Ellis & Larsen-Freeman, 2006).

- *Co-adaptation and interconnectedness of variables*
  Co-adaptation refers to the 'interaction of two or more complex systems, each changing in response to the other' (Larsen-Freeman & Cameron, 2008, p. 67). There is no 'single bullet explanation' for changes or simple cause–effect relationships (N. Ellis & Larsen-Freeman, 2006): variables collectively explain the changes, but not in isolation.

- *Attractors in state space and control parameters*
  An attractor is a 'preferred region of a system's state space into which the system tends to move' (Larsen-Freeman & Cameron, 2008, pp. 50–53). Transitions to an attractor's state are influenced by 'control parameters'. Larsen-Freeman and Cameron illustrate this process with an example of motivation. Motivation could be a control parameter that helps to avoid attractors such as skipping homework and helps L2 learning systems move forward to higher stages of learning.

- *Self-organization*
  Self-organization refers to a sudden shift from one attractor state to another. After reaching a critical stage, systems transform themselves into a new pattern of behavior (de Bot, 2008). Self-organization leads to a new phenomenon called emergence, or the appearance of new properties of systems at a higher level of organization (N. Ellis & Larsen-Freeman, 2006; Larsen-Freeman & Cameron, 2008).

- *Sensitivity to onset conditions*
  L2 development is constrained by the initial condition. Relatively small differences in initial conditions may lead to larger differences in growth trajectories across individuals. The initial condition itself is also in an ongoing state of change (de Bot, 2008; Larsen-Freeman & Cameron, 2008).

These concepts and principles have informed the latest reform in the study of learner characteristics in SLA. In traditional ID research, individual factors have been treated as discrete, fixed variables and have been used to identify linear cause–effect relationships between the variables and learning outcomes in a single timeline. With the advent of the dynamic systems approach, however, variation in learners' performance has since been seen as stemming from individual characteristics mediated by context and time. IDs are no longer viewed as isolated factors independent from one another; instead, they form a complex constellation of factors that interact with each other and with context on multiple levels.

Several models are available for the ID research under the dynamic systems approach. For example, Dörnyei (2009) illustrates a framework that draws on the concept of attractors and attractor states. Cognitive systems of memory and attention—as well as affective factors such as motivation, interest, and attitudes—may serve as powerful attractors that cause the language system to gravitate toward a stable, attractor state. The stability of the system depends on the strength of the attractors, as well as on the size of the region where the attractors are concentrated (i.e. the attractor basin). A combination of individual factors, rather than factors in isolation, can assert great predictive power because they form a broader attractor basin.

Another example of ID research in the dynamic framework is seen in the recent methodological reform in researching individual variation. The volume *Motivational Dynamics in Language Learning* (edited by Dörnyei, Henry, & MacIntyre, 2015) showcases methods for researching L2 motivation when it is treated as a constantly evolving entity. One such example is the method called 'retrodictive qualitative modeling' (RQM) (Dörnyei, 2014; Chan, Dörnyei, & Henry, 2015). Using interviews, RQM reverses the traditional method of pre-selecting predictor variables and tracing their impact on learning outcomes. Instead, RQM locates salient factors retrodictively by analyzing the outcome-state of development to search for the factors that produced the outcome. By tracing salient factors from outcome states, RQM can demonstrate how different factors interact with each other, as well as with the context, in shaping L2 outcomes. The interview method in RQM follows three stages: (1) identifying learner archetypes (for example, an unmotivated learner with poor language ability); (2) selecting prototypical learners of each archetype; and (3) conducting multiple interviews with selected learners.

L2 pragmatics research should benefit from these recent methods that focus on dynamicity and complexity, because—as with learning syntax or lexis—the multiple factors that influence learning pragmatics are inherent to contexts and individuals. Co-adaptation between context and individuals might manifest even more strongly in pragmatics given the complex nature of the construct, which is inseparable from cognitive, social, and personal influences.

In L2 pragmatics, very few studies have attempted an explicit application of the dynamic systems framework. However, findings from several longitudinal, qualitative studies drawing on the language socialization framework reveal interaction among learner characteristics, context, and pragmatic development, and thus can be interpreted from the complex, dynamic perspective.

Gonzales (2013) examined the text-based synchronous CMC conversation closings between native Spanish speakers and an L2 Spanish learner on *Livemocha*, a social networking site designed for language learners, over one academic year. Interestingly, the focal participant, Bill (pseudonym), was a motivated student, but he directly expressed his dislike of participating in the *Livemocha* chat sessions, which was a bi-weekly assignment for his class. Although Bill was familiar with technological tools, he remained 'adamantly opposed to their application in the language class, since he finds them to be boring and not useful' (Gonzales, 2013, p. 108). However, despite his negative attitude, Bill gradually gained competence in conversation-closing strategies, as marked by a shift from foreshortened to extended closings. The following excerpts (Gonzales, 2013) illustrate this change. Bill's closing at the beginning of Figure 6.4 was characterized as foreshortened because he overtly announced his intention to end the conversation, neglecting rapport with the interlocutor. We observe more extended closing sequences toward the end of the study in Figure 6.5, where Bill and his interlocutor close their interaction collaboratively. Here, it is clear that Bill is working to enhance the rapport with his interlocutor by using a variety of positive politeness strategies.

Bill	*es la hora de salir, gracias* [interlocutor's name]!!
	'it's time to leave, thank you [interlocutor's name]!!'
	*** You have been switched to away
Interlocutor	hey, do u have msn??
	*** Interlocutor's IC window is closed

Figure 6.4 Chat log between Bill and his interlocutor: earlier recording (Gonzales, 2013, p. 112)

Bill	[Interlocutor's name], *era un gran placer hablando contigo!*
	Horita tengo que irme, pero te digo un consejo:
	'[Interlocutor's name], it was a great pleasure talking with you! Now I have to leave, but I'll give you some advice:'
Interlocutor	ok
Bill	*Practica tu ingles lo mas posible! Puedes tener lo que quieras si trabajas duro. Buena suerte!* Good Luck!
	'Practice your English as much as possible! You can have whatever you want if you work hard. Good luck! Good luck!'
Bill	*Ciao!*
	'Bye!'
	*** You have been switched to away
	*** interlocutor's IC window is closed
	*** interlocutor's IC window is open
Interlocutor	sorry
Interlocutor	*creo que serre la ventana sin culpa*
	'I think I closed the window on accident'
	*** interlocutor's IC window is closed

Figure 6.5 Chat log between Bill and his interlocutor: later recording (Gonzales, 2013, p. 114)

Despite his skepticism, Bill became socialized into the components of closing sequences in *Livemocha*, owing to his repeated observation of, and participation in, the sequences through online interaction. As Gonzales attests, the theory of communities of practice (Lave & Wenger, 1991; Wenger, 1998) cannot explain these findings, because the theory requires membership as a crucial element in learning, and this was missing in Bill's case. He identified very little with the *Livemocha* activities or participants in the activities. Instead, Gonzales claims that it was the 'affinity spaces' (Gee, 2004), rather than his membership, which created the framework for learning. According to Gee, affinity spaces are those in which 'what people have affinity with (or for) [...] is not first and foremost the other people using the space, but the endeavor or interest around which the space is organized' (Gee, 2004, p. 84). *Livemocha*, the cyberspace where people communicate for the common goal of language learning, fits well under Gee's conceptualization of affinity spaces.

From a dynamic systems perspective, the findings present an insightful illustration of the context–individual interaction. Linear, cause–effect relationships between learner characteristics and L2 development are not in place when interpreting these findings because Bill's reluctance toward the opportunity for practice did not result in non-learning, as the traditional paradigm would have expected. Learning did occur because he participated in systematic practice. It was the context (or Gee's 'affinity spaces') that facilitated pragmatics learning. The findings corroborate the complex theory framework that delegates central power to context in the process of language learning. The individual and context are coupled, and every change to the individual is influenced by context. Larsen-Freeman and Cameron observe:

> ...the context-dependence of complex applied linguistic systems is three-fold: language is developed in context, as use in context shapes language resources; language is applied in context, as context selects the language action to be performed; language is adapted for context, as the experience of past language use is fitted to the here and now. (2008, p. 69)

Although Gonzales's study provides a window through which the dynamic nature of pragmatic development can be observed, Taguchi (2012) more explicitly adopted the complex, dynamic systems approach to L2 pragmatics. This mixed method study traced change in abilities to comprehend implicature and produce speech acts among 48 Japanese EFL students in an English-medium university. Quantitative analyses were cross-examined with qualitative analyses of the developmental patterns observed among the eight informants recruited from the whole participant group. As shown in interviews and observation data, each of the eight cases revealed learners' unique contributions to the ongoing developmental process in their respective contexts.

From a complexity theory perspective, it is essential to understand how variation works at the individual level: why individuals do or do not conform to expected patterns. The cases of Ryota and Asako (pseudonyms), for instance, revealed interesting variation in the development of pragmatic listening. These two students had similar backgrounds and similar previous experiences. They both received grammar-based English instruction and had almost no contact with native-speaker instructors. They were shy, slow to express thoughts, and rarely spoke up in class. They also had meager social networks with other international students. Both had a sense of inferiority about their poor speaking skills as a result of comparing themselves to fluent peers.

After the first semester, Asako showed a dramatic gain in implicature comprehension; her score jumped by 11 points, when the average gain of the entire group was two points, but Ryota's score dropped by five points. While Ryota's social network remained limited, Asako successfully established her membership in the English-speaking community. She became friends with three international students who regularly came to the library to study; and soon after, it became her routine to sit at the same desk as them and do homework while eavesdropping on their conversation. This sustained listening contributed to her gain on the listening test. Asako's library routine started as a way of completing an assignment that involved recording her English-speaking experiences. Because she did not have many English-speaking friends to talk to, she needed to take advantage of her small social circle with three international students so that she could complete this weekly assignment. She sustained this social circle by participating in it every day, although her participation was rather peripheral as an observer.

In Asako's case, access to opportunities for practice was both circumstantial and strategic. It was circumstantial and context-driven because she was under the pressure of completing the assignment and met, by chance, the three international students who were willing to help her with the assignment. At the same time, her access was strategic and learner-driven because she created her own space in the group and maintained it by filling it on a routine basis. This case tells us that a combination of multiple factors—learners' personality, commitment to learning goals, subjectivity to access opportunity, and a circumstance that necessitates such access—interacted with each other and supported pragmatic development.

This case can also be interpreted using Dörnyei's (2005, 2009) L2 motivational self system (see the section on motivation). Three components—ideal L2 self, ought-to L2 self, and L2 learning experience—serve as 'attractor basins' that influence the direction and persistence of a learning behavior (Dörnyei, 2009). Asako had all three of these components in harmony. The gap between her and her fluent peers, and the sense of inferiority that she initially experienced, led to her conceptualization of the ideal L2 self and the ought-to self. Motivation stemmed from these two types of self-image and was reinforced through motivation from the third level: successful engagement with the language learning process. In Ryota's case, the two self-images might have existed, but he did not have access to the context, i.e. the actual experiences.

The eight case histories in Taguchi's book all exemplified the intricate interaction between individuals, context, and changes in pragmatic competence, confirming that there is indeed no 'single bullet explanation' for pragmatic development. These case studies represent the key features of the dynamic systems approach—dynamicity, variability, and context-dependence—and definitely describe pragmatic development when it is examined in a situated manner. A future challenge in this perspective is to go beyond simple description and to construct a concrete research design that facilitates a dynamic analysis of context and individuals in pragmatics learning. Difficulty in conducting such a study was expressed by Dörnyei a few years ago:

> Isn't the DST approach merely a descriptive model without any real explanatory power? Although we can certainly explain away any dynamic movement–stability fluctuation by bringing in concepts such as emergence, self-organization, and attractor states, does this new conceptual system and terminology really help us to understand and predict the details of the learners' behavior? That is, is the attractor landscape a useful model rather than being simply an appealing metaphor?
> (2009, p. 230)

Since this claim was made, SLA and individual difference research have made great advances in how research in a dynamic systems vein is conducted, as seen in several methods books and collections of sample studies that have appeared in the field (Dörnyei et al., 2015; Verspoor et al., 2011). Researchers in L2 pragmatics can benefit from these publications. We can explore creative ways to apply these unique methods to pragmatic analysis as a way of conducting a context-rich, situated analysis of pragmatic development.

Chapter summary and directions for future research

This chapter has discussed research developments in the last decade by describing recent studies on the role of individual characteristics for pragmatics learning and development. Common ID factors of motivation, personality, and cognitive variables (aptitude, working memory, and lexical access skill) were surveyed in the existing L2 pragmatics literature to see whether these factors explain the variation among L2 learners in their process and outcome of pragmatic development. We also discussed the effect of proficiency extensively as one of the most researched ID factors in L2 pragmatics. In the second part of the chapter, shifting from the positivist framework that conceptualizes individual characteristics as independent variables, we reviewed qualitative studies in the domain of identity to reveal how agency and subjectivity influence learners' pragmatic choices and provide a complementary explanation to pragmatic competence and development. Finally, the chapter addressed the recent complex, dynamic systems approach and reconceptualization of individual difference factors, emphasizing that the role of individual characteristics in pragmatic development is best understood with characteristics of context of learning. Below we will offer a summary of the key findings emerging from this review and implications for future research.

Proficiency—understood as knowledge of, and real-time access to, grammar and vocabulary—is a well-researched factor in pragmatics. Having a larger repertoire of grammatical structures, a large vocabulary, and highly automatized access to both helps learners' pragmatics, but effects are not uniform. Proficiency is more facilitative of production than comprehension since producing language requires greater effort, active access to grammar and vocabulary knowledge, and fast output. By contrast, parsing incoming language and judging its pragmatic meaning and appropriateness is a less active and less effortful process. Proficiency is also less important in more sociopragmatic tasks (such as appropriateness judgments of speech acts), which emphasize knowledge of cultural rules and norms, than in pragmalinguistic tasks (such as implicature comprehension), which require careful parsing of language. There is no doubt that proficiency helps but does not subsume pragmatics.

Several cognitive variables were found to underlie pragmatic performance. Lexical access skill was positively related to L2 learners' ability to process implicature quickly. In an instructional setting, working memory correlated with gains in speedy recognition of pragmatic forms; rote memory correlated with gains in planning speed when producing pragmatic forms; and grammatical sensitivity was related to speech rates in pragmatic production. General trends that emerge from these findings are two-fold. First, general cognitive mechanisms support learners' processing of pragmatic meaning and functions, thereby promoting their pragmatic performance, but different aspects of pragmatic performance were related to different cognitive abilities. Second, the effects of cognitive variables seem to be restricted to the fluency aspect of pragmatic performance measured by response time, planning speed, and speech rates, because accuracy in comprehension of implicature or accuracy/appropriacy in production of pragmalinguistic forms had no relationship with the cognitive variables. The existing pool of studies is too small to enable us to draw a definite conclusion from these tendencies, and more studies are necessary to address the interaction between types of cognitive ability and aspects of pragmatic competence. In addition, future research could incorporate a different conceptualization of aptitude, such as the one underlying CANAL-FT, to see whether creative and practical intelligence affects pragmatic abilities that also draw on adaptability and flexibility.

Similar to cognitive variables, studies on personality also exhibited a complex interplay between traits and constructs. The relationship between personality and pragmatic competence is not direct; rather, it is indirect, mediated by other modifying variables such as the aspects of pragmatic competence that are analyzed, modality of the pragmatic task (perception vs. production), learning context, and timescales. Particularly noteworthy is the mixed effect of extraversion and neuroticism on production and perception. Extraversion affected production of speech acts but did not affect perceived psychological difficulty toward the speech act scenarios. In contrast, neuroticism affected perception of speech acts but not production of speech acts. These findings suggest we should consider production and perception separately. Individual personality traits differently affect learners' understanding of pragmatic tasks and their actual performance on the tasks. Future studies can cultivate a concrete research design to explore the traits–constructs interaction.

Dynamic Systems Theory (DST) (de Bot, 2008) is a promising framework for the investigation of individual characteristics in pragmatics learning. It provides a model for exploring an interaction among different learner characteristics, as well as interaction between characteristics and context, which a traditional linear approach cannot offer. The DST perspective can also inform studies in the area of identity that are concerned with the social, historical, and cultural contexts in which pragmatics learning takes place. Future challenges lie in systematically adapting the DST methods to study pragmatics. For instance, several methods have been proposed to capture intra- and inter-individual variability as a developmental yardstick, based on the premise that development can take place only when learners have access to a variety of linguistic forms to choose from. Development is analyzed through stability and variability seen in learners' performance at a given moment, as well as through the resources—both internal and external—that learners draw on in learning. DST-specific concepts and methods such as attractor state and control parameters, correlations among variables, and phase transitions have been applied to investigate variability and non-linearity in L2 development (for example, Baba & Nitta, 2014; Spoelman & Verspoor, 2010). Because these methods typically require long-term observation with a large number of data points, most studies have analyzed genetic language abilities such as complexity and fluency, and used a task such as free writing, which allows a repeated administration of a similar task over time. We encourage future researchers to explore creative ways to apply DST methods to reveal variability, non-linearity, and connected growth among variables in pragmatic development. It is also important for researchers to explore similarities and differences between DST and other socially oriented theories such as language socialization (see Chapter 3).

Aspects of pragmatic competence analyzed in the existing studies are largely limited to speech acts, implicature, speech styles (including honorifics), and sentence-final particles. Expansion on the construct of investigation will expand the scope of literature on the impact of individual characteristics in pragmatics learning. Interactional features that routinely occur in a conversation such as expressions of alignment (for example, nodding, backchannels, and follow-up comments) are good candidates because they indicate learners' interactional competence to create synergy with their interlocutors. Because these features occur frequently, they can be traced over time to accumulate enough data points for a longitudinal analysis under the DST.

Notes

1. TOEFL is the Test of English as a Foreign Language, created by the Educational Testing Service to measure English language readiness for prospective international tertiary students (ETS, 2016). IELTS is the International English Language Testing System, co-owned by Cambridge English Language Assessment, the British Council, and IDP: IELTS Australia. It is designed to ascertain test takers' English language level for education, immigration, or workplace purposes (IELTS, 2016). TOEIC is the Test of English for International Communication, designed for measuring English language proficiency for workplace purposes and run by the Educational Testing Service (ETS, 2014). PTE is the Pearson Test of English, also designed to assess international students' English language readiness for tertiary study in English language universities (Pearson, 2014a). In contrast to the skills focus of these tests, a C-test (Grotjahn, 2014) is a type of integrative cloze procedure, where four to six short texts are used, and the second half of every second word is deleted to obtain 25 gaps per text. Test takers reconstruct the damaged text.

2. For other studies on imposed foreigner identity interfering with learners' access to opportunities for pragmatic practice and development, see Brown (2013), Hassall (2013), and Iino (1996).

7

Contexts for pragmatic development

Introduction

Expanding the scope from the previous chapter's focus on the contribution of individual characteristics to pragmatics learning, this chapter discusses the role of learning contexts in pragmatic development. The last few decades have seen the appearance of a large number of empirical studies that examined pragmatic competence and development in diverse learning contexts, including study abroad contexts, immersion settings, migrant situations, heritage learner environments, technology-enhanced learning contexts, and formal classrooms (see Taguchi, 2015a, for a review). This chapter synthesizes the existing literature in the four contexts where the current findings are concentrated: the study abroad context, the formal classroom, the technology-enhanced learning environment (for example, learning through social networking, virtual interaction, and online gaming), and the immigrant context. We will compare and contrast characteristics of these different learning contexts to highlight what features in each context can promote the learning of pragmatics.

Study abroad contexts for pragmatic development

Study abroad programs, defined as pre-scheduled, educational temporary stays in the country where the target language is spoken, have been the prime area of investigation in SLA research (Isabelli-García, Bown, & Plews, forthcoming; Kinginger, 2011; Llanes, 2011). Instigated by Freed's (1995) seminal volume, _Second language acquisition in a study abroad context_, a number of studies have analyzed the impact of study abroad experiences on L2 learning. The popularity of the study abroad research comes from the assumption that L2 learners benefit both culturally and linguistically from studying in a country where the target language is widely spoken. In a study abroad setting, learners are exposed to linguistic and cultural practices that are not easily available in a domestic classroom setting. Exposure to language input and cultural practices is considered a prime feature of the study abroad context that can facilitate L2 acquisition.

This assumption of the advantages of studying abroad in L2 learning is certainly shared in pragmatics research (see Taguchi 2016 for a review). Freed's (1995) volume has one entire section dedicated to studies dealing with the sociolinguistic aspects of language use. Around two decades later, the most recent volume on study abroad research, edited by Kinginger (2013), devotes one-third of its pages to pragmatics-focused learning (for example, acquisition of Korean honorifics and Japanese hedging expressions).

The study abroad context is considered beneficial for pragmatics learning because it offers opportunities to participate in socioculturally bound linguistic practices, which are limited in a classroom context. These practices, aided by modeling and guidance from local members, can lead to socialization into appropriate pragmatic behaviors. An additional benefit of studying abroad is the diversity of communicative situations available in that context. By interacting with locals from diverse backgrounds in different settings, learners can develop their pragmatic awareness: they come to understand that their linguistic choices are guided by the characteristics of the setting and the person to whom they are speaking, and that those choices have a direct consequence on the outcome of the interaction and interpersonal relationship. In summary, the features of the study abroad context that are believed to assist pragmatic development include: (1) recurrent opportunities to observe local norms of interaction; (2) situated pragmatic practice and instant feedback (implicit or explicit) on that practice; (3) real-life consequences of pragmatic behavior; and (4) exposure to variation in styles and communicative situations.

The benefit of the study abroad context, however, is not an entirely straightforward matter. Many studies have addressed the question 'Is studying abroad effective for pragmatic development?' and have found somewhat inconclusive results. In fact, previous studies found that learners in a study abroad context do not always outperform their counterparts in a domestic instructional context. A line of replication studies of Bardovi-Harlig and Dörnyei's (1998) work is a good illustration of this. Bardovi-Harlig and Dörnyei designed the pragmatic awareness task in which learners watched video scenes and judged grammaticality and appropriateness of speech act utterances. ESL learners in the United States were able to identify more pragmatic errors than their EFL counterparts, supporting the link between study abroad experiences and pragmatic competence. Replicating this study, Schauer's (2006) research also supports the benefits of studying abroad. Compared with EFL learners in Germany, ESL learners in the U.K. detected more pragmatic than grammatical errors, and their pragmatic awareness continued to improve during their nine-month stay in the U.K. In sharp contrast, Niezgoda and Roever's (2001) replication revealed opposite findings: EFL learners in the Czech Republic detected a higher number of both pragmatic and grammatical errors than ESL learners in the United States. The authors explained that EFL learners were sensitive to pragmatic inappropriateness because they constituted a highly motivated group enrolled on a teacher education program taught using a communicative approach.

Using exactly the same instrument, these three studies reached a different conclusion to the central question regarding the advantage of studying abroad for learning pragmatics. The contrasting findings caution that study abroad is not a uniform construct. Whether learners can take advantage of their study abroad experiences for their pragmatic development depends on their individual characteristics and the affordances that the context provides (see also Chapter 6).

We will illustrate the characteristics of the study abroad advantage by organizing extant findings according to two orientations. One is a line of research on the construct–context interaction, which includes studies that revealed mixed study abroad effects on the development of different pragmatic features under investigation. The other is the individual–context interaction. Studies in this group highlight the dynamic nature of the study abroad context, where pragmatic development emerges from an interaction between individuals and resources in the context.

The construct–context interaction in pragmatic development: different gains across pragmatic targets in a study abroad context

A group of quantitative studies using a cross-sectional design have compared pragmatic competence and development between learners in a host country and their counterparts in a domestic, formal instructional context (for example, Bardovi-Harlig & Dörnyei, 1998; Barron, 2003; Félix-Brasdefer, 2013; Félix-Brasdefer & Hasler-Baker, 2015; Matsumura, 2001; Niezgoda & Roever, 2001; Roever, 2005; Schauer, 2006; Ren, 2012; Shimizu, 2009; Taguchi, 2008c, 2011b, 2013). While several studies revealed that study abroad students are at a clear advantage in terms of pragmatic performance, others have revealed no effect or mixed findings depending on the aspects of pragmatic competence examined (for a review, see Xiao, 2015). Findings from the latter group of studies give rise to a generalization that the study abroad effect is not all-encompassing over different pragmatic targets: some aspects of pragmatic competence are more susceptible to changes than others. In this section, we will discuss this differential study abroad effect across pragmatic targets according to three contrasts: comprehension vs. production of routines, fluency vs. accuracy dimension of pragmatic competence, and pragmalinguistic forms vs. semantic strategies in speech acts.

Comprehension vs. production of routines

Routines and formulae have been discussed widely in the SLA literature under a variety of labels, including: prefabricated routines (Hakuta, 1974), formulae (Coulmas, 1981), phrasal chunks (De Cock, 1998), formulaic sequences

(Schmitt, 2004), situation-bound utterances (Kecskes, 2003), and conventional expressions (Bardovi-Harlig, 2009). Some labels refer to fixed forms (for example, 'Good luck'), while others refer to semi-fixed units, such as slot-and-frame patterns or syntactic strings (for example, 'I wanna' + verb). In pragmatics literature, Bardovi-Harlig (2012) defines formulae as recurrent expressions whose occurrence is closely bound to specific situations and communicative functions. Formulae convey the illocutionary force of a communicative act based on tacit agreements on their form, meaning, and use in a speech community.

One area where study abroad students are clearly excelling is the comprehension of routine formulae. Roever's (2005) study is an early attempt at investigating this. He compared ESL and EFL learners on the comprehension of routines, comprehension of implicatures, and production of speech acts. He designed 12 routine items in a written task, which included situational routines (i.e. fixed expressions tied to specific situations, such as 'Can I leave a message?') and functional routines that are not situation-bound (for example, 'Excuse me, do you have the time?'). A significant study abroad effect was found on the comprehension of routines. Proficiency, on the other hand, had no significant effect. In contrast, study abroad had no effect on comprehension of implicatures and production of speech acts, but instead there was a significant effect of proficiency on both. The study abroad advantage on routines was also supported by Taguchi's (2011b) study using a listening task. EFL learners who had studied abroad outperformed their counterparts without study abroad experience on the comprehension of routines.

The advantage of the study abroad context in the comprehension of routines makes intuitive sense, considering the ubiquitous nature of routines that are community-wide in use and tied to ordinary speech events. Because routines permeate our daily communication and assist our social participation, it makes sense that the development of routines is best observed in a place where the target language is spoken as an L1. The study abroad context is beneficial for the learning of routines because learners have abundant opportunities to observe linguistic patterns preferred by native speakers and to practice those patterns through daily participation in social events.

This assumption is supported by previous findings regarding a positive relationship between the amount of social contact learners have and their ability with routine formulae. In Dörnyei, Durow, & Zahran's (2004) study, interview data revealed that the development of competence in using formulae while abroad was closely related to the learners' involvement in the local community, suggesting that formula-learning is to a large extent a function of the learners' cultural integration and social networking. In another study, Bardovi-Harlig and Bastos (2011) investigated the effects of proficiency, length of stay, and intensity of interaction on L2 English learners' knowledge of conventional expressions. Intensity of interaction, measured by the reported amount of target language contact, had a significant effect on both recognition and production of conventional expressions. Interestingly, the length of residence had no effect, suggesting that the quality of social contact while abroad, not the amount of time spent abroad, matters for the development. However, more recently, Roever, Wang, and Brophy (2014) found that, when the length of residence was compared against proficiency and gender, it remained a significant factor for the recognition of routines. Finally, Taguchi, Li, and Xiao's (2013) findings also add to the relationship between formula development and language contact, but with another variable at play, namely initial-level formulaic competence. Over a ten-week study abroad period in Beijing, L2 Chinese learners gained the ability to produce Chinese formulae, but their reported frequency of encounter with target formulae situations bore no relation to the gains. However, there was a significant interaction effect on the gains between the frequency of encounter and the learners' pre-test scores, indicating that the learners who started out with low scores benefited more from the perceived frequency of contact with formula-use situations during the study abroad period. Similarly, a study by Roever (2012) suggests that not all formulae are equal: learners' recognition of some formulae (such as 'No thanks, I'm full.') improved rapidly over a brief stay of fewer than two months, whereas other formulae (such as 'Can I get you anything else?') took two years to acquire.

To summarize, in contrast to speech acts and implicatures, comprehension of routine formulae is highly susceptible to study abroad experiences. Target language exposure in a study abroad context, characterized by features such as amount and intensity of interaction, length of residence, and frequency of participation in formula-use situations, are likely to enhance knowledge of routine formulae. This is because routines are salient linguistic forms in the target language community. Since routines are closely tied to colloquial language use, they are most effectively learned through participation in recurrent communicative events while abroad.

When we turn to the production of routines, however, these generalizations are not as clear-cut. In contrast to the comprehension findings, there is evidence that the study abroad experience alone does not make a unique contribution to the production of routines. The same participants in Taguchi's (2011b) comprehension study completed a spoken DCT (discourse completion task) that presented a series of situations to which EFL learners responded by producing the target routine expressions (Taguchi, 2013). High-proficiency learners who had studied in an English-speaking country performed better than their low-proficiency counterparts with no study abroad experience. However, when equated in proficiency, the groups with and without study abroad experiences achieved the same scores, suggesting that studying abroad alone does not account for target-like production of routines. The critical role of proficiency in production is also supported by Bardovi-Harlig and Bastos (2011), who found that proficiency had a significant effect on the production of conventional expressions, but not on comprehension.

These contrasting findings suggest that the modality (comprehension vs. production) was interacting with the study abroad effect. Comprehension of formulae is possible without precise linguistic parsing, by relying on contextual cues, but the production of the same expression requires some extent of grammatical analysis. Morpho-syntax and lexis must be accurate in production so that the meaning encoded in the expression is understood correctly. Incorrect linguistic representation, as seen in wrong word order or word choice, could lead to misunderstanding. For instance, the utterance 'Do you have the time?' is a common expression when asking about the time of day. Without the article 'the', the utterance meaning changes completely. Because of this demand on grammar, production of formulae is affected by the combination of proficiency and study abroad experiences. Exposure to the target community can lead to the production of native-like patterns. At the same time, high-level proficiency is necessary in production for the control of linguistic expressions. Indeed, Bardovi-Harlig (2009) used a recognition task paired with a production task (oral DCT) and found that learners showed poorer performance on the production of conventional expressions than on recognition.

In summary, the study abroad context is advantageous for the learning of routines and formulae because of their strong associations with social situations. Learners in a study abroad context have exposure to the situations in which routines occur. As a result, they are able to understand the function of highly context-dependent, culture-specific routines. This study abroad advantage, however, does not hold the same across different task modalities. The linguistic demands posed by the production, as opposed to the comprehension, of routines, highlight proficiency as an additional influence on formulaic competence. The degree of native-like selection (Pawlye & Syder, 1983), an index of formulaic competence, seems to reveal more in production than in comprehension because production data shows learners' ability to select exact strings preferred in the speech community.

Fluency vs. accuracy in L2 pragmatics

While small in quantity, a few longitudinal studies have traced development in the knowledge and processing dimensions of pragmatic competence separately, revealing a different pace of development between the two in a study abroad context. In these studies, pragmatic knowledge was operationalized as accurate and appropriate comprehension and production of pragmatic meaning, while pragmatic processing was operationalized as fluent and speedy performance of pragmatic functions (see Chapter 3 for descriptions of these two dimensions).

Using a listening test with multiple-choice questions, Taguchi (2008c) compared development in comprehension of implicature between EFL and ESL learners over a five- to seven-week period. Both groups made significant gains in both comprehension accuracy (measured by scores) and fluency (measured by response times). However, when the effect size was compared, the two groups showed reversed patterns of development. The EFL group made a greater degree of gain on accuracy than on fluency, but for the ESL group the gain size was much larger for fluency than it was for accuracy.

The accuracy–fluency contrast in development while abroad reveals a more complex picture when the initial-level proficiency is included in the analysis. Using a spoken DCT, S. Li (2014) compared development in the speech act of request between intermediate and advanced learners of Chinese during a semester abroad in Beijing. Although both groups made comparable gains on the appropriateness of request (scored on a five-point scale), only the advanced group made gains in fluency (measured by speech rate when producing requests). When the size of gain was compared, the advanced group made a slightly larger improvement on fluency than on accuracy (effect size of .54 for the fluency gain and .49 for the accuracy gain). The results further confirm the study abroad advantage on the processing dimension of pragmatic competence.

These findings suggest that the type of practice available in a study abroad context has differential effects on the development of pragmatic knowledge and processing. The processing of pragmatic functions involves the coordination of a number of underlying processes, including linguistic, cognitive, and pragmatic processes, which must be automatized to achieve speedy comprehension and production. These underlying components may take longer to be automatized in a foreign language context because of the limited processing practice available in that context. In contrast, abundant incidental processing practice available in the target language context provides an advantage for faster-paced progress in performance fluency.

Means vs. forms in speech acts

Another area where study abroad experiences may result in different degrees of learning is that of means vs. forms used to realize a speech act. Clark (1979) distinguishes two types of conventions: conventions of means and conventions of form. Conventions of means are semantic strategies used to realize a speech act. For instance, a speech act of request can be achieved by asking the hearer's ability to perform the activity. It can also be achieved through discourse moves such as preparing the hearer for the upcoming request by saying: 'Can I ask you a favor?' or laying out a problem leading to a request (for example, 'I forgot to bring my cell phone.'). Conventions of form, on the other hand, concern the exact pragmalinguistic forms used to perform a given illocutionary act. Examples include syntactic constructions such as: 'Could you' + verb or 'I wonder if you could' + verb, as well as modification devices used to mitigate the imposition, such as 'if possible' or 'maybe'.

Longitudinal studies conducted in a study abroad context revealed unbalanced development between forms (exact pragmalinguistic forms used in a speech act) and means (semantic strategies used to realize a speech act), with acquisition of the former lagging behind that of the latter. Learners usually start out with a limited range of pragmalinguistic forms, often seen in the overgeneralization of a form across a range of communicative functions. They eventually expand their pragmalinguistic repertoire by adopting a new form–function mapping into their systems, but this process is slow. In contrast to pragmalinguistic development, learners' strategies and tactics in performing the target illocutionary act usually display faster, incremental progress.

A classic study that illustrates this non-parallel development is Bardovi-Harlig and Hartford's (1993a) work, which examined international students' development of suggestions and rejections during academic advising sessions in a U.S. university. Over a semester, learners became able to use discourse moves in advising sessions, for example nominating courses that they wanted to enroll in and offering credible reasons when rejecting advisors' suggestions about courses to choose. However, learners struggled with appropriate pragmalinguistic forms of rejection; indeed, they continued to use direct expressions with no mitigations when rejecting. These findings indicate that learners became familiar with certain strategies that are appropriate for advisees to use, but they did not achieve a full control of the exact pragmalinguistic tools necessary to implement target speech acts. This is likely to be due to the lack of advisor correction and modeling of appropriate pragmalinguistic behaviors, while advisors' reactions helped learners understand which discourse moves were acceptable or unacceptable (for example, a lengthy explanation coming from the advisor when he/she rejected the student's course nomination).

The slow acquisition of forms compared with semantic strategies was also found in more recent studies. Using DCTs, Warga and Schölmberger (2007) traced development of the apology speech act among L2 French learners during a ten-month study abroad period. Learners initially justified their behaviors and did not offer to repair the damage they caused in the speech act. However, learners' use of these strategies improved over time. Justifications decreased in frequency from 80% to 20%, while offers of repair increased from 50% to 70%. In contrast, learners' use of the exact pragmalinguistic forms remained underdeveloped, as shown in their continuing overuse of strong expressions (such as the use of *très* meaning 'very'). In another study, Schauer (2007) examined the use of internal and external modifications in the speech act of request in L2 English over a nine-month study abroad period. The use of external modifiers (for example, small talk, flattering, showing consideration) approached native-level use after four months. What remained underused were internal modifiers involving lexical and syntactic downgraders, such as consultation devices (for example, 'Would you mind') and imposition minimizers (for example, 'a bit').

More recent findings are also consistent with this trend. In Félix-Brasdefer and Hasler-Barker's (2015) study, learners of Spanish expanded on their range of compliment strategies during their eight-week stay in Mexico, approximating native-speaker patterns as seen in the increased use of the *Que* ADJ/ADV NP pattern (What (a/an) ADJ/ADV NP). However, their use of adjectives remained the same. They showed either underuse or overuse of certain adjectives. They frequently used *bello* (lovely) and *bien* (well), which were absent in the native-speaker data, whereas their use of *padre* (cool) remained underused compared with native speakers' use.

Ren's (2012) study, on the other hand, adds to these findings by demonstrating that the salience of strategy type also affects the pace of development. He documented the development of L2 English learners' refusal strategies over one academic year during their stay in England. Development was traced on two aspects: (1) the use of main refusal strategies (strategies that convey the force of a refusal, such as 'I can't make it.' or 'Is it possible to do it next time?'); and (2) adjuncts to refusals (forms that do not carry the force of refusal but modify the main refusal strategies, such as 'I'd love to.'). Learners improved in their use of refusal strategies during study abroad, but they continued to underuse adjuncts. Because the main refusal strategy is a single, necessary component in the refusal, its salient role in the speech act probably assisted the learners' strong development. Adjuncts are optional elements attached to the main strategy and mitigate the force. Because one can still convey the illocutionary force without adjuncts, it is possible that the learners did not attend to them as much as they did to the main strategy. As a result, development of the adjuncts was slower.

In summary, previous findings indicate that learners can improve on their tactics and coping strategies in the target speech act while abroad. Learners in these studies became able to initiate suggestions in advising sessions, which essentially reduced the chance of them rejecting the suggestions coming from their advisors (Bardovi-Harlig & Hartford, 1993a). When apologizing, they learned to offer repair for the damage they had caused rather than justifying their misconduct (Warga & Schölmberger, 2007). They also learned to soften their requests by establishing a friendly atmosphere with small talk and expression of consideration before bringing up the request (Schauer, 2007). Although knowledge of the logistics specific to a pragmatic event may develop relatively quickly, acquisition of the precise pragmalinguistics for encoding illocutionary intentions is a slow process, even while in the target language context.

These findings corroborate the previous literature about characteristics of adults' pragmatic development. Unlike children, whose pragmalinguistic and sociopragmatic competences develop simultaneously, adult learners are already fully competent in L1 pragmatics; they possess a rich foundation of universal pragmatic knowledge and strategies (Levinson, 1983; Mey, 2001). For instance, they already have implicit knowledge of politeness and formality, face-saving strategies, and sociolinguistic variability in linguistic choices. The challenge for adult learners is to relearn new form–function relations appropriate to the L2, which requires that they learn new pragmalinguistic forms, along with the social contexts in which they occur. The study abroad context assists learners in developing an understanding of strategies involved in communicative acts through their daily participation in the acts. But this context may not be sufficient in promoting the learning of the exact syntax and lexis involved in the acts.

If pragmalinguistic sophistication does not occur in parallel to the attainment of semantic strategies, what factors could close the gap between the two? One promising factor is direct feedback and modeling provided by community members. Salience of the target form–function mappings, promoted through direct attention to forms, could facilitate the pace of pragmalinguistic development. Qualitative studies conducted in a study abroad context have revealed a range of social encounters contributing to the acquisition of new form–function associations. We will discuss these qualitative studies in the next section, focusing on the individual's contributions to the context of pragmatics learning.

The context–individual interaction in pragmatic development while abroad: learners' experiences in a study abroad context

The complexity of the study abroad effect demonstrated in the previous section suggests that study abroad and at home contexts cannot be treated as dichotomized categories or be directly compared against each other. It is not the context *per se* but the configuration of the context that requires a close analysis. Moving away from the 'context-as-a-black-box' approach, there is a need to conduct a bottom-up analysis of the elements and resources in the context to uncover how they support pragmatics learning. Such a bottom-up approach can, in turn, shed light on individual variation in pragmatic development. In fact, previous studies found that not all learners gain equally well while abroad, leading to a generalization that learners' individual characteristics and their interface with context mediate pragmatic development (for example, Brown, 2013; Hassall, 2015; Kinginger, 2008).

Research in the past decade has seen a clear shift in the treatment of the study abroad context from a categorical label to a site that involves a complex configuration of elements, including learners, community members, settings, input, social practice, and institutional programs. These elements are dynamic, constantly changing, and shaping the pathway of pragmatic development. Take social practice as an example: social practice is a generic term that refers to community-based activities that learners participate in. Immediacy and frequency of social practice are considered as a prime benefit of a study abroad context. Indeed, previous studies revealed that participation in social practice actually led to strong pragmatic performance. However, the types of social practice examined in those studies are so diverse that the standard term does not cover all the experiences within different practices. We have studies on learners' participation in homestay interactions (for example, Cook, 2008; Kinginger, 2008; McMeekin, 2011; Shively, 2013), service transactions (Shively, 2011), dorm room conversations with a same-age peer (Diao, 2016), conversation sessions with an assigned partner (Salsbury & Bardovi-Harlig, 2000), extra-curricular activities (Taguchi, 2015c), and interaction with tour guides (Jin, 2012). Each of these situations represents a unique configuration of linguistic resources, participant membership, organization of talk, and sociocultural features; and as a result, the form of pragmatics learning occurring in each practice is unique. Hence, it is critical for researchers to investigate what actually goes on in each social practice. A fine-tuned analysis of elements of a practice, when cross-examined with pragmatic gains, could reveal what types of opportunities for pragmatic development are available in each practice and how those opportunities characterize pragmatics learning specific to a given practice.

Several qualitative, longitudinal studies have provided an account of the intricate relationship between pragmatics learning and contextual specifics. Some of these studies have adapted the concept of community of practice (Lave & Wenger, 1991; Wenger, 1998) and the language socialization approach (Duff, 2007; Schieffelin & Ochs, 1986) (see Chapter 3 for the review of the language socialization approach and related studies). The community of practice is defined as a group of people who gather to learn things as they interact regularly. Lave and Wenger argue that only through the process of sharing experiences with the group do the members develop personally and professionally. The language socialization approach, on the other hand, attests that linguistic and sociocultural knowledge develop simultaneously through participation in routine, social activities (Duff, 2007; Schieffelin & Ochs, 1986).

Drawing on these frameworks, several studies have provided micro-genetic analyses of pragmatics learning in situated social practices. Cook (2008), cited in Chapter 3, documented learners' socialization into Japanese speech style through their interactions with their host families. Shively (2011) analyzed service encounter exchanges self-recorded by L2 Spanish learners in Spain. She found that some learners acquired request-making forms in service exchanges by observing other customers and adopting their forms, while others learned the forms through feedback from their host families. Diao (2016) analyzed dorm room conversations between L2 Chinese learners and their Chinese roommates. She revealed learners' developing understanding of affective sentence-final particles as gendered practices through peer socialization (see Chapter 3).

The strength of these studies is that they were able to illustrate a direct connection between context and learning by documenting learning as it was occurring in a social practice. This 'learning-as-participation' perspective is also related to the concept of discursive practices or 'talk activities that people do' (Young, 2008, p. 69). According to Young, learning manifests in our changing engagement in discursive practices. We learn by participating in context-specific discursive practices. During the process of participation, we acquire linguistic and interactional resources that are necessary to construct interaction and enable our participation in practices.

The perspective of discursive practices also informs pragmatics learning. Social practices that learners engage in contain a range of pragmalinguistic and sociopragmatic resources, examples being: request-making forms in service-encounter routines (Shively, 2011), style-shifting in homestay talk (Cook, 2008), and affective particles as a gendered language use (Diao,

2016). These resources are specific to activity, place, and purpose of interaction. Pragmatic competence involves one's ability to use pragmatic resources specific to practice. Pragmatic development takes place when the learner participates in a range of social practices that involve different types of pragmatic resources.

The data from McMeekin (2011) below illustrates the acquisition of pragmatic resources specific to a given practice. This study investigated L2 Japanese learners' socialization into using speech style in a homestay setting. Japanese speech style has two forms: the polite form (the *desu/masu* form) and the plain form (casual form). Because classroom teaching emphasizes the polite form, learners tend to stick to the polite form as their default style and do not attempt to use the plain form. This was also the case with McMeekin's participants, but one participant, Mandy, gradually added the plain form to her repertoire through recurrent participation in a common social practice at home, namely cooking.

During a cooking activity, the plain form often occurs as a way of expressing spontaneous feeling and surprise. For example, the utterance *oishii!* (It's delicious!) usually takes the plain form because it is emphatic and shows excitement. Despite this common use, Mandy was not able to use the plain form for the emphatic purpose at the beginning. Instead, she used the polite *desu/masu* form *oishiidesu*, which resulted in an unnatural sounding tone without emphatic voice. Later recordings showed Mandy in a similar exchange around cooking and food tasting with her host mother. On these occasions, she was gradually socialized into using the plain form by imitating and repeating her host mother's plain form.

Figure 7.1 (McMeekin, 2011) gives an illustration. In line 1, the host mother asks a question in the plain form (*oishii?* Literally, 'Is it good?'). Mandy responds to it by repeating the host mother's plain form. The host mother acknowledges her response in the following turn, signaling that Mandy's response, which includes the plain form, is accepted.

---

1 **HM** *oishii?*
           Is it good?
2 **M**   *un oishii*
           Yes it's good
3 **HM** *yokatta*
           That's good

Figure 7.1 Conversation between Mandy (M) and her host mother (HM): earlier recording (McMeekin, 2011, p. 28)

Figure 7.2, from Mandy's last recording, further illustrates her control of the plain form in expressing emotion (McMeekin, 2011). In line 1, she asks a question in the polite form (*kore wa nan desu ka*). In lines 5 and 7, she shifts to the plain form to express her feeling about the food (*oishii*). This style shift occurs without her host mother's prompting.

1 →	M	*kore wa nan desu ka*
		What is this?
2	HM	*tabete mite kudasai kore wa piman kore hai* ((putting some on plate))
		Try it and see. This is a pepper. Here.
3	M	*doomo*
		Thank you
4	HM	*tabereru?*
		Can you eat it?
5 →	M	*un oishii*
		Yes it's good
6	HM	*oishii?*
		Is it good?
7 →	M	*hai oishii*
		Yes, it's good

Figure 7.2 Conversation between Mandy (M) and her host mother (HM): later recording (McMeekin, 2011, p. 29)

Taguchi (2015c) is another study conducted in a study abroad context on the acquisition of Japanese speech style. She analyzed 18 learners' peer-to-peer conversation data collected before and after study abroad (a period of three months). One participant from China, Lin, demonstrated dramatic progress in the use of different speech forms (polite, plain, and honorific forms). Interview data revealed Lin's sustained involvement in three different communities: a university club, a peer discussion group, and a restaurant where she worked as a waitress. By traversing these social networks composed of distinct settings, goals, memberships, and participant structures, Lin gained access to different types of context-rich speech style practices. The university club served as a place for practicing the polite and plain forms and the senior–junior relationship indexed by the forms. The peer discussion group involved multicultural members who got together to discuss current issues in their common language, Japanese. In this close friendship group, Lin learned how to speak in the plain form, a speech style of which she had almost no experience prior to coming to Japan. Her role in the restaurant, on the other hand, provided opportunities to practice honorifics with customers, which were not available in other places. Lin's case tells us that the local community is structured according to different sub-communities or domains of practice, each of which presents opportunities to practice different patterns of speaking (the polite form, the plain form, and honorifics). Lin had to master forms of speech unique to individual communities in order to participate in their shared social activities and to establish identities within them. In this process, culturally appropriate speech forms were both the means and the outcome of her participation in the social practices.

Finally, Shively's (2013) study documented one L2 Spanish learner's development in understanding and creating humor in a study abroad context. Analyses of the learner's conversations with his host family and a Spanish-speaking friend revealed three changes over one semester: (1) a decrease in failed humor; (2) a decrease in deadpan humor (i.e. humor without contextualization cues); and (3) an increase in humorous revoicing. These changes happened through the learner's observations of others' humor and reflection on others' reactions to his humor. Friendship with the interlocutor, accompanied by shared experiences, attitudes, and interactional styles, were the primary reasons for the learner's humor development, which illustrates the co-adaptation between the individual and resources in context.

As illustrated above, the current literature has confirmed that study abroad experiences are complex and dynamic, and that they interact closely with individual learners in shaping their pragmatic development. Although the study abroad context can provide valuable venues for learning new pragmatic information, which often goes beyond what students learn in textbooks or classroom instruction, the context alone is not sufficient to understand what actually leads to pragmatic development. A close examination of elements and resources involved in a given social practice, as demonstrated in the studies reviewed here, helps to discern the contextual configuration that facilitates pragmatics learning. Pragmalinguistic forms and sociopragmatic norms configured in a given practice are learned through recurrent, sustained participation in the practice. Future research into study abroad contexts should continue to cultivate ways of uncovering this complex context–individual interaction in pragmatic development.

Although we have presented the study abroad context as a useful site for pragmatics practice, we should also be mindful about the learner and community factors that may constrain learners' access to practice while abroad. In terms of the learner factors, a line of studies on identity and subjectivity has shown that learners do not always conform to the pragmatic norms practiced in the local community. They sometimes reject adopting normative use of honorifics, gendered speech, direct ways of speaking, or informal speech when these norms are incongruent with their L1 cultural values or their sense of self (Ishihara & Tarone, 2009; Kim, 2014; Iwasaki, 2011; Shively, 2011; see Chapter 6).

Host community factors may also limit learners' access to practice. Several studies found that race and gender discrimination constrained learners' access to the local community and preferred living arrangements (Churchill, 2003; Knight & Schmidt-Rinehart, 2002). Other studies showed that cultural stereotypes function as a barrier to providing and receiving target language input. Members in the host culture may treat international visitors differently than in-group members and interact with them using different pragmatic norms (Brown, 2013; Hassall, 2013). Brown's (2013) study on L2 Korean honorifics revealed that native-like patterns of honorifics were not available to learners because learners were positioned as foreigners. The 'foreigner' identity assigned to the participants positioned them in the 'peripheries of Korean society' (p. 290), which resulted in patterns of honorific use that flouted native-speaker norms. This was seen when a teacher used *panmal* (honorific forms) when addressing Korean students, whereas she used *contaymal* (non-honorific forms) when addressing the L2 learner. Similarly, Hasall's study (2013) showed how the 'foreigner' identity constrained learners from adopting local norms of address forms during a sojourn in Indonesia. The participants were positioned as *bule*, an Indonesian term referring to western foreigners, which bears a disparaging tone. The identity of 'outsiders' that was assigned to them led to the learners' belief that they did not have to practice appropriate use of the address term system.

These cases of restricted access to social practices further reinforce the complex and dynamic nature of the study abroad context. Pragmatics learning is not always guaranteed for everyone. It is the product of contextual affordances and learners' positioning that determine whether learners can take advantage of the context to grow pragmatically while abroad.

Classroom contexts for pragmatic development

Moving away from the focus on the target language environment, this section turns to formal classroom settings as a site for pragmatics learning. We will focus on incidental pragmatics learning in which pragmatic features are not the focus of instruction but are learned incidentally from naturalistic input and output opportunities in classroom interactions.

The classroom context generally has a poor reputation when it comes to pragmatics. Because of the instructional focus on grammar, vocabulary, and the four skill areas, pragmatics has been an under-represented area of formal learning. A consensus in the literature is that classroom discourse does not provide rich representations of a variety of communication situations and registers. Textbooks often contain unauthentic language samples with limited information about pragmatic norms and sociocultural language use (Diepenbroek & Derwing, 2013; McConachy & Hata, 2013; Nguyen, 2011).

The assumption of the classroom as a pragmatics-poor environment, however, is seriously challenged in the current era of globalization. In a growing number of classes and programs, the target language is used as the medium of instruction and communication. English is a prime example of this trend. With the recognition of English as a world language, teaching *in* English is increasingly emphasized in countries where English has no official status but is the international language for global communication. In these countries, English-medium classes and curricula are expanding rapidly under the national policy goals of internationalization (for a review, see Graddol, 2006; Smit & Dafouz, 2013; Doiz, Lasagabaster, & Sierra, 2013; See Chapter 9). These English-medium classes certainly offer opportunities to use English for authentic communicative purposes, both in academic study and classroom interaction.

Indeed, several studies have examined this English-medium educational context to identify specific types of classroom resources available for pragmatics learning (for example, Kääntä, 2014; Nikula, 2008). These studies have demonstrated that incidental pragmatics learning does occur in an English-medium classroom when pragmatics is not the intended learning target. Nikula (2008) analysed content-based, English-medium physics and biology classes in middle schools in Finland. She described numerous instances of pragmatic practices in English. Students used mitigations ('Well, then...') or discourse markers ('Yeah, but...') when they disagreed with their classmates. They also used rising intonation to soften the tone of disagreement. When asking questions, some students avoided direct questioning and instead used a pre-sequence such as 'Can I ask something?' These instances show how content-based classes support opportunities to practice pragmatics in conversational participation. Through the recurrent speech events of asking questions and discussing academic matters, students learn how to interact in a way that builds a rapport with the teacher and peers.

More recently, Kääntä (2014) described how students in CLIL (Content and Language Integrated Learning) classes in Finnish middle schools correct errors made by a teacher. When students initiate corrections and display their epistemic positioning (i.e. claiming and demonstrating content knowledge), such a situation highlights the asymmetrical epistemic hierarchy, with students momentarily trying to renegotiate the hierarchy by correcting the teacher and the teacher re-establishing a position of authority through his responses to the students.

Kääntä observed that when students notice the teacher's mistakes, they first display an embodied noticing. Their gaze usually shifts from the screen to their materials on the desk, followed by an intensely focused gaze toward the screen, which is sometimes accompanied by facial expressions such as frowning. These physical movements and facial expressions embody students' stance toward the noticed (incorrect) features. Since they are on display in public, they become perceivable to other students and serve as resources for interaction.

When the correction occurs, Kääntä observes that it is produced in a format of a negative interrogative yes/no question, which strongly preferences alignment (Heritage, 2002). This initiation highlights the problem but also 'displays that [the student performing the correction] is a knowing questioner who is orienting to her focal recipients as knowing as well' (p. 98). In the subsequent turn, the teacher thanks the student for pointing out the problem. Here the teacher displays his duty as a teacher, i.e. evaluating the student's correction, which serves to re-establish the teacher's status.

As illustrated above, correction sequences occur seamlessly in routine classroom interactions. Learners perform this face-threatening act in multiple ways, for example by displaying the embodied noticing via gestures and facial expressions, as well as by correcting errors in a negative yes/no question, which is designed to seek alignment from the teacher. This analysis of student-initiated correction goes beyond the simple speech act analysis of who conveys which illocutionary force in what manner. It is the product of how students display their epistemic positions and renegotiate the asymmetrical epistemic hierarchy by demonstrating their knowledge in class. Most notably, the act of correction is co-constructed between the teacher and students: students try to negotiate their epistemic positions and the teacher re-establishes his epistemic status through his reactions to the students.

In addition to these studies conducted in a foreign language environment, classroom-based studies in a second language context have revealed opportunities for incidental pragmatics learning. For instance, Hellermann (2009) documented learners' attempts at rapport-building by recording disagreement and correction strategies employed by an ESL student in a multilingual classroom. Analyses of the student's interaction with her peers revealed that, although the student initially used the direct 'no' to correct her interlocutor, she gradually adopted mitigation devices (for example, hesitation and hedging) and showed her orientation toward mutual face-saving. The student also expanded on the functional use of 'no' by using the form for a variety of discourse functions such as repair and humor.

The three studies described above show that there are certainly occasions for producing a dispreferred response (for example, disagreement and correction) in a classroom where the subject is taught in the target language. Through repeated participation in these face-threatening acts, learners gradually develop understanding of the interpersonal nature of classroom exchanges. These studies also suggest that classroom discourse involves a variety of form–function mappings. As shown in Hellermann's study, the learner's use of 'no' expanded in function over time, from direct correction and disagreement to repair and humor. This finding indicates that, contrary to the previous assumption, the classroom context does indeed offer a rich variety of opportunities for meaning-making in pragmatics. In the case of Kääntä's (2014) study, the speech act of correction is a dynamic, situated, and sequenced activity, emerging from students' position toward co-construction of knowledge with the instructor and peers.

While small in quantity, existing findings exemplify the opportunities for incidental pragmatics learning in an input-rich lesson taught in the target language. These opportunities may be covert, but they do come to the surface through a close analysis of features of classroom discourse and interaction patterns. Previous findings then present counter-evidence to the claim about the pragmatics-poor classroom context. Yet, given the paucity of existing findings, more research is necessary to examine this claim by analyzing classroom discourse and interaction through a pragmatics lens.

It is beneficial for such research to focus on a chain of speech events or forms that occur repeatedly in class. Nikula's analysis of group discussion, Kääntä's analysis of Initiation–Response–Evaluation sequences, and Hellermann's form-to-function analysis of the linguistic unit 'no' serve as a model for such research. This approach also resonates with the framework of discursive practices (Young, 2008) discussed in the previous section. The classroom context comprises numerous discursive practices, all of which have unique characteristics. By participating in those practices, learners acquire pragmatic resources specific to a given practice. Unlike the study abroad context, the classroom context may reveal the practice–learning link more clearly because it is a controlled environment. Class recordings give us complete data of interaction occurring in the classroom. Salient pragmatic behaviors in the data can be traced over time to see how learners develop in pragmatics, and what factors in the classroom—teacher feedback, modeling, and peer-to-peer interaction—contribute to the development.

Another point of consideration for classroom-based pragmatics researchers is the need to attend to both pragmalinguistic and sociopragmatic aspects of development. So far, classroom research has mainly focused on pragmalinguistic changes, and the sociopragmatic aspect has been neglected. We see this tendency in Nikula (2008) and Hellermann's (2009) studies, which analyzed syntactic mitigations and hedging in face-threatening acts. In addition to the studies cited above, R. Ellis (1992) revealed changing linguistic structures in the speech act of request among young ESL learners, and Ohta (2001) revealed learners' progress with acknowledgment to alignment expressions using sentence-final particles in a Japanese classroom. These studies have revealed learners' developing knowledge of form–function mappings, but it is not clear whether their development could extend to form–function–context mappings, or aspects of sociopragmatics, which involves making a linguistic choice corresponding to situational variety. In fact, R. Ellis (1992) concluded that his participants did not develop in sociopragmatics because they used the same request forms, no matter who they were speaking to.

Sociopragmatic development is not easy to investigate in a classroom because learners interact with the same interlocutors—teachers and classmates—in the same classroom setting. Without involving people of different social status and distance, it is difficult to examine how learners change their pragmatic behaviors across settings and participant structures. One possible approach is to observe learners interacting with people outside a typical classroom setting. Some previous work is available in this area (Ishida, 2009; Tateyama & Kasper, 2008). Tateyama and Kasper invited native-speaker guests to a Japanese classroom. They found that a teacher's requests to guests reflected a wider range of interactional sequences, linguistic forms, and speech styles than those used with their students. Hence, by having native-speaker guests or conversation partners, learners can observe how requests are structured differently in different situations and speaker relationships. A challenge in a classroom setting is making this type of practice sustainable so that learners have exposure to different registers and styles.

Technology-enhanced contexts for pragmatic development

In this section we will review recent developments in technology-enhanced environments for pragmatics learning. This section has great relevance to Chapter 8 (teaching and assessing pragmatics), because many of the technology-based studies in the current L2 pragmatics literature are concerned with instruction. Research in the last decade has broadened the body of technology-related literature in SLA, which has demonstrated the potential of technology in expanding the current scope of data collection and analysis, instructional methods, and assessment approaches (for a review, see Chun, Kern, & Smith, 2016). In the area of pragmatics, a range of new venues of research and teaching has emerged from this trend, including computer-assisted pragmatics instruction, social networking sites, online gaming, and mobile-based learning (see Taguchi & Sykes, 2013, for a review). These new forms of environment have expanded the options for researching and teaching pragmatics. At the same time, they have generated new insights about the process and products of pragmatic development.

These technology-enhanced environments are distinct from a study abroad and classroom context in that they provide direct, speedy, and individualized access to situated communicative practice. They can allow participants to develop a sense of community through shared activities. Take a virtual participatory environment as an example, such as multiplayer online games. This type of context can serve as a hybrid environment that takes the learner beyond the limitations of both study abroad and formal classroom settings. A virtual environment can arrange multiple key elements of pragmatics learning in one setting, which a traditional classroom cannot support easily. These elements include contextualized language use, interaction with consequences, self-discovery learning, and experience-based learning. In addition, learners do not have to travel to gain access to the target language community. Learners can log on to the virtual world and simulate a variety of participant roles with built-in avatars in diverse social settings. In a study abroad setting, access to practice is not guaranteed to everyone because learner- and community-driven factors may constrain access. A virtual environment can be leveraged as a solution to such a barrier, as long as researchers strategically incorporate learning objectives through game-based tasks and prompts. By participating in goal-oriented interactions, participants are also socialized into virtual communities. In short, the advantage of virtual interactions is their immediacy and convenience of access to realistic communicative practices directed to individual needs, which is not easily attainable in a classroom or study abroad context.

This section will discuss these technology-enhanced options for pragmatics learning by surveying a range of recent literature in this direction. We will illustrate how recent technological advancements have broadened the provision of opportunities for pragmatics learning through interaction, simulation, and multimedia environments. We will start with the literature in the area of computer-mediated communication (CMC).

Computer-mediated communication (CMC)

CMC involves a collection of tools, for example email, chat, blogs, social networking sites, discussion forums, and video/web conferencing programs such as Skype and Google Hangouts, which allow learners to interact with other language users through computer technology. Unlike standalone software programs or websites, CMC tools typically facilitate interaction using the language produced by the users themselves, rather than the language provided by the computer (Levy & Stockwell, 2006).

CMC technologies have proliferated as a promising tool for the analysis of learner data since the 1990s. Recently, this has been taken to a new level by Web 2.0 applications (for example, Facebook and Twitter), which have made social networking easier and more flexible (Thomas & Peterson, 2014; Wang & Vásquez, 2012). CMC tools have several advantages for research and teaching. First, we can examine learners' naturalistic communication across physical distance with other users of the target language. Such a context often presents a wide range of discourse options, as well as opportunities for peer feedback and modeling. In addition, CMC tools allow us to collect data from multiple sources at once so we can develop triangulated understanding about the L2 learning process. For instance, we can analyze learners' output coupled with the input from their interlocutors. By cross-examining learners' and their peers' linguistic choices, we can examine how input regulates learning and the roles that noticing and attention play in learning.

Taking advantage of these features, a number of recent studies have analyzed CMC for a range of SLA topics, including focus-on-form (Yilmaz, 2012), task-based learning (González-Lloret & Ortega, 2014), multiliteracy skills and sociopragmatic awareness (Blattner & Fiori, 2011), alignment and negotiation (Uzum, 2010; Piirainen-Marsh & Tainio, 2014), and identity (Kitade, 2014). In fact, Wang and Vásquez's (2012) review attests that Web 2.0 technologies have broadened the scope of computer-mediated SLA research, shifting from early studies focusing on language abilities to more recent topics of identity, learner autonomy, online collaboration, interactional alignment, and communities of learning. Several meta-analyses exploring the CMC–SLA link have also appeared. Lin (2014) synthesized findings from 59 primary studies and revealed a positive, medium-sized effect of CMC intervention on L2 learning. However, a range of factors—learner proficiency, interlocutor type (peers, instructors, and native speakers), task type (for example, information gap, decision making), and research setting (second or foreign language context)—moderated the effect of CMC-based interaction.

The benefit of CMC technologies has also been acknowledged in L2 pragmatics. A decade ago, Belz's (2007) seminal article specified three main applications of computer mediation to pragmatics research and teaching: (1) the provision of authentic and meaningful pragmatic practice; (2) the longitudinal documentation of pragmatic development; and (3) the implementation of pedagogical interventions in pragmatics instruction.

Indeed, these three areas have continued to show a powerful growth, as is clear from the sharp increase in empirical studies on pragmatic interaction, development, and teaching, in a wider range of computer-mediated environments. Belz and Kinginger (2003), Kakegawa (2009), and González-Lloret (2008) provided some of the early studies in this trend. These studies analyzed learners' development through rich descriptions of asynchronous dyads between learners and their native-speaker peers. More recently, Gonzales's (2013) study, reviewed in Chapter 6, analyzed pragmatic practices occurring in textual synchronous CMC outside of an instructional context. She analyzed *Livemocha*, a social networking site for language learners, as an affinity space (Gee, 2007) that affords opportunities for L2 use. She documented one L2 Spanish learner's development in the use of politeness strategies in conversation closings (see Chapter 6 for the illustration of the learner's interaction). Jenks (2012) also analyzed online conversations among L2 English speakers, in the chat room *Skypecasts*, and showed that the participants were quick in spotting communication problems. They brought the problems to their partner's attention immediately via laughter, joking, or ridicule, indicating that using reprehensive demeanors was the norm of online chatting examined in the study. Tsai and Kinginger (2015) analyzed advice-giving and -receiving sequences occurring in CMC-based peer review sessions. They showed that the asymmetrical relationship between the advice giver and receiver was compromised through the use of various face-saving strategies and the co-construction of meaning. These pragmatic demeanors emerged from the speakers' concerns toward maintaining interpersonal relationships. Finally, in Cunningham's (2016) study, learners of German in a U.S. university received direct instruction of German request-making forms and participated in web conferences with German-speaking professionals using *Adobe Connect Pro*. There was no significant improvement in the directness level and external/ internal modifications in learners' requests produced during video conferencing immediately after the instruction, but several learners demonstrated a profound development after the instruction.

Takamiya and Ishihara (2013), on the other hand, revealed the benefit of blogging for intercultural communication and pragmatics learning. Blogs are a form of asynchronous CMC in which people express themselves through free-form web posting. A learner of Japanese in a U.S. college first received explicit instruction on speech acts and then discussed what she had learned on blogs with Japanese college students in Japan. The learner's developing pragmatic awareness became apparent over time. Her posts demonstrated instances of noticing Japanese-specific pragmatic behaviors (for example, a white lie used in a refusal) and her struggle with accepting those behaviors. Responses from native-speaker peers helped the learner gain an emic perspective on this culture-specific practice. The advantage of the asynchronous nature of blogging, as opposed to synchronous CMC, is the assisted use of metacognitive strategies such as planning and monitoring: learners can organize their thoughts in advance before making them publicly available, which in turn maximizes their learning opportunity.

More recent work has illustrated pragmatic norms of interaction emerging among participants during computer-mediated exchanges. González-Lloret (2016) analyzed text-based synchronous CMC between L2 Spanish learners and expert Spanish speakers via Yahoo Messenger and WhatsApp (instant messaging mobile applications). The data revealed instances where participants constructed emotion using a variety of linguistic and typographical resources (emoji, laughter, use of capital letters, elongated words, and use of punctuation marks), as well as code-switching.

Figure 7.3, from an interaction between 'Kid', a learner of Spanish and 'Remi', a Spanish speaker, displays such multilingual interaction (González-Lloret, 2016). In lines 144–145, Kid conveys his wish ('I want to go with you') and produces a sad emoji, emphasizing the emotion behind his wish. Remi responds to it by saying 'then come (if you want to come with me)!!' Her response is taken as sarcasm because they both know that Kid cannot come to Remi's place because of the physical distance. In line 147, Kid responds to this sarcasm by changing his sad face to a crying face, which upgrades his emotional stance. However, Remi does not orient to this emoji as Kid's display of sadness. Rather, she attends to the playfulness of Kid's expression and responds with a token of laughter. Following this, she produces the speech act of promise, i.e. a commitment to a future action. The action that Remi commits to is about 'drinking', which is the reason why Kid wants to come to accompany Remi. Although this action is not explicit in Kid's initial wish statement, Remi infers it through Kid's use of sad emoji. Kid accepts Remi's promise as a solution to his 'unhappiness' by changing his sad emoji to a happy face and using the exclamation mark (ok!) in his acceptance token.

144	**Kid** (11:25:07 AM):	*quiero ir contigo*
		I want to go with you
145	**Kid** (11:25:13 AM):	😞
146	**Remi** (11:25:13 AM):	*pues ven!!*
		then come!!
147	**Kid** (11:25:17 AM):	😭
148	**Remi** (11:25:20 AM):	*jajaja*
149	**Remi** (11:25:35 AM):	*no te preocupes, yo me tomare una copa a vuestra salud!!*
		don't worry, I will have a drink to your health!!
150	**Kid** (11:25:40 AM):	*ok!* 😊

Figure 7.3 Chat log between Kid and Remi (González-Lloret, 2016, pp. 299–300)

In a brief 30-second exchange like this, it is remarkable to see how the learner skillfully displays his change of emotion turn-by-turn by manipulating multiple emoji and punctuation marks. The learner produces the emoji in response to his interlocutor's reaction, which indicates that emotions are negotiated and co-constructed sequentially by the learner and the expert speaker during the course of interaction.

Co-construction of pragmatic acts in a CMC environment is also seen in Kim and Brown's (2014) study on the use of Korean address terms and speech forms. Learners of Korean interacted with multiple Korean speakers via email, Facebook, Skype, Twitter, and Kakao Talk (a mobile messaging app) over a three-month period. Transcripts of CMC interactions and retrospective interviews revealed that CMC provided a context for learners to practice address forms with Korean speakers and develop competence in their use. The situated use of the address forms also assisted learners in establishing personal relationships with Korean speakers.

The most notable finding was that the learners manipulated various address terms to modulate specific social meanings and their desired identities, but the identities, and hence the address forms used to project them, were negotiated and co-constructed between the learners and their online interlocutors. When interacting with her former music instructor, Grace, a beginner-level learner, initially used *panmal* (the non-honorific form) and the kinship term *enni* (older sister), which is reserved for family members and intimates of superior age. Grace expressed positive attitudes toward the term ('kinda cute') and used it as a signal of solidarity and closeness. However, her use of this kinship term and *panmal* speech did not follow Korean norms because these forms do not usually apply to a relationship with a status superior, such as an instructor, even if the relationship becomes close. When the instructor replied to Grace's message, she did not downgrade her speech to *panmal*. In addition, she corrected Grace's use of intimate speech to the polite speech style, signaling her 'instructor' identity. Later transcripts showed Grace's use of the honorific form *contaymal* and formal address terms (for example, *sensayngnim* 'esteemed teacher') instead of *enni*. These data indicate that pragmatic norms in CMC encounters are not fixed: they are dynamic and open to negotiation.

The fact that 'appropriateness' is negotiated rather than fixed has important implications for the way that we conceptualize pragmatic competence in CMC environments. Critically, it demonstrates an obvious need for researchers to go beyond crude comparisons between L1 and L2 use when discussing whether L2 use is pragmatically appropriate. When compared directly with L1 usage, Grace's use of *enni* would simply be labeled as inappropriate, incorrect, or deficient. However, when contextual factors (such as Grace's identity and the reactions of her interlocutors) are taken into account, we see that things are more complicated. In some ways, Grace's use of *enni* may actually be appropriate (seeing as Professor Kang was seemingly accepting of it) and socially skillful since it allowed her to create more intimate relationships.

CMC serves as a space for learners to cultivate identity. In the case of Grace, by addressing her instructor as *enni* and using non-honorific speech forms, she tried to 'transit from the identity of student to that of friend' (Kim & Brown, 2014, p. 279). This attempt did not meet with the instructor's approval, eventually leading to Grace's self-corrected pragmatic behaviors. This change in her pragmatic behaviors, however, goes beyond just the level of acquisition of pragmatic forms. It represents an intricate change of her pragmatics state at multiple levels:

using forms strategically to project desired identity, reflecting on the impact of the forms on the interlocutor, and adapting the forms corresponding to the interlocutor's expectations. This negotiation of pragmatic norms and identities becomes apparent in the analysis of naturally occurring CMC interactions.

In summary, CMC has established itself as a profitable context for the analysis of pragmatics learning and pragmatic language use. CMC technologies generate a context-embedded, socially consequential target language practice for L2 learners. Previous research has analyzed learners' use and development in a variety of pragmatic features, for example speech act strategies, address terms, honorifics, conversation closings, interactional particles, and expressions of emotions, in both synchronous and asynchronous interactions. The next section will focus on gaming and immersive digital environments as another type of computer-mediated interaction. Similar to email, chat, and blogs, online digital environments such as multiplayer online games and social virtualities can serve as fertile sites for intercultural communication and socialization into community practices.

Games

Over the last decade, gaming has grown rapidly in diversity and accessibility across the globe. Digital games have thrived along with the expansion of the internet, as seen in the current boom of Massively Multiplayer Online Games (MMOGs) and Social Networking Games (SNGs). Genres of these games are diverse, including action, adventure, and role-play, in different player configurations, such as solo, multiplayer, and massively multiplayer. These games, available in many of the world's major languages, attract millions of users worldwide. Multilingual communication occurs routinely in these global gaming environments as game players interact with each other while engaging in game tasks. This prominence of digital games has sparked strong interest among researchers and instructors who wish to harness the power of digital games for L2 teaching and learning (for example, Cornillie, Thorne, & Desmet, 2012; Gee, 2007; Squire, 2011; Reinhardt & Sykes, 2014; Sykes & Reinhardt, 2013).

Following this trend of game-mediated L2 language learning, Sykes and Reinhardt (2013) proposed a three-dimensional framework that categorizes research on digital games. The framework involves three categories of research: game-enhanced, game-based, and game-informed, which are distinguished mainly by the functional characteristics of the game under investigation.

According to Reinhardt and Sykes, game-enhanced research investigates how commercial games not purposed for education can support opportunities for L2 learning, and how those affordances can inform traditional, formal L2 pedagogy in turn. For example, games such as *World of Warcraft* and *Final Fantasy* provide learners with opportunities to interact with a large number of target language speakers for the purpose of playing games. In these gaming environments, learning is an incidental byproduct of a learner's interactions with the game and its associated activities shared among participants. Game-based research, on the other hand, is concerned with designing a game for pedagogical purposes to elicit specific L2 learner behaviors as learning objects. The advantage of this approach is that researchers can target specific aspects of language by manipulating design features. Designers of game-based environments can draw on insights from vernacular game behaviors and design principles when developing learning activities and tasks. An example of this is *Zon*, a multiplayer online learning environment designed to teach Chinese language and culture through gameplay. It provides a narrative-based curriculum in which learners interact with non-player characters during their journey through China. The last category, game-informed research, aims to apply game-generating qualities, such as playfulness, to rule-based, goal-oriented classroom teaching. Essentially the first two categories guide game-informed research: the game-enhanced research reveals game-specific experiences and interactional characteristics, and the game-based research demonstrates how those features can be applied to a classroom to enhance learning.

Although research on gameplay and its potential for L2 learning has flourished in recent years, pragmatics radically lags behind this trend with only a few studies available in this area, all by Julie Sykes and her colleagues (Holden & Sykes, 2013; Sykes, 2009, 2013). All of Sykes's studies fall into the category of game-based learning, in which the author(s) implemented pedagogical games specifically designed to teach pre-selected pragmatic features in existing Spanish classrooms. Hence, in these studies, interaction did not occur 'in the wild' as in the studies of game-enhanced learning. This semi-structured format of gaming is unlikely to afford the same level of authentic, coherent discourse practice as in the vernacular games. However, the clear objectives and goals embedded in the design of the game could ensure, at least in principle, the type of pragmatics learning that was expected to occur through game-based interaction.

Sykes's (2009, 2013) pioneering work explored the potential of digital games in multi-user virtual environments (MUVEs) as a site for learning speech acts. She developed *Croquelandia*, a three-dimensional, immersive game-based space. This digital space emulated Spanish-speaking worlds where learners can practice requests and apologies while interacting with computer-generated avatars. These pragmatic practices were embedded in the learning space as goal-directed, problem-solving tasks. After a few sessions of gameplay, a written DCT was administered as a measure of learning outcomes. Results revealed only a small change in the choice of speech act strategies. The degree of learning was much greater for apology than request, reflecting the formulaic nature of apology that required less effort to learn. The fact that there was only a minimal change with more complex request-making forms suggests that simple exposure to in-game activities may not prove fruitful without systematic focus-on-form and feedback.

Sykes's more recent work focused on this feedback as part of in-game features. Holden and Sykes (2013) created the mobile video game called

Mentira to teach Spanish pragmatics in a collaborative environment. The goal of the game is to solve a murder mystery by collecting clues from a number of non-player characters (NPCs) in the game. Each NPC has a unique preference of interaction style. Some characters prefer a direct style of communication, while others prefer an indirect manner. Success in getting useful clues depends on learners' abilities in manipulating different pragmatic strategies to interact differently with each character. In addition, learners have to complete various speech acts (for example, agreement, refusal, and apology) with each of the NPCs to progress through in-game tasks. Pragmatically appropriate linguistic choices lead to more clues and successful gameplay, whereas inappropriate pragmatic choices result in roadblocks or game-over experiences.

Mentira was used in fourth-semester Spanish classes in a U.S. university. The efficacy of *Mentira* was evaluated by analyzing gameplay data, in-class observations, interviews, and written feedback. The authors found that learners had difficulty in noticing NPCs' feedback because it was too subtle. As a result, they redesigned in-game interactions to exaggerate the feedback, making it more salient to the learners. This modification, based on learners' experiences, generates invaluable insights for the future design of mobile games for pragmatics learning. When combined with assessment of learning outcomes, such gameplay adjustment can also help to address Reinhardt and Sykes's (2014) original question for game-based learning: how do specific game designs afford particular L2 learner behaviors and learning?

Holden and Sykes's work closely aligns with the trend of mobile technologies in education in general. The last two decades have seen an expansion of literature on mobile technology in language teaching, as seen in the emergence of the acronym MALL (mobile-assisted language learning) (Sotillo & Stockwell, 2013). In addition, over 300 publications have appeared on this topic since the 1990s (Burston, 2013). Mobile devices such as smartphones, iPads, and laptop computers have gained prominence as media of instruction owing to their widespread market and the 'anytime, anywhere' feature of convenience. Mobile devices offer deep connection to place, ubiquity of access, and a personalized learning experience. Holden and Sykes's attempt took advantage of these characteristics of mobile-based learning. The *Mentira*-based curriculum was unique in that it involved a visit to a local neighborhood where the game's story was based. Players gathered clues while visiting local sites to solve the mystery. The connection of the fictional game world and the real world played a critical role for learning, as it made the interaction with simulated characters authentic and meaningful.

Another recent attempt at game-based learning is found in Si's (2015) work on teaching Chinese to heritage learners. Although this study did not specifically target pragmatics, the simulated virtual environments created using the game engine Unity (Unity Technologies, 2015) could profitably serve as an interactive site for pragmatics learning. Si designed four environments with 2.5D graphical projections for children (aged six to eight). Instead of using the mouse-and-keyboard or touchpad interface designed for adult learners, Si incorporated the Microsoft Kinect camera so that the child can use the camera to interact with the system and with other users. The Kinect camera enables embodied interface: by using his/her own physical movements, the user can control the physical movements of a virtual character. Because the characters are modeled in 2.5D, when the Kinect camera is used, the characters directly mimic the user's body movements. As a result, the characters display a richer set of movements compared to those in the 2D environment. Because the Unity game engine does not support voice chat, Si used Teamspeak 3, a popular voice-based chat service for gaming, to create a voice-chat server. With this application, users can talk to each other and communicate using gestures and body language. They can solve problems collaboratively and improve their language skills as a byproduct.

Of the four practice environments developed, the third one, 'school café', can serve as a space for simulated pragmatic practices. In this environment, the user can walk around the school cafeteria and talk about food and school activities in Chinese. The user can also collaborate with another user and they can engage in physical activities together, such as picking up a cup and moving it to the counter, pushing tables around, or moving a heavy box on the ground. We can imagine a variety of speech acts occurring in these activities, such as requesting, suggesting, complaining, and expressing feelings. These activities allow the user to practice sentences and words associated with these speech acts. They are also designed to add fun to the game.

As illustrated above, there is definitely a small but emerging effort being made to develop an interactive, input-rich, self-directed, and playful context that can facilitate learning of pragmatic behaviors. One area where the virtual gaming context excels compared with other technologies or learning contexts (such as study abroad and the classroom) is meaningful, timely, and individualized feedback. Pragmatic feedback is often difficult to provide because of its face-threatening nature. Classroom instructors may correct students' grammar, vocabulary, and pronunciation, but they often hesitate to give negative feedback on pragmatics due to their fear of risking their relationship with students. Teachers' reluctance to correct pragmatics is similar to host country members' avoidance of providing pragmatic feedback to international students and foreign visitors (for example, Barron, 2003).

Digital gaming environments can offer a solution to the challenge of giving pragmatic feedback when the feedback is pre-programmed in a way that the system automatically responds to learners' pragmatic choices. This is seen in Holden and Sykes's work with *Mentira*. When participants make a wrong pragmatic choice, NPCs in the game provide implicit feedback by not conforming to the participants' requests or taking away their rewards (clues). Through these situated interactions, learners become aware of the results of their pragmatic choices and learn to select pragmatic behaviors appropriate to specific situation and character. In-game feedback helps reshape learners' understanding of pragmatics by presenting the opportunity to modify their pragmatic behaviors, based on the NPCs' reactions. As Holden and Sykes (2013, p. 158) claim, 'key to providing meaningful pragmatic feedback for the learner is attaining an emotional response that is indicative of a need or desire to adapt L2 pragmatic behaviors in order to produce the intended illocutionary force and maintain successful interactions'. Feedback in gameplay is likely to cause this emotional effect because it is the direct consequence of learners' own choices of action embedded in their virtual experiences.

Gaming can serve as a place for meaningful, personalized learning, where learners practice pragmatic strategies using available resources, adapt their pragmatic strategies to diverse interactions, and even retry an entire interaction for a different outcome. Holden and Sykes summarize the advantage of game-based pragmatics learning, as opposed to classroom-based learning, in the following:

> ...learners can compare their own pragmatic behaviors with the pragmatic system(s) of the language being learned. Providing individualized learning experiences that are responsive to learner choices and player variability represents a significant step away from the use of one-size-fits-all, memorized semantic formulae towards true pragmalinguistic and sociopragmatic competence.
> (2013, p. 160)

This section has described recent developments in game-based pragmatics learning. Two other areas of research, game-enhanced learning (incidental L2 learning in recreational games) and game-informed learning (application of gamefulness to L2 pedagogy), are still extremely limited in terms of empirical findings. More future research is needed, perhaps with a renewed conceptualization of pragmatic competence in gameplay interaction. Existing research in general SLA areas has situated gaming as a cultural and discursive activity, and analyzed participants' collaborative management of resources during gameplay. Participants construct interactional sequences involving a range of communicative acts, such as complaints, requests, suggestions, assessments, and blaming (for example, Newton, 2011). Sociocultural factors such as power, relationship, role, position, and identity are also in play and affect the patterns of interaction (Piirainen-Marsh & Tainio, 2014). Because there are no stable, isolated speech act strategies that construct a communicative act, it is best to apply the discourse-based approach or the concept of interactional competence (Young, 2008, 2011) to analyze pragmatic interaction in a gameplay environment. Analysis of how players co-construct pragmatic meaning turn-by-turn, by drawing on linguistic and interactional resources available around them, will tell us how game-mediated pragmatics learning occurs 'in the wild'. The resources and patterns of interaction identified in the analysis can turn into game-informed learning when we apply those principles to develop pedagogical materials.

Finally, empirical data is considerably limited regarding the cause-and-effect relationship between learners' participation in CMC and increased pragmatic competence. Sykes (2009, 2013) is the only existing study that directly evaluated the effect of gaming on pragmatic gains using a pre-post design. Results revealed progress in the production of apology strategies, but not with request forms, leading the author to conclude that pragmatic practice in the virtual world did not produce intended outcomes. Given the dearth of available findings, however, this conclusion should be tabled until more studies using an experimental design directly compare the degree of learning between computer-mediated interaction and other instructional settings.

Workplace and immigrant contexts for pragmatic development

The workplace is becoming increasingly mobile and intercultural, and, as a result, communication often extends beyond geographical boundaries, involving people from different cultures and languages. Effective workplace communication is therefore critical in order to establish a collegial community and promote organizational productivity. Workplace communication is institutional and interpersonal in nature (Yates, 2010). It is institutional because it occurs in a goal-oriented situation in which institutional values and roles impact individuals' linguistic choices. (See Drew & Heritage, 1992, for characteristics of institutional talk and Bardovi-Harlig & Hartford, 2005, for empirical studies of institutional talk.) At the same time, workplace communication is interpersonal because it is a means by which individuals connect with each other. This dual nature of workplace language use reiterates the critical role that pragmatics plays within workplace communicative competence. To function effectively toward shared institutional goals, one needs to develop abilities to adapt to institutional norms of interaction and make linguistic choices accordingly, while considering a variety of situations, interlocutors, and modalities of communication.

The multicultural workplace, particularly within the context of immigrant workers, has recently attracted interest as a site for L2 pragmatic analyses and development (for example, Dahm & Yates, 2013; Holmes & Riddiford, 2011; Riddiford & Holmes, 2015; Yates & Major, 2015). Because immigrant workers come to a foreign country as permanent residents or future citizens, their pragmatic needs are inherently different from those of study abroad students or sojourners. Indeed, Yates and Major's (2015) interview data from immigrants in Australia uncovered their unique pragmatic needs, i.e. the types of sociopragmatic and pragmalinguistic skills that they perceived as necessary to function successfully in English. Those pragmatic needs were: participating in small talk, understanding indirectness, being social and informal, and being flexible with pragmatic norms. Timpe-Laughlin, Wain, and Schmidgall (2015) also synthesized a range of social- and business-oriented tasks in the workplace that are critical for employees to master. Those tasks include: emails, reports and proposals, telephoning and phone messaging, small talk, discussions, and presentations. Pragmatic-functional competence has been identified as a critical competence in accomplishing these tasks. The tasks and skills are mostly about how to adapt to the workplace, something that is not addressed in typical L2 pragmatics studies that involve classroom learners. These areas go beyond the level of pragmatic skills, and extend to life skills that immigrants have to master in order to establish membership in the workplace community.

Indeed, the workplace is one of the primary sociocultural contexts in which immigrants become socialized into new pragmatic norms, interactional patterns, and discourse systems. Yet, aside from descriptive studies of workplace pragmatics (for example, Bilbow, 1997; Holmes, 2000; Holmes & Stubbe, 2003; Miller, 2008; Yates, 2005, 2015), studies that examined L2 speakers' pragmatic development and socialization in a workplace context are considerably limited in the literature. D. Li (2000) is one of very few available studies. Adapting the language socialization perspective, the author investigated development of the request-making behavior of one Chinese immigrant woman in an inner-city immigrant job-training program in the United States. The 20-week training program offered clerical courses focusing on office skills, computer literacy, and accounting. The focal participant, Ming, was a newly arrived immigrant, who had a college degree in Chinese language and literature from mainland China. At the end of the training program, she obtained a job as a clerical assistant in a medical equipment company. During the period of study, Ming's request-making behavior, documented through audio recordings of naturalistic interactions, journals, and field notes, exhibited a clear shift from indirect to direct ways of asking. At the beginning, Ming's requests were ambiguous and ineffective to the extent that her interlocutors were not able to understand the illocution. Ming often provided background information and reasons only, and waited until her interlocutors offered to help by guessing her request intention. Her indirect communication style gradually changed as she became socialized into the community norms of directness.

This socialization process was grounded in her strong commitment to adapting to the target culture so she could receive fairness and personal respect. For instance, she asked her boss to hire more people because of the heavy workload imposed on her. After several attempts, she learned that hinting strategies did not work in this type of situation and that she had to express her needs directly. Similarly, when her co-workers treated her disrespectfully, she spoke up at the meeting for better treatment. She gradually adopted the 'American way' of communicating in the workplace, which she described as 'directly, truthful and things a little bit sweet' (D. Li, 2000, p. 75).

This study shows that immigrant workers' pragmatics learning is part of their socialization process into the workplace culture. The request-making behavior that Ming had to acquire was not supplementary pragmatic knowledge often taught in foreign language classrooms or instructional studies. It was grounded in Ming's basic survival needs with important real-life consequences.

Success of this speech act was crucial for her because it had a direct significance for gaining a fair workload and personal respect from her co-workers. This needs-based pragmatic development is a unique characteristic of migrant worker situations. When we analyze pragmatics learning among immigrant workers, we need to explicitly incorporate *consequentiality* as part of the analysis. In instructional studies or classroom settings, researchers primarily focus on 'locution' and 'illocution' of speech acts, i.e. what forms to use to convey what intentions, and often neglect 'perlocution', i.e. the actual effect of an utterance on the listener. In workplace pragmatics, however, the perlocutionary effect is at least equally important. A speech act inevitably produces an effect on the listener, intended or not, and causes the listener to react in a certain way. Appropriateness and effectiveness of a speech act is directly reflected in the perlocution, i.e. whether or not the speaker can convey illocutionary force successfully and can observe the desired outcome of the act.

Riddiford and Joe (2010) documented this needs-based pragmatics development. The study examined immigrant workers' acquisition of requests during a five-week in-class training program followed by a six-week work placement in New Zealand. The in-class training sessions helped participants learn the characteristics of workplace interactions, focusing on several speech acts. During the work placement period, participants came together once a week and discussed pragmatics-related problems that they had encountered while working. Participants' development in request-making behaviors was assessed with DCTs, role-plays, interviews, and recordings of their workplace conversations. Participants' progress in request-making was found in their increased use of various grounders (i.e. instances of providing a reason for a request), external modifiers (for example, 'Excuse me' and 'Can I have a quick word?'), and internal modifiers (for example, 'I wonder if' and 'if possible'). These findings suggest that pragmatic knowledge learned in class becomes relevant once participants enter a workplace, where high-stakes speech acts such as requests occur frequently in everyday interactions.

Because available findings are extremely limited, future research should look toward the workplace to gain unique insights about pragmatics learning specific to workplace culture. Such research will also generate pedagogical implications in terms of how to teach sociopragmatic skills to prepare immigrants for their transition to the local community. Examples in this area can be found in the Skilled Migrant Program in New Zealand, which involves a blend of classroom instruction, individual reflection, and interaction in the workplace (for example, Holmes & Riddiford, 2011; Lam, Cheng, & Kong, 2014; Riddiford & Joe, 2010; Riddiford & Newton, 2010). Instructional materials used in this program incorporated authentic conversations recorded in New Zealand workplaces, which were carefully selected according to participants' needs. Riddiford and Joe's study, cited above, is an example of this blended program.

In another study, Lam et al. (2014) surveyed materials developed by the government and commercial publishers to teach workplace communicative competence in multicultural settings in Hong Kong. Three spoken genres (formal meetings, presentations, and telephoning) and three written genres (emails, memos, and letters) were the most frequently used genres in Hong Kong workplaces in published research (based on a survey of 2,000 working professionals). However, textbook resources tended to overemphasize the communicative function of making and handling complaints at the expense of other genres such as making an appropriate phone call and conducting a meeting. Some materials were also found to be lacking in input (for example, linguistic expressions used to conduct a business meeting) and instead focused on production-based tasks. Examples were often provided in an isolated, decontextualized manner. The boundary between business and personal email writing was not always consistent, as well as the distinction between formal and informal messages. These findings point to areas where current materials are limited and thus require improvement for teaching effective workplace communication.

Job interview skills are another critical area of pedagogy in the workplace context. Louw, Derwing, and Abbott (2010) implemented instructional intervention on job interviews. Participants were Chinese-speaking engineering job candidates in Canada. A panel of experts who had experience with human resources and hiring evaluated the candidates' mock job interviews and identified their problems. The problems were used to prepare instructional materials, which involved explicit teaching of common interview questions and effective interview behaviors. After the instruction, the panel assessed the candidates' skills using a five-point Likert scale over a range of categories (for example, self-introduction, rapport management, tempo, and expression of enthusiasm). This instructional intervention is authentic because it is based on the real-life need to find a job. As such, the consequence of learning is immediate to the participants. The instruction is also authentic in that it is motivated by the societal problem of immigrants being unemployed and needing to improve their potential for obtaining a position. Interview training fills this need, by making candidates aware of the pragmatic rules and rituals of job interviews, and using them to their advantage.

Chapter summary and directions for future research

This chapter has presented the current L2 pragmatics literature in four distinct contexts: study abroad settings, formal classrooms, technology-enhanced environments, and multilingual workplaces. We discussed the benefits of study abroad experiences by analyzing opportunities for pragmatics practice available in the contexts. We reviewed observational classroom-based studies that analyzed patterns of classroom discourse and interaction (for example, teacher talk, routines, and peer-to-peer interaction) from a pragmatic perspective. We also discussed the relationship between digitally mediated technologies and pragmatics learning by surveying literature pertaining to a range of technology-enhanced contexts (i.e.

social networking, mobile games, and virtual environments). The last section highlighted pragmatics learning taking place in the international workplace among immigrant workers.

The current literature best represents the study abroad context as a complex, dynamic environment of multiple elements shifting and interacting with each other in shaping pragmatic development. The study abroad context certainly offers opportunities for direct contact with community members, but whether learners can use these opportunities for their pragmatic advantages depends on their individual characteristics, stance, and investment. We have now established a generalization that not all learners acquire pragmatic competence in an equal manner. Because of the large individual variation in the outcome of study abroad programs, analysis of the individual–context interaction has become the norm of current study abroad research.

We can even extend the analysis to individual–context–construct interaction. Recent studies have revealed variation in the pace of acquisition across pragmatic features. Mixed patterns of development were found in the contrasts between different modalities (comprehension vs. production), aspects of pragmatic competence (knowledge vs. processing), and aspects of speech act realization strategies (forms vs. means). Hence, it seems that the structure of the learning object itself, along with the types of opportunities offered in a study abroad context, determines the course of pragmatic development. Because very few studies have traced change over multiple pragmatic constructs over time, future effort should be concentrated in this direction. When variation in development is actually found in pragmatic targets, a follow-up question to pursue is why such variation has occurred within the same participant group, in the same physical context, over the same time period. This question will help us understand the properties of a study abroad context: why studying abroad facilitates the learning of certain pragmatic features but not others. Understanding the developmental variation across pragmatic constructs could serve as an alternative way to understand the context–construct interaction in L2 pragmatics research.

The domestic formal classroom context, on the other hand, has long been characterized by scant opportunity for pragmatic practice. However, this generalization needs to be revised with a motivated investigation into routine communicative events and activities involved in a classroom. This research direction is important, considering that much second/foreign language learning still takes place in formal classrooms and within school curriculums. As we have illustrated in this chapter, recent studies have analyzed content-based classes, where the instructor and students use the target language (for example, English) for authentic, classroom-based communication. They use L2 as a shared language to discuss academic matters, to present and defend their point of view, to give feedback, to correct mistakes, and to display support for each other. As such, classrooms are full of communicative acts that the teacher and students perform in order to conduct their everyday business of teaching and learning. We would be remiss if we did not target these practices in order to better understand pragmatic development. Routine classroom activities and the types of pragmatic language use involved in those activities should be examined closely in order to meaningfully interpret the process and outcome of pragmatics learning from those activities. A handful of studies described in this section certainly serve as guidelines for researchers who wish to cultivate concrete methods in classroom-based pragmatics research.

The advancement of technology has transformed our way of researching pragmatics. Future research should utilize available technologies in full, and adapt new forms of technology that can be used for investigation. Various tools described in this chapter (for example, CMC, online games, video-conferencing), as well as other under-represented tools (for example, online DCTs and role-plays, corpus linguistics, eye tracking) can be used to enhance investigations of L2 learners' pragmatic language use.

In addition to the scope of technology use in research, the field needs to expand its understanding of the use of technology in teaching. Specifically, a great deal of work needs to be done to uncover how technology-based mediums do (or do not) lead to increased pragmatic abilities. More stream-lined instructional intervention research can be conducted to directly compare gains between technology-based pragmatics learning and other types of learning. Such research could help us understand which features of online participation (for example, interactivity, authenticity, meaningful language use, comprehensible input, self-directed learning) produce strong evidence of learning. A growing number of studies have pursued such investigation in general areas of L2 learning, not specific to pragmatics (deHaan, Reed, & Kuwada, 2010; Piirainen & Tainio, 2009; see Sykes & Reinhardt, 2012, for a review). These studies could certainly inform research design in L2 pragmatics. Pragmatic competence in such a study can be reconceptualized to focus more on interactional features (for example, turn-taking), alignment strategies, discourse competence, adaptability, and responsiveness to better reflect the type of abilities being practiced in technology-based learning contexts.

Finally, in line with global trends, the international labor pool has expanded dramatically. This pool includes immigrant workers and people working for international companies, as well as those who are connected to a global system of networking via technology. We have described how their pragmatic needs are unique compared with adult L2 learners in school settings (the most frequently studied participant population in L2 pragmatics research). The consequentiality of immigrant workers' pragmatic behaviors indicates that pragmatic needs and perlocutionary effects, which are often neglected in mainstream research, should receive more attention in future. Future research could be designed along these two axes—needs-driven pragmatic behaviors and consequences of these behaviors—to examine how the two factors interact with each other and jointly shape pathways of pragmatic development. As found in D. Li's (2000) study on a Chinese immigrant worker, indirect manners of request-making did not satisfy the participant's communicative needs because her intention was often unclear and people were not able to respond to her needs. This perlocutionary reality essentially shaped her learning as she abandoned indirectness in speech and adapted more explicit, conventional request forms.

Language socialization is a suitable theoretical approach to illuminate such a process because pragmatics learning occurs as part of socialization into the norms of workplace interaction. Another useful guiding framework is the functionalist approach to SLA. The functionalist approach emphasizes L2 learners' meaning-making efforts as a driving force of L2 development (Mitchell, Myles, & Marsden, 2013). In other words, L2 learners set out to achieve their personal needs, and in this goal-oriented process they exploit their linguistic and contextual resources to create meaning. The end of this meaning-making process is a shift from pragmatic to syntactic modes of expression, as revealed in the previous studies (for example, Bardovi-Harlig, 2000b; Klein & Perdue, 1992). Learners start out with a heavy reliance on context and scaffolding from others, and gradually shift to more elaborate morpho-syntactic coding when expressing meaning. The functionalist perspective could shed light on pragmatic development among immigrant workers. Instrumental and integrative needs arising from their workplace settings direct their attention to the pragmalinguistic and sociopragmatic resources that are necessary to achieve their needs. Pragmatics learning can be a byproduct of the trial-and-error process of testing these resources to their advantage. Future research is needed to examine this interaction between communicative needs, contextual affordances, and pragmatic development.

Although we have focused our attention in this chapter on these four different contexts, we have no intention of presenting them as exhaustive categories of context in pragmatics research. Instead, we believe that context should go beyond common categories of study abroad programs, classrooms, technology-enhanced platforms, and workplaces, extending to a broader range of instructional arrangements including immersion, cultural exchange programs, heritage speaker communities, and lingua franca interactions. These contexts are distinct on their own, presenting unique challenges and opportunities for pragmatics learning. An immersion context, for example, offers rich, naturalistic in-class input and interaction practice, but it is different from a study abroad context in that it is predominantly composed of speakers of the same language. Hence, learners in this context might operate on their native norms of interaction when speaking in the target language. In a lingua franca context, on the other hand, speakers of different L1s communicate in the shared language. As such, norms of interaction, standards of politeness, and conventions of practice are constantly negotiated among speakers. Pragmatic behaviors emerging in the lingua franca context are not those from either L1 or L2 but are rather hybrids of multiple styles and strategies (see Chapter 9). Heritage speakers also come from unique speech communities. Heritage learners are bilinguals who grow up acquiring two languages—home language and societal/school language—and are concerned with the study and maintenance of their minority languages (Valdés, 2005). This circumstance gives rise to a unique context where pragmatic development occurs concurrently within two languages and cultures (see Chapter 9).

Recent SLA literature has undergone a shift from the traditional reductionist approach that focuses on a simple cause–effect explanation apart from context, to a more ecological approach that considers context as part of the systems under investigation and explores reciprocal relationships between contexts and individuals. This trend is seen in the current theoretical paradigms that take a complex, dynamic systems view toward L2 development (Larsen-Freeman, 2012; Verspoor, de Bot, & Lowie, 2011). Within this framework, the focus is not on the learner or on language but on the learning process in which learners 'soft-assemble' their language resources while interacting with a changing environment (Larsen-Freeman & Cameron, 2008, p. 158). We believe that future pragmatics research should align itself more closely with this complex, dynamic systems perspective, and commit to investigating the intricate interaction between elements, agents, and systems, and their connection with context, as they jointly shape the pathway of pragmatic development.

8

Teaching and assessing L2 pragmatics

Introduction

In this chapter, we will discuss instructed learning of L2 pragmatics in formal settings, as well as assessment of learners' pragmatic ability. The first part of the chapter on teaching L2 pragmatics reviews research on how pragmatics can be taught, what aspects of it are taught, and how teaching relates to learners' development. It discusses teaching approaches under the umbrella of explicit and implicit instruction for speech acts, extended discourse, routine formulae, and implicature. We will also sketch out what aspects of pragmatics can most profitably be taught to learners at different proficiency levels; the aim of this is to encourage reflection on pragmatics from a syllabus design perspective, since curricular thinking on L2 pragmatics instruction is still sorely lacking.

In the second part of the chapter, we will discuss assessment of L2 pragmatics. We will show how pragmatics fits into constructs of communicative competence, and review the work that has been done so far on the testing of pragmatic abilities.

Teaching L2 pragmatics

Research into instruction in L2 pragmatics has been conducted for almost as long as research into uninstructed learning of L2 pragmatics, with the first major instructional study appearing in the mid-1980s (Wildner-Bassett, 1984). In her state-of-the-art article on instruction in L2 pragmatics, Taguchi (2015d) identified 95 studies reporting instructional interventions in L2 pragmatics in the 30 years from Wildner-Bassett's (1984) study to Taguchi's literature search in April 2014. While Taguchi (2015d) focused on research studies, practically oriented resources for teachers have also appeared, with coverage ranging from general teaching ideas (Bardovi-Harlig & Mahan-Tayler, 2005; Ishihara & Cohen, 2010) to more specific areas such as speech acts (Tatsuki & Houck, 2010), natural conversation (Houck & Tatsuki, 2011), and language use in the workplace (Riddiford & Newton, 2010).

This significant interest in the teaching of L2 pragmatics demonstrates that there is a need for instruction in L2 pragmatics, but it is noteworthy that little structured teaching of pragmatics occurs in most courses. Pragmatics rarely forms an explicit part of curricula, and is not commonly formally assessed. This may be due to teachers', curriculum writers', and material designers' unfamiliarity with pragmatics and to the negative washback from the lack of formal assessment, but there is no question that pragmatics is teachable in principle. Taguchi (2015d) reviewed 58 studies that followed a pre-post design and were therefore able to detect instructional effects, and 57 studies did show such effects. Only one study—by Tateyama (2001) on apology formulae in L2 Japanese—did not show effects of instruction, which Taguchi suspects is due to problems with the outcome measure. While this is strong evidence that pragmatics is indeed amenable to instruction, there is a possible file-drawer problem here in that studies not showing significant effects of instruction are much less likely to be published. Still, there is no question that pragmatics can be taught. Having established the teachability of pragmatics, we will follow Roever (2009) in summarizing and discussing research on teaching L2 pragmatics based on three instructional considerations: how to teach, what to teach, and when to teach.

How to teach

While a variety of teaching methods have been used in pragmatics instruction, the most widely explored distinction in research on L2 pragmatics teaching is between explicit and implicit teaching approaches. This echoes research in SLA, which has also long investigated explicit vs. implicit teaching (R. Ellis et al., 2009; Norris & Ortega, 2000; Rebuschat, 2015). This line of research is motivated by findings that communicative language teaching, while effective in promoting fluency and communicative competence, does not necessarily lead to grammatical accuracy (Long, 2015). The challenge for instructional research has been to find ways to enhance communicative language teaching without giving up its positive effects, and this challenge has been most systematically answered by the Focus on Form (FonF) movement (Doughty & Williams, 1998; Long, 2015), which has investigated the benefits of explicit and implicit approaches to instruction within an overall communicative, meaning-focused framework.

Explicit instruction

Explicit teaching is designed for intentional language learning (R. Ellis & Shintani, 2014) and directs learners' attention to the instructional target in order to promote learning with awareness of what is being learned (Schmidt, 2001), often involving understanding of metalinguistic rules. Neurolinguistically, learning from explicit instruction involves the pre-frontal cortex, with explicitly learned knowledge stored in the hippocampus region (N. Ellis, 2008). In the general field of SLA, explicit instruction is operationalized in terms of attention and awareness, and does not necessarily involve explicit rules. However, in the teaching of L2 pragmatics, explicit instruction is typically characterized by provision of metapragmatic explanation (Kasper, 2001), i.e. direct presentation of sociopragmatic rules and pragmalinguistic tools.

Pedagogically, explicit instruction treats a language feature as an object separate from use. This deviates from the fundamental idea of communicative language teaching that instruction should consist of meaningful language use (Richards, 2006). R. Ellis and Shintani (2014, p. 84) characterize the typical teaching approach in explicit instruction as 'Presentation–Practice–Production (PPP)'. However, these phases are not clear-cut, and the practice and production phases frequently overlap.

In the presentation phase, new material is introduced to learners, which, in L2 pragmatics instruction, frequently happens as awareness-raising and metapragmatic explanation. Ishihara and Cohen (2010) list a number of pragmalinguistically and sociopragmatically oriented awareness-raising tasks, and the research literature contains numerous examples. For example, Haugh and Chang (2015) describe a method for awareness-raising of the sociopragmatic norms of teasing in Australian English and Taiwanese Mandarin using transcripts of authentic interactions. They suggest first describing the instructional target, then showing learners authentic examples in the target language and in the learners' L1, and discussing similarities and differences. Of course, this approach depends on learners sharing the same L1; however, it can be effective in not only providing positive evidence of how a pragmatic feature or interactional practice is carried out in the L2, but also precluding negative transfer from L1 since learners are led to notice the differences between the languages.

[margin note: compare & contrast ss' L1 pragmatics & L2 pragmatics]

Nguyen, Do, Nguyen, and Pham's (2015) study on the role of feedback in teaching request emails combined awareness-raising of sociopragmatics and pragmalinguistics. Nguyen et al. split the presentation phase of their instruction into a consciousness-raising phase and a metapragmatic explanation phase. During the consciousness-raising phase, students reflected on their experiences with writing request emails, thinking about the challenges they encountered and the reactions they received from recipients. Students were then given samples of request emails, which they analyzed in terms of structure, formality, and directness, as well as overall politeness. They also speculated on possible recipient reactions. In the subsequent metapragmatic explanation phase, students received explicit instruction about sociopragmatic norms for email discourse and pragmalinguistic speech act strategies for making requests.

[margin note: analyzed e-mails]

A study by Takimoto (2012) demonstrates that explicit instruction does not necessarily have to be deductive (i.e. the teacher providing a rule and the learners applying it), but that it can be done inductively, with the students discovering the rule for themselves. Takimoto's instruction comprised four phases: in the pragmalinguistic phase, learners identified requests in sample

[margin note: ss find out the rules of pragmatics]

dialogues and compared them; in the subsequent sociopragmatic phase, learners were guided to reflect on the relationship between interlocutors; in the third phase, learners judged the appropriateness of the request (connecting sociopragmatics and pragmalinguistics). In the final phase, learners were split into two groups: learners involved in metapragmatic discussion and those who would work alone. Learners in the former group discussed the requests and their metapragmatic features in pairs, and then provided ways to improve the requests, while learners in the latter group wrote improved versions individually. While Takimoto's approach was explicit in that requests were made an object of language-related discussion in the metapragmatic discussion condition, it was also inductive, since no metapragmatic explanation was provided by the teacher.

Awareness-raising can take various forms and incorporate a range of activities, but it most often involves exemplars of the target feature, engagement with these exemplars through analytic activities, comparison with L1 practices or other (possibly less successful) exemplars, and metapragmatic explanation of rules. How awareness-raising is conducted depends on the target feature, its complexity, and the characteristics of the learner group; however, the ultimate goal is for the learners to form theories about the sociopragmatic conditions and pragmalinguistic realizations of the target feature. Once learners have developed knowledge of the target feature through awareness-raising, practice and production activities can help them develop ability for use.

Practice activities can be viewed along a continuum of processing demand, stretching from less demanding, guided, untimed activities focusing on individual aspects of the target to more demanding, integrated, open activities done under time pressure. For example, Huth (2014) describes a teaching unit for L2 German telephone conversation openings, for which the practice phase encompasses three stages. First, learners practice brief and highly standardized summons–answer sequences in pairs, then they practice longer and less constrained 'how are you' sequences, and finally they write an entire conversation. Similarly, Houck and Fujimori (2010) show a step-by-step instructional sequence for advice-giving. After awareness-raising and explanation phases, learners identify advice-giving strategies in spoken dialogue, and then produce advice in a written DCT. Their responses can be collected on the whiteboard and discussed in class before they act out advice-giving situations in role-plays.

In a study on teaching routine formulae, Bardovi-Harlig, Mossman, and Vellenga (2015) used a number of games and activities for learners to practice routine formulae. In groups of three, one learner read a statement, the second agreed with the statement, and the third learner determined if the agreement formula used by the second speaker had been correct. In a pair-work activity, learners were given photographs with unclear objects; one learner hypothesized as to what the object might be, then the other learner agreed or disagreed with the statement. Finally, Bardovi-Harlig et al. (2015) developed a board game where learners moved around the board and landed

[handwritten margin note:] awareness ∨ identification ∨ Product (written Conversation)

on statements to which they responded with a learned expression based on an instruction card that they drew. Both the range of activities that Bardovi-Harlig et al. included and the requirement for learners to evaluate each other led to a great deal of production, repeated reflection, and likely also some metapragmatic discussion.

In order to establish how much practice is needed, S. Li (2013) investigated the effect of practice amount with learners of L2 Mandarin. Following skill acquisition theory (Anderson, 1993; DeKeyser, 2007), S. Li compared an input-based practice group with an output-based practice group and a control group. After all groups had taken a pre-test, the practice groups received four training sessions. Then all groups took a mid-test, followed by another four training sessions, and a post-test. The training for the input-based group involved participants reading a metapragmatic explanation, followed by a judgment task on the grammaticality of requests, and a judgment of degree of imposition based on a request scenario. Learners then read a dialogue which contained two turns. For each turn, learners chose a request from three options: a grammatically correct but pragmatically incorrect option, a pragmatically correct but ungrammatical option, and a pragmatically and grammatically correct option. After choosing, learners received metapragmatic feedback, read the complete dialogue with correct request choices highlighted, and listened to the dialogue. The output-based group followed the same procedure, except that instead of judging the grammaticality of a request after the metapragmatic explanation, this group translated a request sentence into Chinese; and instead of choosing response options to complete the dialogue, they typed their responses. Li used appropriateness judgments to test the input-based group and oral DCTs to test the output-based group, with the control group completing both measures. He found that both practice groups made significant gains from pre-test to mid-test on accuracy but more limited gains from mid- to post-test. They both outperformed the control group. However, their performance did not differ from the control group on measures of response time for the input-based group and response planning time and speech rate for the output-based group.

S. Li's study was based on the fundamental concept underlying PPP: in the presentation phase, learners build declarative knowledge of the target feature, which is knowledge about pragmatics but not ability for use. This ability is developed in the practice phase, where declarative knowledge is converted into increasingly automatized procedural knowledge, enabling real-time production. S. Li found that four practice sessions were sufficient to build accuracy, but even eight practice sessions were not sufficient to improve processing speed.

While explicit instruction aims to move learners from developing knowledge about the target feature that is external to them (pre-structured and imposed by the teacher) to internalized and proceduralized knowledge, implicit teaching leaves the task of learning about the target feature primarily up to the learner, with the teacher mainly acting as a facilitator.

Implicit instruction

Implicit teaching is designed for learning without awareness of what is being learned, and aims to engage sub-conscious processing mechanisms which abstract regularities of the target feature. While implicit learning means learning without awareness, it is not learning without attention in terms of Schmidt's (2001) noticing hypothesis (see Chapter 3 for details). In fact, learners need to attend to the target feature at least momentarily, and the feature needs to enter their working memory; however, they do not need to be able to label it or be aware of it at a level where they could discuss it as an object. Long (2015) considers implicit learning the default learning mechanism, which, after all, is what leads to successful L1 learning. Neurolinguistically, implicit learning involves the perceptual and motor cortex (N. Ellis, 2008), and pedagogically, it is in line with the tenets of communicative language teaching, where the emphasis is on communication rather than forms (Richards, 2006).

Implicit teaching methods do not involve an explanation of the target phenomenon or the provision of a rule. Instead, they aim to draw learners' attention to the target so it can enter working memory and be processed by implicit learning mechanisms. Implicit teaching techniques are designed along a continuum ranging from those that focus learners' attention on the target feature to those that leave noticing entirely up to the learner. Among the former, input enhancement is a common technique, involving the target feature being highlighted in the input, for example by underscoring or bold print. Toward the more learner-directed end of the continuum lie recasts, where an interlocutor repeats a faulty learner utterance with corrections but without explaining how the learner's production was incorrect. The most implicit of implicit methods is simply the provision of input, though the input can be modified to increase the frequency of the target feature, and given massively as an input flood.

Nguyen, Pham, and Pham (2012) combined some of these methods in their ten-week study comparing explicit and implicit teaching of constructive criticism. Their implicitly and explicitly taught groups started the instructional phase with a reflective session on constructive criticism in L1 and L2. The implicit group then received exemplars of constructive criticism in dialogues of native-speaker peer-feedback conversations with the target structures highlighted. They also answered comprehension questions and compared native-speaker criticism with their own. In the subsequent sessions, they practiced criticism with DCTs and spoken activities, and received recasts in the form of confirmation checks from instructors, which clearly identified the problematic part of their production of a target feature and provided a correction but no explanation. Learners also reflected on their output. By contrast, the explicit group received metapragmatic instruction on strategies and modifiers for expressing criticism during the first half of the instructional period. They were also given explanatory handouts, and were specifically instructed on recognizing directness in criticism and softening it.

Subsequently, the learners in the explicit group did the same practice activities as the learners in the implicit group but received explicit feedback on their performance. Nguyen et al. (2012) found that both teaching approaches led to improvements, with learners outperforming a control group; however, the gains under the explicit condition were much larger than under the implicit condition.

For an implicit teaching condition, Nguyen et al.'s approach was quite explicit. Learners were aware of what the target feature was, and the recasts were clearly focused on accuracy rather than being integrated in the flow of communication. It is rare to find studies in L2 pragmatics whose instruction is clearly implicit, with the exception of Q. Li's (2012), Takimoto's (2006, 2009), and Fordyce's (2014) studies. Q. Li taught beginner-level adolescent EFL learners supportive moves for requests under three conditions: explicit instruction with metapragmatic explanation, implicit instruction with input enhancements, and implicit instruction without enhancements. Learners received printed input materials, for which the sociopragmatics–pragmalinguistics mapping was explained by the teacher in the explicit group, whereas the implicit group with input enhancements had dialogues with the head acts and supportive moves highlighted. The unenhanced implicit group had dialogues without highlighting. After the groups had familiarized themselves with the dialogues, they all followed the same practice steps. Q. Li used DCTs to measure instructional effects, and found an overall advantage of the enhanced implicit group and the unenhanced implicit group over the explicit group in a pre-post comparison. Only the unenhanced implicit group showed a durable effect for all features on a delayed post-test six months after treatment, whereas the other groups showed durable effects only for some features.

Takimoto (2009) taught semantic formulae for requests and their sociopragmatic conditions of use under the input processing approach (VanPatten, 2015) and compared three instructional conditions, one of which did not include explicit explanation or metapragmatic discussion. Rather, learners read dialogues containing requests and chose the more appropriate of two options for the requestive head act before listening to a recording of the dialogue and underlining the correct answer. They also read the dialogue aloud and listened to a recording again. Takimoto (2009) found that all instructional conditions worked nearly equally well, with all instructional groups outperforming the control group and not differing significantly from each other.

Fordyce's (2014) study compared the effect of explicit and implicit treatment on L2 English learners' use of epistemic stance markers. The explicit group received teacher explanation of epistemic markers, along with exposure to the targets via enhanced input, consciousness-raising activities, feedback on students' epistemic forms, and a quiz. In contrast, the implicit treatment did not attempt to draw learners' attention to the target pragmatic features; instead, students were simply exposed to texts that contained epistemic forms. Both groups made significant improvements after the treatment, but the explicit group outperformed the implicit group on the frequency and range of the epistemic forms they used in the post-test writing samples.

Explicit vs. implicit treatment

From our discussion above, the picture on the relative effectiveness of explicit vs. implicit treatments may appear diffuse: studies like Nguyen et al. (2015) and Fordyce (2014) suggest a strong advantage of explicit instruction, whereas Q. Li (2012) found implicit instruction more effective, and Takimoto (2006, 2009) found no difference. In fact, Taguchi's (2015d) review suggests that explicit instruction is more effective. Taguchi lists ten studies that compared explicit and implicit instruction, and in nine of these studies the explicit instruction group outperformed the implicit instruction group. This reflects findings from general SLA, where gains in studies using explicit instruction had on average a large effect size, whereas gains in studies using implicit instruction had on average a medium effect size (Go, Granena, Yilmaz, & Novella, 2015). This advantage is likely due to explicit instruction providing regularities and patterns of the target phenomenon to learners and short-cutting the slow and cumbersome process of having to first identify the target phenomenon, building hypotheses about it, and then testing these hypotheses against the input. Explicit instruction can also provide negative evidence to eliminate transfer-based hypotheses early on. Given these advantages of explicit instruction, how can it be explained that implicit instruction is also effective in some studies and at times more effective (for example, Q. Li, 2012; see also Martínez-Flor, 2006)?

One explanation involves the processing demands of the assessment task (Taguchi, 2015d). Where tasks have a high cognitive load because they are productive and online (such as role-plays), explicit instruction gives learners an edge, probably because they can rely on declarative knowledge to supplement whatever implicit, intuitive knowledge they have developed. However, where cognitive load is low in receptive, offline tasks, implicit learning is sufficient to enable learners to recognize appropriate responses.

Another possible explanation relates to the complexity of the target phenomenon and the cognition of the learners. Explicit teaching is generally highly effective in disambiguating target phenomena and showing learners patterns and regularities. This works particularly well for adult learners, whose cognitive system is fully developed, and learners at intermediate and advanced levels of L2 proficiency, who have little trouble comprehending and producing the L2 but may lack pragmatic form–function mapping. However, the learners in Q. Li's (2012) study were young adolescents at beginner level, and Q. Li (2012) suggests that metapragmatic explanation may have actually distracted them from attending to the target features (particularly when the target features are shared between L1 and L2, and are thus easily transferable from L1). In Takimoto's study, the cognitive level of the learners was probably less of an issue, but the target feature was accessible enough through implicit teaching so that the explicit explanation rendered no added value.

It is important to note that the studies we have reviewed were done as research studies to isolate effects of teaching methods. In practice, nothing stops a teacher from mixing explicit and implicit teaching, for example, by taking an inductive approach where learners try to recognize patterns of the target feature in sample dialogues, then discuss their findings in metapragmatic discussion, and eventually are given metapragmatic information, followed by practice. While we appreciate that implicit teaching follows the Focus-on-Form mandate of maintaining an overriding focus on communication (Long, 2015), the greater efficiency of explicit teaching for most learners in most settings means that some degree of metapragmatic explanation is generally helpful in teaching L2 pragmatics.

What to teach

Similar to research on L2 pragmatics learning, the bulk of research on L2 pragmatics teaching concerns speech acts. About half of the studies Taguchi (2015d) reviewed were speech-act based; and, similar to acquisitional studies, requests are the most commonly taught speech act, followed by refusals and apologies. For example, Eslami, Mirzaei, and Dini (2015) report a study of teaching request head acts and supportive moves with two groups of upper-intermediate EFL learners in Iran and graduate student tutors in the United States. Under the explicit teaching condition, tutors provided metapragmatic awareness-raising, feedback and explanation, whereas under the implicit condition, awareness raising was done through input enhancement, and tutors provided recasts and implicit feedback. Eslami et al. also included a control group, which did not receive any particular instruction in pragmatics and was not assigned tutors. Using DCTs as their pre- and post-test, they found that the explicit group's scores showed an immense 89% increase from pre-test to post-test; the implicit group's scores also increased strongly by 66%; and even the control group's scores increased by 16%. Eslami et al. also coded email requests sent by learners from the instructed groups to tutors in the early phase and late phase of instruction, which were authentic, unelicited requests dealing with the actual business of the instructional situation. They found for both groups a drop in direct requests and an increase in indirect requests, with a concomitant greater use of supportive moves in the late phase.

Eslami et al.'s study focused on the implicit/explicit distinction in its approach to pragmatic instruction, and taught speech act strategies for head acts and supportive moves, which is a common instructional target. Their study was unusual in its use of email communication as a teaching tool, although computer-based instruction with a custom-designed system was also used by Sydorenko (2015) in teaching requests. Eslami et al.'s analysis of learners' requests in their emails to tutors supports their findings since it shows that learners apply learned material in real-world communication. However, the asynchronous, written, and DCT-based nature of data collection does not allow conclusions as to learners' ability to use requests in spoken real-world interactions.

While most studies investigate instructional effects on groups of learners, Riddiford and Holmes (2015) report a case study of a Filipino migrant to New Zealand who completed a 12-week course aimed at improving learners' language for the workplace with a particular focus on speech acts. The course followed an explicit approach to teaching speech acts and integrated practice and reflection. Learners also undertook a work placement/internship. Riddiford and Holmes focused on refusals, collecting data via DCTs, role-plays, retrospective interviews, and learner-controlled recordings of workplace interactions at various times in the course and placement. Over the period of the course, role-play data showed that the learner adjusted his refusal practices to New Zealand workplace norms and away from his L1 Filipino norm, which requires apologizing for the refusal and emphasizing willingness to help. While few instances of refusals occurred in the authentic workplace data, the learner employed material practiced in class to show refusal and disaffiliation, notably the word 'actually' to highlight contradiction to the interlocutor's expectations. Interestingly, the learner still expressed uncertainty about the right combination of clarity and deference in refusals during the final interview. Riddiford and Holmes's data collection in the workplace is innovative and important since it provides evidence for the beneficial effect of pragmatics instruction on real-world language use.

The second most widely taught aspect of L2 pragmatics is routine formulae, which overlaps with the teaching of speech acts, discussed above, and the teaching of interactional abilities, discussed below. A focus in the teaching of routine formulae that connects to interactional abilities has been the teaching of gambits (expressions that manage the flow of interaction) in various languages, including German (Wildner-Bassett, 1984, 1986), English (House, 1996; Németh & Kormos, 2001), Japanese (Yoshimi, 2001), and Spanish (Taylor, 2002). While investigations of gambits also included some formulae for speech acts, such as pragmalinguistic markers of agreement, disagreement, and opinion in Németh and Kormos's (2001) study, other studies have specifically focused on semantic formulae for speech acts including apology in English (Olshtain & Cohen, 1990) and Japanese (Tateyama, 2001), requests (Takimoto, 2009), and a range of high-frequency formulae, including formulae for thanking and apologizing (Bardovi-Harlig & Vellenga, 2012).

In their study of routine formulae, Bardovi-Harlig et al. (2015) taught formulae for agreement ('That's right'), disagreement ('Yeah but…'), other-clarification ('You're saying…'), and self-clarification ('What I mean…') to ESL learners. They drew candidate formulae from two sources: previous research by Bardovi-Harlig and Salsbury (2004) and ESL textbooks used as supplementary materials in the course taken by their participants. They then checked the frequency of these formulae in the MICASE corpus (Michigan Corpus of Academic Spoken English; Simpson, Briggs, Ovens, & Swales, 2002), and chose 17 target formulae with at least 10 occurrences per million words. They spread their instruction over four lessons, which started with a noticing activity, followed by explicit metapragmatic instruction, and concluding with practice opportunities. Bardovi-Harlig et al. (2015) taught an experimental group and included a control group, which did not receive specific instruction in routine formulae. They used oral DCTs as pre- and post-test instruments, and found a significant effect of instruction in all four types of formulae for the instructed learners. There were no significant differences between pre- and post-test for the uninstructed control group, but for the instructed learners, other-clarification routines benefited most from instruction, with scores more than doubling, and agreement routines also benefited strongly. Effect sizes of gains were modest for disagreement and self-clarification routines. While the use of nearly all instructed formulae increased, and learners used formulae on the post-test that they had not used on the pre-test (for example, 'I agree, but...'), learners strongly preferred certain expressions, and the most fre- quently used pre-test expression in each category was still the most frequent post-test expression. The instructional intervention mostly served to broaden the learners' pragmalinguistic repertoire, though it did not necessarily con- strain it: learners' use of the bald-on-record disagreement formula 'I disagree' (also rendered as 'I'm disagree') increased from pre-test to post-test, even though this formula is low in frequency in the corpus and was not mentioned in the instruction. Bardovi-Harlig et al. emphasize the need to provide nega- tive evidence to learners as well as positive evidence; otherwise, they have no way of knowing what expressions *not* to use. Provision of negative evidence has not been made a prominent part of instructional L2 pragmatics studies, and Bardovi-Harlig et al.'s study shows that it should be.

Building up from speech acts and routine formulae, a small number of studies have taught learners larger-scale interactional skills to help them build sequences of turns. For example, Liddicoat and Crozet (2001) taught learn- ers of French as a foreign language the interactional norms and practices for making small talk in French. They conducted a pre-test/post-test study and focused on the content aspects of tellings and feedback practices for listeners to show affiliation, such as evaluative responses, receipt tokens, and repeti- tions. They found that learners were able to incorporate content features but made less use of affiliative feedback features. In a delayed post-test, one year after instruction, the use of affiliative feedback features had deteriorated further, but content features remained stable.

While Liddicoat and Crozet (2001) took an interactional sociolinguistics approach and taught cultural norms of small talk as well as interactional practices, Barraja-Rohan (2011) taught sequential organization from a Conversation Analysis perspective (see also Huth, 2006, for a CA approach to teaching German compliment responses). She instructed learners on a wide range of interactional features, including opening and closing conversations, turn-taking, preference organization, topic management, adjacency pairs, and the normativity of second pair parts, as well as listening practices such as use of response tokens and assessments. Her teaching approach incorpo- rated awareness-raising, learner reflection, role-play practice, and completion of written dialogues. Barraja-Rohan's analysis focused on learners' use of response tokens and assessments, as well as second pair part responses, and she found improvements in all three areas, though her data collection relied on analyses of exemplars of learner discourse rather than formal pre- and post-tests. In their course evaluations, learners stressed the usefulness of having developed awareness of the structure of conversation. Barraja-Rohan's study is interesting in that she taught learners about the sequential organization of conversation, of which language users are not likely to be consciously aware. While she did not conduct formal tests to gauge the effect of her instruction, developing and sharpening conversational skills is probably an ongoing project for learners, and would require a longitudinal study to investigate. Making learners aware of the systematics underlying conversation gives them tools to analyze conversations and understand target community practices.

While the teaching of speech acts, routines, and sequential organization of discourse focuses on productive abilities, a limited amount of research has also been done on the teaching of receptive skills such as implicature. While this aspect of pragmatics has been covered in a small number of studies (Bouton, 1999; Padilla Cruz, 2013; Ifantidou, 2013; Kubota, 1995; Murray, 2011), only the studies by Bouton (1999) and Kubota (1995) used a pre-post design that allows conclusions as to the effectiveness of instruction. Bouton (1999) taught two categories of implicature to ESL learners. The first category was idiosyncratic implicature, which encompasses relevance, minimum requirement, and scalar implicature. The second category, formulaic implicature, included the Pope Q, indirect criticism, irony, and sequence implicature. Bouton's experimental group received six weeks of instruction in interpreting the various types of implicature, bracketed by pre- and post-tests. He found very little effect of teaching idiosyncratic implicature with the total score (which was already at 86% at pre-test time) not changing at all; however, there was a strong effect for formulaic implicature, for which the total score increased nearly by half. Bouton concludes that idiosyncratic implicature is easy to learn but hard to teach, whereas formulaic implicature is hard to learn but easy to teach. Bouton's findings emphasize the need to teach explicitly those areas of pragmatics that are otherwise difficult to learn, perhaps because they are opaque (Taguchi, 2015d) or because they require specific background knowledge (as with the Pope Q), since not all learners necessarily have the cultural knowledge about what a pope is and know he is Catholic.

Besides the areas of pragmatics discussed above, instructional studies have been done across a variety of topics, including written requests via email (Alcón Soler, 2015; Nguyen et al., 2015), epistemic stance in writing (Fordyce, 2014), modifiers in criticism (Nguyen, 2013), mitigation in L2 Spanish (Félix-Brasdefer, 2008b), address terms in L2 French (van Campernolle, 2011a), and speech styles in L2 Japanese (Ishida, 2007). Taguchi (2015d) notes that the vast majority of studies have been on English as a target language, with other languages under-explored. Also, the strong focus on speech acts rather than extended discourse means that learners may not necessarily be able to use what they learned in conversation.

When to teach

In terms of curriculum planning, the question of what aspects of pragmatics to teach early on and which ones to teach later is crucial. This question is fundamentally about learnability and processability of pragmatic features, and no study has so far addressed these issues directly. However, some insights can be gleaned from studies on the teaching of L2 pragmatics that compare different aspects of pragmatics, and from studies on learning that look at development.

An obvious constraint on teaching some aspects of pragmatics is learners' general L2 proficiency. This concerns, in particular, speech act formulations that express high levels of politeness; a polite, highly indirect request ('I was wondering if you might be able to spare a minute to take a look at what I've written?') is far more linguistically complex than a less polite, direct request ('Look at this, please.'). There is no point in trying to teach low-proficiency learners complex requestive head acts, which their linguistic competence would not yet allow them to generate creatively. This is not to say that low-proficiency learners are invariably unsuccessful in making requests or would not benefit from instruction—quite the contrary. As Al-Gahtani and Roever (2013, 2014a) showed for learners of L2 English and L2 Arabic, low-proficiency learners can successfully negotiate requests but tend to rely on the interlocutor to ask questions or provide repairs (see Chapter 5). Learners also under-use preliminary moves (i.e. explanations before a request), and this, at times, leads to confusion for the interlocutor since the conventional dispreferred structure of a request (especially delays and preliminary moves) is absent. In Al-Gahtani and Roever's (2014a) study with learners of Modern Standard Arabic, learners' use of preliminary moves increased dramatically within one semester, even among beginner-level learners, which indicates that simple pre-sequences were within the reach even of low-level learners. This indicates that a teaching intervention may well be fruitful.

Another eminently teachable feature at lower proficiency levels is routine formulae. Given that routines can be memorized as chunks, thus allowing learners to outperform their competence, there is no reason why low-proficiency learners could not be taught simple, useful routine formulae. As Bardovi-Harlig (2009) and Roever (2012) show, not all routine formulae are at equal level of difficulty: 'Nice to meet you' is easily learnable at early stages, but 'Thanks for having me' (in Bardovi-Harlig, 2009) and 'Can I get you anything else?' (in Roever, 2012) are not widely recognized until much later. This greater difficulty is likely to be a function of frequency in the input and grammatical complexity of the formula itself, so high-frequency, less complex formulae should be accessible to lower-proficiency learners.

Implicature might be an area that cannot be instructed to learners at low-proficiency levels since, as Roever (2005) suggests, a threshold of comprehension must be met before learners realize that an utterance is intentionally designed to imply non-literal meaning. At lower levels, it is difficult for learners to tell whether an interlocutor's response seems odd by design or because the learner lacks comprehension ability.

At intermediate levels, where most research studies are conducted, a wide range of pragmatic features can be taught, including context–form–function mapping of semantic formulae for speech acts, less frequent and more complex routine formulae, longer pre-sequences for dispreferred social actions (requests, complaints), post-expansions after unsuccessful requests, and different types of formulaic implicature.

Very little research exists on teaching pragmatics for advanced learners; teaching interventions will, in many cases, depend on their specific task needs. As Sykes (2015, personal communication) points out, advanced learners have highly developed linguistic ability but may not know how to harness and configure this ability for pragmatic purposes. For example, university students may benefit from being taught how to write complex emails on delicate topics, for example going back on a promise made to a professor (Roever, Knoch, & Macqueen, 2016). Learners in the workplace can benefit from an explicit understanding of the norms of interaction in the target language culture (Riddiford & Holmes, 2015), and how to engage in small talk interactions, which can remain a problem even for advanced second language speakers (Cui, 2012). Also, the learning of sociopragmatic norms of social roles and the expectations attached to these roles can be greatly aided by instruction. For example, the supervisor–employee relationship and the privileges, duties, and behavioral expectations attached to each role can differ strongly between cultures (Thompson & Twitchin, 1991), but such underlying norms are outside most language users' conscious awareness.

Teaching L2 pragmatics: summary and directions for future research

While a great deal of work has been done in 30 years of research on teaching L2 pragmatics, many tantalizing questions remain. At the center of future research should be the interaction between what to teach, when to teach it, and how, possibly with 'who to teach it to' added in, since no previous research has directly addressed the issue of teaching pragmatics in the foreign language setting vs. the second language setting. (These two settings differ drastically in the amount of input opportunities, interaction, and range of social roles available to learners.)

Apart from a 'who' facet, there is still a great deal of work to be done regarding the 'how' facet, i.e. which teaching methods are most effective. While explicit teaching appears to be more effective and efficient than implicit teaching, we still know far too little about the effectiveness of different modes of presentation (inductive vs. deductive), and different types and amounts of practice. S. Li's study demonstrates that accuracy can be improved with less practice than that needed to improve processing speed, but the exact amount of practice needed to improve processing speed is unknown, and it is also unclear how much practice might be needed for other target phenomena. In addition, the question of 'how much' or 'how long' is relevant to the ongoing explicit vs. implicit/deductive vs. inductive method debate. Existing findings on instructional outcomes largely favor explicit over implicit teaching; but so far, these methods have been compared on the same instructional timescale. It is possible that the implicit condition, which involves learners' own analysis and discovery of pragmatic rules, may require a longer time for internalizing knowledge than the explicit condition, where rules are given directly. Hence, the length and amount of instruction both need to be considered with methods of instruction. Furthermore, the sequencing of practice activities deserves further investigation, as does their cognitive load. Finally, the 'when' facet needs to be taken into account: what type of practice benefits learners at different ability levels?

With regard to what to teach, specific, targeted teaching of particular aspects of conversation (such as opening and closing sequences, preference organization, and topic initiation and closing) has not been sufficiently attended to. While extended conversation requires learners to be at a higher level than beginner proficiency, beginners do have interactions too, and tools for small talk, requests, or responses to requests can be taught. It is surprising that more research has not been done on the teaching of routine formulae, since these benefit learners at any level. Also, sociopragmatic norms of interaction and understandings of social roles are important to teach since they are nearly impervious to uninstructed insight, and can lead to serious cross-cultural misunderstandings. Riddiford and Holmes's (2015) study is exemplary in terms of raising awareness of deeply ingrained sociopragmatic norms and teaching pragmalinguistic tools for functioning effectively in the target culture. Finally, pragmatics for languages other than English looms large as a teaching challenge. This is particularly the case for Mandarin, as learner numbers are increasing dramatically (Confucius Institute/Hanban, 2014).

It remains a concern that L2 pragmatics is not well integrated into curricula and is often just treated incidentally in classrooms. However, it is common for research to take some time to affect practice, so we are hopeful that we will see pragmatics permeate general L2 teaching more strongly in the future.

In the following section we will turn to an area that has an even shorter history than the teaching of L2 pragmatics, namely the assessment of learners' pragmatic ability.

Assessing L2 pragmatics

Research on teaching L2 pragmatics is a fairly recent phenomenon, and assessment of learners' pragmatic knowledge has an even shorter history. The first test battery informed by L2 pragmatics research was created by Hudson, Detmer, and Brown in 1995; 20 years later, no large-scale test, such as the Test of English as a Foreign Language (TOEFL), the International English Language Testing System (IELTS), the Pearson Test of English Academic (PTE Academic), the American Council for the Teaching of Foreign Languages Oral Proficiency Interview (ACTFL OPI), the Test of German as a Foreign Language (TestDaF) or the Chinese Standard Exam (*Hanyu Shuiping Kaoshi*, HSK), has a pragmatics section or gives separate scores for pragmatics. This is problematic since conceptualizations of communicative competence include pragmatic competence, as we will outline below, and the absence of measures of pragmatics means that test scores do not provide information about test takers' communicative competence as a whole. This threatens the validity of decisions based on test scores: tests are done to inform real-world decisions, for example, admission to academic programs, diagnostics to enable pedagogical interventions, or the granting of privileges, such as permanent residence in the target-language country. Language tests that do not include pragmatics run the risk of construct under-representation in Messick's (1989) construct-based model of test validity, and they risk damaging the extrapolation inference in Kane's (2006) argument-based approach to validation. Practically speaking, end users of tests might believe that a test taker is able to function at a high level in the target language, when in fact we only know that they have listening, speaking, reading and writing ability, and not whether they are able to configure and deploy these abilities to perform social actions that attain real-world goals.

Tests of second language pragmatics have been developed to address this shortcoming but have struggled to cover the construct of pragmatics broadly enough to enable useful inferences from scores while still maintaining practicality. Another problem has been the creation of items with sufficient difficulty to discriminate between test takers, especially at the upper levels of the ability spectrum.

In this part of the chapter, we will first discuss how pragmatics has been conceptualized in constructs of communicative competence and as a construct of its own. We will then outline how different tests have tried to measure it.

Pragmatic competence and communicative competence

Pragmatics has featured as part of various constructs of communicative competence, though it has been conceptualized in different ways.

In Canale and Swain's (1980) early but highly influential model of communicative competence (informed by Dell Hymes' work), pragmatics is incorporated in the 'sociolinguistic' component, which exists alongside a grammatical and a strategic component. The sociolinguistic component encompasses sociocultural rules, corresponding roughly to sociopragmatic knowledge and rules of discourse, which govern the combination of several utterances. Canale and Swain leave the issue of discourse rules quite open and unresolved, and seem to have been unaware of the work in Conversation Analysis, which sees the description of the rules of discourse as its major project. Canale's (1983) model of communicative competence was very similar but made discourse competence a component of its own, while limiting the sociolinguistic component to what Canale and Swain (1980) had called 'sociocultural rules'.

Currently, the most influential model, Bachman and Palmer's (2010) model of communicative language ability, is hierarchically organized with strategic competence and language knowledge as the main components. Language knowledge is then split into two major types: organizational knowledge and pragmatic knowledge. The former encompasses knowledge of the language system (grammar, vocabulary, phonetics) as well as text organization. The latter involves knowledge of language functions (which is roughly equivalent to knowing how to carry out speech acts) and sociolinguistic knowledge of genres, dialects, registers, idiomatic expressions, and cultural references.

Rather than postulating separate components, Purpura (2004) focused on grammatical ability but related it to pragmatics by emphasizing how grammar enables pragmatic meanings. While this link is well known to pragmatics researchers as pragmalinguistic knowledge (which draws on grammatical and other types of language knowledge to express illocutions), Purpura subdivides pragmatic knowledge into knowledge of contextual, sociolinguistic, sociocultural, psychological, and rhetorical meaning. He does not discuss sociopragmatics.

While the models discussed so far try to describe communicative competence overall, models also exist that focus on pragmatic competence alone. Historically, the most influential model is Leech's (1983, 2014) distinction between sociopragmatics and pragmalinguistics (see also Thomas, 1983). Leech (2014) sees sociopragmatics as the cultural values that determine the relationship between the participants and their views of the target speech act. Depending on the relationship and the cost (in terms of effort, time, money, face, etc.) involved in the target action, more or less politeness may be required. Leech (2014) defines pragmalinguistics as the total of lexical and grammatical resources and the way they can be deployed for pragmatic purposes. Leech (2014) stresses that both areas of pragmatics are closely connected and that pragmalinguistic meanings need to be mapped onto sociopragmatic values to enable culturally appropriate pragmatic performance.

Leech's model is strongly focused on social rules and politeness, and does not go beyond the level of individual utterances. Timpe-Laughlin, Wain, and Schmidgall (2015) propose a more detailed model that takes discourse into account and has five components:

- sociocultural knowledge: encompasses sociopragmatic knowledge of social rules and norms
- pragmatic-functional knowledge: refers to form–function mapping for generating illocutions and knowledge of the effect of social rules on the use of pragmatic tools
- grammatical knowledge: covers knowledge of the language system, including grammar, vocabulary, morphology, etc.
- discourse knowledge: involves knowledge of how to establish coherence and cohesion (although turn-taking, sequential organization, and repair are not mentioned)

- strategic knowledge: this is a set of mostly compensatory skills for handling insufficient knowledge or communication breakdown.

Timpe-Laughlin, Wain, and Schmidgall's (2015) model tries to outline the connection between overall language competence and pragmatics more explicitly, but does not go into much detail on discourse knowledge or learners' ability to participate in extended interaction.

Ability to engage in extended discourse is much more closely captured in the concept of 'interactional competence' (Kramsch, 1986; Pekarek Doehler & Pochon-Berger, 2015; Young, 2011), which has influenced L2 pragmatics work on learners' participation in extended discourse. Interactional competence is interactants' ability to create intersubjectivity by engaging in mutually recognizable discursive practices (Pekarek Doehler & Pochon-Berger, 2015). Such practices include turn-taking, repair, opening and closing of conversations, sequentially organizing talk, and engaging in preference organization so that, for example, a request sequence is recognizable as such early on and a listener can either deploy tools to aid in bringing it to a successful conclusion or forestall it. Development of interactional competence involves interactants knowing how to engage in discursive practices (Kasper, 2006a), for example being a listener (Ishida, 2009), following up when a problem is not satisfactorily resolved (Al-Gahtani & Roever, 2014b), or giving the interlocutor space to co-construct meaning through the use of incomplete utterances (Taguchi, 2014a). While interactional competence incorporates knowledge of pragmalinguistic tools and sociopragmatic rules, it is competence at the discourse level, and its development is characterized by increased accuracy, efficiency, and a range of tools for engaging in discursive practices across a range of activities (Pekarek Doehler & Pochon-Berger, 2015). Young (2011) and Kasper and Wagner (2011) note that interactional competence can also be viewed as a resource co-constructed and shared by participants, but it is difficult to conceive of such a conceptualization as a framework for assessment, so we will use the term 'interactional competence' as denoting the abilities and knowledge that enable an individual to engage in interaction.

Given that pragmatics is part of all the major conceptualizations of communicative competence, which inform the design of language tests, pragmatic abilities also need to be assessed to provide a well-rounded picture of learners' overall L2 competence. A number of pragmatics tests have been developed, with tests of the first and second generation generally relying on Leech (1983, 2014), and interactive tests of the third generation following an interactional competence orientation or Purpura's (2004) framework.

First generation assessments and predecessors: speech acts and functions

The earliest tests that can be considered to test L2 pragmatics were dissertations in the early and late 1980s: Farhady's (1980) functionally oriented test and Shimazu's (1989) Pragmatic Competence in American English test. Farhady's test followed the notional–functional approach to language analysis and teaching (van Ek, 1976; Wilkins, 1976), whereas Shimazu (1989) integrated some work on pragmatics (especially speech acts). Both tests consisted entirely of multiple-choice items and assessed test takers' recognition of the most grammatically and socially acceptable response option.

The first test development project informed by L2 pragmatics was Hudson, Detmer, and Brown's (1995) test battery. Hudson et al. (1995) designed their test for Japanese learners of English around the speech acts of request, apology, and refusal. They varied power, social distance, and imposition and administered written DCTs, oral DCTs, multiple-choice DCTs, role-play tasks, and two self-assessment scales, one for the DCTs and one for the role-plays. The multiple-choice DCT was scored dichotomously, whereas the other DCTs were rated on six indicators of pragmatic competence: use of the intended speech act, conventionality of expression, amount of speech and information, as well as formality, politeness, and directness. Each role-play contained a request, an apology, and a refusal; these were rated holistically. Hudson (2001) reports on a small-scale validation study with 25 Japanese learners of English, which showed reliabilities for the oral and written DCTs as well as the role-play ranging from .75 to .86, and a pronounced ceiling effect (i.e. the test was too easy for the participants). Hudson (2001) also demonstrated a test method effect, with scores correlating much more strongly between the DCT instruments than between the DCT instruments and the role-play. While some degree of method effect is to be expected, the strength of the method effect Hudson found points to different aspects of pragmatic ability being elicited by DCTs and role-plays.

Hudson et al.'s (1995) instrument was adapted by Yamashita (1996) for English-speaking learners of Japanese, by Ahn (2005) for Korean as a foreign language (see also Brown, 2008; Brown & Ahn, 2011), and used by Yoshitake (1997) with Japanese EFL learners. Hudson et al.'s (1995) battery was a ground-breaking development since it was the first larger-scale test of pragmatics, and relied on research on cross-cultural and L2 pragmatics, especially CCSARP (Blum-Kulka, Kasper & House, 1989; see Chapter 1). Until Hudson et al. developed their test, it was not even clear whether it was possible to test pragmatics reliably. They showed that such a test is possible, and created rating criteria for the productive components. However, their test was limited to ESL learners with L1 Japanese, with some items designed contrastively. Also, the multiple-choice DCT did not work well in Yamashita's and Yoshitake's tests, attaining very low reliabilities, which is unfortunate since it is the most practical part of the test.

The search for a reliable multiple-choice test of speech acts became something of a 'holy grail' in L2 pragmatics assessment research, and two projects developed more reliable multiple-choice instruments. Tada (2005) created a computer-based multiple-choice DCT for Japanese EFL learners supported by video scenarios, and found a satisfactory reliability level of .75 for his multiple-choice items, and a similar inter-rater reliability for his oral DCT items.

Liu (2006, 2007) developed a multiple-choice DCT, employing a bottom-up development approach, where he asked learners from his target population (L1 Mandarin-speaking ESL learners) to describe apology and request scenarios they had encountered. He then collected learner and native-speaker responses with a written DCT, and finally used learner responses as incorrect response options and native-speaker responses as correct options. Liu initially had difficulty attaining agreement among native speakers on the correct response for the multiple-choice items, but when administering his final revised test to learners, he obtained a high reliability score of .88 for the multiple-choice part. McNamara and Roever (2006) question whether Liu's bottom-up test development approach may have inadvertently led to test takers selecting answer choices based on their idiomaticity rather than pragmatic appropriateness.

The first generation of pragmatics tests was very much in the speech act tradition, and scores on these tests can be interpreted as indicative of learners' offline knowledge of politeness and appropriateness for the target speech acts, with proficiency a possible mediating factor in productive sections. These tests do not allow for inferences regarding interactional competence. However, pragmatics encompasses more than just speech acts, and this was reflected in the second generation of tests.

Second generation assessments: a broader construct

The second generation of pragmatics tests built on the work of the first generation, but broadened the construct. In addition to speech acts, these tests also included other aspects of pragmatics, such as comprehension of implicature, recognition of routine formulae, speech acts beyond requests and apologies, and even attempts at more interactive discourse. While broadening the construct, second generation tests are characterized by a strong concern for practicality, i.e. ease of administration and ease of scoring, to make it more likely that pragmatics tests would be used for real-world purposes.

The first test in this tradition was Roever's (2005, 2006) web-based test of ESL pragmalinguistics. Roever's test included multiple-choice sections for recognition of routine formulae and comprehension of implicature, and DCT items with rejoinders testing request, apology, and refusal. Roever used rejoinders to de-emphasize the appropriateness aspect of responses and to focus on the elicitation of speech act strategies, in a similar way to the example item in Figure 8.1.

The scenario makes it clear that Anna is making a request for a ride, but for Bill's response to make sense, Anna's utterance also has to contain an explanation, for example: 'Bill, can you give me a ride to work? My car won't start.' Only if learners had the pragmalinguistic ability to provide both the request and the explanation did they receive a full score. Roever validated his test using Messick's (1989) construct validation approach, and found strong proficiency effects as expected for a pragmalinguistic assessment (see also Roever,

Anna is about to drive to work when her car won't start. Her neighbor, Bill, who works at the same company, is about to drive to work and Anna decides to ask him for a ride. She walks over to Bill and says:

Bill: 'Oh, I hate it when that happens. Sure, I'll give you a ride.'

Figure 8.1 DCT item with rejoinder

Wang, & Brophy, 2014), a factor structure that mirrored the construct, and a high reliability score of .9. The test was practical, with administration taking less than an hour for the entire test, and two of the three sections self-scoring. Finally, Roever's test differed from tests of the first generation in that it was not designed for test takers from a specific L1 background, and was run with test takers from a variety of L1 backgrounds. Subsequent differential item functioning (DIF) analyses showed that L1 background conferred very little advantage (Roever, 2007, 2010).

A second test in this tradition was Itomitsu's (2009) web-based test of the pragmatics of Japanese as a foreign language. It included multiple-choice sections assessing recognition of routine formulae, speech act, speech styles, and grammar. Itomitsu found that learners' scores generally increased with proficiency (as determined by length and level of instruction as well as OPI ratings), and he attained overall high reliability close to .9. It is especially noteworthy that the reliability of the (multiple-choice) speech act section was satisfactory at .7, though Itomitsu's focus in this section was less on appropriateness of response options and more on which response option was most suitable for expressing a particular speech intention in a given scenario, possibly making acceptability decisions more clear-cut. While Itomitsu did not design his test contrastively like tests of the first generation, he also did not systematically include test takers from different L1 backgrounds, making it impossible to tell if his test would be generally usable. However, his test was practical in terms of administration and scoring, taking less than 60 minutes to administer and allowing automatic scoring of items.

A somewhat different approach from Roever's (2005) and Itomitsu's (2009) projects was taken by Roever, Fraser, and Elder (2014) in their web-based test of ESL sociopragmatics. Unlike other tests in the second generation, which are generally pragmalinguistically oriented, Roever et al. focused on socio-pragmatic appropriateness and extended discourse. Since some of their item types had not been previously used, we will provide brief examples below. Their test included four sections:

1 Metapragmatic judgments of the speech acts of request, apology, suggestion, and refusal: test takers judge the final utterance in a situation in terms of its appropriateness to provide information on their sociopragmatic awareness, as in Figure 8.2.

Jane needs to buy some stamps at the post office. She goes up to the counter, and the man behind the counter says: 'Hi, how can I help you?'
Jane: 'Hi, I'm terribly sorry to bother you, but I was wondering if you might be so kind as to give me ten 50-cent stamps.'

Look at the final utterance. Do you think it is…?
Very impolite/very harsh
Not quite polite/soft enough
Completely appropriate
A little too polite/soft
Far too polite/soft

Figure 8.2 Metapragmatic judgment item (Roever, Fraser, & Elder, 2014, p. 274)

2 Metapragmatic judgments of second pair parts (responses to offers, news tellings, compliments, requests, etc.), with correction of inappropriate ones: test takers judge the final utterance and provide corrections where they judge it incorrect. This item type, shown in Figure 8.3, tests sociopragmatic awareness and pragmalinguistic knowledge.

Two friends are meeting at F1's new flat.
F1 So, do you like my new flat?
F2 It's very small. My flat's much bigger.

Is F2 responding appropriately? Yes / No
How should F2 respond? _____

Figure 8.3 Metapragmatic judgment for second pair parts (Roever, Fraser, & Elder, 2014, pp. 274–275)

3 Completion of multi-turn DCTs: test takers fill in one interlocutor's turns in a conversation, as shown in Figure 8.4. This assesses primarily pragmalinguistic and discursive abilities.
4 Choice between two dialogues in terms of normativity of sequential organization: this very experimental item type asked learners to choose which of two dialogues was more successful, as in Figure 8.5. It assesses knowledge of discourse structure.

Roever et al. attained an overall acceptable reliability of .8 but found that their test was easy for their participants, echoing Brown's (2001) findings for the battery developed by Hudson et al. (1995). The highest-difficulty section was the correction of inappropriate second pair parts, which is an interesting finding that points to a need for productive items testing a wide variety of utterance types, rather than just standard speech acts like requests, apologies, and refusals. Roever et al. (2014) included speakers from a wide range

Max and Julie are at a party. They don't know each other but happen to stand next to each other and start chatting.

Max 'Hi, I'm Max.'
Julie _____

Max 'I'm good, thanks. Are you enjoying the party?'
Julie _____

Max 'Yeah, it's fun. So what line of work are you in, Julie?'
Julie _____

Max 'Really? Investment banking, sounds exciting.'
Julie _____

Max 'I'm a dentist.'
(conversation continues)

Figure 8.4 Multi-turn DCT (Roever, Fraser, & Elder, 2014, p. 275)

Employee	Do you have a minute?
Boss	Sure.
Employee	I just wanted to ask you about this afternoon.
Boss	What's up?
Employee	Can I take one of the laptops and work from home?
Boss	Ok, how come?
Employee	The IT department is upgrading my computer today but I need to finish these reports and email them out to everyone on the team by 4.
Boss	Sounds sensible. No problem. Let me know when you're leaving.
Employee	Thanks, will do.

Employee	Can I ask you a question?
Boss	Sure.
Employee	My child's school has been completely flooded after the storm this afternoon.
Boss	Oh, that sounds terrible.
Employee	The school is actually not that far from here.
Boss	Right.
Employee	It would be difficult to get someone else to pick him up.
Boss	You mean as a regular thing?
Employee	No, I need to leave early just for today.

Which of the two interactions is more successful in terms of the communication skills used?

Figure 8.5 Dialogue choice item (Roever, Fraser, & Elder, 2014, p. 276)

of native languages in their sample, and administration of their test took an average of 47 minutes for the target ESL sample. However, the need for human scoring of the productive components lowered practicality.

The tests of the second generation have extended and deepened the assessed construct of L2 pragmatics, providing a more comprehensive picture of learners' pragmatic ability. A challenge that remains is to create items of sufficient difficulty for ESL learners, who are frequently international students with a fairly high level of overall target language proficiency. Including a wider range of proficiency levels is likely to increase item difficulty and improve reliability, but may introduce construct-irrelevant variance by turning tests into measures of general proficiency (reading, vocabulary, grammar, speed of access) rather than tests of pragmatic knowledge.

While the second generation can be seen as an extension and broadening of the first generation, the third generation shifted its emphasis to extended discourse.

Third generation: extended discourse

Tests of the third generation focus on interactional abilities, generally elicited through role-plays. While Hudson et al. (1995) also included role-plays as part of their test battery, they used them to elicit specific target speech acts (request, apology, refusal), which were rated. By contrast, tests in this generation rate extended discourse performances as a whole.

The first test in this tradition was Grabowski's (2009, 2013), which consisted of four role-plays, acted out between an ESL learner and a trained native-speaker interlocutor. Grabowski's construct of pragmatic knowledge was based on Purpura's (2004) types of pragmatic meaning (i.e. contextual, sociolinguistic, sociocultural, psychological, and rhetorical meaning), which also underpinned the rating criteria. Grabowski attained high internal consistency and inter-rater reliabilities above .9, and her tasks were slightly more difficult than those in other tests that were similarly limited to learners at the intermediate level or above, and which had struggled with tasks being too easy for test takers. While Grabowski's test worked well as a measurement instrument, the need for raters to score large amounts of spoken discourse made it less practical than the computer-delivered tests of the second generation.

Youn (2013, 2015) developed a test of extended discourse that included both role-plays and a monologic task. Youn standardized parts of her role-plays by providing role-play conductors and participants with instructions on what social action to perform during the conversations, which included asking a professor for a recommendation letter and arranging with a classmate to collaborate on a project. For the monologic task, participants provided feedback on an email written by an imaginary classmate as an extended monologue. Youn also included two monologic tasks (similar to TOEFL speaking tasks) that were not pragmatically oriented and served as measures of general proficiency.

Youn took an interactional competence perspective and derived her rating criteria for role-plays using a bottom-up approach, analyzing discourse from her tasks, and extracting the following features that differentiate learners:

- content delivery: smoothness and fluidity of turn initiations and transitions
- language use: range of pragmalinguistic tools in terms of structures, modals to express indirectness

- sensitivity to the situation: recipient-designing contributions, for example by including accounts and explanations with a higher-power interlocutor
- engagement with the interaction: understanding of previous turns and active recipiency
- turn organization: completeness of adjacency pairs and appropriateness of pauses.

She adapted criteria for her monologic task from the TOEFL speaking rubric (Educational Testing Service, 2014). Youn used multi-faceted Rasch measurement as her main approach for quantitative analysis and found strong reliability of examinee ability measures; but, similar to other previous instruments, Youn's test was also somewhat easy for test takers.

While Youn's and Grabowski's instruments were entirely productive, Walters (2007, 2009) attempted to create a test encompassing comprehension and production. The test was strongly rooted in the CA tradition with a listening comprehension section requiring test takers to understand sequential organization, while in the speaking section they delivered responses to assessments (in the CA sense of utterances that demonstrate the speakers' evaluation of a target). For example, in the listening test, test takers' understanding of pre-sequences was examined through multiple-choice items, such as the pre-invitation in the aurally delivered dialogue in Figure 8.6 (Walters, 2009).

In the speaking part of the test, a test taker and an examiner conversed with each other, with the latter injecting a compliment, an assessment, and a pre-sequence at appropriate points in the conversation. The test taker's response to the examiner utterance (for example, response to a compliment, response to an assessment) was later scored by raters, though Walters (2007) did not analyze responses to pre-sequences as they 'evinced frequent problems with examinee uptake' (p. 167).

While innovative, Walters' test had very low reliabilities, possibly due to the homogenous test taker sample or due to little variation in abilities with regard to the pragmatic targets. It is also not clear what would constitute different

---

1	**M**	Hi Jane, this is Dick.
2	**W**	Hi Dick.
3	**M**	How ya doin-<uh what'r you guys doing.
4	**W**	Well we're about to leave for class. Why.

In the conversation, what do you think the man will most probably do NEXT?
(a) suggest going to class with the woman and the others
(b) offer to carry the woman's heavy book bag for her
*(c) explain that he had intended to make an invitation ***
(d) invite the woman and the other students to do something

Figure 8.6 Pre-sequence comprehension item (Walters, 2009, p. 39)

levels of ability in responses to assessments or compliments. Finally, it is especially questionable whether learners' common-sense knowledge of sequential organization can be tested as explicitly as Walters attempted. Testing interactional features as isolated instances is not likely to be a fruitful approach, as Walters' studies suggest.

Finally, Timpe (2013) integrated elements of the second and third generation by administering a computer-based multiple-choice test of sociopragmatics, encompassing speech acts, routine formulae, and idioms, and combining this test with four role-plays carried out via Skype. The role-plays varied the context variables of power and social distance, and were rated on the two main criteria of pragmatic performance and discourse performance, with subscales for the former based on Hudson et al. (1995) and the latter derived from the literature and data. Both parts had strong reliabilities in the mid-.8 region and, like many previous tests, were somewhat easy for Timpe's fairly high-proficiency sample of German ESL learners. It is noteworthy that Timpe's role-plays correlated more strongly with her multiple-choice section than with a proficiency measure, indicating a stronger pragmatics than proficiency effect in the role-plays, whereas both were about equally strong for the multiple-choice section. Timpe took a different approach to the testing of speech acts than previous studies by assessing test takers' comprehension of offers and requests, rather than having them judge appropriateness. However, the reliability for the speech act section was still quite low at .5, and the section was the easiest one in the test. In terms of practicality, the test is also a hybrid of the first and second generations: the multiple-choice sections had a time limit of 35 minutes, with the spoken tasks adding another 20 minutes, amounting to less than an hour's administration time. However, the spoken tasks require rater scoring.

As described above, tests in the third generation added extended discourse as an important new part of the construct to pragmatics testing. While tests combining elements of all three generations, like Timpe's, probably have the widest construct coverage, the integration of extended discourse reduces practicality and requires administration and rating by human testers. At the same time, great strides are being made in human–machine interactions using intelligent agents (Suendermann-Oeft, Ramanarayanan, Teckenbrock, Neutatz, & Schmidt, 2015), as well as in automated scoring of speaking (Zechner, Higgins, Xi, & Williamson, 2009). If these developments can aid in solving practicality problems, cost-efficient testing of a more well-rounded construct of L2 pragmatics is a distinct possibility.

Assessing L2 pragmatics: summary and directions for future research

Testing of L2 pragmatic ability has made significant progress in the 20 years since its inception. A range of tests has been developed covering most aspects of L2 pragmatic competence. However, several challenges remain, especially the balance between construct coverage and practicality, the role of proficiency, and the real-world predictiveness of pragmatics tests.

The issue of practicality is an eternal problem for tests of pragmatics. Establishing context is essential for pragmatics testing, both in terms of situational context and discourse context. Situational context concerns the relationship between interlocutors in terms of power, social distance, and imposition, but also the physical target language use situation. This can be best established through video or computer simulation (for example, Tada, 2005), both of which are resource-intensive to design and create. Discourse context is the actual sequential unfolding of interactions, and this is difficult to standardize without compromising the natural flow of the interaction, although Youn (2013) tried to do so. The solution in both cases is probably interaction with intelligent agents in a virtual reality environment, but the technology to implement this cheaply is still several years away.

Another conundrum is the relationship between proficiency and pragmatics (see Chapter 6 for a detailed discussion). Pragmatics is always somewhat mediated by proficiency since pragmatic meaning is primarily expressed linguistically. So to some extent, proficiency is likely to 'mask' pragmatic ability; to reduce that effect, several studies (Grabowski, 2009, 2013; Roever et al., 2014; Timpe, 2013; Youn, 2013, 2015) have limited their learner sample to intermediate-level learners and above. While this is likely to ensure that learners have sufficient proficiency to express pragmatic intentions, it curtails the range of learner abilities and lowers test reliability. Furthermore, it makes it challenging to create items of sufficient difficulty: higher-proficiency learners are also likely to have greater pragmatic ability, which explains the ceiling effect found in many studies. We need to use more difficult pragmatics items, and we need to know what makes pragmatics items difficult. For routine formulae, this is likely to be their frequency and transparency: less frequent and more opaque formulae are more difficult. Similarly, with implicatures, formulaic implicatures (Bouton, 1988) such as indirect criticism are more difficult than non-formulaic ones. But with speech acts, it appears that difficulty is to a large extent a function of the amount of language required, which takes us back to proficiency. In the case of extended discourse, there is some work being done to identify different levels of ability for a range of aspects, for example Youn's criteria, Galaczi's (2014) distinguishing features for elicited conversations rated at different levels of the Common European Framework of Reference for Languages (CEFR), and Roever's (2015) markers of interactional competence. Still, what features of extended discourse tasks make some tasks more challenging than others remains unclear.

A final problem, in some ways the most fundamental one, concerns extrapolation of test scores to target domains. In Kane's (2006) model of validation, inferences from tests concern the strength of the trait-in-domain, but very little knowledge exists about what is pragmatically required in domains like academic settings, 'everyday talk', medical settings, or offices. While there are corpora for academic genres that have been used in designing proficiency tests (Biber et al., 2004; Biber, 2006), domain characteristics that underlie pragmatics tasks have mostly been chosen based on the researcher's intuition and personal experience, rather than an empirically supported notion of representativeness. Understanding how pragmatics testing relates to real-world performance and how this relationship can be strengthened should be at the heart of future research on testing L2 pragmatics.

9

L2 pragmatics and globalization

Introduction

The previous eight chapters have presented a comprehensive review of L2 pragmatics research by surveying diverse topics within the current literature. We have discussed definitions and conceptualizations of pragmatic competence, theories of pragmatic development and descriptions of the development, research methods for examining pragmatic competence, and instructional, individual, and contextual influences on pragmatics learning. By surveying an array of these topics, we have examined the current state of pragmatics literature and identified the issues that must be taken further in future research.

In this chapter, we take a wider perspective and focus on three areas of applied linguistics literature that hold substantial implications for L2 pragmatics research. These areas belong to a broader domain of globalization. Globalization has brought momentous changes to the linguistic and cultural make-up of the world. National borders for languages, cultures, and norms are quickly disappearing, as people around the globe are more promptly and intensively connected than ever before. This phenomenon has compelled us to reconsider established assumptions about language use. As Kramsch (2014, p. 296) claims, the 'modernist tenets' of our profession—the stability of nation-states, the existence of stable grammar and codified norms of language, and the presence of clear boundaries between native and foreign languages—are now questioned and have to go through 'deep changes'.

Likewise, L2 pragmatics needs to find ways to respond to rapidly emerging globalization realities. In this chapter, we will first outline what those globalization realities are by presenting background literature in three areas: English as a lingua franca, intercultural competence, and heritage language learning. We have selected these areas because they represent the current globalization trends in applied linguistics, and concurrently their impact has started to be revealed in L2 pragmatics research. In other words, these areas have led to certain issues, trends, and concerns being uncovered, resulting in a transformation in traditional practices of pragmatics research. In each of these areas, we will review background literature and then discuss its relevance to pragmatics research. We will conclude each section with implications for future pragmatics research, teaching, and assessment.

Pragmatics in English as a lingua franca

English as a lingua franca: background

A lingua franca is a language that is adopted as a medium of communication between <u>speakers who do not share a native language</u> (Samarin, 1987). Historically, lingua francas emerged as contact languages for commercial purposes (also known as 'trade languages') and have spread to cultural, religious, and diplomatic domains as a means of exchanging information between people of different L1s. Although examples of lingua francas are numerous and exist in all continents, <u>English is currently the dominant lingua franca of international business, science, technology, diplomacy, aviation, and seafaring</u> (Crystal, 2006). According to recent statistics, 1.5 billion people speak English, of whom over 1.1 billion are non-native speakers of English (Statista, 2016). When native and non-native speakers are combined, English is the most widely spoken language: one in four of the world's population can speak English at functional level. Given this international demand, English as a lingua franca is both the <u>consequence of globalization and the medium</u> of <u>globalizing processes</u> (Jenkins, Cogo, & Dewey, 2011).

This definition of English as a lingua franca highlights the fact that the vast majority of <u>English users are not native speakers of English</u>. Seidlhofer (2011, p. 7) defines English as a lingua franca (ELF) as 'any use of English among speakers of different first languages for whom <u>English is the communicative medium of choice</u>, and often the only option'.[1] ELF speakers are from the Outer and Expanding Circles; they use English as a global medium of communication among themselves rather than with native English speakers.[2] Because native speakers are the minority group of ELF users, their English no longer serves as the single reference standard in ELF communication (Jenkins, 2015; Seidlhofer, 2011). Instead, ELF is considered to have a number of *similects*, which are contact varieties of English spoken by people of different L1s with features transferred from their L1s (Mauranen, 2012, p. 29). This concept further emphasizes the hybrid, plurilingual, and diversified nature of ELF.

The recent rapid growth of ELF as a medium of intercultural communication has meant that research on the use of ELF has expanded dramatically. A cursory database search with WorldCat brings up over 2,000 books and articles on the topic. The *Journal of English as a Lingua Franca* is into its fourth volume. The first book series on ELF, *Developments of English as a Lingua Franca* (de Gruyter Mouton), has produced nine volumes since 2013. In addition to publications, linguistics corpora have expanded rapidly. Four corpora of ELF have been compiled: the Vienna–Oxford International Corpus of English (Seidlhofer, 2002), ELF in Academic Settings (Mauranen, 2003), the Written Corpus of ELF in Academic Settings (Mauranen, 2015), and the Asian Corpus of English (Kirkpatrick, 2010). These corpora have facilitated linguistic descriptions of ELF, contributing to the recognition of ELF as language use in its own right, without reference to native-speaker English (Seidlhofer, 2011).

These worldwide, multi-level developments in ELF research have led to a critical mass of debates, controversies, and reconsiderations of conventional attitudes to English. One visible controversy is the ownership debate, which revolves around the question: Who owns English today? Currently, non-native speakers outnumber native speakers of English by a ratio of three to one. Hence, most communication in English takes place within and across the Outer and Expanding Circles rather than within the Inner Circle (based on Kachru's three circles of English, 1992). Given these realities, scholars have argued that native English speakers no longer own English or have the right to determine how English should be used (Widdowson, 1994).

Correspondingly, the native-speaker authority and the monolingual normality have been questioned and often disputed in a number of publications (for example, Canagarajah, 2006, 2013; Cook, 2002; Firth & Wagner, 1997; Jenkins, 2007; Pennycook, 1994; Rampton, 2006; Seidlhofer, 2011). Although English used by the Inner Circle speakers has been regarded as the only legitimate object of learning, and used as a benchmark for evaluating non-native speakers' English for a long time, this traditional practice presents an obvious mismatch with the actual use of English among ELF speakers, whose main aim is to use English for successful intercultural communication. As Seidlhofer (2011, p. 50) contends, for non-native ELF speakers, 'being able to use the language like native speakers and without traces of their L1 is increasingly perceived as unnecessary, unrealistic, and at least by some, as positively undesirable'.

Instead of adhering to pre-established native-speakers norms, ELF speakers operate according to their own standards, which are emergent, and contingent upon their communicative needs (Jenkins, 2015; Seidlhofer, 2011). Norms are negotiated and established *ad hoc*, depending on participants' resources and purposes in the context of interaction. L2 speakers' communication is often successful despite the non-standard forms they produce. Communication ability, i.e. the ability to adjust language for the mutual benefit of their interlocutors, is much more important for successful ELF communication than the ability to emulate native-speaker forms.

Creativity, adaptability, and contingency—the core characteristics of ELF interactions—have been well documented in the literature. Non-native-like features of ELF are not regarded as 'errors' or 'deficits'. Instead, they are viewed as resources that ELF speakers draw on to achieve mutual intelligibility. Previous studies have revealed numerous linguistic phenomena supporting this. (For a review, see Jenkins, 2015; Jenkins et al., 2011; Mauranen, 2012; Mackenzie, 2014; Seidlhofer, 2004, 2011.) For instance, ELF speakers often drop the third person singular -*s* and use the relative pronouns *who* and *which* interchangeably. These simplifications occur because they prioritize communicative effectiveness and economy over native-speaker-like forms. Similarly, ELF speakers omit the definite article *the* when it is practically redundant (for example, omitting *the* from *the best*), but maintain it when they want to add emphasis to a referent. This additive redundancy is also found in the overuse of a preposition, as in *discuss about* and *reject against*. These prepositions are non-standard but communicatively effective because they highlight the object of the verb. Lexical innovation is another characteristic of ELF. ELF speakers often produce non-standard forms such as *examinate* and *bigness* by applying morphological systems in unconventional ways. While not standard, these forms are perfectly functional.

Besides these lexico-grammatical features, the literature has uncovered accommodation strategies that ELF speakers employ to promote mutual intelligibility and solidarity. ELF speakers adjust and modify their verbal and non-verbal behaviors so these become more accessible and acceptable to each other. They try to make their messages explicit by repeating, rephrasing, and simplifying. They also use a range of convergence strategies. Firth (1996, 2009) observed that in ELF conversations, participants orient to the institutionalized goals of getting business done, and deflect attention from problematic language usage. For example, when their interlocutor produces a marked, non-standard form, ELF speakers often incorporate the non-standard form into their own turn rather than correcting the form. Another technique ELF speakers use is to provide an embedded repair by producing the standard form in their subsequent turn, rather than overtly correcting the non-standard form. They co-opt each other's non-standard usage or provide repair only implicitly, because the goal of talk is not to mimic native-speaker competence but to co-construct meaning with the available resources.

As illustrated above, various instances of non-standard language use found in ELF communication are indeed purposeful and functionally motivated, meeting the contextual and communicative requirements (Seidlhofer, 2011). These linguistic and discourse characteristics are indicative of the context-dependent, meaning-driven nature of ELF communication, whose primary goal is to maximize clarity, effectiveness, and economy of information exchange. ELF speakers 'adjust and calibrate their own language use for their interlocutors' benefit' (Seidlhofer, 2011, p. 109). Hence, the criteria of what is correct, appropriate, and acceptable do not subscribe to idealized native-speaker conventions; rather, they are determined *in situ* among local users based on what is feasible and practical for them. ELF is a representation of contingent creativity and adaptation in intercultural communication-in-progress.

Pragmatics in English as a lingua franca

How have these empirical descriptions of ELF, as well as controversies surrounding standard language ideology, affected L2 pragmatics research? Despite the overwhelming amount of literature on ELF in general, empirical descriptions of ELF pragmatics are under-represented in the literature. In her seminal paper in 2004, Seidlhofer acknowledged that, compared with the rich descriptions of ELF phonology that are available in the field, pragmatics is 'less manageable in research' because it does not contain 'a closed set of features for study', and violations of pragmatic norms 'rarely lead to loss of intelligibility' (Seidlhofer, 2004, p. 217). In this paper, she presented only a cursory summary of three generalizations about ELF pragmatics: (1) misunderstandings do not occur frequently in ELF interactions because speakers use compensatory strategies to handle them; (2) L1 interference of interactional norms rarely occurs because speakers suspend their L1-based expectations; and (3) ELF interactions are cooperative and consensus-driven, oriented toward mutual intelligibility. Seidlhofer called for future research documenting more generalizable patterns of ELF pragmatics based on a larger corpus. Yet her monograph in 2011 still presents a minimal treatment of ELF pragmatics. The author observes the same methodological challenge, saying that, unlike phonology, which involves a finite set of phonemes and intonation counters, analyzing 'the whole' of pragmatics is less feasible (Seidlhofer, 2011, p. 218). Although the book has a complete section devoted to idiomatic usage in ELF, pragmatics issues are largely subsumed within accommodation and convergence strategies.

We will return to this point in the 'future directions' section, but first let us review available findings on ELF pragmatics. We have categorized the literature into three areas: (1) intercultural pragmatics, (2) identity in pragmatic choices, and (3) pragmatic norms in English-medium schools. The first area is a direct representation of pragmatics research in ELF. The other two are re-interpretations of previous findings using the lingua franca framework.

Intercultural pragmatics

Intercultural pragmatics[3] is a field of research concerned with language use between speakers of different cultural backgrounds (Kecskes, 2012, 2014) (see Chapter 1). It studies how people of different L1s communicate using a common language, and what pragmatic principles manifest in their communication. Kecskes (2014) takes the socio-cognitive approach by combining the cognitive-philosophical perspective, which views intention as an a priori mental state of the speaker, and the sociocultural-interactional perspective, which views intention as a *post factum* phenomenon jointly constructed by the speaker and hearer in interaction. According to Kecskes, speakers resort to their prior cultural repertoires, but these repertoires blend with situationally emergent elements and develop into new intercultures.

Under the socio-cognitive approach, intercultural pragmatics is not just about, for example, how Chinese and Arabic speakers apologize to each other in English, what L1-based norms they bring to the act of apologizing, and whether those norms are in agreement or in conflict. Rather, the field's focus is on revealing how speakers from different cultures find common ground and co-construct norms of interaction unique to their communicative situations.

Although people's interactional norms are closely tied to their prior experiences as members of certain cultural groups, intercultural communication allows for new, hybrid, multicultural norms to emerge during interaction. As Kecskes (2014, p. 13) claims, intercultural communication goes beyond simply understanding cultural differences; it extends to 'creating a "third culture" that combines elements of each of the participants' original cultures in novel ways'.

Intercultural pragmatics is one area where ELF and pragmatics clearly intersect. This is because ELF itself is a process of intercultural pragmatics. In fact, Cogo and House (2017) named ELF as the context where most current work of intercultural pragmatics is located. The authors categorized findings in four areas of intercultural pragmatics strategies: negotiation of meaning, interactional management, creative idiomaticity, and use of multilingual resources. These are incorporated in our review below. From these topics, we learn that studies of intercultural pragmatics in ELF primarily focus on how speakers construct and negotiate mutual understanding while coping with problems of miscommunication and non-understanding.

Current ELF pragmatics research is concentrated in the area of negotiation of meaning. Research has revealed that ELF speakers use a variety of communication strategies to pre-empt potential communication problems or to solve problems after non-understanding has occurred. These strategies include paraphrasing, repeating, checking comprehension, and providing a repair. Among these strategies, the so-called 'represents' (Edmondson, 1981) (or other-repetitions) have been the focus of a number of studies (for example, Björkman, 2013; Cogo, 2009; Gotti, 2014; House, 2010; Kaur, 2012; Mauranen, 2012). In ELF talk, a part of the previous speaker's utterance is sometimes repeated or 'represented' (House, 2010, p. 373). Hence, the 'represents' strategy involves echoing or shadowing previous speakers' turns. By repeating what the interlocutor said, speakers can signal comprehension, emphasize the message, and, at the same time, develop coherence in discourse. ELF speakers' frequent use of these strategies indicates that mutual understanding is not assumed in ELF communication; it is co-constructed and monitored turn-by-turn.

Besides these compensatory strategies, ELF speakers often employ strategies for interactional management and solidarity building. Linguistic convergence and accommodation (which were discussed in the previous section) are some example strategies contributing to interactional management and solidarity building. By letting unclear utterances pass, or by adopting the interlocutor's nonstandard forms, the speakers display alignment and cooperation (Firth, 1996, 2009). Accommodation practice is also found in the use of L1-based resources. ELF speakers promote a shared sense of non-nativeness through code-switching and use of cognates. These strategies help to display their intercultural identities and accommodation to each other's cultural backgrounds (Hülmbauer, 2011). House (2010) illustrated a case of ELF speakers code-switching from English to L1 German. This typically occurred during small talk as phatic expressions, as well as in opening and closing rituals. Ife (2008) revealed frequent instances of code-switching from Spanish to ELF in college-level Spanish classes in the

U.K., which involved instructors and students from different L1s. Students often shifted to their common language, ELF, as an aid for learning and communication. This code-switching projected a range of pragmatic meanings, for example, regret, irony, and humor, indicating that students used ELF as a mutual resource for rapport-building and collaborative learning.

Another example of interactional management is found in the use of discourse markers. House (2009, 2010, 2013) documented how ELF speakers exploited intersubjectivity and connectivity through their skilled use of discourse markers 'yes/yeah', 'so', 'you know', and 'okay'. Speakers used these markers to reinforce their own perspectives and to organize discourse. Functional use of these markers in ELF conversations was greater than in those of native speakers, indicating the hybrid and poly-functional nature of ELF talk. In another study, Metsä-Ketelä (2016) found that ELF speakers use general extenders (for example, 'so on', 'or something like that') to express intersubjectivity in a variety of manners, including indicating hesitation and politeness, organizing discourse, and paraphrasing. Hiramoto (2012) adds a case of the discourse marker 'can' in Singaporean English: an example of a pragmatic marker becoming localized by adopting features from a regional language. Singaporeans use the marker 'can' in sentence-final position to project attitude and stance. This marker serves the interactional function because it helps the speaker emphasize his/her proposition to the hearer. Other studies examined overlapping as an indicator of active involvement in talk. Konakahara's (2015) analysis of ELF in British universities showed that overlapping questions occurred frequently to develop mutual understanding and interpersonal relationships.

Finally, idioms and chunks are also prominent features of intercultural management strategies. Although idioms are pervasive in any speech community, ELF speakers are unique in that they engage in the 'idiomatizing process' by adopting a portion of an existing idiom and customizing it to create a new one (Seidlhofer, 2011, p. 138). Newly invented idioms, which are non-conventional from the Standard English standpoint, serve as a shared repertoire, contributing to solidarity and in-group membership. Kecskes (2007) reported a case of ELF speakers using the phrase *Native Americans* to refer to native speakers of American English. Although this mistake was brought to the speakers' attention, the mistaken use remained and became incorporated into the group's repertoire, suggesting that this expression became part of the interculture being created. In another study, Mauranen (2009) documented ELF speakers' creative use of the chunk 'in my point of view'. This chunk and its alternative form 'in my opinion' were far more frequent than in comparable native-speaker corpora. These chunks showed greater expressiveness in ELF talk as a device to signal divergence of opinion and counter-argument.

These descriptions indicate that the pragmatic aspect of ELF is revealed most in strategies that are used to facilitate joint meaning-making. In ELF talk, pragmatics extends beyond the notions of politeness and face management, or pragmalinguistic and sociopragmatic knowledge, which L2 pragmatics research often focuses on. Besides these concepts, ELF pragmatics addresses how speakers use various conversation moves, communication strategies, and own and others' linguistic resources to support smooth interaction. Hence, pragmatic success in ELF is essentially about interactional success, i.e. whether speakers are able to achieve mutual understanding and build rapport by using a variety of resources in a creative, flexible manner.

In intercultural communication involving different L1s and cultural norms, the amount of shared knowledge and background information is limited. Hence, speakers need to willingly seek and co-construct common ground by developing shared understanding. Kecskes (2014) contends that this is the basic difference between intercultural and intracultural communication. Because in intercultural communication people do not know what to expect as common ground, they have to explicitly orient to and work toward it. Strategies for pre-empting and repair, interactional management, convergence, and accommodation are tools used to secure mutual understanding, which serves as a base for common ground. Intersubjectivity is contingent and achieved collaboratively during the process of common ground building.

In summary, pragmatics in ELF closely aligns with the socio-cognitive approach in intercultural pragmatics. As Kecskes (2014) claims, intercultural pragmatics involves the study of two types of intention in synergy: prior intention and emergent intention. ELF speakers bring assumptions and expectations from their own cultures, but those prior individual experiences are negotiated and redefined in their actual situational experiences in interaction. Norms of interaction are synergetic and situationally emergent: they reflect individual speakers' perspectives and stance, but those individual norms eventually develop into new, hybrid norms, reflecting the dynamics of interaction. Various standards of politeness and directness are constantly negotiated among ELF speakers, and speakers develop their own communicative styles while using a shared language.

Gu, Patkin, and Kirkpatrick's (2014) study is a clear illustration of this socio-cognitive approach in intercultural pragmatics. The authors analyzed a conversation between a librarian (a Hong Kong Chinese person) and two academic staff members (a British person and a Singaporean Chinese person) in a university in Hong Kong. These speakers negotiated their power relations and professional identities by drawing on their institutional roles and personal histories. When the librarian was explaining the multilingual function in the search engine, the British speaker said that he does not understand other languages because he is a 'native speaker' of English, implying a link between being a native English speaker and monolingualism. He continued that English is the official language in Singapore, and other languages (for example, Chinese) are secondary. The librarian responded that in Hong Kong, where he is from, people have to speak three languages, thereby reinforcing his multilingual identity. In this way, speakers constantly drew on their personal backgrounds and culturally conditioned norms to position themselves and others in the discourse. But interestingly, even in these face-threatening circumstances, the speakers still pursued alignment and common ground by taking into consideration each other's histories and values, and establishing a commonality based on their shared multicultural context. Hence, ELF communication provides a context for speakers to re-evaluate their histories and cultural backgrounds and, at the same time, to establish new attitudes, relationships, and identities.

Identity in pragmatic choices

As discussed in Chapter 6, previous studies have repeatedly found that learner identity and agency affect pragmatic choices. Learners do not blindly conform to the pragmatic norms practiced in the local community. In contrast, they reject adopting certain pragmatic practices, like the use of honorifics, gendered speech, or informal language, when these norms are incongruent with their L1-derived cultural values or their sense of self (for example, Brown, 2013; Iwasaki, 2011; Kim, 2014). For instance, Kim's study revealed instances of accommodation and divergence from target pragmatic norms among Korean learners of English in the United States. Because of their Asian identity and L1-based value of modesty, students felt uncomfortable with accepting a compliment in English by saying just 'Thank you'. To avert awkward feelings, they added humble expressions in their compliment responses. Similarly, when making a request to someone younger, they resisted target norms of using indirect strategies. Instead, they intentionally used direct forms (imperative requests) to position themselves as an older interlocutor with authority.

These non-normative speech act behaviors, resulting from L2 learners' conflicting identities, highlight the agency of learners who make their own linguistic decisions. Because ELF speakers use a language as a means of intercultural communication, not as a way of conforming, they maintain their L1 identity by confronting native speakers' sociopragmatic values (Clyne, 2006). Since native-speaker norms do not serve as reference points or models in ELF communication, deviations from target standards are irrelevant as discussion points. More precisely, instances of nonconformity to the norm should *not* be regarded as deviations. If L2 speakers are indeed aware of normative pragmatic patterns but still opt out, it can be assumed that they are exercising agency. L2 speakers often express their social and cultural identity, and they do so by selecting certain pragmalinguistic forms and sociopragmatic norms that suit them.

An important implication from ELF research, which we should keep in mind when interpreting identity-related literature, is that learners' linguistic choices are not fixed. Because ELF is fluid and contingent upon speakers' resources and needs specific to the context of interaction, language use in ELF presents both regularities and variations. Patterns of ELF gleaned from corpus-based analyses, such as dropping the third person -*s* or using the relative pronouns 'who' and 'which' interchangeably, while frequent and regular, are not stable patterns and thus cannot be codified (Jenkins, 2015). These features change according to the situation, because ELF speakers constantly exploit the potential of language systems as they focus on the purpose of interactions and on their interlocutors (Seidlhofer, 2009).

These descriptions apply to pragmatics too. Pragmatic choices that L2 speakers make reflect their understanding of the self, others, and context at the moment of interaction. These choices are localized and negotiated *in situ*. L2 speakers might opt for different pragmatic choices as their interlocutors and context of interaction change, and they position themselves differently. The ELF research provides sites in which this dynamic, fluid nature of L2 identity and pragmatic choices can be examined.

Pragmatic norms in English-medium institutions

With the recent expansion of English-medium education worldwide, international universities have become prime sites of ELF use. These universities involve a large number of international students, staff, and instructors of different nationalities and L1 backgrounds. English is used as the global lingua franca on a daily basis for both academic study and social interactions. This trend has resulted in a large amount of research on the linguistic implications of English-medium education, as represented in book-length monographs and edited volumes on the topic (Björkman, 2013; Doiz, Lasagabaster, & Sierra, 2013; Jenkins, 2014; Mauranen, 2012, Smit, 2010; Smit & Dafouz, 2013; Taguchi, 2014b).

While language use in English-medium academic communities has been documented in these publications, less has been revealed about the pragmatics of ELF in these communities. In this section we will present Taguchi's (2012) year-long longitudinal study on pragmatic development conducted in an English-medium university in Japan. We focus on this study because it revealed the precise characteristics of ELF communication, i.e. contingency and adaptability, in pragmatics. The study showed how Japanese ESL students and instructors in this particular ELF community suspended idealized pragmatic norms and instead co-constructed pragmatic norms unique to their needs and situations. Findings thus confirm that norms of interaction are locally negotiated and emergent, and do not necessarily follow native-speaker conventions.

The study traced changes in 48 Japanese students' speech acts through cyclical administration of an oral DCT task. Combined with qualitative data collected via interviews and observations, the study revealed pragmatic experiences available in the ELF context and the ways they shaped students' pragmatic development. After a year, students' high-imposition speech acts (making a high-stakes request of a teacher or expressing an opinion to a teacher on a serious matter) showed little progress. Critically, the patterns found in the DCT task were also observed in their interactions with native-speaker instructors. In the real-life pragmatics of expressing a complaint about a class, students often used explicit expressions of dislike ('I don't like X.') and strong modals ('should' and 'must'). Although instructors were aware of the students' rudeness, they never reacted to it. They focused on getting students' feedback on the class and did not care about the manner in which the feedback was delivered.

These findings highlight the contingent and adaptive nature of ELF communication. During the process of socialization and cultural adjustment, teachers and students co-adapted to each other's needs and circumstances. Teachers adapted to the Japanese students' tendency of being shy about speaking up, which comes from the students' L1-based cultural practices, and responded to it by accepting their impoliteness when they did speak up. Japanese students adapted to the Western mode of education that promotes partnership with teachers for creating a productive learning environment. They learned that it is acceptable to complain about a class directly as long as their comments are constructive. During this socialization process, sociopragmatic dimensions of communication—politeness and formality—were not an issue for students or instructors. Direct interaction styles were accepted and appropriated. Those norms were context-driven, needs-based, and co-constructed according to the participants' mutual benefit.

Further striking evidence of emergent pragmatic norms is found in the case history of Tomoyo (pseudonym). Tomoyo started out with fairly competent speech act production at the beginning of the study. Unlike other students, she was able to use elaborate pragmalinguistic expressions furnished with syntactic mitigations and indirect forms (for example, she used the bi-clausal request-making form 'I wonder if' + clause). However, her pragmatic knowledge diminished over time. The target pragmalinguisitic forms, which were in her repertoire at the onset of the study, disappeared in the last DCT task. Instead, she used direct forms and informal linguistic markers (for example, contractions such as 'wanna' and 'gonna') in high-imposition speech acts. This change, however, perfectly corresponded to the kind of interactional experiences that Tomoyo accumulated in this ELF context.

[margin note: adapt her speech ∴ interaction w/ NS]

Because Tomoyo had extensive contact with English speakers in her high school, she was already fluent when she entered the English-medium university. Her competent English skills, combined with her open, candid personality, worked to her advantage in developing a rapport with ESL instructors and gaining their trust as a student who could understand and respond to their concerns. Over time, her relationship with teachers became close and informal, and, as a result, her manner of speech became direct and casual. In her real-life context, formal, high-imposition situations, such as those encoded in the DCT task, did not exist. Her sociopragmatic assessment of these situations changed. Consequently, indirect, elaborate expressions disappeared from her systems in both real-life and DCT tasks.

Tomoyo's case is a concrete illustration of adaptation and accommodation. Norms regarding what is appropriate and acceptable as a way of speaking were negotiated *ad hoc*, corresponding to the purposes of communication. By doing away with formal, elaborate ways of speaking, Tomoyo effectively positioned herself in the community where local members (students and teachers) orient to the institutionalized goals and adapt their linguistic means to achieve these goals. Conformity to the idealized pragmatic conventions, as expected in the DCT task (for example, using mitigations and indirect expressions), was indeed unnecessary and even dysfunctional in this ELF context. Exercising her agency, Tomoyo distanced herself from the pre-determined norms and engaged in authentically appropriate ways of speaking, which were negotiated and determined by local members. These findings support Seidlhofer's (2011) point that ELF talk is not about forms but about the functions and the goals it fulfills.

If we conceptualize pragmatic competence as the ability to communicate appropriately in a situation, Tomoyo did indeed demonstrate such an ability by moving away from the idealized norms and adapting to the local norms. Her pragmatic demeanors were completely appropriate, effective, and reciprocating in her context of use. These findings reiterate that the right to determine what is appropriate and desirable belongs to local users of the language, not to idealized native speakers. ELF users exploit possibilities to produce linguistic forms that are appropriate and effective in their context of use. Norms are co-constructed and revised among those who are directly involved in the process.

Future directions in lingua franca pragmatics

The previous sections have surveyed key findings from ELF literature and discussed their relevance to L2 pragmatics research. In concluding this section, we will present two major directions for future research: expanding the database of ELF pragmatics features and moving away from native-speaker norms as a single model of pragmatic competence.

Analyzing pragmatics in lingua franca communication

One direction for future research is to expand the scope of pragmatics analyses in ELF communication. Aside from studies on accommodation, communication strategies, and interactional management, we do not have many studies focusing on the use of forms for social-interpersonal functions in a situation, i.e. the primary area of investigation in pragmatics research. We discussed the difficulty of documenting ELF pragmatics earlier in this section by referring to Seidlhofer's (2011) observation that pragmatics is not practical to study because of the open set of features available for study. Because of a lack of a closed set of features, pragmatics is left to search for its own methods and approaches in ELF research. One possible approach is to focus on those pragmatic features that occur most frequently. For example, address terms, discourse markers, hedging, and routines are searchable in a larger corpus. By analyzing how ELF speakers use them in interaction with other ELF users, researchers can reveal characteristics of ELF talk—contingency, adaptability, and creativity—reflected in pragmatics. There are a few studies on discourse markers, but given the small database, future research is needed in this direction.

Another approach to researching ELF pragmatics is to commit to small-scale qualitative analyses of pragmatic language use in ELF talk. This approach is seen in studies of intercultural pragmatics, which revealed how pragmatic principles manifest in interactions between people who operate on different cultural norms and backgrounds. Researchers can start from pragmatics-related concepts such as face-saving, politeness, and solidarity, and analyze how these concepts are realized linguistically and interactionally among ELF speakers (for example, see Maíz-Arévalo, 2014; Schnurr & Zayts, 2013). Alternatively, pragmatic acts of an interpersonal nature (for example, disagreements, confrontations, and complaints) can be sampled in ELF and analyzed for pragmalinguistic and sociopragmatic features characterizing those acts.

Such analyses can expand the body of ELF findings and add new questions: how accommodation and convergence emerge in consensus-oriented, cooperative ELF talk; whether participants draw on their L1-based pragmatic norms or suspend their norms; and how they co-construct mutual standards of what is appropriate and accepted in pragmatic acts. These analyses are available in the domain of intercultural pragmatics, but by adding the ELF framework more explicitly, we can certainly strengthen the connection between ELF and pragmatics.

Searching for alternative approaches to the native-speaker ideal

A critical mass of ELF research has led to a substantial reassessment of traditional assumptions and approaches to the study of language learning. One of those assumptions is native-speaker authority. A non-refutable generalization emerging in the literature is that ELF speakers use English not just to identify with native English speakers, but to achieve communicative goals, develop personal relationships, and express identity in intercultural communication. Because ELF speakers focus on mutual intelligibility and efficiency of communication, rather than native-speaker correctness, native-speaker norms are often irrelevant and do not serve as a reference point (Seidlhofer, 2011).

Native-speaker norms have been problematized in L2 pragmatics literature as well. Mori (2009) challenges assumptions of uniform native-speaker norms in the current pragmatics research. Following the SLA tradition, mainstream practice in pragmatics has been to collect data from a sample of native speakers and use it as baseline data to which L2 learners' pragmatic behaviors are compared. When selecting a native-speaker sample, researchers typically draw on Davies's (1995, p. 156) 'bio-developmental definition', i.e. that native speakers are born to the language spoken in the community. Although native speakers come from a variety of regions, professions, and generations, these variations are often discounted, and their pragmatic performance as a group is regarded as an ideal model.

The central problem with this practice is the assumption that native speakers operate under identical standards in judging and projecting the appropriateness of pragmatic behaviors. In fact, they do not. An immediate example is a conversation between a contributor and the volume editor (Taguchi, 2009, personal communication). The author wrote a chapter about L2 Japanese learners' use of honorifics (Ikeda, 2009). Three native speakers evaluated learners' honorific usage on a five-point rating scale. When reporting the findings, the author initially used a sum of the scores from the three raters, rather than the averaged score, although the latter is more conventional in the practice of assessment. The author used the sum because of the large variation observed in their scores. The raters were highly subjective in judging appropriateness of honorifics, demonstrating the extent to which the use of honorifics is dependent on personality and individual style. Because there was no solid consensus, the author opted for a composite score to respect individual raters' judgments. This episode reiterates variation among native speakers in assessing pragmatics.

Aside from this anecdote, there is empirical evidence supporting extensive native-speaker variation in honorifics usage. Okamoto (2011) analyzed blog postings and found that there are no socially agreed-upon rules of honorifics that all speakers follow corresponding to contextual specifics (for example, hierarchy and social distance). Japanese speakers showed different beliefs about how honorifics should be used, which made the author conclude that 'it is ultimately the speaker and not the context that determines the choice of honorific and plain forms' (Okamoto, 2011, p. 368). The meanings of speech forms are diverse and ambiguous, reflecting one's language ideology and contextual contingencies.

The Japanese honorifics system is a perfect vehicle for disclosing native-speaker variation. The honorifics system is socioculturally complex. Speakers use honorifics not just to conform to socially agreed norms in a situation, but they use them strategically to construct their social identity. In other words, the degree of honorifics used by individual speakers is, to some extent, a reflection of the social self that they want to project, i.e. how polite or casual they want to sound in a certain situation, which leads to immense individual variation in their use.

If there are no uniform native-speaker standards, or if the standards are not valid or relevant in evaluating L2 pragmatic abilities, what alternative approaches exist for assessing and teaching pragmatics? By whose criteria should appropriateness be determined and evaluated? If the assumption of idealized native speakers is in question, can teachers still transmit ideological beliefs about community norms to students? In our search for answers, we can turn to the ELF literature, where various scholars have engaged in the discussion on alternative models. Several scholars have made an attempt to replace the label 'native speaker'. Leung, Harris, and Rampton (1997) proposed the term 'expert speaker' to describe the fluent user of English. Jenkins (2015), on the other hand, proposed the terms 'monolingual speakers' to refer to native speakers and 'bilingual speakers' to refer to non-native speakers.

More intense discussion on alternative approaches to native-speaker norms is found in the area of assessment (for example, Jenkins & Leung, 2014; McNamara, 2011; Hall, 2014). By problematizing current language testing ideology found in high-stakes assessments (for example, TOEFL, IELTS), Jenkins and Leung (2014) argue that benchmarks used to evaluate ELF have to be updated. The authors recommend moving away from a narrow focus on native-like correctness. They suggest cultivating ways to assess communicative success, effectiveness, and accommodation skills, because these features help to determine whether ELF users' language is indeed fit for ELF use.

Researchers in pragmatics can certainly benefit from this ongoing debate as they re-evaluate what counts as socially appropriate language behavior. Appropriateness can be reconceptualized according to a local context of use, i.e. speakers' communicative needs, resources, and goals of interaction, rather than idealized norms of native speakers who are not part of the local context. To do so, we echo Ishihara and Cohen's (2010) suggestion that we need to first assess who the L2 speakers are, with whom they use the language, and what needs they have for their language use. Through such needs analyses, norms respective to the local community will emerge, to which learners have to commit for a successful intercultural exchange.

Another implication coming from ELF research relates to the aspects of ability to be evaluated in pragmatics. Now that there is clear evidence about the flexibility and adaptability involved in ELF communication, we can focus our evaluation on these aspects that are critical for a successful interaction (success based on mutual intelligibility). Likewise, it is important that we assess a pragmatic act for effectiveness in its entirety within a communicative event, rather than based on pieces of isolated pragmalinguistic forms appearing in the act. This implication corresponds to the recent emphasis on discursive pragmatics (Kasper, 2006b), interactional competence (Young, 2011), and intercultural pragmatics (Kecskes, 2014). This body of literature has highlighted the shifting view of pragmatic competence from 'pragmatics-within-individuals' to 'pragmatics-in-interaction-in-context'. Pragmatic acts are dynamic and negotiated among speakers of different cultural backgrounds. Strategies for accommodation, intelligibility, and co-construction of meaning revealed in ELF analyses can provide a useful framework to examine and evaluate such pragmatics-in-interaction.

These new concepts and epistemologies emerging from ELF research offer several implications for teaching pragmatics. In order to develop flexibility and adaptability, learners can practice pragmatics in authentic, less controlled dialogic activities, where they have choices to adapt their pragmatic resources to ongoing interactions. Likewise, when teaching pragmatics, instructors can incorporate a range of performance-oriented, interactional features, not just typical pragmalinguistic forms and semantic strategies. We can find those interactional features in the empirically based strategies used in ELF, which Murray (2012) recommends as a pragmatics toolkit. Those strategies include:

pedagogy

developing tolerance toward ambiguity and infelicities of language; teaching communication strategies that help to pre-empt problems; de-emphasizing one's own politeness parameters; and practicing accommodation by tuning into the interlocutor's turns and linguistic/non-linguistic behaviors.

Because of the monolingual orientations in SLA research, interactions with native speakers have been regarded as an ideal condition for L2 learning for some time. This conventional thinking requires transformation because of the current multilingual reality and international use of English. As the vast majority of English use around the world occurs between L2 English speakers, and not with native speakers of English, instructors should set up tasks that simulate interactions between speakers of different varieties of ELF. Pragmatic acts in those tasks should reflect what ELF speakers are likely to encounter in everyday intercultural communication. Critically, tasks should be designed according to the institutionalized goal of getting business done so that learners' task performance can be evaluated for clarity, effectiveness, and co-construction of pragmatic acts. Recent technology, such as social networking, blogging, and other tools of digitally mediated communication, can be used to create opportunities for pragmatic practice in intercultural communication (see also Chapter 7).

Intercultural competence

The previous section discussed pragmatic competence in lingua franca communication by highlighting how pragmatic acts are dynamic and emergent in discourse between intercultural speakers. In this section, we will continue with the topic of intercultural pragmatics, but we will shift our focus from the process of intercultural communication to the construct of intercultural competence.[4] Specifically, we will discuss current conceptualizations of intercultural competence by surveying definitions and key characteristics; we will then propose a relationship between intercultural competence and pragmatic competence.

Conceptualization of L2 communicative competence has evolved over the last four decades, shifting from the individualistic view of competence to a more interaction-oriented understanding of construct (see Chapter 8). We propose that communicative competence can be situated more broadly within the concept of 'intercultural speakers' (Byram, 1997, 2012; Kramsch, 2011). With globalization, the goal of language learning has shifted from the learner approximating native-speaker norms to an attempt, on the part of an intercultural speaker (who is sensitive to other cultures and aware of his/her own cultural position), to mediate across linguistic and cultural boundaries (Wilkinson, 2012). An intercultural speaker possesses two distinct competences: communicative competence and intercultural competence (Byram, 1997). The former involves the ability to communicate effectively and appropriately in intercultural interactions, while the latter entails certain personality traits, attitudes, and worldviews that help individuals to engage with

[handwritten margin note: definition of CC and intercultural competence]

cultural differences.)These two competences jointly assist people's ability to navigate communication in intercultural spaces.

Intercultural competence: background

As intercultural competence has become a prime concern among international and domestic communities, a number of definitions, theoretical models, and assessment measures of intercultural competence have appeared in the field (Fantini, 2006, 2012; Leung, Ang, & Tan, 2014; Sinicrope, Norris, & Watanabe, 2007; Spitzberg & Chagnon, 2009). Much of this work is highly interdisciplinary, with definitions and frameworks coming from a variety of fields, including intercultural psychology, personality studies, international business and management, global leadership, intercultural communication, and international education.

Currently, there are more than 30 models of intercultural competence over 300 related constructs (Leung et al., 2014). Although this proliferation is overwhelming, a closer inspection reveals some commonality among definitions. For instance, Wiseman (2002, p. 208) defines intercultural competence as 'the knowledge, motivation and skills to interact effectively and appropriately with members of different cultures'. In Fantini's (2006, p. 12) definition, intercultural competence refers to 'a complex of abilities needed to perform effectively and appropriately when interacting with others who are linguistically and culturally different from oneself'. Johnson et al. (2006, p. 530) define intercultural competence as 'an individual's effectiveness in drawing upon a set of knowledge, skills, and personal attributes in order to work successfully with people from different national cultural backgrounds at home or abroad'.

The similarity between these three definitions is two-fold, in that intercultural competence: (1) is situated in the context of cultural differences; and (2) refers to knowledge, skills, attitudes, and personal traits that help us communicate effectively and appropriately while engaging with cultural differences. To be sure, the concept of cultural differences is not simply limited to geographical boundaries. The idea more generally refers to diverging orientations between any groups of people. This claim is clearly reflected in Spitzberg & Chagnon's (2009, p. 7) definition of intercultural competence: 'the appropriate and effective management of interaction between people who, to some degree or another, represent different or divergent cognitive, affective, and behavioral orientations to the world'.

As with the scope of definitions, theoretical models of intercultural competence are also diverse. Some models take a developmental view of intercultural competence, while other models take a componential approach (see Sincrope et al., 2007, for a review). A representative model of the developmental orientation is the Developmental Model of Intercultural Sensitivity (DMIS) (Bennett, 1993; Bennett et al., 1999). The DMIS views intercultural competence as 'the general ability to transcend ethnocentrism, appreciate other cultures, and generate appropriate behavior in one or more different cultures' (Bennett et al., 1999, p. 13). In the DMIS, intercultural adaptation is seen in the process of moving from an ethnocentric (one's culture as central) to ethnorelative (one's culture as one of many) worldview. The six stages in the model—denial, defense, minimization, acceptance, adaptation, and integration—present a continuum that illustrates the way in which people gradually develop the ability to construe cultural differences in more complex ways.

The other componential approach is more prominent in the field. A number of models taking this approach emphasize core elements that form the basis of one's potential to succeed in intercultural communication. For example, Byram's (1997) model includes five dimensions. The first dimension, attitudes, refers to the personal traits of flexibility and openness, which help a person appreciate others' cultural values. The second dimension, knowledge of self and others, refers to knowledge of cultural rules and practices. The third dimension, skills of interpreting and relating, involves the ability to interpret, explain, and relate events from another culture. The fourth dimension, skills of discovery and interaction, includes one's ability to acquire knowledge of a new culture. Finally, cultural awareness refers to the ability to draw on practices in one's own culture and other cultures when making evaluations. In a similar way, Fantini (2006) conceptualizes intercultural competence as consisting of three major components: personal traits, abilities in different domains and dimensions, and language proficiency.

Another example of a componential model is Kelley and Meyers's (1995) model. Like Byram's and Fantini's, this model includes several personal traits as components: flexibility and openness, emotional resilience (ability to react positively to new experiences), and autonomy (one's sense of self as a unique entity). However, unlike others, this model addresses the ability to communicate more directly by including perceptual acuity as one of the components. Perceptual acuity refers to one's ability to pay attention to verbal and non-verbal cues in intercultural communication. A range of factors—differences in language systems, communication styles, and values encoded in language—may lead to communication difficulties. Perceptual acuity is considered to help ease these difficulties.

Another way to classify models is by content. According to Leung et al. (2014), diverse characteristics of intercultural competence in the existent models can be divided into three areas: (1) traits, (2) attitudes and worldviews, and (3) capabilities. Traits involve personal characteristics that determine a stable pattern of behaviors. Flexibility, openness, and emotional resilience (mentioned above) belong to this category, along with other traits such as inquisitiveness (Bird et al., 2010), patience (Kealey, 1996), and ambiguity tolerance (Deardoff, 2006). Attitudes and worldviews, on the other hand, focus on how people perceive other cultures. Bennett's (1993) ethnocentric–ethnorelative worldviews concept is an example. The last area, capabilities, refers to what people can do to be effective in intercultural communication. Some examples include learning about other cultures (in Byram and Fantini's models), developing perceptual acuity (in Kelley and Myer's model), as well as adapting to communication (Gudykunst, 1993), and developing social flexibility (Bird et al., 2010).

To sum up, intercultural competence specifies knowledge, skills, and personal qualities that are useful for individuals to function effectively in culturally diverse settings. Common elements of intercultural competence include minimum ethnocentrism, flexibility and openness to new experiences, ambiguity tolerance, empathy, and communication skill. These elements are postulated as culturally generic attitudes that are considered useful in any cultural encounter.

Intercultural competence in L2 communication

Communication skill is situated as a core constituent of intercultural competence. Fantini (2006, 2012) argues that intercultural competence and language competence together can promote full access to a new culture. Similarly, Byram (2012, p. 89) contends that successful intercultural communication involves 'both intercultural competence and linguist/communicative competence, in any task of mediation where two distinct languacultures are present'. However, existing models do not usually specify the actual linguistic skills required for a successful intercultural encounter. For instance, Fantini (2012) simply makes a reference to ACTFL guidelines as a measure of language proficiency and does not stipulate how linguistic abilities work with other personal traits or cultural knowledge to facilitate intercultural communication. Most measures of intercultural competence are designed to collect indirect evidence of linguistic proficiency using a self-report survey, and very few studies have actually assessed linguistic abilities as part of intercultural competence.

This construct-level separation between the discussion of intercultural competence and linguistic competence is also noticeable in the literature of communicative competence.[5] In the four decades' worth of discussion on communicative competence models, the concept of intercultural competence has been largely absent. A notable exception is Usó-Juan and Martínez-Flor's (2006, p. 161) model, which includes intercultural competence as a component of communicative competence, along with linguistic, pragmatic, and strategic competences. They define intercultural competence as 'the knowledge of how to interpret and produce a spoken or written piece of discourse within a particular sociocultural context'. Cultural knowledge and awareness, operationalized as knowledge of sociocultural conventions, dialects, and non-verbal signals, are key aspects of intercultural competence. Although this conceptualization does not extend to personal traits and attitudes, explicit attention to the intercultural concern in L2 competence is noteworthy.

To further expand on Usó-Juan and Martínez-Flor's model, SLA researchers can draw on a larger discourse of intercultural communication to specify the elements of intercultural competence, while maintaining their core concern about communicative competence. Building on Leung et al.'s (2014) synthesis, intercultural competence can be conceptualized involving three dimensions: (1) intercultural capabilities, (2) intercultural traits, and (3) intercultural attitudes/worldviews. The first area, intercultural capabilities, involves cultural knowledge that helps L2 learners understand the target cultural norms and practices. At the same time, these capabilities refer to the ability to communicate, which can be operationalized at the level of grammatical, pragmatic, interactional, and strategic competences that enable learners to attend to linguistic and semiotic cues, and co-construct meaning during interaction. Drawing on the literature on lingua franca discourse (for example, Seidlhofer, 2011; Jenkins, et al., 2011) and interactional competence (Young, 2008), the ability to communicate can focus on how communicative acts are interactionally managed and negotiated by participants *in situ*.

The second dimension, intercultural traits, entails personal characteristics that affect intercultural behaviors. Key characteristics include flexibility and open-mindedness, emotional resilience, ambiguity tolerance, empathy, and curiosity. The last dimension, intercultural attitudes/worldviews, focuses on how people perceive cultures outside their own. Culturally competent individuals are usually distant from an ethnocentric view of cultural differences and similarities, and they take a more ethnorelative, global worldview. In the SLA literature, these traits and attitudes are typically discussed as individual difference factors. However, given the extensive content validity evidence found in the literature beyond SLA, these individual characteristics can be situated as critical dimensions of intercultural competence.

These three dimensions (capabilities, traits, and attitudes/worldviews) inform intercultural effectiveness, as reflected in the degree of one's cultural adjustment and performance. While this framework is largely drawn from the fields of intercultural communication, business, and global leadership, the contribution from SLA is seen in fine-tuned specifications of intercultural capabilities. To become effective in intercultural interactions, one needs cultural knowledge and awareness (Usó-Juan & Martínez-Flor, 2006), linguistic and pragmatic knowledge (Bachman & Palmer, 2010), and interactional abilities (Celce-Murcia, 2007; Young, 2008).

These skills and knowledge, together with intercultural traits and attitudes/worldviews, essentially assist one's growth as an intercultural speaker. The successful intercultural speaker is one who possesses intercultural communicative competence, critical cultural awareness, and skills of discovery and interpreting cultures (for example, Byram, 1997; Kramsch, 2011; Wilkinson, 2012). Intercultural competence can directly address this concern by specifying capability, trait, and attitude-based characteristics of an effective intercultural speaker.

Intercultural competence in pragmatics

The previous section discussed the construct of intercultural competence and the placement of communicative competence within that construct. In this section, we will more directly situate pragmatic competence within the discourse of intercultural competence. The connection between these two competences is evident from what we have discussed so far. Intercultural capabilities involve the ability to engage in intercultural communication; pragmatic knowledge, a component of communicative competence, can directly contribute to that ability. Hence, pragmatic competence in intercultural settings can be viewed as a constituent of intercultural competence. By situating pragmatics within intercultural competence, pragmatic competence goes beyond the traditional focus on how L2 learners perform a pragmatic act, and it extends to a broader understanding of how L2 learners participate in intercultural interactions. <u>The connection between pragmatic and intercultural competences can also elevate the practice of L2 pragmatics research from SLA matters alone to the area of global citizenship</u> (Taguchi, 2017).

Several studies have investigated the direct relationship between intercultural and pragmatic competence. Cohen et al. (2005) found significant correlations between speech act gains and cultural learning strategies (for example, paying attention to gestures; using a different cultural perspective to understand meaning) among Spanish and French learners while abroad. In another study, Shively and Cohen (2008) used Hammer et al.'s (2003) Intercultural Developmental Inventory (a survey based on Bennett's DMIS) to assess intercultural development among L2 Spanish learners. Learners showed gains in their speech acts and intercultural sensitivity during a semester abroad, but no correlation was found between these constructs. Taguchi (2015b), on the other hand, examined the relationship between cross-cultural adaptability (based on Kelley & Meyers, 1995) and speech acts in L2 Japanese learners while abroad. A significant relationship was found between the initial-level cultural adaptability and gains in appropriate speech act production, but there was no relationship with gains in appropriate use of speech style (polite or plain form). Given this small pool of research, we need more studies that examine the relationship between pragmatic competence and intercultural competence.

The relationship between these two competences is conceptually plausible because of common features shared between these constructs. Key traits of intercultural competence, i.e. flexibility, openness, empathy, and ability to interpret cultural cues, essentially draw on the notion of adaptability. Individuals with these qualities are often tolerant and non-judgmental, and thus are able to adapt to different ways of thinking and behaving, which leads to a successful cultural adaptation.

Likewise, pragmatic competence assumes the notion of adaptability, or, more precisely, linguistic adaptability to context. It is the ability to adapt linguistic resources to different contexts and perform a communicative act appropriately. Different contexts presume different types of linguistic strategies and interactional cues depending on the goals and settings of the interaction. Part of pragmatic competence is to understand contextual specifics (for example, setting, speaker relationship, degree of formality) and decide which linguistic and interactional resources to use to accomplish a communicative act. Learners' linguistic choices essentially reflect their pragmatic adaptability, i.e. their ability to maneuver between different contexts with linguistic resources. In addition, contextual specifics are not fixed variables. They change within a sequential context of discourse corresponding to participants' responses to each other's contributions to a talk. They also change over time, corresponding to participants' changing attitudes and relationships as time goes by. Here, pragmatic adaptability refers to the ability to maneuver between *changing* contexts with linguistic resources.

Adaptability, a common feature of pragmatic and intercultural competences, can be explored further with an explicit focus on addressing the relationship between these two competences. In addition to these two constructs, social contact can be included in the research design. As an indicator of cultural adjustment, social contact is often theorized as part of behavioral outcomes in intercultural competence models. Factors such as the number of intercultural friends people have (Hammer, 2005), their amount of multicultural activity (Van Oudenhoven & Van der Zee, 2002), and the degree to which they show intercultural cooperation (Mor et al., 2013) have been identified as some of the outcomes of intercultural effectiveness.

The link between intercultural competence, pragmatic competence, and social contact has theoretical significance. Because intercultural competence involves skills for functioning effectively in a new culture, greater intercultural competence is likely to lead to greater social networking. Pragmatic competence may improve as a byproduct of this social networking process. Successful social interaction in the host community, supported by a high level of intercultural competence, could result in numerous opportunities for pragmatic practice, leading to pragmatic development. Amount of social contact is a relevant variable to examine because the construct of pragmatic competence is socially grounded. Exposure to diverse social situations and interaction types is critical for pragmatics learning, and such exposure is likely to arise in the extent of social networks that learners are able to establish in the community.

Future directions in intercultural competence in pragmatics

While the relationship between intercultural competence, pragmatic competence, and social contact is plausible, the connection has not been fully attested in the current literature, and thus remains an agenda for future research. To our knowledge, Taguchi, Xiao, and Li (2016) produced the only existing study that investigated the effects of intercultural competence and social contact on pragmatic knowledge in a longitudinal design. The study examined the contribution of intercultural competence and amount of social contact in speech act development among L2 Chinese learners in a study abroad program. All variables were treated as time-varying variables and measured twice over a semester abroad. Latent Growth Curve Modeling analysis showed that intercultural competence (Kelley and Meyers's cross-cultural adaptability) and social contact together explained 26% of speech act gains. Social contact had direct effects on speech act gains. Intercultural competence had no direct effects, but had indirect effects through social contact, indicating that social contact mediated the effect of intercultural competence to speech act development. These findings provide important implications for the structural relationship among intercultural competence, learning context, and pragmatic development. Intercultural competence, as an individual learner characteristic, promotes access to social contact, with a byproduct of this exposure being increased pragmatic knowledge. Clearly, more research is needed to test the causality link between intercultural competence and pragmatic development.

Along with this investigation, an important issue to consider is the assessment of pragmatic competence, or, more precisely, who should assess learners' pragmatic competence. Mainstream practice has been that native-speaking researchers or language instructors evaluate learners' pragmatic competence. This common practice needs to be appraised using the literature of intercultural competence, which states that evaluation of intercultural competence is grounded in people's perception. Koester and Lusting (2015, p. 20) claim that perception of intercultural competence is 'a social judgment that is somewhat analogous to the concept of "face" in interpersonal relations'. Hence, when assessing intercultural development, perceptions coming from local members in intercultural encounters are critical. Fantini (2012) also distinguishes between communicating 'effectively' and 'appropriately': the former is a judgment from one's own perspective, whereas the latter is based on a judgment from the host community's perspective.

In the context of intercultural speakers, individuals who are most likely to develop perceptions about learners' pragmatic appropriateness are not researchers or class instructors: they are target community members. Researchers and teachers can help develop learners' ability to communicate appropriately, but it is the real-life contact in the target community that provides learners with opportunities to try out what they have acquired in class. Because community members' expectations may have consequences for how learners' pragmatic behaviors are perceived, and whether their communicative needs are met, future research should explore creative ways of incorporating host members' perspectives into the evaluation of L2 pragmatic behaviors. Because of the consequential nature of communication with target community members, host members may provide meaningful and expedient assessment of learners' ability to communicate appropriately in intercultural encounters. Future research is necessary in this direction.

Finally, the concept of intercultural competence offers implications for intercultural training and teaching. Various models and approaches to intercultural training are available in the field (for example, Byram, Nichols, & Stevens, 2001; Byram, Gribkova, & Starkey, 2002; Garrett-Rucks, 2016; Jackson, 2015). These training programs are designed to help people understand the factors involved in intercultural effectiveness and improve on those factors. The programs also provide insight into one's propensity to be success-ful in an international assignment. If research indeed reveals a relationship between cultural adaptability and pragmatic competence, intercultural train-ing could serve as part of a pre-departure orientation program for students planning to study abroad. Cultural training can be combined with strategy training for pragmatics learning (Shively, 2010). Using ethnographic methods such as fieldwork and reflective journals, instructors can implement aware-ness-raising activities by having students look for pragmatic practices while abroad. They can encourage students to analyze, interpret, and reflect upon pragmatic behaviors in relation to interactional norms of the local culture. Intercultural training and strategy training combined could have a positive impact on pragmatic development. Intercultural training can provide stu-dents' access to opportunities for pragmatic practice, while strategy training can help students make the most of those opportunities.

Heritage learner pragmatics

In this last section about pragmatics and globalization, we will turn to a rather under-represented population in L2 pragmatics research: heritage language speakers. Heritage language learners are immigrants or children of immigrants who are exposed to their first-learned language through interaction with family and community members, but are educated in a dominant (societal) language (Kondo-Brown, 2006). Heritage language edu-cation has become a primary concern among policy makers, practitioners, and researchers because of the recent expansion of immigrant populations. Taking the United States as an example, foreign-born residents account for 13% or nearly 40 million of the population (U.S. Census Bureau, 2012).[6] Latin America is the largest region of provenance, accounting for 53% of all foreign-born residents, followed by Asia (28%) and Europe (12%). This demographic shift has led to a dramatic increase in the number of children who speak a language other than English at home. Over 57 million people in the United States speak a language other than English at home. In California, the state with the largest immigrant population, 27% of children five years and older are foreign-born.

   This immigration movement, along with increasing cultural and linguistic diversity, has changed people's attitudes toward minority languages. Although the focus on assimilation to the mainstream society remains, the traditional belief behind it (i.e. that newcomers should give up their language and culture in the process of assimilation) has been challenged by recent groups of immi-grants (Peyton, Ranard, & McGinnis, 2001). As a result, society has developed a more inclusive view toward minority languages. This view is best repre-sented in the area of heritage language learning. There has been a society-wide effort to preserve heritage speakers' pride and competence in their ancestral languages and cultures through educational policies and tailored curricula (Brinton, Kagan, & Bauckus, 2008; Peyton, Ranard, & McGinnis, 2001).

Heritage language learners have been the focus of research because of their unique needs and potentials. The ever-expanding population of immigrants presents a need to help their children to function in the dominant language, as well as to preserve their linguistic and cultural heritage. Needs and potentials specific to heritage speakers certainly expand the scope of L2 pragmatics research. This section will highlight what this particular L2 group adds to our understanding of the nature and process of pragmatics learning by surveying recent empirical findings. Before we discuss pragmatics in heritage learning, we will first present general definitions of heritage language learners and their linguistic profiles.

Heritage language learners: background

The term 'heritage language', broadly defined as a language spoken by a linguistic minority, has a relatively short history in the literature. Originating in Canada in the 1970s (Cummins, 2005), the term first gained prominence in the United States in the publication of the *Standards for Foreign Language Learning* (ACTFL, 1996). Until then, other terms, such as 'home language', 'mother tongue', 'quasi-native language', and 'community language' have been used interchangeably (Valdés, 2001). According to Polinsky and Kagan (2007), heritage language has been conceptualized both broadly and narrowly. The broad conceptualization emphasizes historical and personal connection to a language through family interaction (Fishman, 2006; Wiley, 2001).[7] Critically, this conceptualization highlights 'heritage motivation' or motivation to, and investment in, maintaining one's ancestral language for future generations (Van Deusen-Scholl, 2003). The narrow conceptualization, on the other hand, is found in Valdés's (2001) well-accepted definition. Valdés (2001, p. 38) contends that heritage language speakers in the North American context are 'individuals raised in homes where a language other than English is spoken and who are to some degree bilingual in English and the heritage language'.

While these all-purpose definitions can be useful, we need to be aware that <u>heritage language speakers are a heterogeneous population who exhibit tremendous *inter*-individual variation in their backgrounds, motivations, attitudes, and linguistic abilities</u> (He, 2015; Polinsky & Kagan, 2007; Van Deusen-Scholl, 2003). A recently arrived immigrant may have dominant skills in their heritage language, whereas a second or third generation immigrant might be dominant in the societal language while retaining minimum proficiency in the heritage language. Valdés (2005), on the other hand, emphasizes the *intra*-individual variation among heritage language learners. Heritage language learners are bilinguals who exhibit different levels of strength in their two languages. They move between two languages across different domains of interaction, and their transition hinges on their preference or perceived strengths of the languages. Both intra- and inter-level variations reinforce the complexity involved in conceptualizing heritage learners' competence and pinpointing their linguistic and educational needs.

Previous SLA research has examined a range of linguistic traits among heritage learners, including phonetic/phonological abilities, grammar, vocabulary knowledge, and literacy skills (for example, He, 2015; Montrul, 2010; Polinsky & Kagan, 2007). Research has found that heritage learners do not often acquire their home language completely because language contact usually shifts to their societal language during childhood (Montrul, 2010; Polinsky & Kagan, 2007). Incomplete acquisition of native-like proficiency is often attributed to the quality and quantity of input available for heritage speakers. These speakers are usually exposed to their home language early in life, but the exposure undergoes a dramatic reduction when formal schooling begins. Other than input, a range of factors affect the maintenance of a heritage language: family involvement, status of the heritage language in the community, availability of a speech community beyond the family, attitudes toward the language, and access to formal education in the language (Kondo-Brown, 2006; Montrul, 2008).

Pragmatics and heritage language learners

An assortment of issues relating to heritage language competence and acquisition are relevant to L2 pragmatics. As in other areas of language ability, commonplace SLA terms such as 'mother tongue', 'first language', and 'second language' are problematic when explaining the pragmatic competence of heritage language learners. These traditional concepts draw on 'built-in assumptions about monolingualism and separable L1 and L2 competences' (Block, 2003, p. 44) and thus do not perfectly apply to heritage language speakers who grow up being exposed to two languages, i.e. their home language and the societal language. Because heritage learners exhibit unique characteristics of pragmatic competence, different from those of second or foreign language learners, a first-hand framework is necessary in order to understand and explain the nature of their pragmatic abilities.

Pragmatics is particularly relevant to the study of heritage learners because of its focus on language use in social contexts. Availability of home language input implies that heritage speakers may have attained high-level oral skills and knowledge of informal speech in their heritage language, but these skills and knowledge, acquired at home, may not directly transfer to their performance in a formal, academic context. This is simply because the genres, speech events, and speech styles involved in these two linguistic contexts are different. Diglossia is prominent in heritage speakers' communities: the high variety of the societal language is used to carry out all the formal, public exchanges (for example, bank transactions, academic activities), whereas the heritage language is used primarily in casual, informal interactions (Lynch, 2003; Valdés, 2001).

Because home language environment alone does not provide sufficient experiences and practices in a range of registers and communicative situations, heritage speakers whose linguistic contact concentrates at home may not develop a full range of linguistic abilities with a wide repertoire of styles and registers. Valdés (2001, p. 44) observes that heritage speakers' language use often contains 'a number of features typical of casual and informal registers of the language that are totally inappropriate in the classroom'. Because heritage learners are often considered to have more exposure to informal, casual varieties of the heritage language than a formal register of that language, they are likely to face a challenge in developing the ability to speak appropriately in a range of social contexts, including both formal and informal contexts. In addition, simultaneous access to two languages (home language and societal language) implies that pragmatic transfer, especially bi-directional transfer, may be a prominent characteristic of heritage learner pragmatics. Heritage speakers may develop a hybrid pragmatic system by blending two sets of pragmalinguistic forms and sociopragmatic concepts.

The language shift that usually occurs with formal schooling may also characterize heritage learners' pragmatic development because the shift to the societal language occurs while they are still developing pragmatic competence in their first-learned language. Socialization at home into basic pragmatic knowledge (for example, speech act strategies, conversation mechanisms, and routine formulae in communicative events) may get interrupted during the transition to the societal language. In turn, the societal language provides a space to continue growing in basic pragmatic competences, but this situation indicates that heritage learners, just like adult L2 learners, need to relearn these competences in their heritage language after they have grown up. The process of relearning does not take place naturally or effortlessly; this is because of the reduction in home language input and, more specifically, a restricted range of communicative functions and their contextual distributions in the heritage language community.

The unique situations involved in heritage language acquisition further reiterate that it is not useful to discuss heritage learner pragmatics from the discrete point of L1 vs. L2. The focus should be on bilingual pragmatic competence. In the next section, we will synthesize existing findings on heritage learners' pragmatic competence. This small but emerging line of literature represents an effort toward theorizing bilingual pragmatic competence and extending the scholarly inquiry of heritage linguistic traits to the area of pragmatics.

Empirical findings in heritage learner pragmatics

Unlike other areas of linguistics, pragmatics has not yet fully emerged in the common goal of better understanding the nature of heritage speakers' language. Existing findings are limited and are also largely inconclusive. Some studies have revealed the distinct advantage of heritage learners over foreign language learners, while other findings suggest that heritage learners are no different from foreign language learners. Still others have revealed that heritage speakers fall between two monolingual speaker groups, i.e. speakers of the home language and speakers of the societal language, symbolizing the nature of their bilingual pragmatic competence. In the following, we will illustrate existing findings on heritage learner pragmatics in the United States, where the dominant societal language is English.

Ahn (2005) and Youn (2008) (reported in Youn, 2013) assessed speech acts among adult Korean heritage and non-heritage learners by using multiple measures: a written DCT, a spoken DCT, and a role-play task. Heritage language learners in Ahn's study outperformed their non-heritage counterparts in all items, regardless of the test type. However, heritage learners in Youn's (2008) study fell short on several items in the written DCT compared with those in the spoken version of the test. These findings indicate the noteworthy modality effect and variation in heritage learners' pragmatic performance, lending support to the unique linguistic profiles of heritage learners.

Studies on learners of Chinese as a heritage language also add to the variation of heritage learner pragmatics. Hong (1997) analyzed heritage and non-heritage learners' request strategies in Chinese on two aspects: *accessibility* (clarity of request intentions) and *acceptability* (appropriateness of request-making expressions in situations). Both groups were similar in their production rates of *accessible* requests, but the rates of *acceptable* requests were much higher for the heritage than the non-heritage group. However, heritage learners were still limited in their use of internal and external modifications (for example, use of 'please' and 'excuse me' in Chinese), suggesting their limited experience with formal expressions. In Taguchi, Li, and Liu's (2013) study on comprehension of implicature, heritage learners outperformed non-heritage learners on accuracy of comprehension in Chinese. They also demonstrated a uniform performance across implicature types. However, the heritage group did not excel at comprehension speed: regardless of item type, no difference was found between the two groups with regard to the amount of time taken to respond to items correctly, although native Chinese speakers were significantly faster in their comprehension. In another study, Taguchi, Zhang, and Li (forthcoming) found that Chinese heritage learners outperformed their foreign language counterparts on comprehension and production of speech acts in Chinese (for example, requests and suggestions), but the effect size was smaller for speech acts in formal situations than for those in informal situations. Analyses also revealed limited use of target pragmalinguistic forms (sentence-final particles) among heritage learners compared with native speakers of Chinese. Finally, using a corpus of Chinese heritage learners' blogs, Xiao-Desai and Wong (forthcoming) revealed variation in heritage learners' use of epistemic stance markers in Chinese. Although token frequency of epistemic markers increased along with proficiency levels, variation in frequency was found across three categories: epistemic adverbs (for example, the Chinese equivalent of 'not necessarily'), 'I' + cognitive verbs (for example, the Chinese equivalent of 'I think'), and epistemic modals (for example, the Chinese equivalents of 'probably' and 'maybe'). Frequency of epistemic adverbs increased with proficiency, but that of 'I' + cognitive verb constructions decreased.

Variation in pragmatic performance was also found in Spanish heritage learners in the United States, but this time in the realization strategies of speech acts in Spanish. Using a Spanish and English version of a written DCT, Pinto and Raschio (2007) compared the speech act of request among heritage Spanish learners (in Spanish), native Spanish speakers (in Spanish), and native English speakers (in English). Heritage learners were significantly more indirect than Spanish monolinguals in their choice of request head acts, while no difference was found between heritage learners and English speakers. Qualitative analysis revealed instances of transfer from English to Spanish. Heritage speakers used more speaker-oriented strategies than hearer-oriented strategies. They also used the conditional clause instead of the past subjunctive, although it is not the normative use in Spanish. One area where heritage learners were similar to Spanish monolinguals was in the use of downgraders in Spanish request-making: both groups produced downgraders less frequently than monolingual English speakers.

Pinto and Raschio's (2008) study on the speech act of complaint reached similar conclusions. Spanish heritage learners used fewer openers (for example, greetings) in Spanish, but more justification of a problem than monolingual Spanish speakers, which essentially approximated English speakers' patterns. In addition, like English speakers, heritage learners used multiple mitigating devices to reduce the potential face-threat. They also revealed a trace of transfer from English on their unique use of subjectivizers and consultative devices as mitigation.

These findings are indicative of the influence coming from the societal language in heritage learners' pragmatic performance. Transfer was found to be primarily unidirectional, from English to Spanish. Like English speakers, heritage speakers were indirect in a request and often justified their motive in a complaint. Particularly notable was the transfer of English-based pragmalinguistic forms to Spanish (for example, speaker-oriented strategies and conditional clauses) when they were not at all conventional in Spanish. Although there was a tendency for heritage speakers to use very few Spanish downgraders, they made up for it by transferring English-derived mitigating devices. The great degree of interference from the societal language, English, is notable because these heritage speakers were exposed to Spanish at home and were enrolled in upper-level courses in Spanish linguistics. Hence, these findings are considered as a reflection of accommodation rather than attrition. Heritage learners demonstrated linguistic competence with regard to speech acts, but they opted for less normative strategies, emulating the speech characteristics of the dominant English-speaking community.

Pinto and Raschio's findings also indicate that, as in other areas of linguistic competence, pragmatic competence among heritage learners is found in the continuum between two ends of monolingual speakers: speakers of the home language (Spanish) and speakers of the societal language (English). Heritage learners used distinct speech act strategies and mitigations, which are unique enough to distinguish them from monolingual Spanish speakers.

But they were not completely in line with English speakers because they did not use as many downgraders. These findings confirm that heritage pragmatic competence is a 'bicultural hybrid system' (Blum-Kulka, 1990, p. 277) and has a 'unique intercultural style' (Pinto & Raschio, 2007, p. 135), reflecting knowledge of conventions practiced in both home and public contexts. Pinto and Raschio (2008) argue that the profile of heritage speaker speech acts is unpredictable due to the simultaneous contact with Spanish and English. Since pragmatics is closely intertwined with the knowledge of conventions and norms of speaking in the local community, heritage pragmatic competence is inevitably shaped by their experiences in two different communities, i.e. the community of the heritage language and that of the societal language. Hence, it is not surprising to find their pragmatic competence to be a hybrid of two language systems, which reflect different norms of interaction and social practices.

The degree and nature of hybridity, however, is open to future investigation. Heritage speakers have different types of linguistic exposure and practice in two communities because the goals of interaction, social settings (for example, participant relationships, roles, and topics), and communicative functions are largely different depending on whether interactions take place inside or outside the home. Heritage speakers move across different social contexts and accumulate different pragmatic practices while shifting between two languages. In order to understand their unique pragmatic traits, it is critical to turn our attention to the context of practice. Linguistic exposure, oral practice, rich cultural input, feedback and modeling, and socialization (all common labels used to characterize the heritage learner's environment) need to be scrutinized to reveal the types of pragmatic practice available in the context and to examine how they shape heritage learners' pragmatic development.

To date, studies on heritage learners' contexts are largely confined to the quantitative approach. Previous studies used a survey to document how often and in what capacity the heritage language is used (for example, Hayashi, 2006; Kim, 2006). These studies found that the amount of heritage language use is the single most significant predictor of heritage language ability among other factors (for example, motivation, attitudes, and length of formal education). Given the paucity of these studies in pragmatics (but see Taguchi, Zhang, & Li, forthcoming), future research should grow in exploring a direct connection between social contact and pragmatic competence among heritage learners.

More critically, we need qualitative studies that reveal learners' intricate engagement in the heritage language context in promoting (or not promoting) their pragmatics learning. Very few studies exist in this area. Park (2006) documented the pragmatic socialization of Korean immigrant families of three generations. Triangulated data from audio-/video-recorded family conversations, on-site observations, and interviews revealed numerous instances where children were socialized into the proper use of Korean honorifics, i.e. linguistic forms that signal relational social status. In this socialization

1 *MOT *Halmeonihante juse-yo irae ya-ji.*
        [(You) should say to grandmother like this, 'give me.']
2 *CHI *Juse-yo!*
        [Give me!]
   %act Following grandmother, who is going to the hall to sit
3 *MOT *Juse-yo, halmeoni.*
        [Give me, Grandma]
   %act In high pitch, imitating Emily

Figure 9.1 Mother modeling honorific verb suffix for her child (Park, 2006, p. 75)

process, the grandparents' role was critical. Park illustrated how grandparents transmitted the linguistic and cultural practice of politeness to children through daily routines of serving and eating food. For example, at the dinner table, a younger or lower-status member has to wait for an older person to start eating. By observing this practice, children were socialized to learn the age-based hierarchy among family members. Explicit linguistic teaching often occurred during these routine activities. Adults frequently modeled an utterance with the honorific verb suffix *yo* directed to a higher-status member and told children to repeat it. This is shown in the conversation in Figure 9.1 between a mother (MOT) and her child (CHI), Emily. In line 1, the mother explicitly tells Emily to use the suffix *yo* when asking her grandmother for something. She demonstrates the utterance again in line 3, imitating Emily's voice. (Note that in this paper, '%act' means 'actions'.)

These analyses clearly show that routine activities at home serve as a site for pragmatic practice in heritage language learning. Family members play an essential role in socializing children into appropriate linguistic demeanors. As a follow-up, future research can investigate heritage learners' developing understanding of sociocultural norms and abilities to use pragmatic features across diverse social situations and relationships, extending beyond those in private sphere interactions. Because the contexts where a heritage language is used are restricted, a question remains regarding the extent to which heritage learners can sustain their pragmatic knowledge learned at home and apply it to contexts outside the home. This question regarding the sustainability of knowledge also calls for a further in-depth analysis of context. Pragmatics practice in a heritage language can be documented to reveal the exact type, nature, and intensity of practice that is likely to result in robust pragmatic knowledge.

Future directions in heritage learner pragmatics

In concluding this section, we would like to revisit Valdés's (2005) seminal paper that argues for the reconceptualization and expansion of the SLA field by exploring intersections between SLA and heritage language acquisition. The field of L2 pragmatics certainly aligns with this call and welcomes opportunities to re-examine some of the well-established notions of pragmatics learning from the heritage language perspective. Heritage pragmatic competence should be examined as a hybrid system of home and societal languages under the framework of bilingual pragmatics. As such, issues such as transfer, interference, and ultimate attainment emerge as salient areas of research in heritage languages.

Because characteristics of heritage learner pragmatics are still under-represented areas, more research is needed to shed light on how these speakers perform pragmatic acts. Comparing the pragmatic competence of heritage and non-heritage learners will add to the existing knowledge about possibilities and challenges facing heritage speakers in their mastery of pragmatic competence. Unbalanced pragmatic performance across task modalities and dimensions found in the previous research certainly suggests that the profiles of heritage learner pragmatics are best examined by using multiple tasks tapping into different aspects of pragmatic knowledge and abilities. In addition, we can explore the unique nature of heritage speakers' pragmatics by examining variation in their language contact and experiences. Types of linguistic practice across different social settings can be analyzed concurrently with pragmatic performance to explore the context–competence link in heritage learner pragmatics.

In addition, the context of learning needs to be expanded to include the home as a primary site where pragmatics learning takes place. Typical instruments used to document social contact in a study abroad context (for example, survey, diary, and log) require revisions to situate home language contact as the central construct. Critical elements of home language exposure include parental language use and community support, proportion of the heritage and societal language used at home, and types and range of social activities and registers, which can be incorporated into the design of an instrument (see Hayashi, 2006, and Kim, 2006).

When analyzing context, the language socialization theory offers a useful framework for interpreting heritage learners' pragmatic development. Language socialization reveals how transmission of cultural and linguistic practice takes place through interaction with competent members in the community. Because formal instruction is limited in a heritage language, pragmatics learning is likely to occur through informal socialization processes. Like Park's (2006) study, future studies can identify recurrent discourse practices to reveal how pragmatic norms are learned in a situated, sustained interaction. In this process, the role of parental involvement is likely to emerge as a unique influence on pragmatic development, adding to the existing literature on the role of context in pragmatics learning. The language socialization perspective can be applied to a classroom context as well. He (2015) analyzed teacher–student interaction in a classroom of Chinese as a heritage language to show how emergent, creative language use in classroom discourse promotes heritage learners' socialization into literacy.

There are a number of other issues of heritage language acquisition that could bring about a transformative view toward traditional research practice in L2 pragmatics. Instruction and curriculum are some of those areas. Some scholars advocate the need for developing a heritage language-specific curriculum (for example, Carreira & Kagan, 2011; Polinsky & Kagan, 2007; for a review, see Brinton, Kagan, & Bauckus, 2008). Because of home language exposure and practice, heritage language learners often acquire their language at an accelerated pace. On the other hand, exposure to home language, combined with limited formal schooling, can mean that they are strong on oral skills but weak in literacy skills. Because regular foreign language pedagogy and materials do not usually suit these unique characteristics of heritage learners, innovative programs that serve the needs of heritage language students have been argued as being a necessity. L2 pragmatics research has not caught up with this trend yet. Empirical findings are still too few to determine heritage learners' pragmatic needs. Pedagogical theory about pragmatic instruction in a heritage language cannot be developed until more research is undertaken to identify pragmatic features of heritage languages that are particularly under-developed. We hope that the field continues to add to the body of empirical studies so that pedagogical implications for teaching pragmatics to heritage speakers can be generated.

Chapter summary and directions for future research

This chapter has situated L2 pragmatics research within the larger scope of globalization. We have surveyed literature in three areas—English as a lingua franca (ELF), intercultural competence, and heritage language learners—to describe current globalization realities and to illustrate how pragmatics research is responding to those realities. New concepts, ideas, and challenges emerging from these areas have compelled researchers to evaluate and revise some of the conventional thinking of pragmatic competence and approaches to researching pragmatics.

The emergence of ELF as a global phenomenon has called for a reconsideration of established concepts and assumptions, particularly those related to norms, community, and language competence. English in today's world belongs to the global community of non-native speakers who use the language for intercultural communication. This international status of English has affirmed that communicative competence can no longer be described in relation to the norms of particular native-speaker communities. Rather, competence is determined based on how skillfully speakers can navigate the communicative demands by using a variety of strategies of accommodation and linguistic convergence, while expressing their own identities.

These findings have important implications for pragmatics research. We have acquired sites and methods to investigate intercultural pragmatics, with an explicit focus on adaptability and contingency as speakers co-construct pragmatic meanings using available resources. Together with the framework

individual v joint action

of discursive pragmatics and interactional competence, the study of pragmatics in the domain of ELF has transformed our understanding of pragmatics from 'individual work' to 'joint action'. In addition, the recognition that pragmatic norms are co-constructed and locally negotiated has led us to question the mainstream practice of using native-speaker norms for assessing and teaching pragmatics. Suggestions for alternative approaches in the ELF literature (for example, to focus on communicative success rather than correctness, to reward functional effectiveness, and to set realistic goals that meet the local users' needs of the language) are helpful as our field paves the way to examine L2 pragmatics in its own right, without a reference to native-speaker models.

Theoretical models of intercultural competence have enhanced our understanding of intercultural communication by specifying traits and abilities possessed by competent intercultural speakers. Intercultural speakers subsume ELF speakers, as the former refers to people who are able to mediate across linguistic and cultural boundaries, and the latter is an example category of such people who use English as a tool for mediation. Indeed, the primary features of successful ELF communication, i.e. adaptability, flexibility, and contingency, are also found in the components of intercultural competence, which reinforces the status of ELF speakers as intercultural speakers. This finding also suggests that other components of intercultural competence, such as ethnorelative attitudes and cultural awareness, can also serve to characterize ELF speakers.

The concept of intercultural competence is relevant to our conceptualization of pragmatic competence because much pragmatic interaction in the global society occurs in intercultural encounters. Speakers from different languages and cultural backgrounds negotiate different interactional norms, standards of politeness and directness, communication styles, and cultural conventions. In such intercultural interactions, people's pragmatic competence is at stake because they need to know how utterances work to project social meaning and mediate interpersonal relationships. The theoretical connection between intercultural and pragmatic competences is a timely agenda to pursue with a greater empirical effort because it helps us understand the interdependence of these constructs promoting intercultural adjustment.

Finally, heritage language learners provide a venue where bilingual/multilingual pragmatic competence can be explored. Because heritage language learners grow up being exposed to two languages—their home language and the societal language—pragmatic socialization occurs in two different speech communities. Hence, traditional SLA concepts such as native language and second language do not perfectly explain heritage learner pragmatics. Because of the simultaneous exposure to two linguistic systems and routine transitions between them, heritage speakers develop a hybrid pragmatic competence by blending pragmatic systems from two languages and cultures, which is different from those of native speakers or foreign language learners.

The three lines of literature reviewed in this chapter help us to go beyond the commonplace categories of second language/foreign language learners, reaching out to a broader range of participant populations, i.e. lingua franca users, intercultural speakers, and heritage language learners. These different participant categories highlight unique backgrounds, needs, and potentials of pragmatics learning that we must consider in relation to global realities. Perhaps the most important implication coming from these bodies of research is that <u>pragmatic competence is a hybrid system reflecting multiple languages, communities, and competences</u>. Pragmatic competence is also highly fluid and dynamic, and it is not limited to a fixed body of pragmalinguistic and sociopragmatic knowledge. (Pragmatically competent speakers can adapt and calibrate their linguistic resources for the benefit of their interlocutors, communicative needs, and goals of interaction, and use their resources to mediate across cultural and linguistic boundaries) This renewed conceptualization of pragmatic competence suggests a variety of new possibilities and challenges involved in pragmatics research as it moves into the next decade. We hope that future directions and implications for teaching and assessment provided throughout this chapter will help to move the field forward as we cultivate appropriate frameworks and methods for the investigation of L2 pragmatics issues in the global era.

Notes

1. The current definition of ELF speakers includes native English speakers communicating with non-native English speakers because the former also participate in ELF communication (Jenkins, 2015; Seidlhofer, 2011).
2. Kachru (1992) categorized World Englishes into three concentric circles: the Inner Circle (countries such as the U.K. and the U.S., where English is used as a mother tongue), the Outer Circle (former colonies such as India and Nigeria, where English is not the mother tongue but has institutional use), and the Expanding Circle (countries such as China, Japan, and Turkey, where English is used as an international language for business and educational purposes).
3. Kecskes (2014) distinguishes intercultural pragmatics from pragmatic competence: the former is concerned with language use in intercultural communication, whereas the latter is language competence that affects intercultural communication.
4. Although a variety of labels exist in the field to describe intercultural competence (for example, intercultural communicative competence, intercultural sensitivity, cross-cultural adaptability, ethnorelativity, cultural sensitivity), these terms broadly refer to a similar concept (Fantini, 2006). For example, according to Bradford, Allen, and Beisser's (2000) meta-analysis, intercultural competence and intercultural communicative competence are conceptually equivalent. Literature in the domain of communication studies tends to use the label 'intercultural communicative competence', whereas the literature beyond that domain often uses the label 'intercultural competence'.

5. Although the construct of intercultural competence and linguistic competence has been discussed separately, there is a body of pedagogically oriented literature that addresses the development of intercultural competence in L2 teaching (for example, Cantó, de Graff, & Jauregui, 2014; Chun, 2011; Garrett-Rucks, 2016; Jackson, 2015).
6. The term 'foreign-born residents' includes both foreign-born naturalized U.S. citizens and lawful permanent residents.
7. For reasons of ancestral connection, some researchers include indigenous and colonial languages in their definition, not just immigrant languages (for example, see Fishman, 2006).

10

Conclusion

The field of L2 pragmatics started in the early 1980s and began to expand rapidly in the early 1990s with research guided by a paradigm of interlanguage pragmatics as 'nonnative speakers' (NNSs') comprehension and production of speech acts, and how their L2-related speech act knowledge is acquired' (Kasper & Dahl, 1991, p. 216). Almost three decades after this definition appeared, the field has accumulated a large body of international literature, which has expanded the scope of L2 pragmatics research beyond a study of 'comprehension and production of speech acts', and has given increasing attention to interactional abilities under an interactional competence paradigm (Hall & Pekarek Doehler, 2011; Young, 2011). This book has reviewed three decades' worth of substantive findings from the research literature. In addition to the theoretical and historical background of L2 pragmatics work, we have presented methodological and empirical developments in L2 pragmatics research within seven broad topics: (1) theories of pragmatics learning; (2) research methods; (3) longitudinal research and developmental trajectories; (4) individual variation in pragmatic development; (5) instruction and assessment; (6) contexts of pragmatics learning; and (7) L2 pragmatics in the era of globalization.

In our discussion of theories, we noted that SLA theories have been instrumental because they have provided a framework with which we can trace changing patterns of learners' pragmatic systems and factors contributing to those changes. SLA theories have also provided principled guidelines for designing instructional methods so we can observe their effects on pragmatic development. Although Schmidt's (1993, 2001) noticing hypothesis has dominated the literature since the 1990s, the field has grown in its diversity through an incorporation of new theoretical frameworks for longitudinal and instructional investigations. The cognitive orientation of the noticing hypothesis has been complemented by another cognitivist camp: skill acquisition theories (Anderson, 1993). The field has also added socially oriented theories that view learning as a situated, dialogic activity (Swain & Lapkin's [1998] collaborative dialogue and Vygotsky's [1978] sociocultural theory).

Conversation Analysis (Kasper & Wagner, 2011) has added a micro-analytic sociological perspective but is not designed to accommodate the concept of learning. By contrast, language socialization theory (Ochs & Schieffellin, 1984) has learning as a core concern, and it has grown multifold with a large amount of findings emerging in study abroad settings. This social trend in L2 pragmatics has recently expanded with the application of the complex, dynamic systems approach (Larsen-Freeman & Cameron, 2008).

Although these theories are characterized by different epistemologies and assumptions, all of them essentially try to describe and account for the mechanisms that build pragmatic knowledge. The noticing hypothesis focuses on attention and consciousness as primary conditions that determine whether pragmatic input leads to intake and acquisition. Skill acquisition theories view repeated practice of form–function–context mappings as a force for the consolidation of pragmatic knowledge. Collaborative dialogue and sociocultural theory consider verbalization as a means for externalizing the understanding of pragmatics, which, in turn, facilitates internalization of pragmatic knowledge. Within the language socialization paradigm, pragmatic knowledge becomes strengthened through routine participation in social activities with competent members in the local community. Critically, these theories have mutually enriched our understanding of the process (as opposed to the object) of pragmatics learning, thereby advancing the research focus from descriptions to explanations of pragmatic development.

Parallel to the increasing variety in theoretical paradigms, research methods have also diversified over time. We have presented an array of methodological options for data collection and analysis, including written and spoken DCTs, role-play, multiple-choice tests, appropriateness judgment surveys, think-aloud protocols, and naturalistic data. These methods and data types can be categorized according to area of investigation. Spoken and written DCTs, role-plays, and naturalistic recording of speech samples (audio or video, as well as those recorded in diaries or field notes) can reveal L2 learners' production of pragmatic meaning, while multiple-choice tests and judgment surveys are used to examine learners' comprehension and recognition of pragmatic meaning. Interviews and think-aloud protocols are also used for analyses at the level of metapragmatics, revealing learners' awareness and understanding of their own pragmatic language use. Unlike DCTs, open role-play, elicited conversations, and naturalistic data do not typically focus on the presence or absence of particular pragmatic features (for example, speech act strategies or discourse markers) in learners' production data. Rather, these methods focus on features of interaction by revealing how learners co-construct a social action with their interlocutors across turns. We do not consider this diversity in terms of new methods superseding and replacing older ones. Instead, we think of these existing methods as complementary, as long as researchers are aware of the kind of research questions a specific data collection method and associated analytical approach can answer. For example, if researchers are interested in a learner's repertoire of gratitude formulae, a DCT with a speech act coding analysis may be sufficient. However, if they are interested in how learners express gratitude in spoken interaction and deal with interlocutor responses, they will need to collect interactions and apply a discursive technique like Conversation Analysis. Having a variety of methods at our disposal expands our options for research so we can generate quality data, and at the same time accommodate new topics to move the field forward.

Analysis of L2 pragmatic performance, guided by SLA theories and methods, has generated SLA-related insights such as the trajectory of L2 learners' pragmatic development or the relationship between general proficiency and pragmatic competence. Extensive research into speech acts has shown that learners' productive ability moves from direct speech acts with little supportive material to indirect speech acts with adjuncts and supportive moves. With increasing development, learners' awareness of sociopragmatic rules and norms also increases; then their understanding of how to act in specific contexts expands, and they become increasingly able to deploy fine-tuned pragmalinguistic tools that fit a specific communicative situation.

In addition to producing increasingly sophisticated speech acts, learners also develop their ability to embed these speech acts in interactions, and to make interactional contributions more generally. While they initially tend to produce their core message early on in an interaction without preliminary accounts, explanations or background, learners increasingly set the scene for the interlocutor, foreshadow their core message, and create a shared understanding of what social action they are carrying out. They also become increasingly able to participate actively as listeners and engage with the interlocutor on developing topics while maintaining conversational flow.

Development in other areas of pragmatics is more varied. Learners rapidly recognize some high-frequency routine formulae in the target language context but their development of implicature comprehension is closely tied to proficiency, with some types of implicature learned slowly or not at all.

Findings on development have informed research on pedagogy and assessment. In terms of instructed pragmatics, it is now well established that pragmatic development can be accelerated through classroom instruction. In addition, the majority of studies have confirmed the advantages of explicit teaching approaches over implicit ones in L2 pragmatics (Taguchi, 2015d), similar to findings in SLA. Providing metapragmatic information and thereby jump-starting learners' noticing seems to aid learning, though it is important to note that implicit instruction can also be effective. Semantic formulae for speech acts, routine formulae, and opaque types of implicature are profitable teaching targets. It is also possible to teach aspects of discourse such as conversation opening, making small talk, and even more abstract practices like preference organization.

Assessment of L2 pragmatics is a recent area of research. It began with a focus on speech acts, followed by an expansion to include routine formulae, implicature, sociopragmatic awareness, and speech styles, and it has recently incorporated testing of extended discourse abilities. Eliciting pragmatic performance that allows conclusions to be drawn about real-world performance is complex, first due to the context-sensitivity of pragmatic performance, and secondly due to the fact that real-world assessment needs to ensure practicality. Overall, research on the testing and teaching of pragmatics is an important endeavor since pragmatic ability is a component of all conceptualizations of communicative competence, but it has not received the same attention as other areas such as grammar.

In the chapter on the context of pragmatics learning, we discussed the nature of input and practice available in a second language context, mainly in study abroad settings, where empirical findings are heavily concentrated. Previous studies took diverse approaches to conceptualizing the study abroad context. According to Taguchi's (2016) classification, some studies treated the study abroad context as a categorical label by comparing a group of learners in a study abroad program with their counterparts in a domestic instructional setting. Other studies have examined the context for the amount of language contact and practice available to learners (typically as the 'perceived' amount of contact assessed through a self-report survey) and documented its impact on pragmatic development. Still others have conceptualized the context as a site for situated pragmatic practice and learning. There is a trend in the literature that involves a move away from the quantitative approach of analyzing study abroad as a categorical label; instead, researchers are increasingly undertaking qualitative studies, documenting how contextual resources and individuals' investments in those resources jointly shape developmental trajectories. The types of social practice available in a study abroad context present a wide range of settings, including homestay, service encounters, dorm room interactions, club activities, and part-time jobs. These settings involve unique configurations of such aspects as participant memberships, activities, and structures of interaction. As such, the object of learning involved in each setting is unique. Specific pragmalinguistic forms and sociopragmatic norms are configured to characterize a certain social practice. These forms and norms are learned through direct participation in that practice.

The connection between context, language use, and pragmatic development found in the study abroad research is also found in other contexts of learning. Descriptions of classroom interactions in CLIL (content and language integrated learning) and ELF (English as a lingua franca) indicate that formal classrooms are filled with speech acts specific to classroom interactions (for example, presenting one's point of view, persuading others, giving feedback, and correcting others). Learners' classroom participation facilitates their acquisition of these speech acts. Similarly, the workplace environment presents a unique context for pragmatics. Research suggests that immigrants and international workers consider small talk to be the most critical pragmatic task to master (Yates & Major, 2015). This task is central to maintaining social relationships in the workplace context. We are aware of about three dozen longitudinal studies in L2 pragmatics, but to our knowledge, none of these studies trace the development of the ability to make small talk. It is precisely an area like small talk which would be a good target for instruction in L2 pragmatics, since small talk is important to learners in the target language setting and involves a particular discourse structure, specific formulaic expressions, and a predictable range of topics.

The heritage learner context also presents a unique community for pragmatic practice. For heritage learners, pragmatic development occurs simultaneously in two language use contexts—home language and societal language—which differ in the range of speech genres and events involved. Because of their concurrent access to two distinct speech communities, heritage learners are considered to display a unique, hybrid pragmatic system.

Availability of sociocultural input and practice in context, however, does not guarantee accessibility of input and practice. Whether or not learners can take advantage of social practices in various contexts depends on their individual characteristics. Learner characteristics such as motivation, personality, attitudes, learner agency, proficiency, and aptitude mediate access to opportunities for pragmatic practice, leading to variation in the process and outcome of development. In our discussion of individual characteristics, we have conceptualized the current literature involving two distinct lines of research. One is a group of quantitative studies under the cognitive-componential approach, which treat individual characteristics as fixed variables that are measurable as general tendencies through the use of experimental instruments. These studies have examined descriptive and predictive relationships between individual variables and learners' pragmatic competence. The other line of studies takes a dynamic, interactive approach to individual characteristics. Adopting a qualitative design, these studies analyze the interaction between individual characteristics and other individual traits to reveal how multiple characteristics shift dynamically as learners interact with a context. According to this approach, individual characteristics are not viewed as stable, distinct variables separate from context; rather, they are viewed as evolving in interaction between learners and contexts of learning. These two approaches present fundamentally different ways of conceptualizing individual characteristics in pragmatic development. However, they are complementary, and jointly bolster the connection between L2 pragmatics and SLA. Furthermore, while individual factors and contexts of learning have been discussed here in two separate chapters, these two areas of research can be discussed together. As the current complex, dynamic systems theories contend, the role of individual factors in pragmatic development is best understood in conjunction with characteristics of the context of learning (Dörnyei, 2005).

With globalization, the area of individual characteristics in the L2 pragmatics literature has expanded to include intercultural competence. Theoretical models of intercultural competence are diverse, with numerous definitions co-existing across disciplines. However, they all emphasize cultural/linguistic knowledge, personality traits (for example, flexibility, risk-taking, empathy), and ethnorelative worldviews as critical elements that help people mediate linguistic and cultural differences. Within the intercultural framework, communicative competence is defined as the ability to communicate effectively and appropriately in intercultural interactions (Byram, 1997, 2012). Hence, pragmatic competence, which refers to the ability to operate in different social contexts with appropriate linguistics resources, can directly contribute to intercultural communication. By situating pragmatics within the scope of intercultural competence, research can extend its analytical focus beyond how L2 speakers perform pragmatic acts to how they participate in intercultural communication using their pragmatic competence.

Appropriateness in pragmatic acts, however, needs to be reconceptualized in the era of globalization. As we discussed in Chapter 9, the surge in production of literature on English as a lingua franca (ELF) and intercultural pragmatics has compelled us to re-evaluate our commonplace practice. As the concept of uniform native-speaker norms is increasingly challenged, we are compelled to explore alternative approaches to examining pragmatic competence. Moving away from using native-speaker baseline data, we can use local norms as alternatives by incorporating community members' needs, resources, and goals of interaction to conceptualize what counts as appropriate language behavior. In addition, analysis of a pragmatic act should incorporate more process-oriented views by focusing on how participants mutually achieve communicative goals in interaction. Politeness, formality, and appropriateness have served as typical dimensions of pragmatic analyses, but equally important is a set of strategies that speakers employ to accomplish a pragmatic act. Recent findings from the ELF literature suggest such strategies. Solidarity-based strategies for accommodation and linguistic convergence, as well as communication-based strategies for conversation management and meaning negotiation, provide a new framework with which to analyze pragmatic language use in intercultural communication.

As summarized above, this book has traced the rapid development of the L2 pragmatics literature in the last three decades. As the field enters its fourth decade, new topics and challenges have emerged. At the end of each chapter, we have detailed those challenges as directions for future research. On the topic of theories, the growing theoretical diversity in the current literature is a welcome tendency, but several theoretical frameworks are still underrepresented in terms of empirical findings. To advance our understanding of the mechanisms behind pragmatics learning, more empirical data is necessary within some of the more recent theoretical paradigms (collaborative dialogue, sociocultural theory, Dynamic Systems Theory, Conversation Analysis, and the Cognition Hypothesis).

In the areas of contexts of learning and developmental pragmatics, the notion of pragmatics-specific-to-discursive-practice can be explored further with a focus on revealing the types of pragmatic resources available in specific contexts. By attending to the relationship between context and pragmatic language use, our view will shift from context as a stable background to a part of the ecological system that characterizes patterns of pragmatic development.

Further studies in under-researched contexts such as workplace environments, heritage language learning, and intercultural communication will help us to explore the link between contextual resources and patterns of pragmatic development. Contextual resources can be analyzed together with individual resources to explore how learner characteristics (such as proficiency, motivation, personality, aptitude, etc.) interact with contextual affordances and jointly explain patterns and variation in pragmatics learning.

Individual learner characteristics are also important for future research in the area of pragmatics teaching. Recent reviews (for example, Roever, 2009; Takahashi, 2010) have situated a dynamic interaction of learnability, pragmatic targets, instructional methods, and learning outcomes as a critical area of investigation for future instructed pragmatics research. So far, only a few studies have compared learning outcomes among learners who differ in a particular learner characteristic (for example, Fordyce's [2014] learners differed in their general proficiency; Li's [in press] learners differed in their aptitude; Takahashi's [2015] learners differed in their motivation). Further research can investigate what pragmatic features should be taught to what kinds of learners (in terms of individual difference factors) using what kinds of methods (for example, implicit or explicit; collaborative or individual-based; input-based or output-based). This line of research will advance our understanding of the relationship between learnability and instructional intervention in L2 pragmatics.

Most instructed pragmatics research focuses on one particular feature (for example, a specific speech act) and then contrasts more explicit and more implicit teaching approaches. It is now time for research to move on to the implementation of a full-scale pragmatics curriculum, extending from beginner to advanced level. Developing such a curriculum needs to take into account the learner's developmental trajectory by initially teaching brief, formulaic realizations of social actions, and increasingly broadening learners' repertoires and the complexity of social situations. Integration of such a comprehensive curriculum in suites of textbooks would go a long way to ensuring that learners develop the ability to use language for social purposes.

The assessment of learners' pragmatic ability has made significant steps forward, but this area struggles with the tension between providing adequate contextualization and eliciting rich data on the one hand and keeping tests practical on the other. This tension has a direct impact on the range of conclusions that pragmatics tests can support: where a test is limited to diagnosing learners' pragmatic knowledge, its range of uses is less broad than for a test that includes performance aspects. However, the extent to which test performance is indicative of real-world performance needs to be carefully investigated, as it is currently a weak link in the validation of most pragmatics tests. A more technical issue has been the challenge of designing pragmatics test tasks that are sufficiently difficult for learners at intermediate proficiency levels or above, and research is needed to establish what task features influence the difficulty of pragmatics tasks.

Finally, we should recognize that pragmatic competence and multicultural competence share common features of adaptability, flexibility, and variability as constituents. As Canagarajah (2007, p. 932) says, '[M]ultilingual competence is open to unpredictability. It refers to the ability to find a fit or an alignment between the linguistic resources they bring and the context of communication.' Flexibility and adaptability are also important characteristics of pragmatic competence, which entails the ability to adapt linguistic resources to the context of interaction. However, these aspects have not been fully incorporated into L2 pragmatics research. This is because many traditional studies tend to assign fixed, stable variables to context (power, social distance, and degree of imposition) and draw a one-to-one correspondence between context and forms, neglecting multiplicity and dynamicity of context and pragmatic competence. To move away from this tradition, future research can explore creative ways of designing tasks that can reveal learners' ability to move across different contexts and to adapt and align their pragmatic resources to a dynamic context (Taguchi, 2017).

Although each chapter proposes distinct future directions in its area, an overarching challenge is to fully incorporate the interdisciplinary stance in our research practice. As the field has become radically diversified, no single definition, theory, or method can adequately explain what it means to be pragmatically competent in L2. Research topics themselves are interrelated. We have a number of different theoretical paradigms, but they are all oriented toward the same goal of explicating how pragmatic knowledge is built. Longitudinal and instructional investigations adopt different research designs, but they share the central concern of capturing a change within L2 pragmatic systems and identifying the mechanisms behind the change. Individual characteristics and contexts of learning can conjointly explain patterns of pragmatic development and variation in the development. Pragmatic, interactional, intercultural, and multicultural competences present distinct definitions, but they share common characteristics of adaptability and variability that characterize L2 pragmatic behaviors. We hope that our book will inspire future eclectic researchers who can explore connections between different theories, methods, and topics of investigation, advancing the field into new, exciting areas as we move into the fourth decade of L2 pragmatics research.

References

Achiba, M. (2002). *Learning to request in a second language: A study of child interlanguage pragmatics.* Clevedon, UK: Multilingual Matters.

ACTFL (1996). *Standards for foreign language learning: Preparing for the 21st century.* Yonkers, NY: National Standards in Education Project.

Ahn, R. C. (2005). *Five measures of interlanguage pragmatics in KFL (Korean as foreign language) learners* (Unpublished doctoral dissertation). University of Hawaii at Manoa, Honolulu, HI.

Alcón Soler, E. (2013a). Mitigating e-mail requests in teenagers' first and second language academic cyber-consultation. *Multilingua, 32*(6), 779–799.

Alcón Soler, E. (2013b). Teachability and bilingual effects on third language knowledge of refusals. *Intercultural Pragmatics, 9,* 511–541.

Alcón Soler, E. (2015). Pragmatic learning and study abroad: Effects of instruction and length of stay. *System, 48,* 62–74.

Al-Gahtani, S., & Roever, C. (2009). *Role-playing L2 requests: head acts and sequential organization.* (Unpublished data).

Al-Gahtani & Roever (2011). *Refusals in second language interaction.* (Unpublished data).

Al-Gahtani, S., & Roever, C. (2012). Role-playing L2 requests: head acts and sequential organization. *Applied Linguistics, 33*(1), 42–65.

Al-Gahtani, S., & Roever, C. (2013). 'Hi doctor, give me handouts': low-proficiency learners and requests. *ELT Journal, 67*(4), 413–424.

Al-Gahtani, S., & Roever, C. (2014a). Insert and post-expansion in L2 Arabic requests. *System, 42*(1), 189–206.

Al-Gahtani, S., & Roever, C. (2014b). Preference structure in L2 Arabic requests. *Intercultural Pragmatics, 11,* 619–643.

Al-Gahtani, S., & Roever, C. (2015a). The development of requests by L2 Learners of Modern Standard Arabic: A longitudinal and cross-sectional study. *Foreign Language Annals, 48*(4), 570–583.

Al-Gahtani, S., & Roever, C. (2015b). Multiple requests in Arabic as a second language. *Multilingua, 34*(3), 405–432.

Aljaafreh, A., & Lantolf, J. P. (1994). Negative feedback as regulation and second language learning in the Zone of Proximal Development. *Modern Language Journal, 78,* 465–483.

Allami, H., & Naeimi, A. (2011). A cross-linguistic study of refusals: An analysis of pragmatic competence development in Iranian EFL learners. *Journal of Pragmatics, 43*(1), 385–406.

Anderson, J. R. (1993). *Rules of the mind.* Hillsdale, NJ: Lawrence Erlbaum Associations.

Anderson, J. R., Bothell, D. Byrne, M. D., Douglass, S., Lebiere, C., & Qin, Y. (2004). An integrated theory of the mind, *Psychological Review, 111,* 1036–1060.

Archer, D. (1983). The encoding of meaning: A test of three theories of social interaction. *Sociological Enquiry, 50,* 393–419.

Austin, J. L. (1962). *How to do things with words.* Oxford: Oxford University Press.

Baba, K., & Nitta, R. (2014). Phase transitions in development of writing fluency from a complex dynamic systems perspective. *Language Learning, 64,* 1–35.

Bachman, L. F. (1990). *Fundamental considerations in language testing.* New York: Oxford University Press.

Bachman, L. F., & Palmer, A. S. (1996). *Language testing in practice: Designing and developing useful language tests.* Oxford: Oxford University Press.

Bachman, L. F., & Palmer, A. S. (2010). *Language assessment in practice: developing language tests and justifying their use in the real world.* Oxford: Oxford University Press.

Bakhtin, M. (1981). *The dialogic imagination: Four essays by M. M. Bakhtin.* Austin, TX: University of Texas Press.

Bandura, A. (1986). *Social foundations of thought and action.* Englewood Cliffs, NJ: Prentice-Hall.

Bardovi-Harlig, K. (1999). Exploring the interlanguage of interlanguage pragmatics: A research agenda for acquisitional pragmatics. *Language Learning, 49,* 677–713.

Bardovi-Harlig, K. (2000a). Pragmatics and second language acquisition. In R. B. Kaplan (Ed.), *Oxford handbook of applied linguistics* (pp. 182–192). Oxford: Oxford University Press.

Bardovi-Harlig, K. (2000b). Tense and aspect in second language acquisition: Form, meaning and use. *Language Learning, 50,* 1.

Bardovi-Harlig, K. (2001). Evaluating the empirical evidence: Grounds for instruction in pragmatics? In K. Rose & G. Kasper (Eds.), *Pragmatics in language teaching* (pp. 13–32). Cambridge: Cambridge University Press.

Bardovi-Harlig, K. (2009). Conventional expressions as a pragmalinguistic resource: Recognition and production of conventional expressions in L2 pragmatics. *Language Learning, 59,* 755–795.

Bardovi-Harlig, K. (2010). Exploring the pragmatics of interlanguage pragmatics: Definition by design. In A. Trosborg (Ed.), *Pragmatics across languages and cultures* (pp. 219–260). Berlin: De Gruyter Mouton.

Bardovi-Harlig, K. (2012). Formulas, routines, and conventional expressions in pragmatics research. *Annual Review of Applied Linguistics, 32,* 206–227.

Bardovi-Harlig, K. (2013). Developing L2 pragmatics. *Language Learning, 63,* 68–86.

Bardovi-Harlig, K. (2014). Awareness of meaning of conventional expressions in second-language pragmatics. *Language Awareness, 23*(1–2), 41–56.

Bardovi-Harlig, K., & Bastos, M.T. (2011). Proficiency, length of stay, and intensity of interaction and the acquisition of conventional expressions in L2 pragmatics. *Intercultural Pragmatics, 8,* 347–384.

Bardovi-Harlig, K., & Dörnyei, Z. (1998). Do language learners recognize pragmatic violations? Pragmatic versus grammatical awareness in instructed L2 learning. *TESOL Quarterly, 32,* 233–259.

Bardovi-Harlig, K., & Hartford, B. (1993a). Learning the rules of academic talk: A longitudinal study of pragmatic development. *Studies in Second Language Acquisition, 15,* 279–304.

Bardovi-Harlig, K., & Hartford, B. S. (1993b). Refining the DCT: Comparing open questionnaires and dialogue completion tasks. In L.F. Bouton (Ed.), *Pragmatics and Language Learning, 4* (pp. 143–165). Urbana, Ill.: DEIL.

Bardovi-Harlig, K., & Hartford, B. (2005). *Interlanguage pragmatics: Exploring institutional talk.* Mahwah, NJ: Lawrence Erlbaum.

Bardovi-Harlig, K., & Mahan-Taylor, R. (2005). *Teaching pragmatics.* Retrieved from http://americanenglish.state.gov/resources/teaching-pragmatics

Bardovi-Harlig, K., & Salsbury, T. (2004). The organization of turns in the disagreements of L2 learners: a longitudinal perspective. In D. Boxer & A. D. Cohen (Eds.), *Studying speaking to inform second language learning* (pp. 199–227). Bristol: Multilingual Matters.

Bardovi-Harlig, K., & Vellenga, H. E. (2012). The effect of instruction on conventional expressions in L2 pragmatics. *System, 40*(1), 77–89.

Bardovi-Harlig, K., Mossman, S., & Vellenga, H. E. (2015). The effect of instruction on pragmatic routines in academic discussion. *Language Teaching Research, 19*(3), 324–350.

Barkaoui, K. (2011). Think-aloud protocols in research on essay rating: An empirical study of their veridicality and reactivity. *Language Testing, 28*(1), 51–75.

Barraja-Rohan, A. M. (2011). Using conversation analysis in the second language classroom to teach interactional competence. *Language Teaching Research, 15*(4), 479–507.

Baron-Cohen, S. (1995). *Mindblindness: An essay on autism and theory of mind.* Oxford: Oxford University Press.

Barron, A. (2003). *Acquisition in interlanguage pragmatics. Learning how to do things with words in a study abroad context.* Amsterdam/Philadelphia: John Benjamins.

Barron, A. (2006). Learning to say "you" in German: The acquisition of sociolinguistic competence in a study abroad context. In M. A. Dufon & E. Churchill (Eds.), *Language learners in study abroad contexts* (pp. 59–88). Clevedon, UK: Multilingual Matters.

Barron, A. (2007). 'Ah no honestly we're okay': Learning to upgrade in a study abroad context. *Intercultural Pragmatics, 4,* 129–166.

Bataller, R. (2010). Making a request for a service in Spanish: Pragmatic development in the study abroad setting. *Foreign Language Annals, 43*(1), 160–175.

Bataller, R. (2013). Role-plays vs. natural data: asking for a drink at a cafeteria in peninsular Spanish. *Íkala, revista de lenguaje y cultura, 18*(2), 111–126.

Baumgarten, N., & House, J. (2010). I think and I don't know in English as lingua franca and native English discourse. *Journal of Pragmatics, 42*(5), 1184–1200.

Beebe, L. M., & Cummings, M. C. (1996). Natural speech act data versus written questionnaire data: How data collection method affects speech act performance. In S. M. Gass, & J. Neu (Eds.), *Speech acts across cultures* (pp. 65–86). Berlin: Walter de Gruyter.

Bella, S. (2012). Pragmatic development in a foreign language: A study of Greek FL requests. *Journal of Pragmatics, 44*(13), 1917–1947.

Bella, S. (2014). Developing the ability to refuse: A cross-sectional study of Greek FL refusals. *Journal of Pragmatics, 61,* 35–62.

Belz, J. (2007). The role of computer mediation in the instruction and development of L2 pragmatic competence. *Annual Review of Applied Linguistics, 27,* 45–75.

Belz, J., & Kinginger, C. (2003). Discourse options and the development pragmatic competence by classroom learners of German: The case of address forms. *Language Learning, 53,* 591–647.

Bennett, J. M., Bennett, M. J., & Allen, W. (1999). Developing intercultural competence in the language classroom. In R. M. Paige, D. L. Lange, & A. Y. Yershova (Eds.), *Culture as the core: Integrating culture into the language curriculum. CARLA working paper 15* (pp. 13–45). Minneapolis, MN: Center for Advanced Research on Language Acquisition.

Bennett, M. J. (1993). Towards ethnorelativism: A developmental model of intercultural sensitivity, In R. M. Paige (Ed.), *Education for the intercultural experience* (pp. 21–71). Yarmouth, ME: Intercultural Press.

Bialystok, E. (1990). The competence of processing: Classifying theories of second language acquisition. *TESOL Quarterly, 24,* 635–648.

Bialystok, E. (1993). Symbolic representation and attentional control in pragmatic competence. In G. Kasper & S. Blum-Kulka (Eds.), *Interlanguage pragmatics* (pp. 43–63). New York: Oxford University Press.

Bialystok, E. (1994). Analysis and control in the development of second language proficiency. *Studies in Second Language Acquisition, 16,* 157–168.

Biber, D., Conrad, S., Reppen, R., Byrd, P., Helt, M., Clark, V., Cortes, V., Csomay, E., & Urzua, A. (2004). *Representing language use in the university: Analysis of the TOEFL 2000 spoken and written academic language corpus.* (TOEFL Monograph Series, MS-25). Princeton, NJ: Educational Testing Service.

Biber, D. (2006). *University language: A corpus-based study of spoken and written registers* (Vol. 23). Amsterdam: John Benjamins.

Bilbow, G.T. (1997). Cross-cultural impression management in the multicultural workplace: The special case of Hong Kong. *Journal of Pragmatics, 28,* 461–487.

Billmyer, K., & Varghese, M. (2000). Investigating instrument-based pragmatic variability: Effects of enhancing discourse completion tests. *Applied Linguistics, 21*(4), 517–552.

Bird, A., Mendenhall, M., Stevens, M. J., & Oddou, G. (2010). Defining the content domain of intercultural competence for global leaders. *Journal of Management Psychology, 25,* 810–828.

Björkman, B. (2013). *English as an academic lingua franca.* Berlin: De Gruyter.

Blattner, G., & Fiori, M. (2011). Virtual social network communities: An investigation of language learners' development of sociopragmatic awareness and multiliteracy skills. *CALICO Journal*, 29(1), 24–43.

Block, D. (2003). *The social turn in second language acquisition*. Edinburgh: Edinburgh University Press.

Block, D. (2007). The rise of identity in SLA research, post Firth and Wagner (1997), *Modern Language Journal*, 91, 863–876.

Blum-Kulka, S., & House, J. (1989). Cross-cultural and situational variation in requesting behavior. In S. Blum-Kulka, J. House & G. Kasper (Eds.), *Cross-cultural pragmatics: Requests and apologies* (pp. 123–154). Norwood, NJ: Ablex.

Blum-Kulka, S. (1990). Don't touch your lettuce with your fingers. *Journal of Pragmatics*, 14, 259–288.

Blum-Kulka, S., House, J., & Kasper, G. (1989). *Cross-cultural pragmatics: Requests and apologies*. Norwood, NJ: Ablex.

Bolden, G. B. (2015). Transcribing as research: "manual" transcription and conversation analysis. *Research on Language and Social Interaction*, 48(3), 276–280.

Bourdieu, P. (1977). *Outline of a theory of practice*. Cambridge: Cambridge University Press.

Bouton, L. (1994). Conversational implicature in the second language: Learned slowly when not deliberately taught. *Journal of Pragmatics*, 22, 157–167.

Bouton, L. (1999). Developing nonnative speaker skills in interpreting conversational implicatures in English. In E. Hinkel (Ed.), *Culture in second language teaching and learning* (pp. 47–70). Cambridge: Cambridge University Press.

Bouton, L. F. (1988). A cross-cultural study of ability to interpret implicatures in English. *World Englishes*, 7(2), 183–196.

Bowles, M. A. (2010). *The think-aloud controversy in second language research*. London: Routledge.

Boxer, D. (2005). Discourse issues in cross-cultural pragmatics. *Annual Review of Applied Linguistics*, 22, 150–167.

Boxer, D. (2010). How to gripe and establish rapport. In A. Martínez-Flor & E. Usó-Juan (Eds.), *Speech act performance: Theoretical, empirical and methodological issues* (pp. 163–178). Amsterdam: John Benjamins.

Bradford, L., Allen, M., & Beisser, K. (2000). An evaluation and meta-analysis of intercultural communication competence research. *World Communication*, 29, 28–51.

Bravo, D. (2001). Sobre la cortesía lingüística, estratégica y conversacional en Español (On linguistic, strategic and conversational politeness in Spanish). *Oralia: Análisis del discurso oral*, 4, 299–314.

Bravo, D. (2012). Cortesía lingüística y comunicativa. In S. de los Heros & M. Niño-Murcia (Eds.), *Fundamentos y modelos del estudio pragmático y sociopragmático del español* (pp. 83–115). Washington, D.C.: Georgetown University Press.

Brinton, D., Kagan, O., & Bauckus, S. (2008). *Heritage language education. A new field emerging*. New York: Routledge.

Brock, M. N., & Nagasaka, Y. (2005). Teaching pragmatics in the EFL classroom? SURE you can! *TESL Reporter*, 38, 27–41.

Brown, A. (2003). Interviewer variation and the co-construction of speaking proficiency. *Language Testing*, 20 (1), 1–25.

Brown, J. D. (2001). Six types of pragmatics tests in two different contexts. In K. R. Rose & G. Kasper (Eds.), *Pragmatics in language teaching* (pp. 301–325). Cambridge: Cambridge University.

Brown, J. D. (2008). Raters, functions, item types and the dependability of L2 pragmatics tests. In E. Alcón Soler & A. Martínez-Flor (Eds.), *Second language acquisition research series* (Vol. 30). *Investigating pragmatics in foreign language learning, teaching and testing* (pp. 224–248). Bristol: Multilingual Matters.

Brown, J. D. (2011). Likert items and scales of measurement. *SHIKEN: JALT Testing & Evaluation SIG Newsletter*, 15(1), 10–14.

Brown, J. D., & Ahn, R. C. (2011). Variables that affect the dependability of L2 pragmatics tests. *Journal of Pragmatics*, 43(1), 198–217.

Brown, L. (2013). Identity and honorifics use in Korean study abroad. In C. Kinginger (Ed.), *Social and cultural aspects of language learning in study abroad* (pp. 269–298). Amsterdam/New York: John Benjamins.

Brown, P., & Levinson, S. D. (1978). Universals in language use: politeness phenomena. In E. N. Goody (Ed.), *Questions and politeness: strategies in social interaction* (pp. 56–289). New York: Cambridge University Press.

Brown, P., & Levinson, S. D. (1987). *Politeness: Some universals in language usage* (2nd ed.). Cambridge: Cambridge University Press.

Brown, R. (1973). *A first language: The early stages*. Cambridge, MA: Harvard University Press.

Burston, J. (2013). Mobile-assisted language learning: a selected annotated bibliography of implementation studies 1994–2012. *Language Learning & Technology, 17*, 157–225.

Byon, A. S. (2004). Sociopragmatic analysis of Korean requests: pedagogical settings. *Journal of Pragmatics, 36*, 1673–1704.

Byram, M. (1997). *Teaching and assessing intercultural communicative competence.* Philadelphia: Multilingual Matters.

Byram, M. (2012). Conceptualizing intercultural (communicative) competence and intercultural citizenship. In J. Jackson (Ed.), *The Routledge handbook of language and intercultural communication* (pp. 85–98). Oxford: Routledge.

Byram, M., Gribkova, B., & Starkey, H. (2002). *Developing the intercultural dimension in language teaching. A practical introduction for teachers.* Strasbourg: Council of Europe.

Byram, M., Nichols, A., & Stevens, D. (2001). *Developing intercultural competence in practice.* Clevedon, UK: Multilingual Matters.

Cadierno, T., & Eskildsen, S. W. (Eds.). (2015). *Usage-based perspectives on second language learning.* Berlin: Walter de Gruyter.

Canagarajah, S. (2006). Negotiating the local in English as a lingua franca. *Annual Review of Applied Linguistics, 26*, 197–218.

Canagarajah, S. (2007). Lingua franca English, multilingual communities, and language acquisition. *Modern Language Journal, 91*, 923–939.

Canagarajah, S. (2013). *Translingual practice: Global Englishes and cosmopolitan relations.* Milton Park: Routledge.

Canale, M. (1983). From communicative competence to communicative language pedagogy. In J. Richards, & R. Schmidt (Eds.), *Language and communication* (pp. 2–27). London: Longman.

Canale, M., & Swain, M. (1980). Theoretical bases of communicative approaches to second language teaching and testing. *Applied Linguistics, 1*, 1–47.

Cantó, S., de Graff, R., & Jauregui, K. (2014). Collaborative tasks for negotiation of intercultural meaning in virtual worlds and video-web communication. In M. González-Lloret & L. Ortega (Eds.), *Technology-mediated TBLT: researching technology and tasks* (pp. 183–212). Amsterdam, Philadelphia: John Benjamins.

Carifio, J., & Perla, R. J. (2007). Ten common misunderstandings, misconceptions, persistent myths and urban legends about Likert scales and Likert response formats and their antidotes. *Journal of Social Sciences, 3*(3), 106–116.

Carreira, M., & Kagan, O. (2011). The results of the national heritage language survey: Implications for teaching, curriculum design, and professional development. *Foreign Language Annals, 44*, 40–64.

Carroll, J. B. (1974). The aptitude-achievement: The case of foreign language aptitude and proficiency. In D. Green (Ed.), *The aptitude achievement distinction* (pp. 289–303). Monterey, CA: McGraw-Hill.

Carroll, J. B., & Sapon, S. (1959). *The Modern languages aptitude test.* San Antonio, TX: Psychological Corporation.

Cekaite, A. (2007). A child's development of interactional competence in a Swedish L2 classroom. *The Modern Language Journal, 91*(1), 45–62.

Celce-Murcia, M. (2007). Rethinking the role of communicative competence in language Teaching (pp. 41–57). In E. Alcón Soler & M. P. Safont Jordà (Eds.), *Intercultural language use and language learning* (pp. 7–22). Springer.

Celce-Murcia, M., Dörnyei, Z., & Thurrell, S. (1995). Communicative competence: A pedagogically motivated model with content specifications. *Issues in Applied Linguistics, 6*(2), 5–35.

Chan, L., Dörnyei, Z., & Henry, A. (2015). Learner archetypes and signature dynamics in the language classroom: A retrodictive qualitative modelling approach to studying L2 motivation. In Z. Dörnyei, P. MacIntyre, & A. Henry (Eds.), *Motivational dynamics in language learning* (pp. 238–259). Bristol: Multilingual Matters.

Chang, Y. F. (2009). How to say no: An analysis of cross-cultural difference and pragmatic transfer. *Language Sciences, 31*(4), 477–493.

Chang, Y. F. (2010). 'I no say you say is boring': the development of pragmatic competence in L2 apology. *Language Sciences, 32*(3), 408–424.

Chang, Y. F. (2011). Refusing in a foreign language: An investigation of problems encountered by Chinese learners of English. *Multilingua, 30*(1), 71–98.

Chen, R. (2010). Compliment and compliment response research: A cross-cultural survey. In A. Trosborg (Ed.), *Pragmatics across languages and cultures* (pp. 79–101). New York/Berlin: De Gruyter Mouton.

Chen, Y. (2015). Chinese learners' cognitive processes in writing email requests to faculty. *System, 52*, 51–62.

Chun, D. (2011). Developing intercultural communicative competence through online exchanges. *CALICO Journal, 28*(2), 392–419.

Chun, D., Kern, R., & Smith, B. (2016). Technology in language use, language teaching, and language learning. *Modern Language Journal, 100*, 64–80.

Churchill, E. (2003). Competing for the floor in the American home: Japanese students sharing host families. *Kanagawa University Studies in Language, 25*, 185–202.

Clark, H. H. (1979). Responding to indirect speech acts. *Cognitive Psychology, 11*, 430–477.

Clayman, S. E., & Heritage, J. (2002). Questioning presidents: Journalistic deference and adversarialness in the press conferences of Eisenhower and Reagan. *Journal of Communication, 52*(4), 749–775.

Clyne, M. (2006). Some thoughts on pragmatics, sociolinguistic variation, and intercultural communication. *Intercultural Pragmatics, 3*, 95–105.

Cogo, A. (2009). Accommodating difference in ELF conversations: A study of pragmatic strategies. In A. Mauranen & E. Ranta (Eds.), *English as a lingua franca: Studies and findings* (pp. 254–273). Newcastle upon Tyne: Cambridge Scholars Publishing.

Cogo, A., & Dewey, M. (2012). *Analysing English as a lingua franca. A corpus-driven investigation.* London: Continuum.

Cogo, A., & House, J. (2017). Intercultural pragmatics. In A. Barron, Y. Gu., & G. Steen (Eds.), *Routledge handbook of pragmatics* (pp. 168–183). London/New York: Routledge.

Cohen, A. D. (2013). Verbal report. In C. Chapelle (Ed.), *The encyclopedia of applied linguistics.* Oxford: Wiley Blackwell.

Cohen, A. D., & Olshtain, E. (1981). Developing a measure of sociocultural competence: the case of apology. *Language Learning, 31*(1), 113–134.

Cohen, A. D., & Shively, R. L. (2002). Measuring speech acts with multiple rejoinder DCTs. *Language Testing Update, 32*, 39–42.

Cohen, A. D., Paige, R. M., Shively, R. L., Emert, H., & Hoff, J. (2005). *Maximizing study abroad through language and culture strategies: Research on students, study abroad program professionals, and language instructors.* Minneapolis, MN: Center for Advanced Research on Language Acquisition, University of Minnesota. http://www.carla.umn.edu/maxsa/documents/MAXSAResearchReport_000.pdf

Cole, M. (1996). *Cultural psychology.* Cambridge, MA: Harvard University Press.

Confucius Institute/Hanban (2014). Confucius Institute annual development report 2014. Beijing: Hanban. Retrieved from http://www.hanban.edu.cn/report/pdf/2014_final.pdf

Cook, H. (2001). Why can't learners of Japanese as a foreign language distinguish polite from impolite speech styles? In K. Rose & G. Kasper (Eds.), *Pragmatics in language teaching* (pp. 80–102). Cambridge: Cambridge University Press.

Cook, H. (2008). *Socializing identities through speech style*. New York/Bristol: Multilingual Matters.

Cook, M., & Liddicoat, A. J. (2002). The development of comprehension in interlanguage pragmatics: The case of request strategies in English. *Australian Review of Applied Linguistics, 25*(1), 19–39.

Cook, V. (2002). *Portraits of the L2 user*. Clevedon, UK: Multilingual Matters.

Cornillie, F., Thorne, S., & Desmet, P. (2012). Special issue: Digital games for language learning: Challenges and opportunities. *ReCALL, 24*(3).

Costa, P. T., & McCrae, P. R. (1985). *The NEO personality inventory manual*. Odessa, FL: Psychological Assessment Resources, Inc.

Coulmas, F. (1981). *Conventional routine: Exploration in standardized communication situations and prepatterned speech*. The Hague: Mouton.

Council of Europe (2001). *Common European framework of reference for languages: Learning, teaching, assessment*. Cambridge: Cambridge University Press.

Crookes, G., & Schmidt, R. (1991). Motivation: Reopening the research agenda. *Language Learning, 41*, 469–512.

Crystal, D. (1997). *The Cambridge encyclopedia of language* (2nd ed.). New York: Cambridge University Press.

Crystal, D. (2006). *Language and the internet* (2nd ed.). Cambridge: Cambridge University Press.

Cui, X. (2012). *Problematic Chinese–Australian social interactions at work* (Unpublished doctoral dissertation). The University of Melbourne, Melbourne, Australia.

Cummins, J. (2005). A proposal for action: Strategies for recognizing language competence as a learning resource within the mainstream classroom. *Modern Language Journal, 89*, 585–591.

Cunningham, J. D. (2016). Request modification in synchronous computer-mediated communication: The role of focused instruction. *Modern Language Journal, 100*(2), 484–507.

Curl, T., & Drew, P. (2008). Contingency and action: A comparison of two forms of requesting. *Research on Language and Social Interaction, 41*(2), 129–153.

Curl, T., & Drew, P. (2008). Contingency and action: A comparison of two forms of requesting. *Research on Language and Social Interaction, 41*(2), 129–153.

Dahm, M. R., & Yates, L. (2013). English for the workplace: Doing patient-centred care in medical communication. *TESL Canada Journal, 30*, 21–44.

Davies, A. (1995). Proficiency or the native speaker: What are we trying to achieve in ELT? In G. Cook & B. Seidlhofer (Eds.), *Principles and practice in applied linguistics* (pp. 145–157). Oxford: Oxford University Press.

Dalmau, M. S., & Gotor, C. H. (2007). From 'sorry very much' to 'I'm ever so sorry': Acquisitional patterns in L2 apologies by Catalan learners of English. *Intercultural Pragmatics, 4*(2), 287–315.

de Bot, K. (2008). Introduction: Second language development as a dynamic process. *Modern Language Journal, 92*, 166–178.

De Cock, S. (1998). A recurrent word combination approach to the study of formulae in the speech of native and non-native speakers of English. *International Journal of Corpus Linguistics, 3*, 59–88.

de Jong, N., & Perfetti, C. (2011). Fluency training in the ESL classroom: An experimental study of fluency development and proceduralization. *Language Learning. 61*(2), 533–568

de Jong, N., Steinel, M., Florijn, A., Schoonen, R., & Hulstijn, J. (2012). Facets of speaking proficiency. *Studies in Second Language Acquisition, 34*(1), 5–34.

Deardorff, D. K. (2006). Identification and assessment of intercultural competence as a student outcome of internationalization. *Journal of Studies in International Education, 10*, 241–266.

L292

DeCapua, A., & Dunham, J. F. (2007). The pragmatics of advice giving: Cross-cultural perspectives. *Intercultural Pragmatics*, 4(3), 319–342.

Deci, E., & Ryan, R.M. (1985). The general causality orientations scale: Self-determination in personality. *Journal of Research in Personality*, 19, 109–34.

DeHaan, J., Reed, M., & Kuwada, K. (2010). The effect of interactivity with a music video game on second language vocabulary recall. *Language Learning & Technology*, 14, 74–94. http://www.tesl-ej.org/ej43/a1.pdf.

DeKeyser, R. (2007). *Practice in a second language: Perspectives from applied linguistics and cognitive psychology*. Cambridge: Cambridge University Press.

DeKeyser, R., & Koeth, J. (2011). Cognitive aptitudes for second language learning. In E. Hinkel (Ed.), *Handbook of research in second language teaching and learning* (pp. 395–406). New York: Routledge.

Dennis, A., Philburn, R., & Smith, G. (2013). *Sociologies of interaction*. Oxford: John Wiley & Sons.

Dewaard, L. (2012). Learner perception of formal and informal pronouns in Russian. *The Modern Language Journal*, 96(3), 400–418.

Dewaele, J. M. (2016). Thirty shades of offensiveness: L1 and LX English users' understanding, perception and self-reported use of negative emotion-laden words. *Journal of Pragmatics*, 94, 112–127.

Dewey, J. (1970). The development of American pragmatism. In *Philosophy and Civilization*, (pp. 13–35). New York: G.P. Putnam's. (Original work published 1931)

Diao, W. (2016). Peer socialization into gendered Mandarin practices in a study abroad context: Talk in the dorm. *Applied Linguistics*, 37(5), 599–620.

Diepenbroek, L., & Derwing, T. (2013). To what extent do popular EFL textbooks incorporate oral fluency and pragmatic development. *TESL Canada Journal*, 30, 1–20.

Dippold, D. (2011). Argumentative discourse in L2 German: A sociocognitive perspective on the development of facework strategies. *The Modern Language Journal*, 95(2), 171–187.

Do, H. T. T. (2013). Complaints in Vietnamese by native and non-native speakers. In C. Roever & H.T. Nguyen (Eds.), *Pragmatics of Vietnamese as native and target language* (pp. 111–134). Honolulu, HI: National Foreign Language Resource Center, University of Hawaii.

Dobao, A. F. (2012). Collaborative dialogue in learner–learner and learner–native speaker interaction. *Applied Linguistics*, 33, 229–256.

Doiz, A., Lasagabaster, D., & Sierra J. M. (2013). *English-medium instruction at universities: Global challenges*. Bristol: Multilingual Matters.

Dörnyei, Z. (2000). Motivation in action: Towards a process-oriented conceptualisation of student motivation. *British Journal of Educational Psychology*, 70, 519–538.

Dörnyei, Z. (2001). *Teaching and researching motivation*. London: Longman.

Dörnyei, Z. (2005). *The psychology of the language learner*. Mahwah, NJ: Lawrence Erlbaum.

Dörnyei, Z. (2007). Creating a motivating classroom environment. In J. Cummins & C. Davison (Eds.), *International handbook of English language teaching*, (Vol. 2, pp. 719–731). New York: Springer.

Dörnyei, Z. (2009). *The psychology of second language acquisition*. Oxford/New York: Oxford University Press.

Dörnyei, Z. (2014). Researching complex dynamic systems: 'Retrodictive qualitative modelling' in the language classroom. *Language Teaching*, 47, 80–91.

Dörnyei, Z., & Chan, L. (2013). Motivation and vision: An analysis of future L2 self images, sensory styles, and imagery capacity across two target languages. *Language Learning*, 63, 437–462.

Dörnyei, Z., & Ottó, I. (1998). Motivation in action: A process model of L2 motivation. *Working Papers in Applied Linguistics (Thames Valley University, London)*, 4, 43–69.

Dörnyei, Z., & Skehan, P. (2003). Individual differences in second language learning. In C. Doughty & M. Long (Eds.), *The handbook of second language acquisition* (pp. 589–630). Oxford: Blackwell.

Dörnyei, Z., Henry, A., & Muir, C. (2015). *Motivational currents in language learning: Frameworks for focused interventions.* London: Routledge.

Dörnyei, Z., Durow, V., & Zahran, K. (2004). Individual differences and their effects on formulaic sequence acquisition. In N. Schmitt (Ed.), *Formulaic sequences* (pp. 87–106). Amsterdam/Philadelphia: PA: John Benjamins.

Dörnyei. Z., Henry, A., & MacIntyre, P. (2015). *Motivational dynamics in language learning.* Bristol: Multilingual Matters.

Doughty, C., & Williams, J. (Eds.) (1998). *Focus on form.* Cambridge: Cambridge University Press.

Doughty, C., Campbell, S., Bunting, M., Mislevy, M., Bowles, A., & Koeth, J. (2010). Predicting near-native L2 ability. *Proceedings of the 2008 Second Language Research Forum.* Cascadilla Press. Retrieved from: http://www.lingref.com/cpp/slrf/2008/index.html

Drew, P., & Couper-Kuhlen, E. (2014). *Requesting in social interaction* (Vol. 26). Amsterdam: John Benjamins.

Drew, P., & Heritage, J. (1992). Analyzing talk at work: An introduction. In P. Drew & J. Heritage (Eds.), *Talk at work: Interaction in institutional settings* (pp. 3–65). New York: Cambridge University Press.

Duff, P. A. (2003). New directions in second language socialization research. *Korean Journal of English Language and Linguistics, 3,* 309–339.

Duff, P. A. (2012). Identity, agency and second language acquisition. In S. M. Gass & A. Mackey, (Eds.), *The Routledge handbook of second language acquisition* (pp. 410–426). Abingdon: Routledge.

Duff, P. A. (2007). Second language socialization as sociocultural theory: Insights and issues. *Language Teaching, 40,* 309–319.

Duff, P. A., & Talmy, S. (2011). Language socialization approaches to second language acquisition: Social, cultural, and linguistic development in additional languages. In D. Atkinson (Ed.), *Alternative approaches to second language acquisition* (pp. 95–116). Abington: Routledge.

DuFon, M. (2010). The socialization of leave-taking in L2 Indonesian. In G. Kasper, H. T. Nguyen, & D. R. Yoshimi (Eds.), *Pragmatics and language learning* (Vol. 12, pp. 91–112). Honolulu, HI: University of Hawaii National Language Resource Center.

Dulay, H. C., & Burt, M. K. (1973). Should we teach children syntax? *Language Learning, 23*(2), 245–258.

Economidou-Kogetsidis, M. (2010). Cross-cultural and situational variation in requesting behaviour: Perceptions of social situations and strategic usage of request patterns. *Journal of Pragmatics, 42*(8), 2262–2281.

Economidou-Kogetsidis, M. (2013). Strategies, modification and perspective in native speakers' requests: A comparison of WDCT and naturally occurring requests. *Journal of Pragmatics, 53,* 21–38.

Edmondson, W. (1981). *Spoken discourse: A model for analysis.* London: Longman.

Edmondson, W., & House, J. (1991). Do learners talk too much? The waffle phenomenon in interlanguage pragmatics. In R. Phillipson, E. Kellerman, L. Selinker, M. Sharwood Smith, & M. Swain (Eds.), *Foreign/second language pedagogy research: A commemorative volume for Claus Færch* (pp. 273–287). Clevedon, UK: Multilingual Matters.

Educational Testing Service (2014). *TOEFL ibT scoring guides (rubrics) for speaking responses.* Retrieved from http://www.ets.org/s/toefl/pdf/toefl_speaking_rubrics.pdf

Edwards, J. A., & Lampert, M. D. (1993). *Talking data: Transcription and coding in discourse research.* New York: Psychology Press.

Eisenstein, M., & Bodman, J. (1993). Expressing gratitude in American English. In G. Kasper, & S. Blum-Kulka (Eds.), *Interlanguage pragmatics* (pp. 64–81). Oxford: Oxford University Press.

Ellis, N. C. (2008). Implicit and explicit knowledge about language. In J. Cenoz & N. H. Hornberger (Eds.), *Encyclopedia of language and education* (Vol. 6, pp. 1–13). New York: Springer.

Ellis, N., & Larsen-Freeman, D. (2006). Language emergence: Implications for applied linguistics—introduction to the special issue. *Applied Linguistics, 27*, 558–589.

Ellis, R. (1992). Learning to communicate in the classroom: A study of two learners' requests. *Studies in Second Language Acquisition, 14*, 1–23.

Ellis, R. (2005). Individual differences in second language learning. In A. Davies & C. Elder (Eds.), *The handbook of applied linguistics* (pp. 525–551). Oxford: Blackwell.

Ellis, R. (2009). *The study of second language acquisition, second edition.* Oxford: Oxford University Press.

Ellis, R. (2015). *Understanding second language acquisition.* Oxford: Oxford University Press.

Ellis, R., & Shintani, N. (2014). *Exploring language pedagogy through second language acquisition research.* London: Routledge.

Ellis, R., Loewen, S., Elder, C., Philp, J., Reinders, H., & Erlam, R. (2009). *Implicit and explicit knowledge in second language learning, testing and teaching.* Bristol: Multilingual Matters.

Ericsson, K., & Simon, H. (1993). *Protocol analysis: Verbal reports as data* (2nd ed.). Boston: MIT Press.

Eslami, Z. E. (2010). Refusals: how to develop appropriate refusal strategies. In A. Martínez-Flor & E. Usó-Juan (Eds.), *Speech act performance: Theoretical, empirical and methodological issues* (pp. 217–236). Amsterdam: John Benjamins.

Eslami, Z. R., Mirzaei, A., & Dini, S. (2015). The role of asynchronous computer mediated communication in the instruction and development of EFL learners' pragmatic competence. *System, 48*, 99–111.

Ewald, J. D. (2012). 'Can you tell me how to get there?': Naturally occurring versus role-play data in direction giving. *Pragmatics, 22*(1), 79–102.

Eysenck, H. J., & Eysenck, M.W. (1985). *Personality and individual differences.* New York: Plenum.

Faerch, C., & Kasper, G. (1984). Pragmatic knowledge: Rules and procedures. *Applied Linguistics, 5*, 214–225.

Fairclough, N. (2013). *Critical discourse analysis: The critical study of language.* London: Routledge.

Fantini, A. E. (2006). *Exploring and assessing intercultural competence.* Retrieved February 15, 2012, from http://www.sit.edu/publications/docs/feil_research_report.pdf

Fantini, A. E. (2012). Multiple strategies for assessing intercultural communicative competence. Language: an essential component of intercultural competence. In J. Jackson (Ed.), *The Routledge handbook of language and intercultural communication* (pp. 390–406). Oxford: Routledge.

Farhady, H. (1980). *Justification, development, and validation of functional language testing* (Unpublished doctoral dissertation). University of California, Los Angeles.

Félix-Brasdefer, J. C. (2004). Interlanguage refusals: Linguistic politeness and length of residence in the target community. *Language Learning, 54*(4), 587–653.

Félix-Brasdefer, J. C. (2007). Pragmatic development in the Spanish as a FL classroom: A cross-sectional study of learner requests. *Intercultural Pragmatics, 4*(2), 253–286.

Félix-Brasdefer, J. C. (2008a). Perceptions of refusals to invitations: Exploring the minds of foreign language learners. *Language Awareness, 17*(3), 195–211.

Félix-Brasdefer, J. C. (2008b). Teaching pragmatics in the classroom: Instruction of mitigation in Spanish as a foreign language. *Hispania, 91*, 479–494.

Félix-Brasdefer, J. C. (2010). Data collection methods in speech act performance: DCTs, role plays, and verbal reports. In A. Martínez-Flor & E. Uso-Juan (Eds.), *Speech act performance: Theoretical, empirical and methodological issues* (pp. 41–56). Amsterdam/Philadelphia, PA: John Benjamins.

Félix-Brasdefer, J. C. (2012). E-mail requests to faculty: E-politeness and internal modification. In M. Economidou-Kogetsidis & H. Woodfield (Eds.), *Interlanguage request modification* (pp. 87–118). Amsterdam: John Benjamins.

Félix-Brasdefer, J. C. (2013). Refusing in L2 Spanish: The effects of the context of learning during a short-term study abroad program. In O. Martí Andándiz & P. Salazar-Campillo (Eds.), *Refusals in instructional contexts and beyond* (pp. 147–173). Amsterdam: Rodopi.

Félix-Brasdefer, J. C., & Hasler-Barker, M. (2015). Complimenting in Spanish in a short-term study abroad context. In E. Alcón Soler & L. Yates (Eds.), *Pragmatic learning across contexts.* Special issue. *System, 48*, 75–85.

Fernandez, J. (2013). *Social networks and colloquial language development in study abroad* (Unpublished doctoral dissertation). Penn State University, State College, PA.

Firth, A. (1996). The discursive accomplishment of normality: On 'lingua franca' English and conversation analysis. *Journal of Pragmatics, 26*, 237–259.

Firth, A. (2009). Doing *not* being a foreign language learner: English as a *lingua franca* in the workplace and (some) implications for SLA. *International Review of Applied Linguistics, 47*, 127–156.

Firth, A., & Wagner, J. (1997). On discourse, communication and (some) fundamental concepts in SLA research. *Modern Language Journal, 81*, 285–300.

Fishman, J. (2006). Acquisition, maintenance and recovery of heritage languages. In G. Valdés, J. Fishman, R. Chávez, & W. Pérez (Eds.), *Developing minority language resources: The case of Spanish in California* (pp. 12–22). Clevedon, UK: Multilingual Matters.

Flick, U. (2014). *The SAGE handbook of qualitative data analysis.* London: SAGE.

Flores Salgado, E. (2011). *The pragmatics of requests and apologies: Developmental patterns of Mexican students.* Amsterdam: John Benjamins.

Fordyce, K. (2014). The differential effects of explicit and implicit instruction on EFL learners' use of epistemic stance. *Applied Linguistics, 35*, 6–28.

Fraser, B., Rintell, E., & Walters, J. (1981). An approach to conducting research on the acquisition of pragmatic competence in a second language. In D. Larsen-Freeman (Ed.), *Discourse analysis* (pp. 75–81). Rowley, MA: Newbury House.

Freed, B. (1995). *Second language acquisition in a study abroad context.* Amsterdam: John Benjamins.

Fukkink, R., Hulstijn, J., & Simis, A. (2005). Does training in second-language word recognition skills affect reading comprehension? An experimental study. *Modern Language Journal, 89*, 54–75.

Gal'perin, P. I. (1989). Organization of mental activity and the effectiveness of learning. *Soviet Psychology, 27*, 65–82.

Gal'perin, P. I. (1992). Stage-by-stage formation as a method of psychological investigation. *Journal of Russian and East European Psychology, 30*, 60–80.

Galaczi, E. D. (2008). Peer–peer interaction in a speaking test: The case of the first certificate in English examination. *Language Assessment Quarterly, 5*, 89–119.

Galaczi, E. D. (2014). Interactional competence across proficiency levels: How do learners manage interaction in paired speaking tests? *Applied Linguistics, 35*(5), 553–574.

Gan, Z. (2010). Interaction in group oral assessment: A case study of higher- and lower-scoring students. *Language Testing, 27*, 585–602.

Garcia, P. (2004). Developmental differences in speech act recognition: A pragmatic awareness study. *Language Awareness, 13*, 96–115.

Gardner, R. C. (1985). *Social psychology and second language learning: The role of attitudes and motivation.* London: Edward Arnold.

Garrett-Rucks, P. (2016). *Intercultural competence in instructed language learning.* Charlotte, NC: Information Age Publishing Inc.

Gass, S. M., & Houck, N. (1999). *Interlanguage refusals: A cross-cultural study of Japanese-English.* Berlin: Mouton.

Gass, S. M., & Mackey, A. (2000). *Stimulated recall methodology in second language research.* Mahwah, NJ: Lawrence Erlbaum.

Gass, S., & Selinker, L. (2008). *Second language acquisition: An introductory course.* New York: Routledge.

Gee, J. P. (2004). *Situated language and learning: A critique of traditional schooling.* New York: Routledge.

Gee, J. P. (2007). *Good video games and good learning.* New York: Peter Lang.

Geyer, N. (2007). Self-qualification in L2 Japanese: An interface of pragmatic, grammatical, and discourse competences. *Language Learning, 57*(3), 337–367.

Go, J., Granena, G., Yilmaz, Y., & Novella, M. (2015). Implicit and explicit instruction in L2 learning. In P. Rebuschat (Ed.), *Implicit and explicit learning of languages* (pp. 443–482). Amsterdam: John Benjamins.

Goffman, E. (1967). *Interaction ritual: Essays in face-to-face behaviour.* Chicago, IL: Aldine.

Goffman, Erving (1955). On face-work: An analysis of ritual elements of social interaction. *Psychiatry: Journal for the Study of Interpersonal Processes, 18*(3), 213–231.

Golato, A. (2003). Studying compliment responses: A comparison of DCTs and naturally occurring talk. *Applied Linguistics, 24*, 90–121.

Golato, A., & Golato, P. (2013). Pragmatics research methods. In C. Chapelle (Ed.), *The encyclopedia of applied linguistics.* Oxford: Wiley-Blackwell.

Goldberg, L. R. (1992). The development of markers for the big-five factor structure. *Psychological Assessment, 4*, 26–42.

Gonzales, A. (2013). Development of politeness strategies in participatory online environments: A case study. In N. Taguchi & J. Sykes (Eds.), *Technology in interlanguage pragmatics research and teaching* (pp. 101–120). Philadelphia, PA: John Benjamins.

González-Lloret, M. (2008). Computer-mediated learning of L2 pragmatics. In E. Alcón Soler and A. Martínez-Flor (Eds.), *Investigating pragmatics in foreign language learning, teaching and testing* (pp. 114–32). Clevedon, UK: Multilingual Matters.

González-Lloret, M. (2011). Conversation analysis of computer-mediated communication. *CALICO Journal, 28*(2), 308–325.

González-Lloret, M. (2016). The construction of emotion in multilingual computer-mediated interaction. In M. Prior & G. Kasper (Eds.), *Emotion in multilingual interaction* (pp. 291–313). Amsterdam/Philadelphia, PA: John Benjamins.

González-Lloret, M., & Ortega, L. (2014). *Technology-mediated TBLT: Researching technology and tasks.* Amsterdam/Philadelphia, PA: John Benjamins.

Gotti, M. (2014). Explanatory strategies in university courses taught in ELF. *Journal of English as a Lingua Franca, 3*(2), 337–361.

Göy, E., Zeyrek, D., & Otcu, B. (2012). Developmental patterns in internal modification of requests: a quantitative study on Turkish learners of English. In M. Economidou-Kogetsidis & H. Woodfield (Eds.), *Interlanguage request modification* (pp. 51–86). Amsterdam: John Benjamins.

Grabowski, K. (2009). *Investigating the construct validity of a test designed to measure grammatical and pragmatic knowledge in the context of speaking* (Unpublished doctoral dissertation). Teachers College, Columbia University, New York, NY.

Grabowski, K. (2013). Investigating the construct validity of a role-play test designed to measure grammatical and pragmatic knowledge at multiple proficiency levels. In S. Ross & G. Kasper (Eds.), *Assessing second language pragmatics* (pp. 149–171). New York: Palgrave MacMillan.

Graddol, D. (2006). *English next: Why global English may mean the end of 'English as a foreign language.'* London: British Council.

Granena, G., & Long, M. (Eds.). (2013). *Sensitive periods, language aptitude, and ultimate L2 attainment.* Amsterdam: John Benjamins.

Grice, H. P. (1975). Logic and conversation. In P. Cole & J. Morgan (Eds.), *Syntax and semantics* (Vol. 3, pp. 41–58). New York: Academic Press.

Grieve, A. M. (2015). The impact of host family relations and length of stay on adolescent identity expression during study abroad. *Multilingua, 34*(5), 623–657.

Grigorenko, E., Sternberg, R., & Ehrman, E. E. (2000). A theory-based approach to the measurement of foreign language learning ability: The Canal-F theory and test. *Modern Language Journal, 84*, 390–405.

Grotjahn, R. (2014). *The C-test: current trends.* Frankfurt: Peter Lang.

Gu, M., Patkin, J., & Kirkpatrick, A. (2014). The dynamic identity construction in English as lingua franca intercultural communication: A positioning perspective. *System, 46*, 131–142.

Gumperz, J. J., & Cook-Gumperz, J. (2012). Interactional sociolinguistics: Perspectives on intercultural communication. In C. B. Paulston, S. F. Kiesling & E. S. Rangel (Eds.), *The handbook of intercultural discourse and communication* (pp. 63–76). Oxford: Wiley-Blackwell.

Hakuta, K. (1974). Prefabricated patterns and the emergence of structure in second language acquisition. *Language Learning, 24*, 287–298.

Hall, C. (2014). Moving beyond accuracy: From tests of English to tests of Englishing. *ELT Journal, 68*, 376–385.

Hall, J. K., & Pekarek Doehler, S. (2011). L2 interactional competence and development. In J. K. Hall, J. Hellermann, & S. Pekarek Doehler (Eds.), *L2 interactional competence and development* (pp. 1–15). Bristol: Multilingual Matters.

Halliday, M. A. K., & Matthiessen, C. (2004). *An introduction to functional grammar* (3rd ed.). London: Arnold.

Hammer, M. R. (2005). *Assessment of the impact of the AFS study abroad experience*. New York: AFS Int.

Hammer, M. R., Bennett, M. J., & Wiseman, R. (2003). Measuring intercultural sensitivity: The intercultural development inventory. *International Journal of Intercultural Relations, 27*(4), 421–443.

Hanafi (2015). *Comparing interactional competence between learners and native speakers of Indonesian* (Unpublished doctoral dissertation). The University of Melbourne, Melbourne, Australia.

Hassall, T. (1997). *Requests by Australian learners of Indonesian* (Unpublished doctoral dissertation). Australian National University, Canberra, ACT.

Hassall, T. (2006). Learning to take leave in social conversations: A diary study. In M. DuFon & E. Churchill (Eds.), *Language learners in study abroad contexts* (pp. 31–58). Clevedon, UK: Multilingual Matters.

Hassall, T. (2013). Pragmatic development during short-term study abroad: The case of address terms in Indonesian. *Journal of Pragmatics, 55*, 1–17.

Hassall, T. (2015). Individual variation in L2 study-abroad outcomes: A case study from Indonesian pragmatics. *Multilingua, 34*, 33–59.

Haugh, M., & Chang, W. L. M. (2015). Understanding im/politeness across cultures: an interactional approach to raising sociopragmatic awareness. *International Review of Applied Linguistics in Language Teaching, 53*(4), 389–414.

Hauser, E. (2011). On the danger of exogenous theory in CA-for-SLA: A response to Hellermann and Cole (2009). *Applied Linguistics, 32*(3), 348–352.

Hayashi, A. (2006). Japanese English bilingual children in three different educational environments. In K. Kondo-Brown (Ed.), *Heritage language development: Focus on East Asian Iimmigrants* (pp. 145–174). Amsterdam: John Benjamins.

He, A. (2015). Literacy, creativity, and continuity: A language socialization perspective on heritage language classroom interaction. In N. Markee (Ed.), *Handbook of classroom interaction* (pp. 304–318). Malden, MA: Wiley-Blackwell.

Heath, C., & Luff, P. (2013). Embodied action and organizational activity. In J. Sidnell & T. Stivers (Eds.), *The handbook of conversation analysis* (pp. 281–307). Oxford: Blackwell.

Hellermann, J. (2007). The development of practices for action in classroom dyadic interaction: Focus on task openings. *The Modern Language Journal, 91*(1), 83–96.

Hellermann, J. (2008). *Social actions for classroom language learning*. Bristol: Multilingual Matters.

Hellermann, J. (2009). Practices for dispreferred responses using *no* by a learner of English. *International Review of Applied Linguistics in Language Teaching, 47*, 95–126.

Hellermann, J. (2011). Members' methods, members' competencies: Looking for evidence of language learning in longitudinal investigation of other-initiated repair. In J. K. Hall, J. Hellermann, & S. Pekarek Doehler (Eds.), *L2 interactional competence and development* (pp. 147–172). Bristol: Multilingual Matters

Hellermann, J., & Cole, E. (2009). Practices for social interaction in the language-learning classroom: Disengagements from dyadic task interaction. *Applied Linguistics*, 30(2), 186–215.

Hepburn, A., & Bolden, G. B. (2013). The conversation analytic approach to transcription. In J. Sidnell & T. Stivers (Eds.), *The handbook of conversation analysis* (pp. 57–76). Oxford: Blackwell.

Heritage, J. (1984). *Garfinkel and ethnomethodology*. Cambridge: Polity Press.

Heritage, J. (1990). Intention, meaning and strategy: Observations on constraints on interaction analysis. *Research on Language & Social Interaction*, 24(1–4), 311–332.

Heritage, J. (2002). The limits of questioning: Negative interrogatives and hostile question content. *Journal of Pragmatics*, 34, 1427–1446.

Heritage, J., Robinson, J. D., Elliott, M. N., Beckett, M., & Wilkes, M. (2007). Reducing patients' unmet concerns in primary care: the difference one word can make. *Journal of General Internal Medicine*, 22(10), 1429–1433.

Hill, T. (1997). *The development of pragmatic competence in an EFL context* (Unpublished doctoral dissertation). Temple University Japan, Tokyo.

Hiramoto, M. (2012). Pragmatics of the sentence-final uses of *can* in colloquial Singapore English. *Journal of Pragmatics*, 44, 890–906.

Hồ, G. A. (2013). Apologizing in Vietnamese as a native and a target language. In C. Roever & H. T. Nguyen (Eds.), *Pragmatics of Vietnamese as native and target language* (pp. 77–110). Honolulu, HI: National Foreign Language Resource Center, University of Hawaii.

Holden, C., & Sykes, J. M. (2013). Complex L2 pragmatic feedback via place-based mobile games. In N. Taguchi & J. M. Sykes (Eds.), *Technology in Interlanguage pragmatics research and teaching* (pp. 155–184). John Benjamins, Amsterdam/Philadelphia, PA.

Holmes, J. (2000). Doing collegiality and keeping control at work: Small talk in government departments. In J. Coupland (Ed.), *Small talk* (pp. 32–61). London: Continuum.

Holmes, J., & Riddiford, N. (2011). From classroom to workplace: tracking sociopragmatic development. *ELT Journal*, 65(4), 376–386.

Holmes, J., & Stubbe, M. (2003). Doing disagreement at work: A sociolinguistic approach. *Australian Journal of Communication*, 30, 53–77.

Holtgraves, T. (2007). Second language learners and speech act comprehension. *Language Learning*, 57(4), 595–610.

Hong, W. (1997). Sociopragmatics in language teaching: with examples of Chinese requests. *Journal of the Chinese Language Teachers Association*, 32, 95–107.

Houck, N. R., & Fujimori, J. (2010). Teacher, you should lose some weight: advice giving in English. In D. H. Tatsuki & N. R. Houck (Eds.), *Pragmatics: teaching speech acts* (pp. 89–104). Alexandra, VA: TESOL.

Houck, N. R., & Tatsuki, D. (2011). *Pragmatics: teaching natural conversation*. New York: TESOL.

House, J. (1996). Developing pragmatic fluency in English as a foreign language: Routines and metapragmatic awareness. *Studies in Second Language Acquisition*, 18, 225–252.

House, J. (2008). What is an 'intercultural speaker'? In E. Alcón Soler & M. P. Safont Jordà (Eds.), *Intercultural language use and language learning* (pp. 7–22). Springer.

House, J. (2009). Subjectivity in English as lingua franca discourse: The case of *you know*. *Intercultural Pragmatics*, 6, 171–194.

House, J. (2010). The pragmatics of English as a lingua franca. In A. Trosborg (Ed.), *Handbook of pragmatics VII* (pp. 363–387). Berlin: De Gruyter Mouton.

House, J. (2013). Developing pragmatic competence in English as a lingua franca: Using discourse markers to express (inter)subjectivity and connectivity. *Journal of Pragmatics*, 59, 57–67.

Huang, A. C. Y. (2011). The work of play. *Meaning-making in video games*. New York: Peter Lang.

Hudson, T. (2001). Indicators for cross-cultural pragmatic instruction: some quantitative tools. In K. Rose, & G. Kasper (Eds.), *Pragmatics in language teaching* (pp. 283–300). Cambridge: Cambridge University Press.

Hudson, T., Detmer, E., & Brown, J. D. (1995). *Developing prototypic measures of cross-cultural pragmatics* (Technical Report #7). Honolulu: University of Hawaii, Second Language Teaching and Curriculum Center.

Hülmbauer, C. (2011). 'Old friends? – Cognates in ELF communication. In A. Archibald, A. Cogo, & J. Jenkins (Eds.), *Latest trends in ELF research* (pp. 139–161). Newcastle upon Tyne: Cambridge Scholars Publishing.

Hulstijn, J.H. (2011). Language proficiency in native and nonnative speakers: an agenda for research and suggestions for second-language assessment. *Language Assessment Quarterly*, 8(3), 229–249.

Hulstijn, J. H., Schoonen, R., de Jong, N. H., Steinel, M. P., & Florijn, A. (2012). Linguistic competences of learners of Dutch as a second language at the B1 and B2 levels of speaking proficiency of the common European Framework of Reference for Languages (CEFR). *Language Testing*, 29(2), 203–221.

Hutchby, I., & Wooffit, R. (2008). *Conversation analysis* (2nd ed.). Cambridge, UK: Polity Press.

Huth, T. (2006). Negotiating structure and culture: L2 learners' realization of L2 compliment–response sequences in talk-in-interaction. *Journal of Pragmatics*, 38, 2025–2050.

Huth, T. (2010). Intercultural competence in conversation: Teaching German requests. *Die Unterrichtspraxis/Teaching German*, 43(2), 154–166.

Huth, T. (2014). "When in Berlin...": teaching German telephone openings. *Die Unterrichtspraxis/Teaching German*, 47(2), 164–179.

Hymes, D. H. (1972). On communicative competence. In J. B. Pride & J. Holmes (Eds.), *Sociolinguistics* (pp. 269–293). Baltimore, MD: Penguin Books Ltd.

Hynninen, N. (2013). ICL at the micro level: L2 speakers taking on the role of language experts. In U. Smit & E. Dafouz (Eds.), *Intergrating content and language in higher education: Gaining insights into English-medium instruction at European universities* (pp. 13–29). Amsterdam/Philadelphia, PA: John Benjamins.

Ide, S. (1989). Formal forms and discernment: Two neglected aspects of universals of linguistic politeness. *Multilingua*, 8(2–3), 223–248.

Ide, S. (2005). How and why honorifics can signify dignity and elegance: The indexicality and reflexivity of linguistic rituals. In R. Lakoff & S. Ide (Eds.), *Broadening the horizon of linguistic politeness* (pp. 45–64). Amsterdam: John Benjamins.

IELTS (2016). IELTS. Retrieved from https://www.ielts.org/

Ifantidou, E. (2013). Pragmatic competence and explicit instruction. *Journal of Pragmatics*, 59, 93–116.

Ife, A. (2008). A role for English as a lingua franca in the foreign language classroom? In E. Alcón Soler & M. P. Safont Jordà (Eds.), *Intercultural language use and language learning* (pp. 79–100). Springer.

Iino, M. (1996). *"Excellent Foreigner!" Gaijinization of Japanese language and culture in contact situations – an ethnographic study of dinner table conversations between Japanese host families and American students* (Unpublished doctoral dissertation). University of Pennsylvania, Philadelphia, PA.

Ikeda, K. (2009). Advanced learners' honorific styles in emails and telephone calls. In N. Taguchi (Ed.) *Pragmatic competence* (pp. 69–100). Berlin: Mouton de Gruyter.

Ikeda, N. (2016). *Measuring L2 oral pragmatic abilities for use in social contexts: Development and validation of an assessment instrument for L2 pragmatics performance in university settings* (Unpublished doctoral dissertation). The University of Melbourne, Melbourne, Australia.

Intachakra, S. (2004). Contrastive pragmatics and language teaching: apologies and thanks in English and Thai. *RELC Journal*, 35(1), 37–62.

International English Language Testing System (n.d.). *IELTS speaking band descriptors public version*. Retrieved from https://www.ielts.org/PDF/UOBDs_SpeakingFinal.pdf

Isebelli-Garcia, C. (2006). Study abroad social networks, motivation and attitude: Implications for second language acquisition. In M. A. DuFon & E. Churchill (Eds.), *Language learners in study abroad contexts* (pp. 231–258). Clevedon, UK: Multilingual Matters.

Isabelli-García, C., Bown, J., & Plews, J. K. (forthcoming). Language learning and study abroad. *Language Teaching.*

Ishida, K. (2007). Developing understanding of how the *desu/masu* and plain forms express one's stance. In D. R. Yoshimi & H. Wang (Eds.), *Selected papers from the conference on pragmatics in the CJK classroom: The state of the art.* Honolulu: University of Hawaii, 181–202.

Ishida, K. (2009). Indexing stance in interaction with Japanese *desu/masu* and plain forms. In N. Taguchi (Ed.), *Pragmatic competence in Japanese as a second language* (pp. 41–68). Berlin/New York: Mouton de Gruyter.

Ishida, M. (2009). Development of interactional competence: Changes in the use of *ne* in L2 Japanese during study abroad. In H. T. Nguyen & G. Kasper (Eds.), *Talk-in-interaction: Multilingual perspectives* (pp. 355–385). Honolulu: University of Hawaii, National Foreign Language Resource Center.

Ishida, M. (2011). Engaging in another person's telling as a recipient in L2 Japanese: Development of interactional competence during one-year study abroad. In G. Pallotti & J. Wagner (Eds.), *L2 Learning as social practice: Conversation-analytic perspectives* (pp. 45–85). Honolulu, HI: University of Hawaii, National Foreign Language Resource Center.

Ishihara, N., & Tarone, E. (2009). Subjectivity and pragmatic choice in L2 Japanese: Emulating and resisting pragmatic norms. In N. Taguchi (Ed.), *Pragmatic competence in Japanese as a second language* (pp. 101–128). Berlin: Mouton de Gruyter.

Ishihara, N. (2010). Compliments and responses to compliments: Learning communication in context. In A. Martínez-Flor & E. Usó-Juan (Eds.), *Speech act performance: Theoretical, empirical and methodological issues* (pp. 179–198). Amsterdam: John Benjamins.

Ishihara, N., & Cohen, A. (2010). *Teaching and learning pragmatics: Where language and culture meet.* Harlow, UK: Pearson Longman.

Itomitsu, M. (2009). *Developing a test of pragmatics of Japanese as a Foreign Language* (Unpublished doctoral dissertation). Ohio State University, Columbus, Ohio.

Iwasaki, N. (2011). Learning L2 Japanese "politeness" and "impoliteness": Young American men's dilemmas during study abroad. *Japanese Language and Literature, 45,* 67–106.

Jackson, J. (2015). Becoming interculturally competent: Theory to practice in international education. *International Journal of Intercultural Relations, 48,* 91–107

James, W. (1907). Pragmatism: A new name for some old ways of thinking. *Popular lectures on philosophy.* New York: Longmans, Green & Co.

Jamieson, S. (2004). Likert scales: how to (ab)use them. *Medical Education, 38,* 1212–1218.

Jefferson, G. (1984a). On stepwise transition from talk about a trouble to inappropriately next-positioned matters. In J. Heritage & J. M. Atkinson (Eds.), *Structures of social action: Studies in conversation analysis* (pp. 191–222). Cambridge: Cambridge University Press.

Jefferson, G. (1984b). On the organization of laughter in talk about troubles. In J. M. Atkinson & J. Heritage (Eds.), *Structures of social action* (pp. 346–369). Cambridge: Cambridge University Press).

Jefferson, G. (2004). Glossary of transcript symbols with an introduction. In G. H. Lerner (Ed.), *Conversation analysis: Studies from the first generation* (pp. 13–31). Philadelphia, PA: John Benjamims.

Jenkins, J. (2007). *English as a lingua franca: Attitude and identity.* Oxford: Oxford University Press.

Jenkins, J. (2014). *English as a lingua franca in the international university. The politics of academic English language policy.* London: Routledge.

Jenkins, J. (2015). *Global Englishes* (3rd ed.). London: Routledge.

Jenkins, J., & Leung, C. (2014). English as a lingua franca. In A. Kunnan (Ed.), *The companion to language assessment* (pp. 1607–1616). Malden, MA: John Wiley & Sons.

Jenkins, J., Cogo, A., & Deway, M. (2011). Review of developments in research into English as a lingua franca. *Language Teaching, 44,* 281–315.

Jenks, C. (2010). Adaptation in online voice-based chat rooms: Implications for language learning in applied linguistics. In P. Seedhouse, S. Walsh, & C. Jenks (Eds.), *Conceptualising 'learning' in applied linguistics* (pp. 147–162). New York: Palgrave Macmillan.

Jenks, C. J. (2011). *Transcribing talk and interaction: Issues in the representation of communication data*. Amsterdam: John Benjamins.

Jenks, C. J. (2012). Doing being reprehensive: Some interactional features of English as a lingua franca in a chat room. *Applied Linguistics, 33*, 386–405.

Jeon, E-H., & Kaya, T. (2006). Effects of L2 instruction on interlanguage pragmatic development. In N. John & L. Ortega (Eds.), *Synthesizing research on language learning and teaching* (pp. 165–211). Philadelphia, PA: John Benjamins.

Jin, L. (2012). When in China, do as the Chinese do? Learning compliment responding in a study abroad program. *Chinese as a Second Language Acquisition Research, 1*, 211–240.

John, O. P., Naumann, L. P., & Soto, C. J. (2008). Paradigm shift to the integrative big-five trait taxonomy: History, measurement, and conceptual issues. In O. P. John, R. W. Robins, & L. A. Pervin (Eds.), *Handbook of personality: Theory and research* (pp. 114–158). New York: Guilford Press.

Johnson, J. P., Lenartowicz, T., & Apud, S. (2006). Cross-cultural competence in international business: Toward a definition and a model. *Journal of International Business Studies, 37*, 525–543.

Johnston, B., Kasper, G., & Ross, S. (1998). Effect of rejoinders in production questionnaires. *Applied Linguistics, 19*(2), 157–182.

Judd, E. (1999). Some issues in the teaching of pragmatic competence. In E. Hinkel (Ed.), *Culture in second language teaching and learning* (pp. 152–166). Cambridge: Cambridge University Press.

Juffs, A. (2014). Working memory and sentence processing: A commentary. In Z. Wen, M. B. Mota, & A. McNeil (Eds.), *Working memory in second language acquisition and processing* (pp. 125–136). New York/Bristol: Multilingual Matters.

Juffs, A., & Harrington, M. W. (2011). Aspects of working memory in L2 learning. *Language Teaching, 47*, 137–166.

Kääntä, L. (2014). From noticing to initiating correction: Students' epistemic displays in instructional interaction. *Journal of Pragmatics, 66*, 86–105.

Kachru, B. B. (1992). Models for non-native Englishes. In B. B. Kachru (Ed.), *The other tongue. English across cultures* (2nd ed., pp. 48–74). Urbana, IL: University of Illinois Press.

Kakegawa, T. (2009). Development of the use of Japanese sentence final particles through email correspondence. In N. Taguchi (Ed.), *Pragmatic competence in Japanese as a second langauge* (pp. 301–334). Berlin/New York: Mouton de Gruyter.

Kanagy, R. (1999). Interactional routines as a mechanism for L2 acquisition and socialization in an immersion context. *Journal of Pragmatics, 31*, 1467–92.

Kane, M. T. (2006). Validation. In R. L. Brennan (Ed.), *Educational measurement, fourth edition* (pp. 17–64). Westport, CT: American Council on Education/Praeger Publishers.

Kane, M.T. (2012). All validity is construct validity. Or is it? *Measurement: Interdisciplinary Research and Perspectives, 10*(1–2), 66–70.

Kant, I. (1781). *Kritik der reinen Vernunft* [Critique of pure reason]. Retrieved from https://korpora.zim.uni-duisburg-essen.de/kant/aa03/523.html

Kasper, G. (1979). Errors in speech act realization and use of gambits. *Canadian Modern Language Review, 35*(3), 395–406.

Kasper, G. (1981). *Pragmatische Aspekte in der Interimsprache*. Tübingen: Narr.

Kasper, G. (1992). Pragmatic transfer. *Second Language Research, 8*, 203–231.

Kasper, G. (1995). Wessen Pragmatik? Für eine Neubestimmung sprachlicher Handlungskompetenz. *Zeitschrift für Fremdsprachenforschung, 6*, 1–25.

Kasper, G. (2001). Four perspectives on L2 pragmatic development. *Applied Linguistics, 22*, 502–530.

Kasper, G. (2006a). Beyond repair: Conversation analysis as an approach to SLA. *AILA Review, 19*(1), 83–99.

Kasper, G. (2006b). Politeness in interaction. Introduction. Special Issue. *Multilingua, 25*, 243–248.

Kasper, G. (2006c). Speech acts in interaction: Towards discursive pragmatics. In K. Bardovi-Harlig, J. C. Félix-Brasdefer, & A. S. Omar (Eds.), *Pragmatics and Language Learning: 11* (pp. 281–314). University of Hawaii at Manoa: National Foreign Language Resource Center.

Kasper, G. (2008). Data collection in pragmatics research. In H. Spencer-Oatey (Ed.), *Culturally speaking* (2nd ed., pp. 279–303). London & New York: Continuum.

Kasper, G. (2009). Locating cognition in second language interaction and learning: Inside the skull or in public view? *IRAL – International Review of Applied Linguistics in Language Teaching, 47*(1), 11–36.

Kasper, G., & Blum-Kulka, S. (1993). *Interlanguage pragmatics*. New York: Oxford University Press.

Kasper, G., & Dahl, M. (1991). Research methods in interlanguage pragmatics. *Studies in Second Language Acquisition, 13*, 215–247.

Kasper, G., & Rose, K. (1999). Pragmatics and SLA. *Annual Review of Applied Linguistics, 19*, 81–104.

Kasper, G., & Rose, K. (2002). *Pragmatic development in a second language*. Oxford, UK: Blackwell.

Kasper, G., & Schmidt, R. (1996). Developmental issues in interlanguage pragmatics. *Studies in Second Language Acquisition, 18*, 149–169.

Kasper, G., & Wagner, J. (2011). A conversation-analytic approach to second language acquisition. In D. Atkinson (Ed.), *Alternative approaches to second language acquisition* (pp. 117–142). New York: Routledge.

Kasper, G., & Wagner, J. (2011). A conversation-analytic approach to second language acquisition. In D. Atkinson (Ed.), *Alternative approaches to second language acquisition* (pp. 117–142). London: Routledge.

Kasper, G., & Wagner, J. (2014). Conversation analysis in applied linguistics. *Annual Review of Applied Linguistics, 34*, 171–212.

Kaur, J. (2012). Saying it again and again: Enhancing clarity in English as a lingua franca (ELF) talk through self-repetition. *Text & Talk, 32*, 593–613.

Kealey, D. J. (1996). The challenge of international personnel selection. In D. L. Landis & R. S. Bhagat (Eds.), *Handbook of intercultural training* (pp. 81–105). Thousand Oaks, CA: SAGE.

Kecskes, I. (2003). *Situation-bound utterances in L1 and L2*. Berlin: Mouton de Gruyter.

Kecskes, I. (2007). Formulaic language in English lingua franca. In I. Kecskes & L. R. Horn (Eds.), *Explorations in pragmatics: Linguistic, cognitive and intercultural aspects* (pp. 191–219). Berlin/New York: Mouton de Gruyter.

Kecskes, I. (2012). Interculturality and intercultural pragmatics. In J. Jackson (Ed.), *The Routledge handbook of language and intercultural communication* (pp. 67–84). Oxford: Routledge.

Kecskes, I. (2014). *Intercultural pragmatics*. New York: Oxford University Press.

Kecskes, I. (2015). Intracultural communication and intercultural communication: Are they different? *International Review of Pragmatics, 7*(2), 171–194.

Keirsey, D. (1998). *Please understand me II: Character and temperament types*. Del Mar, CA: Prometheus Nemesis Book Company.

Kelley, C., & Meyers, J. (1995). *Cross-cultural adaptability inventory manual*. Arlington, VA: Vangent.

Kim, E-J. (2006). Heritage language maintenance by Korean-American college students. In K. Kondo-Brown (Ed.), *Heritage language development: Focus on East Asian immigrants* (pp. 175–208). Amsterdam: John Benjamins.

Kim, E-Y., & Brown, L. (2014). Negotiating pragmatic competence in computer mediated communication: The case of Korean address terms. *CALICO, 31*, 264–284.

Kim, H. Y. (2014). Learner investment, identity, and resistance to second language pragmatic norms. *System, 45*, 92–102.

Kim, Y. (2009). The Korean discourse markers – nuntey and kuntey in native–nonnative conversation: an acquisitional perspective. In T. H. Nguyen & G. Kasper (Eds.), *Talk-in-interaction: Multilingual perspectives* (pp. 317–350), Honolulu: University of Hawaii Press.

Kim, Y. (2012). Practices for initial recognitional reference and learning opportunities in conversation. *Journal of Pragmatics, 44*, 709–729.

Kim, Y., & Taguchi, N. (2015). Promoting task-based pragmatics instruction in EFL classroom context: The role of task complexity. *Modern Language Journal, 99*, 656–677.

Kim, Y., & Taguchi, N. (2016). Learner–learner interaction during collaborative pragmatic tasks: The role of cognitive and pragmatic task demands. *Foreign Language Annals, 49*, 42–57.

Kinginger, C. (2008). Language learning in study abroad: Case studies of Americans in France. *Modern Language Journal, 92*, Supplement S1.

Kinginger, C. (2011). Enhancing language learning in study abroad. *Annual Review of Applied Linguistics, 31*, 58–73.

Kinginger, C. (2013). *Social and cultural aspects of language learning in study abroad.* Amsterdam/New York: John Benjamins.

Kinginger, C., & Belz, J. (2005). Sociocultural perspectives on pragmatic development in foreign language learning: Case studies from telecollaboration and study abroad. *Intercultural Pragmatics, 2*, 369–421.

Kirkpatrick, A. (2010). *English as a lingua franca in ASEAN.* Hong Kong: University of Hong Kong Press.

Kitade, K. (2014). Second language teachers' identity development through online collaboration with L2 learners. *CALICO, 31*, 83–103.

Kitzinger, C. (2013). Repair. In J. Sidnell & T. Stivers (Eds.), *The handbook of conversation analysis* (pp. 229–256). Oxford: Blackwell..

Klein, W., & Perdue, C. (1992). *Utterance structure: Developing grammars again.* Amsterdam: John Benjamins.

Knapp, A. (2011). Using English as a lingua franca for (mis-)managing conflict in an international university context: An example from a course in engineering. *Journal of Pragmatics, 43*, 978–90.

Knight, S. M., & Schmidt-Rinehart, B. C. (2002). Enhancing the homestay: Study abroad from the host family's perspective. *Foreign Language Annals, 35*, 190–201.

Koester, J., & Lustig, M. W. (2015). Intercultural communication competence: Theory, measurement, and application. *International Journal of Intercultural Relations, 48*, 20–21.

Konakahara, M. (2015). An analysis of overlapping questions in casual EFL conversation: Cooperative or competitive contribution. *Journal of Pragmatics, 84*, 37–53.

Kondo, S. (2010). Apologies: Raising learners' cross-cultural awareness. In A. Martínez-Flor & E. Usó-Juan (Eds.), *Speech act performance: Theoretical, empirical and methodological issues* (pp. 145–162). Amsterdam: John Benjamins.

Kondo-Brown, K. (2005). Differences in language skills: Heritage language learner subgroups and foreign language learners. *Modern Language Journal, 89*, 563–581.

Kondo-Brown, K. (2006). Chapter 1, Introduction. In K. Kondo-Brown (Ed.), *Heritage language development: Focus on East Asian immigrants* (pp. 1–12). Amsterdam/ Philadelphia: John Benjamins.

Kotthoff, H. (1993). Disagreement and concession in disputes: On the context sensitivity of preference structures. *Language in Society, 22*, 193–216.

Kramsch, C. (1986). From language proficiency to interactional competence. *The Modern Language Journal, 70*(4), 366–372.

Kramsch, C. (1993). *Context and culture in language teaching.* Oxford: Oxford University Press.

Kramsch, C. (2011). The symbolic dimensions of the intercultural. *Language Teaching, 44*, 354–367.

Kramsch, C. (2014). Teaching foreign languages in an era of globalization: Introduction. *Modern Language Journal, 98*, 296–311.

Krashen, S. D. (1985). *The input hypothesis: Issues and implications.* New York: Longman.

Kreutel, K. (2007). "I'm not agree with you." ESL learners' expressions of disagreement. *TESL-EJ: Teaching English as a Second or Foreign Language, 11*(3). Retrieved from http://tesl-ej.org/ej43/a1.html

Kubota, M. (1995). Teachability of conversational implicatures to Japanese EFL learners. *IRLT Bulletin, 9*, 35–67.

Kuriscak, L. M. (2006). *Pragmatic variation in L2 Spanish: Learner and situational effects* (Unpublished doctoral dissertation). Indiana University, Bloomington, IN.

Lafford, B. (Ed.). (2007). Ten years after Firth & Wagner (1997). *Modern Language Journal, 91*(5). Special issue.

Lam, P., Cheng, W., & Kong, K. C. C. (2014). Learning English through workplace communication: An evaluation of existing resources in Hong Kong. *English for Specific Purposes, 34*, 68–78.

Lantolf, J. P., & Thorne, S. L. (2006). Sociocultural theory and the genesis of L2 development. Oxford: Oxford University Press.

Lantolf, J., & Beckett, T. (2009). Research timeline. Sociocultural theory and second language acquisition. *Language Teaching, 42*, 459–475.

Larsen-Freeman, D. (2012). Complexity theory. In S. Gass & A. Mackey (Eds.), *The Routledge handbook of second language acquisition* (pp. 73–87). New York: Routledge.

Larsen-Freeman, D., & Cameron, L. (2008). *Complex systems and applied linguistics.* Oxford/New York: Oxford University Press.

Lave, J. (1988). *Cognition in practice.* Cambridge, UK: Cambridge University Press.

Lave, J., & Wenger, E. (1991). *Situated learning: Legitimate peripheral participation.* Cambridge: Cambridge University Press.

Lee, H. (2013). The influence of social situations on fluency difficulty in Korean EFL learners' oral refusals. *Journal of Pragmatics, 50*(1), 168–186.

Lee, Y. A., & Hellermann, J. (2014). Tracing developmental changes through conversation analysis: Cross-sectional and longitudinal analysis. *TESOL Quarterly, 48*(4), 763–88.

Leech, G. (1983). *Principles of pragmatics.* London: Longman.

Leech, G. (2014). *The pragmatics of politeness.* Oxford: Oxford University Press.

Leontiev, A. N. (1981). *Problems of the development of mind.* Moscow: Progress Publishers.

Leung, C., Harris, R., & Rampton, B. (1997). The idealized native speaker; reified ethnicities and classroom realities. *TESOL Quarterly, 31*, 543–560.

Leung, K., Ang, S., & Tan, M-L. (2014). Intercultural competence. *Annual Review of Organizational Psychology and Organizational Behavior, 1*, 489–519.

Levinson, S. C. (1983). *Pragmatics.* Cambridge: Cambridge University Press.

Levinson, S. C. (2013). Action formation and ascription. In T. Stivers, & J. Sidnell (Eds.), *The handbook of conversation analysis* (pp. 103–130). Malden, MA: Wiley-Blackwell.

Levinson, S. C. (2016). Turn-taking in human communication – origins and implications for language processing. *Trends in Cognitive Sciences, 20*(1), 1–14.

Levy, M., & Stockwell, G. (2006). *CALL dimensions: Options and issues in computer-assisted language learning.* Mahwah, NJ: Erlbaum.

Li, D. (2000). The pragmatics of making requests in the L2 workplace: A case study of language socialization. *Canadian Modern Language Review, 57*, 58–87.

Li, E. S. H. (2010). Making suggestions: A contrastive study of young Hong Kong and Australian students. *Journal of Pragmatics, 42*(3), 598–616.

Li, Q. (2012). Effects of instruction on adolescent beginners' acquisition of request modification. *TESOL Quarterly, 46*, 30–55.

Li, S. (2012). The effects of input-based practice on pragmatic development of requests in L2 Chinese. *Language Learning, 62*, 403–438.

Li, S. (2013). Amount of practice in pragmatic development of request-making in L2 Chinese. In N. Taguchi & J. M. Sykes (Eds.), *Technology in interlanguage pragmatics research and teaching* (pp. 43–70). Amsterdam/Philadelphia, PA: John Benjamins.

Li, S. (2014). The effects of different levels of linguistic proficiency on the development of L2 Chinese request production during study abroad. *System, 45*, 103–116.

Li, S. (forthcoming). The role of language aptitude in teaching request-making in L2 Chinese. *Chinese as a Second Language Research*.

Li, S., & Taguchi, N. (2014). The effects of practice modality on the development of pragmatic performance in L2 Chinese. *Modern Language Journal, 98*, 794–812.

Liao, S. (2009). Variation in the use of discourse markers by Chinese teaching assistants in the US. *Journal of Pragmatics, 41*, 1313–1328.

Liddicoat, A. J., & Crozet, C. (2001). Acquiring French interactional norms through instruction. In K. R. Rose & G. Kasper (Eds.), *Pragmatics in language teaching* (pp. 125–144). Cambridge: Cambridge University Press.

Lin, C. Y., Woodfield, H., & Ren, W. (2012). Compliments in Taiwan and Mainland Chinese: The influence of region and compliment topic. *Journal of Pragmatics, 44*(11), 1486–1502.

Lin, H. (2014). Establishing an empirical link between computer-mediated communication (CMC) and SLA: A meta-analysis of the research. *Language Learning & Technology, 18*, 120–147.

Linck, J. A., Hughes, M. M., Campbell, S. G., Silbert, N. H., Tare, M., Jackson, S. R., Smith, B. K., Bunting, M. F., & Doughty, C. J. (2013). Hi-LAB: A new measure of aptitude for high-level language proficiency. *Language Learning, 63*, 530–566.

Liu, J. (2006). *Measuring interlanguage pragmatic knowledge of EFL learners*. Frankfurt: Peter Lang.

Liu, J. (2007). Developing a pragmatics test for Chinese EFL learners. *Language Testing, 24*, 391–415.

Liu, J., & Ren, W. (2016). Apologies in emails: Interactions between Chinese EFL learners and their foreign peers. In Y. S. Chen, D. H. Rau & G. Rau (Eds.), *Email discourse among Chinese using English as a lingua franca* (pp. 205–228). Singapore: Springer.

Llanes, A. (2011). The many faces of study abroad: An update on the research on L2 gains emerged during a study abroad experience. *International Journal of Multilingualism, 8*, 189–215.

LoCastro, V. (2003). *An introduction to pragmatics: Social action for language teachers*. Ann Arbor, MI: The University of Michigan Press.

Lochner, M. (2013). Politeness. In C. Chapelle (Ed.), *Encyclopedia of Applied Linguistics*. Oxford: Blackwell.

Long, M. H. (1996). The role of the linguistic environment in second language acquisition. In R. William & T. Bhatia (Eds.). *Handbook of second language acquisition* (pp. 413–468). San Diego: Academic Press.

Long, M. H. (2007). *Problems in SLA*. Mahwah, NJ: Lawrence Erlbaum Associates.

Long, M. H. (2015). *Second language acquisition and task-based language teaching*. Oxford: Wiley-Blackwell.

Long, M. H., Gor, K., & Jackson, S. (2012). Linguistic correlates of proficiency: Proof of concept with ILR 2-3 in Russian. *Studies in Second Language Acquisition 34*(1), 99–126.

Louw, K. J., Derwing, T. M., & Abbott, M. L. (2010). Teaching pragmatics to L2 learners for the workplace: The job interview. *The Canadian Modern Language Review 66*, 739–758.

Lynch, A. (2003). The relationship between second and heritage language acquisition: Notes on research and theory building. *Heritage Language Journal, 1*, 26–43.

Lowie, W., & Verspoor, M. (2015). Variability and variation in second language acquisition orders: A dynamic reevaluation. *Language Learning, 65*, 63–88.

Mackenzie, I. (2014). *English as a lingua franca: Theorizing and teaching English*. New York: Routledge.

Mackey, A., & Gass, S. M. (2011). *A guide to research methods in second language acquisition*. London: Basil Blackwell.

Mackey, A., Philp, J., Egi, T., Fujii, A., & Tatsumi, T. (2002). Individual differences in working memory, noticing of interactional feedback and L2 development. In P. Robinson (Ed.), *Individual differences and instructed language learning* (pp. 181–210). Amsterdam: John Benjamins.

MacWhinney, B. (2006). Emergentism – use often with care. *Applied Linguistics, 27,* 729–740.

Maeshiba, N., Yoshinaga, N., Kasper, G., & Ross, S. (1996). Transfer and proficiency in interlanguage apologizing. In S. M. Gass, & J. Neu (Eds.), *Speech acts across cultures* (pp. 155–187). Berlin: Mouton de Gruyter.

Maíz-Arévalo, C. (2014). Expressing disagreement in English as a lingua franca: Whose pragmatic rules? *Intercultural Pragmatics, 11,* 199–224.

Malamed, M. H. (2010). Disagreement: How to disagree agreeably. In A. Martínez-Flor & E. Usó-Juan (Eds.), *Speech act performance: Theoretical, empirical and methodological issues* (pp. 199–216). Amsterdam: John Benjamins.

Manes, J. (1983). Compliments: A mirror of cultural values. In N. Wolfson & E. Judd (Eds.), *Sociolinguistics and language acquisition* (pp. 96–102). Rowley, MA: Newbury House.

Markee, N., & Kunitz, S. (2013). Doing planning and task performance in second language acquisition: An ethnomethodological respecification. *Language Learning, 63*(4), 629–664.

Markee, N., & Seo, M. S. (2009). Learning talk analysis. *IRAL – International Review of Applied Linguistics in Language Teaching, 47*(1), 37–63.

Martínez-Flor, A. (2006). The effectiveness of explicit and implicit treatments on EFL learners' confidence in recognizing appropriate suggestions. In K. Bardovi-Harlig, C. Félix-Brasdefer & A. S. Omar (Eds.), *Pragmatics and language learning* (Vol. 11, pp. 199–225). Honolulu, HI: University of Hawaii Press.

Martínez-Flor, A. (2010). Suggestions: How social norms affect pragmatic behavior. In A. Martínez-Flor & E. Usó-Juan (Eds.), *Speech act performance: Theoretical, empirical and methodological issues* (pp. 257–274). Amsterdam: John Benjamins.

Martínez-Flor, A. (2013). Learners' production of refusals: Interactive written DCT versus oral role-play. *Utrecht Studies in Language & Communication, 25,* 175–211.

Masuda, K. (2011). Acquiring interactional competence in a study abroad context: Japanese language learners' use of the interactional particle *ne*. *Modern Language Journal, 95,* 519–540.

Matsumoto, Y. (1988). Reexamination of the universality of face: Politeness phenomena in Japanese. *Journal of Pragmatics, 12,* 403–426.

Matsumoto, Y. (1989). Politeness and conversational universals – observations from Japanese. *Multilingua: Journal of Cross-Cultural and Interlanguage Communication, 8*(2–3), 207–222.

Matsumura, S. (2001). Learning the rules for offering advice: A quantitative approach to second language socialization. *Language Learning, 51,* 635–679.

Matsumura, S. (2003). Modelling the relationships among interlanguage pragmatic development, L2 proficiency, and exposure to L2. *Applied Linguistics, 24*(4), 465–491.

Mauranen, A. (2003). The corpus of English as a lingua franca in academic settings. *TESOL Quarterly, 37,* 513–527.

Mauranen, A. (2009). Chunking in ELF: Expressions for managing interaction. *Journal of Intercultural Pragmatics, 6,* 217–233.

Mauranen, A. (2012). *Exploring ELF: Academic English shaped by non-native speakers.* Cambridge: Cambridge University Press.

Mauranen, A. (2015, July). *Corpus work on a complex language: A case of ELF.* Plenary talk given at British Association of Applied Linguistics Sig. Conference. Edinburgh, Scotland.

McConachy, T., & Hata, K. (2013). Addressing textbook representations of pragmatics and culture. *ELT Journal, 67,* 294–301.

McCrae, R. R., & Costa, P. T. (2003). *Personality in adulthood: A five-factor theory perspective* (2nd ed.). New York: Guilford Press.

McMeekin, A. L. (2011, March). *Japanese L2 learners' use and acquisition of the plain form during study abroad.* Paper presented at the meeting of the American Association for Applied Linguistics. Chicago, IL.

McNamara, T. (2011). Managing learning: Authority and language assessment. *Language Teaching, 44,* 500–515.

McNamara, T. F., & Roever, C. (2006). *Language testing: The social dimension.* Malden, MA: Blackwell.

Mehan, H. (1979). *Learning lessons: Social organization in the classroom*. Cambridge, MA: Harvard University Press.

Messick, S. (1989). Validity. In R. L. Linn (Ed.), *Educational measurement* (3rd ed., pp. 13–103). New York: American Council on Education/Macmillan.

Metsä-Ketelä, M. (2016). Pragmatic vagueness. Exploring general extenders in English as a lingua franca. *Intercultural Pragmatics, 13*, 325–351.

Mey, J. L. (2001). *Pragmatics: An introduction* (2nd ed.). Oxford: Blackwell.

Miles, M. B., Huberman, A. M., & Saldana, J. (2014). *Qualitative data analysis: A methods sourcebook*. Los Angeles, CA: SAGE.

Miller, L. (2008). Negative assessment of Japanese–American workplace interaction. In H. Spencer-Oatey (Ed.), *Culturally speaking: Culture, communication and politeness theory* (2nd ed., pp. 240–254). London: Continuum.

Mitchell, R., Myles, F., & Marsden, E. (2013). *Second language learning theories* (3rd ed.). London: Edward Arnold.

Miyake, A., & Friedman, D. (1998). Individual differences in second language proficiency: Working memory as language aptitude. In A. F. Healy & L. E. Bourne (Eds.), *Foreign language learning: Psycholinguistic studies on training and retention*. Mahwah, NJ: Lawrence Erlbaum Associates.

Montrul, S. (2008). *Incomplete acquisition in bilingualism. Re-examining the age factor*. Amsterdam: John Benjamins.

Montrul, S. (2010). Current issues in heritage language acquisition. *Annual Review of Applied Linguistics, 30*, 3–23.

Moody, S. (2014). Should we teach rules for pragmatics? Explicit instruction and emergent pragmatic awareness of Japanese plain and polite forms. *Japanese Language & Literature 48*(1), 39–69.

Moore, R. J. (2015). Automated transcription and conversation analysis. *Research on Language and Social Interaction, 48*(3), 253–270.

Mor, S., Morris, M., & Joh, J. (2013). Identifying and training adaptive cross-cultural management skills: The crucial role of cultural metacognition. *Academy of Management Learning Education, 12*, 453–475.

Mori, J. (2009). The social turn in second language acquisition and Japanese pragmatics research: Reflection on ideologies, methodologies and instructional implications. In N. Taguchi (Ed.), *Pragmatic competence in Japanese as a second language* (pp. 335–338). Berlin/New York: Mouton de Gruyter.

Morita, N. (2004). Discourse socialization through oral classroom activities in a TESL graduate program. *TESOL Quarterly, 34*, 279–310.

Morita, N. (2009). Language, culture, gender, and academic socialization. *Language and Education, 23*, 443–460.

Morris, C. (1938). Foundations of the theory of signs. In O. Neurath, R. Carnap, & C. Morris (Eds.), *International encyclopedia of unified science* (pp. 77–138). Chicago, IL: University of Chicago Press.

Murray, J. C. (2011). Do bears fly? Revisiting conversational implicature in instructional pragmatics. *TESL-EJ: Teaching English as a Second or Foreign Language, 15*(2). Retrieved from http://www.tesl-ej.org/wordpress/issues/volume15/ej58/ej58a4/

Murray, N. (2012). English as a lingua franca and the development of pragmatic competence. *ELT Journal, 66*, 318–326.

Myers, I., & Briggs, K. (1976). *The Myers-Briggs type indicator, form G*. Paolo Alto, CA: Consulting Psychologists Press.

Negueruela-Azarola, E. (2008). Revolutionary pedagogies: Learning that leads development in the second language classroom. In J. P. Lantolf & M. Poehner (Eds.), *Sociocultural theory and the teaching of second languages* (pp. 189–227). London: Equinox.

Németh, N., & Kormos, J. (2001). Pragmatic aspects of task-performance: The case of argumentation. *Language Teaching Research, 5*(3), 213–240.

Nerlich, B., & Clarke, D. D. (1996). *Language, action and context: The early history of pragmatics in Europe and America, 1780–1930*. Philadelphia, PA: John Benjamins.

Netz, H., & Lefstein, A. (2016). A cross-cultural analysis of disagreements in classroom discourse: Comparative case studies from England, the United States, and Israel. *Intercultural Pragmatics, 13*, 211–255.

Newton, L. (2011). Multimodal creativity and identities of expertise in the digital ecology of a World of Warcraft guild. In C. Thurlow & K. Mroczek (Eds.), *Digital discourse: Language in the new media* (pp. 309–341). Oxford: Oxford University Press.

Nguyen, M. T. T. (2014). Using conversation tasks and retrospective methodology to investigate L2 pragmatics development: The case of EFL criticisms and responses to criticisms. *The Language Learning Journal,* 1–19.

Nguyen, M. T. T. (2011). Learning to communicate in a globalized world: To what extent do school textbooks facilitate the development of intercultural pragmatic competence? *RELC Journal, 42*, 17–30.

Nguyen, T. T. M. (2013). Instructional effects on the acquisition of modifiers in constructive criticisms by EFL learners. *Language Awareness, 22*, 76–94.

Nguyen, T. T. M., Do, T. T. H., Nguyen, A. T., & Pham, T. T. T. (2015). Teaching email requests in the academic context: a focus on the role of corrective feedback. *Language Awareness, 24*(2), 169–195.

Nguyen, T. T. M., Pham, T. H., & Pham, M. T. (2012). The relative effects of explicit and implicit form-focused instruction on the development of L2 pragmatic competence. *Journal of Pragmatics, 44*(4), 416–434.

Nguyen, T. T. M. (2013). Instructional effects on the acquisition of modifiers in constructive criticisms by EFL learners. *Language Awareness, 22*, 76–94.

Niezgoda, K., & Roever, C. (2001). Pragmatic and grammatical awareness: A function of the learning environment? In K. Rose & G. Kasper (Eds.), *Pragmatics in language teaching* (pp. 63–79). New York: Cambridge University Press.

Nikula, T. (2008). Learning pragmatics in content-based classrooms. In E. Alcón Soler & A. Martínez-Flor (Eds.), *Investigating pragmatics in foreign language learning, teaching and testing* (pp. 94–113). Bristol/New York: Multilingual Matters.

Norris, J., & Ortega, L. (2000). Effectiveness of L2 instruction: A research synthesis and quantitative meta-analysis. *Language Learning, 50*, 417–528.

Norton Peirce, B. (1995). Social identity, investment, and language learning. *TESOL Quarterly, 29*, 9–31.

Norton, B., & McKinney, C. (2011). An identity approach to second language acquisition. In Atkinson, D. (Ed.), *Alternative approaches to second language acquisition* (pp. 73–94). London: Routledge.

Norton, B. (1997). Language, identity, and the ownership of English. *TESOL Quarterly, 31*, 409–429.

Norton, B. (2013). *Identity and language learning: Extending the conversation* (2nd ed.). Bristol: Multilingual Matters.

Ochs, E. (1979). Transcription as theory. *Developmental Pragmatics, 10*(1), 43–72.

Ochs, E. (1988). *Culture and language development: Language acquisition and language socialization in a Samoan village.* Cambridge: Cambridge University Press.

Ochs, E., (1996). Linguistic resources for socializing humanity. In J. J. Gumperz & S. C. Levinson (Eds.), *Rethinking linguistic relativity* (pp. 407–437). Cambridge: Cambridge University Press.

Ochs, E., & Schieffelin, B. (1984). Language acquisition and socialization on grammatical development. In P. Fletcher & B. MacWhinney (Eds.), *The handbook of child language* (pp. 73–94). Oxford: Blackwell.

Ohta, A. (2001). *Second language acquisition processes in the classroom: Learning Japanese.* Mahwah, NJ: Lawrence Erlbaum.

Okada, Y. (2010). Role-play in oral proficiency interviews: Interactive footing and interactional competencies. *Journal of Pragmatics, 42*(6), 1647–1668.

Okamoto, S. (2011). The use and interpretations of addressee honorifics and plain forms in Japanese: Diversity, multiplicity, and ambiguity. *Journal of Pragmatics, 43*, 3673–3688.

Olshtain, E., & Cohen, A. (1983). Apology: A speech act set. In N. Wolfson & E. Judd (Eds.), *Sociolinguistics and language acquisition* (pp. 18–35). Rowley, MA: Newbury House.

Olshtain, E., & Cohen, A. (1990). The learning of complex speech act behavior. *TESL Canada Journal*, 7, 45–65.

Olshtain, E., & Weinbach, L. (1987). Complaints: A study of speech act behavior among native and non-native speakers of Hebrew. In J. Verschueren, & M. Bertucelli-Papi (Eds.), *The pragmatic perspective* (pp. 195–208). Amsterdam: John Benjamins.

Ortega, L. (2011). SLA after the Social Turn: Where cognitivism and its alternatives stand. In D. Atkinson (Ed.), *Alternative approaches to second language acquisition* (pp. 167–180). New York: Routledge.

Padilla Cruz, M. (2013). Metapsychological awareness of comprehension and epistemic vigilance of L2 communication in interlanguage pragmatic development. *Journal of Pragmatics*, 59, 117–135.

Park, E. (2006). Grandparents, grandchildren, and heritage language use in Korean. In K. Kondo-Brown (Ed.), *Heritage language development: Focus on East Asian immigrants* (pp. 57–87). Amsterdam: John Benjamins.

Pavlenko, A., & Blackledge, A. (2003). Introduction: new theoretical approaches to the study of negotiation of identities in multilingual contexts. In A. Pavlenko & A. Blackledge (Eds.), *Negotiation of identities in multilingual contexts* (pp. 1–33). New York: Multilingual Matters LTD.

Pawley, A., & Syder, F. (1983). Two puzzles for linguistic theory: Native-like selection and native-like fluency. In J. Richards & R. Schmidt (Eds.), *Language and communication* (pp. 191–226). London: Longman.

Pearson (2014a). *PTE*. Retrieved from http://pearsonpte.com/

Pearson (2014b). *PTE Academic score guide*. Retrieved from http://pearsonpte.com/wp-content/uploads/2014/07/PTEA_Score_Guide.pdf

Pekarek Doehler, S., & Pochon-Berger, E. (2011). Developing 'methods' for interaction: a cross-sectional study of disagreement sequences in French L2. In J. K. Hall, J. Hellermann & S. Pekarek Doehler (Eds.), *L2 interactional competence and development* (pp. 206–243). Clevedon, UK: Multilingual Matters.

Pekarek Doehler, S., & Pochon-Berger, E. (2015). The development of L2 interactional competence: evidence from turn-taking organization, sequence organization, repair organization and preference organization. In T. Cadierno & S. W. Eskildsen (Eds.), *Usage-based perspectives on second language learning* (pp. 233–268). Berlin: Mouton de Gruyter.

Pennycook, A. (1994). *The cultural politics of English as an international language*. London: Longman.

Pérez-Vidal, C. (2014). Language acquisition in study abroad and formal instruction contexts. Amsterdam: John Benjamins

Peyton, J. K., Ranard, D. A., & McGinnis, S. (2001). *Heritage languages in America: Preserving a national resource*. McHenry, IL: Delta Systems and Center for Applied Linguistics.

Piirainen-Marsh, A., & Tainio, L. (2009). Other-repetition as a source for participation in the activity of playing a video game. *Modern Language Journal*, 93, 153–169.

Piirainen-Marsh, A., & Tainio, L. (2014). Asymmetries of knowledge and epistemic change in social gaming interaction. *Modern Language Journal*, 98, 1022–1038.

Pimsleur, P. (1966). *The Pimsleur language aptitude battery*. New York: Harcourt, Brace, Jovanovic.

Pinto, D. (2005). The acquisition of requests by second language learners of Spanish. *Spanish in Context*, 2(1), 1–27.

Pinto, D., & Raschio, R. (2007). A comparative study of requests in heritage speaker Spanish, L1 Spanish, and L1 English. *International Journal of Bilingualism*, 11, 135–155.

Pinto, D., & Raschio, R. (2008). "Oye, ¿qué onda con mi dinero?" An analysis of heritage speaker complaints. *Sociolinguistic Studies*, 2, 221–249.

Pizziconi, B. (2003). Re-examining politeness, face and the Japanese language. *Journal of Pragmatics, 35,* 1471–1506.

Plakans, L., & Gebril, A. (2012). A close investigation into source use in integrated second language writing tasks. *Assessing Writing, 17*(1), 18–34.

Polinsky, M., & Kagan, O. (2007). Heritage languages: In the 'wild' and in the classroom. *Language and Linguistics Compass, 1,* 368–395.

Pomerantz, A. (1984). Agreeing and disagreeing with assessments: some features of preferred/dispreferred turn shapes. In J. M. Atkinson & J. Heritage (Eds.), *Structures of social action: Studies in conversation analysis* (pp. 57–101). New York: Cambridge University Press.

Pomerantz, A., & Heritage, J. (2013). Preference. In J. Sidnell & T. Stivers (Eds.), *The handbook of conversation analysis* (pp. 210–228). Oxford: Blackwell.

Psathas, G. (1995). *Conversation analysis: The study of talk-in-interaction.* Los Angeles, CA: SAGE.

Purpura, J. (2004). *Assessing grammar.* Cambridge: Cambridge University Press.

Rampton, B. (2006). *Language in late modernity: Interaction in an urban school.* Cambridge: Cambridge University Press.

Ranta, L., & Lyster, R. (2007). A cognitive approach to improving immersion students' oral language abilities: The awareness-practice-feedback sequence. In R. DeKeyser (Ed.), *Practice in a second language: Perspectives from Applied Linguistics and Cognitive Psychology* (pp. 141–160). Cambridge: Cambridge University Press.

Rebuschat, P. (Ed.) (2015). *Implicit and explicit learning of languages.* Amsterdam: John Benjamins.

Rees-Miller, J. (2000). Power, severity, and context in disagreement. *Journal of Pragmatics, 32*(8), 1087–1111.

Reid, T. (1872). *The complete works of Thomas Reid.* Edinburgh: Maclachlan and Stewart. (Original work published 1785)

Reinhardt, J., & Sykes, J. (2014). Special issue on game-informed L2 teaching and learning. *Language Learning & Technology, 18*(2).

Ren, W. (2012). Pragmatic development in Chinese speakers' L2 English refusals. *EUROSLA Yearbook, 12,* 63–87.

Ren, W. (2014). A longitudinal investigation into L2 learners' cognitive processes during study abroad. *Applied Linguistics, 35*(5), 575–594.

Richards, J. (2006). *Communicative language teaching today.* Cambridge: Cambridge University Press.

Riddiford, N., & Joe, A. (2010). Tracking the development of sociopragmatic skills. *TESOL Quarterly, 44,* 195–205.

Riddiford, N., & Holmes, J. (2015). Assisting the development of sociopragmatic skills: Negotiating refusals at work. *System, 48,* 129–140.

Riddiford, N., & Newton, J. (2010). *Workplace talk in action: An ESOL resource.* School of Linguistics and Applied Language Studies, Victoria University of Wellington.

Robinson, M. A. (1992). Introspective methodology in interlanguage pragmatics research. In G. Kasper (Ed.), *Pragmatics of Japanese as a native and target language* (pp. 27–82). Honolulu, HI: University of Hawaii at Manoa, Second Language Teaching and Curriculum Center.

Robinson, P. (2001). Individual differences, cognitive abilities, aptitude complexes and learning conditions in second language acquisition. *Second Language Research, 17,* 368–392.

Robinson, P. (2005). Aptitude and second language acquisition. *Annual Review of Applied Linguistics, 25,* 46–73.

Robinson, P. (2007). Aptitudes, abilities, contexts, and practice. In R. M. DeKeyser (Ed.), *Practice in second language learning: Perspectives from applied linguistics and cognitive psychology.* (pp. 256–286). New York/Cambridge: Cambridge University Press.

Robinson, P. (2011). Task-based language learning: A review of issues. *Language Learning, 61,* 1–36.

Robinson, P. (2012). Individual differences, aptitude complexes, SLA processes, and aptitude test development. In M. Pawlak (Ed.), *New perspectives on individual differences in language learning and teaching* (pp. 57–75). Berlin/Heidelberg: Springer-Verlag.

Roever, C. (2005). *Testing ESL pragmatics*. Frankfurt: Peter Lang.

Roever, C. (2006). Validation of a web-based test of ESL pragmalinguistics. *Language Testing* 23, 229–256.

Roever, C. (2007). DIF in the assessment of second language pragmatics. *Language Assessment Quarterly*, 4(2), 165–189.

Roever, C. (2009). Teaching and testing pragmatics. In M. H. Long & C. J. Doughty (Eds.), *Handbook of language teaching* (pp. 560–577). Malden, MA: Wiley-Blackwell.

Roever, C. (2010). Effects of native language in a test of ESL pragmatics: A DIF approach. In G. Kasper, H. thi Nguyen, D. R. Yoshimi, & J. Yoshioka (Eds.), *Pragmatics & Language Learning* (Vol. 12, pp. 187–212). Honolulu, HI: National Foreign Language Resource Center.

Roever, C. (2011). Tests of second language pragmatics: past and future. *Language Testing*, 28, 463–481.

Roever, C. (2012). What learners get for free (and when): Learning of routine formulae in ESL and EFL environments. *ELT Journal*, 66, 10–21.

Roever, C. (2013). Testing implicature under operational conditions. In G. Kasper, & S. Ross (Eds.), *Assessing second language pragmatics* (pp. 43–64). New York: Palgrave-McMillan.

Roever, C. (2015). Researching second language pragmatics. In B. Paltridge, & A. Phakiti (Eds.), *Companion to research methods in Applied Linguistics* (pp. 387–402). London: Continuum.

Roever, C. (2015). *Diagnose pragmatischer Fähigkeiten: Vorschläge aus einer multilingualen englischsprachigen Welt* [Diagnosing pragmatic abilities: Suggestions from a multilingual English-speaking context]. Paper presented at the 3rd International FiSS Spring Conference, Hamburg, Germany.

Roever, C., & Al-Gahtani, S. (2015). The development of ESL proficiency and pragmatic performance. *ELT Journal*, 69(4), 395–404.

Roever, C., Fraser, C., & Elder, C. (2014), *Testing ESL sociopragmatics: Development and validation of a web-based test battery*. Frankfurt: Peter Lang.

Roever, C., Knoch, U., & Macqueen, S. (2016). *Writing pragmatically: second language pragmatic ability and email communication*. Unpublished manuscript, School of Languages & Linguistics, The University of Melbourne, Australia.

Roever, C., Wang, S., & Brophy, S. (2014). Learner background factors and learning of second language pragmatics. *International Review of Applied Linguistics*, 52, 377–401.

Rose, K. (1992). Speech acts and questionnaires: The effect of hearer response. *Journal of Pragmatics*, 17, 49–62.

Rose, K. (2000). An exploratory cross-sectional study of interlanguage pragmatic development. *Studies in Second Language Acquisition*, 22, 27–67.

Rose, K. R. (2009). Interlanguage pragmatic development in Hong Kong, phase 2. *Journal of Pragmatics*, 41(11), 2345–2364.

Rose, K. R., & Ng, K. F. (2001). Inductive and deductive teaching of compliments and compliment responses. In K. R. Rose & G. Kasper (Eds.), *Pragmatics in language teaching* (pp.145–169). Cambridge, UK: Cambridge University Press.

Ross, S. J., & O'Connell, S. P. (2013). The situation with complication as a site for strategic competence. In G. Kasper & S. Ross (Eds.), *Assessing second language pragmatics* (pp. 311–326). New York: Palgrave Macmillan.

Ross, S., & Kasper, G. (2013). *Assessing second language pragmatics*. New York: Palgrave Macmillan.

Sabaté i Dalmau, M., & Curell i Gotor, H. (2007). From 'sorry very much' to 'I'm ever so sorry': Acquisitional patterns in L2 apologies by Catalan learners of English. *Intercultural Pragmatics*, 4(2), 287–315.

Sacks, H. (1984). Notes on methodology. In: J. M. Atkinson & J. Heritage (Eds.), *Structures of social action: Studies in conversation analysis* (pp. 21–27). Cambridge: Cambridge University Press.

Sacks, H. (1992). *Lectures on conversation*. Oxford: Basil Blackwell.

Sacks, H., & Schegloff, E. (1979). Two preferences in the organization of reference to persons and their interaction. In G. Psathas (Ed.), *Everyday languages: Studies in ethnomethodology* (pp. 15–21). New York: Irvington.

Sacks, H., Schegloff, E. A., & Jefferson, G. (1974). A simplest systematics for the organization of turn-taking for conversation. *Language, 50*(4), 696–735.

Saito, H., & Beecken, M. (1997). An approach to instruction of pragmatic aspects: Implications of pragmatic transfer by American learners of Japanese. *Modern Language Journal, 81*, 363–377.

Salsbury, T., & Bardovi-Harlig, K. (2000). Oppositional talk and the acquisition of modality in L2 English. In B. Swierzbin, F. Morris, M. E. Anderson, C. A. Klee, & E. Tarone (Eds.), *Social and cognitive factors in second language acquisition: Selected proceedings of the 1999 second language research forum* (pp. 57–76). Somerville, MA: Cascadilla Press.

Samarin, W. (1987). Linga franca. In U. Ammon, N. Dittmar, & K. Mattheier (Eds.), *Sociolinguistics: An international handbook of the science of language and society* (pp. 371–374). Berlin: Walter de Gruyter.

Sasaki, M. (1998). Investigating EFL students' production of speech acts: A comparison of production questionnaires and role plays. *Journal of Pragmatics, 30*(4), 457–484.

Sasaki, T. (2008). Concurrent think-aloud protocol as a socially situated construct. *IRAL – International Review of Applied Linguistics in Language Teaching, 46*(4), 349–374.

Savić, M. (2015). "Can I very please borrow it?": Request development in young Norwegian EFL learners. *Intercultural Pragmatics, 12*(4), 443–480.

Scarcella, R. (1979). On speaking politely in a second language. In C. A. Yorio, K. Perkins, & J. Schachter (Eds.), *On TESOL '79* (pp. 275–287). Washington, D.C.: TESOL.

Schauer, G. A. (2004). May you speak louder maybe? *EUROSLA Yearbook, 4*, 253–273.

Schauer, G. A. (2006). Pragmatic awareness in ESL and EFL contexts: Contrast and development. *Language Learning, 56*(2), 269–318.

Schauer, G. (2007). Finding the right words in the study abroad context: The development of German learners' use of external modifiers in English. *Intercultural Pragmatics, 4*, 193–220.

Schauer, G.A. (2009). *Interlanguage pragmatic development: The study abroad context.* London: Continuum.

Schegloff, E.A. (1980). Preliminaries to Preliminaries: 'Can I ask you a question?'. *Sociological Inquiry, 50*, 104–152.

Schegloff, E. A. (1992). Conversation. In J. R. Searle (Ed.), *(On) Searle on conversation* (pp. 7–30). Amsterdam: John Benjamins.

Schegloff, E. A. (1993). Reflections on quantification in the study of conversation. *Research on language and social interaction, 26*(1), 99–128.

Schegloff, E. A. (2007). *Sequence organization in interaction: a primer in conversation analysis.* Cambridge: Cambridge University Press.

Schegloff, E. A., Jefferson, G., & Sacks, H. (1977). The preference for self-correction in the organization of repair in conversation. *Language, 53*, 361–382.

Schieffelin, B. B., & Ochs, E. (1986). *Language socialization across cultures.* Cambridge: Cambridge University Press.

Schmidt, R. (1983). Interaction, acculturation, and the acquisition of communicative competence: A case study of an adult. In N. Wolfson & E. Judd (Eds.), *Sociolinguistics and language acquisition* (pp. 137–174). Rowley, MA: Newbury House.

Schmidt, R. (1993). Consciousness, learning and interlanguage pragmatics. In G. Kasper & S. Blum-Kulka, (Eds.), *Interlanguage pragmatics* (pp. 21–42). New York: Oxford University Press.

Schmidt, R. (1995). Consciousness and foreign language learning: A tutorial on the role of attention and awareness in learning. In R. Schmidt (Ed.), *Attention and awareness in foreign language learning* (pp. 1–63). Honolulu: University of Hawaii at Manoa, Second Language Teaching & Curriculum Center.

Schmidt, R. (2001). Attention. In P. Robinson (Ed.), *Cognition and second language instruction* (pp. 3–32). Cambridge: Cambridge University Press.

Schmidt, R. (2010). Attention, awareness, and individual differences in language learning. In W. M. Chan, S. Chi, K. N. Cin, J. Istanto, M. Nagami, J. W. Sew, T. Suthiwan, & I. Walker (Eds.), *Proceedings of CLaSIC 2010*, Singapore, December 2–4 (pp. 721–737). Singapore: National University of Singapore, Centre for Language Studies.

Schmitt, N. (2004). *Formulaic sequences.* Amsterdam: John Benjamins.

Schnurr, S., & Zayts, O. (2013). "I can't remember them ever not doing what I tell them!": Negotiating face and power relations in 'upward' refusals in multicultural workplaces in Hong Kong. *Intercultural Pragmatics, 10,* 593–616.

Schreier, M. (2014). Qualitative content analysis. In U. Flick (Ed.), *The SAGE handbook of qualitative data analysis.* (pp. 170–184). London: SAGE.

Schumann, J. (1978). The acculturation model for second language acquisition. In R. Gingras (Ed.), *Second language acquisition and foreign language teaching* (pp. 27–50). Arlington, VA: Center for Applied Linguistics.

Searle, J. R. (1969). *Speech acts: An essay in the philosophy of language.* Cambridge: Cambridge University Press.

Searle, J. R. (1976). A classification of illocutionary acts. *Language in Society, 5,* 1–23.

Searle, J. R. (1992). To Searle on conversation: a note in return. In J. R. Searle (Ed.), *(On) Searle on conversation* (pp. 113–126). Amsterdam: John Benjamins.

Seidlhofer, B. (2002). Habeas corpus and divide et impera: "Global English" and applied linguistics. In K. Spelman Miller & P. Thompson (Eds.), *Unity and diversity in language use* (pp. 198–217). London: Continuum.

Seidlhofer, B. (2004). Research perspectives on teaching English as a lingua franca. *Annual Review of Applied Linguistics, 24,* 209–239.

Seidlhofer, B. (2009). ELF findings: form and function. In A. Mauranen & E. Ranta (Eds.), *English as a lingua franca: Studies and findings* (pp. 37–59). Newcastle upon Tyne: Cambridge Scholars.

Seidlhofer, B. (2011). *Understanding English as a lingua franca.* Oxford: Oxford University Press.

Selinker, L. (1972). Interlanguage. *International Review of Applied Linguistics, 10,* 209–231.

Shardakova, M. (2005). Intercultural pragmatics in the speech of American L2 learners of Russian: Apologies offered by Americans in Russian. *Intercultural Pragmatics, 2*(4), 423–451.

Shimazu, T. (2009). Influence of learning environment on L2 pragmatic realization: A comparison between JSL and JFL learners' compliment responses. In N. Taguchi (Ed.), *Pragmatic competence in Japanese as a second language* (pp. 167–198). Berlin/New York: Mouton de Gruyter.

Shishavan, H. B., & Sharifian, F. (2016). The refusal speech act in a cross-cultural perspective: A study of Iranian English-language learners and Anglo-Australian speakers. *Language & Communication, 47,* 75–88.

Shively, R. L. (2010). From the virtual world to the real world: A model of pragmatics instruction for study abroad. *Foreign Language Annals, 45,* 105–137.

Shively, R. L. (2011). L2 pragmatic development in study abroad: A longitudinal study of Spanish service encounters. *Journal of Pragmatics, 43*(6), 1818–1835.

Shively, R. L. (2013). Learning to be funny in Spanish study abroad: L2 humor development. *Modern Language Journal, 97,* 939–946.

Shively, R., & Cohen, A. (2008). Development of Spanish requests and apologies during study abroad. *Íkala: Revista de Lenguaje y Cultura, 13*(20), 57–118.

Si, M. (2015). A virtual space for children to meet and practice Chinese. *International Journal of Artificial Intelligence in Education, 25,* 271–290.

Sidnell, J. (2010). *Conversation analysis: An introduction.* Oxford: Wiley-Blackwell.

Siegal, M. (1994). *Learning Japanese as a second language in Japan and the interaction of race, gender, and social context* (Unpublished doctoral dissertation). University of California-Berkley, San Francisco, CA.

Siegal, M. (1996). The role of learner subjectivity in second language sociolinguistic competency: Western women learning Japanese. *Applied Linguistics, 17,* 356–382.

Silverstein, M. (1976). *Shifters, linguistic categories and cultural description.* In K. H. Basso & H. A. Selby (Eds.), *Meaning in anthropology* (pp. 11–55). Albuquerque: University of New Mexico Press.

Simpson, R. C., Briggs, S. L., Ovens, J., & Swales, J. M. (2002). *The Michigan corpus of academic spoken English.* Ann Arbor, MI: The Regents of the University of Michigan.

Sinicrope, C., Norris, J., & Watanabe, Y. (2007). Understanding and assessing intercultural competence: A summary of theory, research, and practice (technical report for the foreign language program evaluation project). *Second Language Studies, 26*, 1–58.

Smit, U. (2010). *English as a lingua franca in higher education*. Berlin: De Gruyter Mouton.

Smit, U., & Dafouz, E. (2013). Integrating content and language in higher education: Gaining insights into English-medium instruction at European universities. *AILA review, 25*. Amsterdam/Philadelphia, PA: John Benjamins.

Sotillo, S., & Stockwell, G. (2013). Special issue on mobile-assisted language learning. *Language Learning & Technology, 17*.

Spencer-Oatey, H. (2010). Intercultural competence and pragmatics research: Examining the interface through studies of intercultural business discourse. In A. Trosborg (Ed.), *Handbook of pragmatics: Pragmatics across languages and cultures* (pp. 189–218). Berlin: Mouton de Gruyter.

Spencer-Oatey, H., & Franklin, P. (2009). *Intercultural interaction*. New York: Palgrave MacMillan.

Spitzberg, B. H., & Chagnon, G. (2009). Conceptualizing intercultural communication competence. In D. K. Deadorff (Ed.), *The SAGE handbook of intercultural competence* (pp. 2–52). Thousand Oaks, CA: SAGE.

Spoelman, M., & Verspoor, M. (2010). Dynamic patterns in development of accuracy and complexity: A longitudinal case study in the acquisition of Finnish. *Applied Linguistics*, 1–22.

Squire, K. (2011). *Video games and learning: Teaching and participatory culture in the digital age*. New York: Teachers College Press.

Statista. (2016). The most spoken languages worldwide. Retrieved on August 5, 2016, from http://www.statista.com/statistics/266808/the-most-spoken-languages-worldwide/

Sternberg, R. J. (2002). The theory of successful intelligence and its implications for language aptitude testing. In P. Robinson (Ed.), *Individual differences and instructed language learning* (pp. 13–43). Amsterdam: John Benjamins.

Stivers, T. (2015). Coding social interaction: A heretical approach in conversation analysis? *Research on Language and Social Interaction, 48*(1), 1–19.

Stokoe, E. (2013). The (in)authenticity of simulated talk: comparing role-played and actual interaction and the implications for communication training. *Research on Language and Social Interaction, 46*(2), 165–185.

Su, I. (2010). Transfer of pragmatic competence. *The Modern Language Journal, 94*, 87–102.

Suendermann-Oeft, D., Ramanarayanan, V., Teckenbrock, M., Neutatz, F., & Schmidt, D. (2015). HALEF: An open-source standard-compliant telephony-based modular spoken dialog system: A review and an outlook. In G. Geunbae Lee, H. Kook Kim, M. Jeong & J. H. Kim (Eds.), *Natural language dialog systems and intelligent assistants* (pp. 53–61). New York: Springer.

Svennevig, J. (2000). *Getting acquainted in conversation: a study of initial interactions*. Amsterdam: John Benjamins.

Swain, M. (1998). Focus on form through conscious reflection. In C. Doughty & J. Williams (Eds.), *Focus on form in classroom second language acquisition* (pp. 64–81). Cambridge: Cambridge University Press.

Swain, M. (2000). The output hypothesis and beyond: Mediating acquisition through collaborative dialogue. In J. P. Lantolf (Ed.), *Sociocultural theory and second language learning* (pp. 97–114). Oxford: Oxford University Press.

Swain, M. (2006). Languaging, agency and collaboration in advanced second language proficiency. In H. Byrnes (Ed.), *Advanced language learning: The contribution of Halliday and Vygotsky* (pp. 95–108). London: Continuum.

Swain, M. (2011). The inseparability of cognition and emotion in second language learning. *Language Teaching, 28*, 11–13.

Swain, M., & Lapkin, S. (1995). Problems in output and the cognitive processes they generate: A step towards second language learning. *Applied Linguistics, 16*, 371–391.

Swain, M., & Lapkin, S. (1998). Interaction and second language learning: Two adolescent French immersion students working together. *Modern Language Journal, 82*, 320–337.

Swain, M., & Watanabe, Y. (2013). Collaborative dialogue as a source of learning. In C. Chapelle (Ed.), *The encyclopedia of applied linguistics*. Oxford, UK: Wiley-Blackwell.

Sweeney, E., & Hua, Z. (2016). Discourse completion tasks. In Z. Hua (Ed.), *Research methods in intercultural communication: A practical guide* (pp. 212–222). Oxford: Wiley-Blackwell.

Sydorenko, T. (2015). The use of computer-delivered structured tasks in pragmatic instruction: An exploratory study. *Intercultural Pragmatics, 12*(3), 333–362.

Sykes, J. M. (2009). Learner request in Spanish: Examining the potential of multiuser virtual environments for L2 pragmatics acquisition. In L. Lomika & G. Lord (Eds.), *The second generation: Online collaboration and social networking in CALL* (pp. 199–234). CALICO Monograph. San Marcos, TX: CALICO.

Sykes, J. M. (2013). Multiuser virtual environments: Apologies in Spanish. In N. Taguchi & J. M. Sykes (Eds.), *Technology in interlanguage pragmatics research and teaching* (pp. 71–100). Amsterdam/Philadelphia, PA: John Benjamins.

Sykes, J. M., & Reinhardt, J. (2012). *Language at play: Digital games in second and foreign language teaching and learning*. New York: Pearson-Prentice Hall.

Tada, M. (2005). *Assessment of ESL pragmatic production and perception using video prompts* (Unpublished doctoral dissertation). Temple University, Philadelphia, PA.

Taguchi, N. (2005). Comprehension of implied meaning in English as a second language. *Modern Language Journal, 89*, 543–562.

Taguchi, N. (2006). Analysis of appropriateness in a speech act of request in L2 English. *Pragmatics, 16*(4), 513–533.

Taguchi, N. (2007). Development of speed and accuracy in pragmatic comprehension in English as a foreign language. *TESOL Quarterly, 41*(2), 313–338.

Taguchi, N. (2008a). Cognition, language contact, and development of pragmatic comprehension in a study-abroad context. *Language Learning, 58*, 33–71.

Taguchi, N. (2008b). The effect of working memory, semantic access, and listening abilities on the comprehension of conversational implicatures in L2 English. *Pragmatics and Cognition, 16*, 517–538.

Taguchi, N. (2008c). The role of learning environment in the development of pragmatic comprehension: A comparison of gains between EFL and ESL learners. *Studies in Second Language Acquisition, 30*, 423–452.

Taguchi, N. (2009). Corpus-informed assessment of comprehension of conversational implicatures in L2 English. *TESOL Quarterly, 43*(4), 738–749.

Taguchi, N. (2010). Longitudinal studies in interlanguage pragmatics. In A. Trosborg (Ed.), *Handbook of pragmatics* (Vol. 7, pp. 333–361). Berlin: Mouton de Gruyter.

Taguchi, N. (2011a). Do proficiency and study-abroad experience affect speech act production? Analysis of appropriateness, accuracy, and fluency. *IRAL – International Review of Applied Linguistics in Language Teaching, 49*(4), 265–293.

Taguchi, N. (2011b). The effect of L2 proficiency and study-abroad experience in pragmatic comprehension. *Language Learning, 61*, 904–939.

Taguchi, N., (2011c). Teaching pragmatics: Trends and issues. *Annual Review of Applied Linguistics, 31*, 289–310.

Taguchi, N. (2012). *Context, individual differences, and pragmatic competence*. New York/Bristol: Multilingual Matters.

Taguchi, N. (2013). Production of routines in L2 English: Effect of proficiency and study-abroad experience. *System, 41*, 109–121.

Taguchi, N. (2014a). Development of interactional competence in Japanese as a second language: Use of incomplete sentences as interactional resources. *The Modern Language Journal, 98*(2), 518–535.

Taguchi, N. (2014b). English-medium education in the global society. Special Issue. *International Review of Applied Linguistics, 52*(2).

Taguchi, N. (2014c). Personality and development of second language pragmatic competence. *Asian EFL Journal, 16,* 203–221.

Taguchi, N. (2015a). "Contextually" speaking: A survey of pragmatic learning abroad, in class and online. *System, 48,* 3–20.

Taguchi N. (2015b). Cross-cultural adaptability and development of speech act production in study abroad. *International Journal of Applied Linguistics, 25*(3), 343–365.

Taguchi, N. (2015c). *Developing interactional competence in a Japanese study abroad context.* Bristol/New York: Multilingual Matters.

Taguchi, N. (2015d). Instructed pragmatics at a glance: Where instructional studies were, are, and should be going. *Language Teaching, 48,* 1–50.

Taguchi, N. (2016). Contexts and pragmatics learning: Findings and implications of study abroad research. *Language Teaching.*

Taguchi, N. (2017). Interlanguage pragmatics. In A. Barron, P. Grundy, & G. Yueguo (Eds.), *The Routledge handbook of pragmatics* (pp. 153–167). Oxford/New York: Routledge.

Taguchi, N., Gomez-Laich, P. M., & Arrufat-Marqués, M. J. (2016). Comprehension of indirect meaning in Spanish as a foreign language. *Foreign Language Annals 49,* 677–698.

Taguchi, N., & Kim, Y. (2016). Collaborative dialogue in learning pragmatics: Pragmatics-related episodes as an opportunity for learning request-making. *Applied Linguistics, 37,* 416–437

Taguchi, N., & Kim, Y. (Eds.) (in preparation). Task-based approaches to teaching and assessing pragmatics. Philadelphia, PA: John Benjamins.

Taguchi, N., & Sykes, J. M. (Eds.). (2013). *Technology in interlanguage pragmatics research and teaching.* Philadelphia: John Benjamins.

Taguchi N., Li, S., & Liu, Y. (2013). Comprehension of conversational implicature in L2 Chinese. *Pragmatics and Cognition, 21,* 139–157.

Taguchi, N., Li, S., & Xiao, F. (2013). Production of formulaic expressions in L2 Chinese: A developmental investigation in a study abroad context. *Chinese as a Second Language Research Journal, 2,* 23–58.

Taguchi, N., Xiao, F., & Li, S. (2016). Development of pragmatic knowledge in L2 Chinese: Effects of intercultural competence and social contact on speech act production in a study abroad context. *Modern Language Journal.*

Taguchi, N., Zhang, H., & Li, Q. (forthcoming). Pragmatic competence of heritage learners of Chinese and its relationship to social contact. *Chinese as a Second Language Research Journal.*

Tajeddin, A., & Moghadam, A. Z. (2012). Interlanguage pragmatic motivation: Its construct and impact on speech act production. *RELC Journal, 43,* 353–372.

Tajfel, H. (1974). Social identity and intergroup behavior. *Social Science Information, 13,* 65–93.

Takahashi, S. (2005). Pragmalinguistic awareness: Is it related to motivation and proficiency? *Applied Linguistics, 26,* 90–120.

Takahashi, S. (2010). Assessing learnability in second language pragmatics. In A. Trosborg (Ed.), *Handbook of pragmatics* (Vol. 7, pp. 391–421). Berlin: Mouton de Gruyter.

Takahashi, S. (2015). The effects of learner profiles on pragmalinguistic awareness and learning, *System, 48,* 48–61.

Takamiya, Y., & Ishihara, N. (2013). Blogging: Cross-cultural interaction for pragmatic development. In N. Taguchi & J. M. Sykes (Eds.), *Technology in interlanguage pragmatics research and teaching* (pp. 185–214). Amsterdam/Philadelphia, PA: John Benjamins.

Takenoya, M. (2003). *Terms of address in Japanese: An interlanguage pragmatics approach.* Sapporo, Japan: Hokkaido University Press.

Takimoto, M. (2006). The effects of explicit feedback on the development of pragmatic proficiency. *Language Teaching Research, 10*(4), 393–417.

Takimoto, M. (2009). Exploring the effects of input-based treatment and test on the development of learners' pragmatic proficiency. *Journal of Pragmatics, 41*(5), 1029–1046.

Takimoto, M. (2012). Metapragmatic discussion in interlanguage pragmatics. *Journal of Pragmatics, 44*(10), 1240–1253.

Tateyama, Y. (2001). Explicit and implicit teaching of pragmatic routines. In K. Rose & G. Kasper (Eds.), *Pragmatics in language teaching* (pp. 200–222). Cambridge, UK: Cambridge University Press.

Tateyama, Y., & Kasper, G. (2008). Talking with a classroom guest: opportunities for learning Japanese pragmatics. In E. Alcón Soler & A. Martínez-Flor (Eds.), *Investigating pragmatics in foreign language learning, teaching, and testing* (pp. 45–71). Clevedon, UK: Multilingual Matters.

Tatsuki, D., & Houck, N.R. (2010). *Pragmatics: teaching speech acts.* New York: TESOL.

Taylor, G. (2002). Teaching gambits: The effect of instruction and task variation on the use of conversation strategies by intermediate Spanish students. *Foreign Language Annals, 35,* 171–189.

ten Have, P. (2007). *Doing conversation analysis.* Los Angeles: SAGE.

Thomas, J. (1983). Cross-cultural pragmatic failure. *Applied Linguistics, 4,* 91–111.

Thomas, J. (1995). *Meaning in interaction: An introduction to pragmatics.* London: Longman.

Thomas, M., & Peterson, M. (2014). Web 2.0 and language learning. Special issue. *CALICO, 31.*

Thompson, A. (2013). The interface of language aptitude and multilingualism: Reconsidering the bilingual/multilingual dichotomy. *Modern Language Journal, 97,* 685–701.

Thompson, F., & Twitchin, J. (Producers) (1991). *Crosstalk at work.* Available from http://www.bbcactivevideoforlearning.com/1/TitleDetails.aspx?TitleID=505

Timpe, V. (2013). *Assessing intercultural language learning.* Frankfurt: Peter Lang.

Timpe-Laughlin, V., Wain, J., & Schmidgall, J. (2015). Defining and operationalizing the construct of pragmatic competence: Review and recommendations. *ETS Research Report Series 2015(1),* 1–43. Princeton, NJ: ETS.

Tomlin, R.S., & Villa, V. (1994). Attention in cognitive science and second language acquisition. *Studies in Second Language Acquisition, 16,* 183–203.

Tran, V. T. T. (2013a). Address forms in Vietnamese: Learners' sociolinguistic competence. In C. Roever & H. T. Nguyen (Eds.), *Pragmatics of Vietnamese as native and target language* (pp. 136–176). Honolulu, HI: National Foreign Language Resource Center, University of Hawaii.

Tran, V. T. T. (2013b). *Second language interactional competence: Solicitation effects on suggestions* (Unpublished doctoral dissertation). The University of Melbourne, Melbourne, Australia.

Tremblay, P. F., & Gardner, R. C. (1995). Expanding the Motivation Construct in Language Learning. *Modern Language Journal, 79,* 505–518.

Trosborg, A. (1987). Apology strategies in natives/non-natives. *Journal of Pragmatics, 11,* 147–167.

Trosborg, A. (1995). *Interlanguage pragmatics: Requests, complaints and apologies.* Berlin: Mouton de Gruyter.

Tsai, M. H., & Kinginger, C. (2015). Giving and receiving advice in computer-mediated peer response activities. *CALICO, 32,* 82–112.

United States Census Bureau. (2012). *The foreign-born population in the United States: 2010.* Washington D.C.: U.S. Department of Commerce.

Unity Technologies. (2015). http://unity3d.com/unity

Ushioda, E. (2009). A person-in-context relational view of emergent motivation, self and identity. In Z. Dörnyei & E. Ushioda (Eds.), *Motivation, language identity and the L2 self* (pp. 215–228). Bristol: Multilingual Matters.

Ushioda, E. (2016). Language learning motivation through a small lens: A research agenda. *Language Teaching.*

Usó-Juan, E., & Martínez-Flor, A. (2006). Approaches to language learning and teaching: Towards acquiring communicative competence through the four skills. In E. Usó-Juan & A. Martínez-Flor (Eds.), *Current trends in the development and teaching of the four language skills* (pp. 3–25). Berlin, Germany: Mouton de Gruyter.

Uzum, B. (2010). An investigation of alignment in CMC from a sociocognitive perspective. *CALICO, 28,* 135–155.

Valdés, G. (2001). Heritage language students: Profiles and possibilities. In J. K. Peyton, D. Ranard, & S. McGinnis (Eds.), *Heritage languages in America: Preserving a national resource* (pp. 37–80). McHenry, IL: Delta Systems and Center for Applied Linguistics.

Valdés, G. (2005). Bilingualism, heritage language learners, and SLA research: Opportunities lost or seized? *Modern Language Journal, 89*, 410–426.

van Compernolle, R. A. (2011a). Developing second language sociopragmatic knowledge through concept-based instruction: A microgenetic case study. *Journal of Pragmatics, 43*, 3267–3283.

van Compernolle, R. A. (2011b). Responding to questions and L2 learner interactional competence during language proficiency interviews: A microanalytic study with pedagogical implications. In J. K. Hall, J. Hellermann & S. Pekarek Doehler (Eds.), *L2 interactional competence and development* (pp. 117–144). Clevedon, UK: Multilingual Matters.

van Compernolle, R. A. (2014). *Sociocultural theory and instructed L2 pragmatics*. Bristol/ New York: Multilingual Matters.

Van Deusen-Scholl, N. (2003). Toward a definition of heritage language: Sociopolitical and pedagogical considerations. *Journal of language, identity, and education, 2*, 211–230.

van Ek, J. A. (1976). *The threshold level for modern language learning in schools*. London: Longman.

Van Oudenhoven, J. P., & Van der Zee, K. I. (2002). Predicting multicultural effectiveness of international students: The multicultural personality questionnaire. *International Journal of Intercultural Relations, 26*, 679–694.

VanPatten, B. (2015). Foundations of processing instruction. *International Review of Applied Linguistics in Language Teaching, 53*(2), 91–109.

Verhoeven, L., & Vermeer, A. (2002). Communicative competence and personality dimensions in first and second language learners. *Applied Psycholinguistics, 23*, 361–374.

Verschueren, J. (1999). *Understanding pragmatics*. New York: Oxford University Press.

Verschueren, J. (2008). Intercultural communication and the challenges of migration. *Language and Intercultural Communication, 8*, 21–35.

Verschueren, J. (2009). Introduction: The pragmatic perspective. In J. O. Östman & J. Verschueren (Eds.), *Key notions for pragmatics* (pp. 1–27). Amsterdam: John Benjamins.

Verspoor, M., de Bot, K., & Lowie, W. (2011). *A dynamic approach to second language development: Methods and techniques*. Amsterdam/Philadelphia, PA: John Benjamins.

Vilar Beltrán, E., & Melchor-Couto, S. (2013). Refusing in second life. In O. M. Arnándiz & P. Salazar Campillo (Eds.), *Refusals in instructional contexts and beyond* (pp. 23–40). Amsterdam: Rodopi.

Villarreal, D. (2014). Connecting production to judgments: T/V address forms and the L2 identities of intermediate Spanish learners. *Journal of Pragmatics, 66*, 1–14.

Vygotsky, L. S. (1978). *Mind in society: The development of higher psychological processes*. Cambridge, MA: Harvard University Press.

Vygotsky, L. S. (1987). *The collected works of L. S. Vygotsky: Volume 1, Thinking and speech*. New York: Plenum Press.

Vygotsky, L. S. (1997). *The collected works of L. S. Vygotsky, Volume 4: The history of the development of higher mental functions* (R. W. Rieber, Vol. Ed; M. J. Hall, Trans.). New York: Plenum Press. (Original work published 1941)

Walters, F. S. (2007). A conversation-analytic hermeneutic rating protocol to assess L2 oral pragmatic competence. *Language Testing, 27*(2), 155–183.

Walters, F. S. (2009). A conversation analysis-informed test of L2 aural pragmatic comprehension. *TESOL Quarterly, 43*(1), 29–54.

Wang, S., & Vásquez, C. (2012). Web 2.0 and second language learning: What does the research tell us? *CALICO, 29*, 412–430.

Wang, S., Brophy, S., & Roever, C. (2014). Learner background factors and learning of second language pragmatics. *International Review of Applied Linguistics, 52*(4), 377–401.

Warga, M., & Schölmberger, U. (2007). The acquisition of French apologetic behavior in a study abroad context. *Intercultural Pragmatics, 4*, 221–251.

Waring, H. Z. (2013). 'How was your weekend?': developing the interactional competence in managing routine inquiries. *Language Awareness*, 22(1), 1–16.

Wei, M. (2011). Investigating the oral proficiency of English learners in China: A comparative study of the use of pragmatic markers. *Journal of Pragmatics*, 43(14), 3455–3472.

Wenger, E. (1998). *Communities of practice: Learning, meaning and identity*. Cambridge: Cambridge University Press.

Wertsch J. (1991). *Voices of the mind: A sociocultural approach to mediated action*. Cambridge, MA: Harvard University Press.

Widdowson, H. G. (1994). The ownership of English. *TESOL Quarterly*, 28, 377–389.

Wierzbicka, A. (1994). "Cultural script": A semantic approach to cultural analysis and cross-cultural communication. In L. Bouton & Y. Kachru (Eds.), *Pragmatics and language learning monograph series* (Vol. 5, pp. 1–24). University of Illinois at Urbana-Champagne.

Wildner-Bassett, M. (1984). *Improving pragmatic aspects of learners' interlanguage*. Tübingen: Gunter Narr.

Wildner-Bassett, M. (1986). Teaching and learning "polite noises": Improving pragmatic aspects of advanced adult learners' interlanguage. In G. Kasper (Ed.), *Learning, teaching and communication in the foreign language classroom* (pp. 163–78). Aarhus, Denmark: Aarhus University Press.

Wiley, T. (2001). On defining heritage languages and their speakers. In J. K. Peyton, D. Ranard, & S. McGinnis (Eds.), *Heritage languages in America: Preserving a national resource* (pp. 29–36). McHenry, IL: Delta Systems and Center for Applied Linguistics.

Wilkins, D.A. (1976). *Notional syllabuses*. London: Oxford University Press.

Wilkinson, J. (2012). The intercultural speaker and the acquisition of intercultural/global competence. In J. Jackson (Ed.), *The Routledge handbook of language and intercultural communication* (pp. 296–309). Oxford: Routledge.

Wiseman, R. L. (2002). Intercultural communication competence. In W. B. Gudykunst & B. Mody (Eds.), *Handbook of international and intercultural communication* (2nd ed, pp. 207–224). Thousand Oaks, CA: SAGE.

Wolfson, N. (1983). An empirically based analysis of complimenting in American English. In N. Wolfson and E. Judd, (Eds.), *Sociolinguistics and Language Acquisition*, (pp. 82–95). Rowley, MA: Newbury.

Woodfield, H. (2008). Problematising Discourse Completion Tasks: Voices from verbal report. *Evaluation & Research in Education*, 21(1), 43–69.

Woodfield, H. (2010). What lies beneath?: Verbal report in interlanguage requests in English. *Multilingua: Journal of Cross-Cultural and Interlanguage Communication*, 29(1), 1–27.

Woodfield, H. (2012). Pragmatic variation in learner perception: The role of retrospective verbal report in L2 speech act research. In J. C. Félix-Brasdefer & D. Koike (Eds.), *Pragmatic variation in first and second language contexts: Methodological issues* (pp. 209–237). Amsterdam/Philadelphia: PA: John Benjamins.

Wootton, A. J. (1997). *Interaction and the development of mind*. Cambridge: Cambridge University Press.

Xiao, F. (2015). Adult second language learners' pragmatic development in the study abroad context: A review. *Frontiers: Interdisciplinary Journal of Study Abroad*, 25. http://frontiersjournal.org/past-volumes/vol-xxv/

Xiao-Desai, Y., & Wong, K. F. (forthcoming). Epistemic stance in Chinese heritage language writing – A developmental view. *Chinese as a Second Language Research Journal*.

Yamanaka, J. (2003). Effects of proficiency and length of residence on the pragmatic comprehension of Japanese ESL Learners. *Second Language Studies*, 22(1), 107–175.

Yamashita, S. O. (1996). *Six measures of JSL pragmatics* (Technical Report #14). Honolulu: University of Hawaii, Second Language Teaching and Curriculum Center.

Yates, L. (2005). Negotiating an institutional identity: Individual differences in NS and NNS teacher directives. In K. Bardovi-Harlig & S. Hartford (Eds.), *Interlanguage pragmatics: Exploring institutional talk* (pp. 67–99). Mahwah, NJ: Erlbaum.

Yates, L. (2010). Speech act performance in workplace settings. In A. Martínez-Flor & E. Uso-Juan (Eds.), *Speech act performance: Theoretical, empirical, and methodological issues* (pp. 109–126). Amsterdam/Philadelphia: John Benjamins.

Yates, L. (2015). Intercultural communication and the transnational: Managing impressions at work. *Multilingua, 34,* 773–796.

Yates, L., & Major, G. (2015). "Quick-chatting", "smart dogs", and how to "say without saying": Small talk and pragmatic learning in the community. *System, 48,* 141–152.

Yilmaz, Y. (2012). The relative effects of explicit correction and recasts on two target structures via two communication modes. *Language Learning, 62,* 1134–1169.

Yoshimi, D. (2001). Explicit instruction and JFL learners' use of interactional discourse markers. In K. R. Rose, & G. Kasper (Eds.), *Pragmatics in language teaching* (pp. 223–244). Cambridge, MA: Cambridge University Press.

Yoshitake, S. (1997). *Interlanguage competence of Japanese students of English: A multi-test framework evaluation* (Unpublished doctoral dissertation). Columbia Pacific University, San Rafael, CA.

Youn, S. J. (2008). *Rater variation in paper vs. web-based KFL pragmatic assessment using FACETS analysis* (Unpublished manuscript). University of Hawaii, Honolulu, HI.

Youn, S. J. (2013). *Validating task-based assessment of L2 pragmatics in interaction using mixed methods* (Unpublished doctoral dissertation). University of Hawaii at Manoa, Honolulu, Hawaii.

Youn, S. J. (2015). Validity argument for assessing L2 pragmatics in interaction using mixed methods. *Language Testing, 32*(2), 199–225.

Youn, S. J., & Brown, J. D. (2013). Item difficulty and heritage language learner status in pragmatic tests for Korean as a foreign language. In S. Ross & G. Kasper (Eds.), *Assessing second language pragmatics* (pp. 98–123). New York: Palgrave Macmillan.

Young, L. (1994). *Crosstalk and culture in Sino-American communication.* Cambridge: Cambridge University Press.

Young, R. (2002). Discourse approaches to oral language assessment. *Annual Review of Applied Linguistics, 19,* 105–132.

Young, R. (2008). *Discursive practices in language learning and teaching.* Malden, MA and Oxford: Wiley-Blackwell.

Young, R. (2011). Interactional competence in language learning, teaching, and testing. In E. Hinkel (Ed.), *Handbook of research in language learning and teaching* (pp. 426–443). New York: Routledge.

Zechner, K., Higgins, D., Xi, X., & Williamson, D. M. (2009). Automatic scoring of non-native spontaneous speech in tests of spoken English. *Speech Communication, 51*(10), 883–895.

Zhang, Y. (2016). *Development of second language interactional competence: Agreement and disagreement negotiation by learners of Mandarin* (Unpublished doctoral dissertation). The University of Melbourne, Melbourne, Australia.

Zhu, W. (2012). Polite requestive strategies in emails: An investigation of pragmatic competence of Chinese EFL learners. *RELC Journal: A Journal of Language Teaching and Research, 43*(2), 217–238.

Zimmermann, D. (1999). Horizontal and vertical comparative research in language and social interaction. *Research on Language and Social Interaction, 32,* 195–203.

Zuengler, J., & Cole, K. (2005). Language socialization and second language learning. In E. Hinkel (Ed.), *Handbook of research in second language teaching and learning* (pp. 301–316). Mahwah, NJ: Lawrence Erlbaum.

Zuengler, J., & Miller, E. R. (2006). Cognitive and sociocultural perspectives: Two parallel SLA worlds? *TESOL Quarterly, 40,* 35–58.

Index

(Page numbers annotated with 'f' or 'n' refer to figures or notes respectively.)